Americans View
Their Mental Health

This is a volume in the Arno Press collection

HISTORICAL ISSUES IN MENTAL HEALTH

Advisory Editor
Gerald N. Grob

Editorial Board
David Mechanic
Jacques M. Quen
Charles E. Rosenberg

See last pages of this volume for a complete list of titles

Americans View Their Mental Health

GERALD GURIN
JOSEPH VEROFF
SHEILA FELD

ARNO PRESS
A New York Times Company
New York • 1980

362.2
G979

Editorial Supervision: Brian Quinn

Reprint Edition 1980 by Arno Press Inc.
Copyright © 1960 by Basic Books, Inc.
Reprinted by permission of Basic Books, Inc.
HISTORICAL ISSUES IN MENTAL HEALTH
ISBN for complete set: 0-405-11900-3
See last pages of this volume for titles.
Manufactured in the United States of America

Library of Congress Cataloging in Publication Data

Gurin, Gerald, 1922-
    Americans view their mental health.

    (Historical issues in mental health)
    Reprint of the ed. published by Basic Books,
New York, issued as no. 4 of the Joint Commission
on Mental Illness and Health Monograph series.
    1. Mental health--United States. 2. Mental
health--United States--Public opinion. 3. Public
opinion--United States. I. Veroff, Joseph,
1929-   joint author. II. Feld, Sheila,
1932-   joint author. III. Title. IV. Series.
V. Series: Joint Commission on Mental Illness
and Health. Monograph series ; no. 4.
[RA790.6.G87 1979] 301.15'43'614580973   78-22564
ISBN 0-405-11918-6

AMERICANS VIEW THEIR MENTAL HEALTH

Joint Commission
on Mental Illness and Health

MONOGRAPH SERIES / NO. 4

Americans View Their Mental Health

A Nationwide Interview Survey

GERALD GURIN
JOSEPH VEROFF
SHEILA FELD

A REPORT TO THE STAFF DIRECTOR, JACK R. EWALT
1960

Basic Books, Inc., Publishers, New York

© 1960 BY BASIC BOOKS, INC.

MANUFACTURED IN THE UNITED STATES OF AMERICA

Foreword

THIS IS the fourth of a series of monographs to be published by the Joint Commission on Mental Illness and Health as part of a national mental health survey that will culminate in a final report containing findings and recommendations for a national mental health program.

The present document constitutes a report of the project director to the staff director of the Joint Commission.

Titles of the monograph series, together with the principal authors, are listed here in the order of expected publication:

1. *Current Concepts of Positive Mental Health*
   Marie Jahoda, Ph.D., Basic Books, 1958.

2. *Economics of Mental Illness*
   Rashi Fein, Ph.D., Basic Books, 1958.

3. *Mental Health Manpower Trends*
   George W. Albee, Ph.D., 1959.

4. *Americans View Their Mental Health. A Nationwide Interview Survey*
   Gerald Gurin, Ph.D., Joseph Veroff, Ph.D., and Sheila Feld, Ph.D.

5. *Community Resources in Mental Health*
   Reginald Robinson, Ph.D., David F. DeMarche, Ph.D., and Mildred K. Wagle, M.S.S.A.

6. *Epidemiology and Mental Illness*
   Richard J. Plunkett, M.D., and John E. Gordon, M.D.

7. *The Role of Schools in Mental Health*
   Wesley Allinsmith, Ph.D., and George W. Goethals, Ed.D.

8. *The Role of Religion in Mental Health*
   Richard V. McCann, Ph.D.

9. *New Perspectives of Mental Patient Care*
    Morris S. Schwartz, Ph.D., Charlotte Green Schwartz, M.A., Mark G. Field, Ph.D., Elliot G. Mishler, Ph.D., Simon S. Olshansky, M.A., Jesse R. Pitts, Ph.D., Rhona Rapoport, Ph.D., and Warren T. Vaughan, Jr., M.D.

10. *Research Resources in Mental Health*
    William F. Soskin, Ph.D.

These monographs, each a part of an over-all study design, will contain the detailed information forming the basis of a final report. From the data in the individual studies and other relevant information, the headquarters staff will prepare a summary document incorporating its findings and recommendations for national and state mental health programs. This summary document will have the approval of the Joint Commission before its publication in the form of an official report.

This final report will be published by Basic Books and transmitted to the United States Congress, the Surgeon General of the Public Health Services, and the Governors of the States, together with their representatives in the public health and mental health professions, in accordance with the provisions of the Mental Health Study Act of 1955.

Participating organizations, members, and officers of the Joint Commission and the headquarters staff are listed in Appendix III at the end of the book.

The Joint Commission, it may be seen, is a nongovernmental multidisciplinary, nonprofit organization representing a variety of national agencies concerned with mental health. Its study was authorized by a unanimous resolution of Congress and is financed by grants from the following sources:

American Association on Mental Deficiency
American Association of Psychiatric Clinics for Children
American Legion
American Medical Association
American Occupational Therapy Association
American Orthopsychiatric Association, Inc.
American Psychiatric Association

FOREWORD

American Psychoanalytic Association
Association for Physical and Mental Rehabilitation
Carter Products Company
Catholic Hospital Association
Field Foundation
Henry Hornblower Fund
National Association for Mental Health
National Committee Against Mental Illness
National Institute of Mental Health
National League for Nursing
National Rehabilitation Association
Rockefeller Brothers Fund
Benjamin Rosenthal Foundation
Smith, Kline and French Foundation

Additional copies of *Americans View Their Mental Health* may be purchased from the publisher or from book dealers.

JOINT COMMISSION ON MENTAL ILLNESS AND HEALTH

Staff Review

In evaluating national resources for coping with the human and economic problems of mental illness, as directed by the Congress, the staff of the Joint Commission on Mental Illness and Health became aware at the outset that no nationwide information was available on what the American people themselves thought of their mental health.

How well or badly adjusted do they consider themselves to be? Are they happy or unhappy, worried or unworried, optimistic or pessimistic in their outlook? Do they feel strong or weak; adequate or inadequate? What troubles Americans, as they see themselves?

And what do people do about their troubles? Do they solve their problems by themselves? Do they learn to live with them? Do they turn to someone for help?

When they feel the need for help, where do they turn? What kind of help do they get? How effective do they think this help is?

To be sure, answers to such questions about psychological well-being constitute only one measure of "mental health" or "mental illness" inasmuch as the person interviewed might see his troubles or lack of them quite differently from the way the professional expert or other outsiders, such as the person's friends, might view them. Indeed, this recognition that we require an insight and perspective greater than our own is implicit in help-seeking.

Yet such answers have more value than that of simple human interest, as interested as we are in "how it is for the other fellow." In a democracy, the needs of the people—as they themselves feel them, come to understand them, and express them—ultimately determine the ways in which organized efforts will be made to meet these needs. Expressed needs also will serve as a measure of how much of a given need is being met or remains unmet. These needs also serve to predict the extent of self-initiated help-seeking.

Many counts were at hand on how many persons in various walks of life are diagnosed as mentally ill as they come to professional attention in various official agencies. These will be reviewed in a forthcoming monograph, *New Perspectives of Mental Patient Care,* as well as in the Joint Commission's Final Report.

Also, an intriguing variety of estimates is available on how many persons in the general population suffer from what the psychiatrist, psychologist, or social scientist would define as a psychiatric or psychosomatic disorder, psychological maladjustment, or socially deviant behavior. In sampling surveys of several communities, such symptoms of mental or emotional disturbance or distress appear to affect anywhere from 10 to 75 per cent of the population, depending on the orientation of the investigators and whether major or major *and* minor ills are counted. A forthcoming monograph, *Epidemiology and Mental Illness,* will review these community surveys.

In the interest of objectivity and a broader view, we saw the desirability of turning the problem around and looking at the nation's mental health in this instance through the eyes not of the expert in mental disease but of the normal adult population, as interpreted by the expert in normal behavior. Our first monograph, *Current Concepts of Positive Mental Health,* dealing with the meaning of mental health, suggested the value of this approach—for one reason because there is no general agreement among the experts on what constitutes mental health or mental illness; mental health means many things to many people—to some, the absence of mental illness, itself often ill-defined. The present monograph not only considers the individual's own estimate of his mental well-being, in contrast to the evaluation of the expert in mental diseases; it also explores the ways in which the individual can evaluate his own well-being—such as his happiness, absence of worries, feelings of self-satisfaction.

The Joint Commission staff, in its design of the National Mental Health Study, conceived that each individual has within his life span a given potential for mental health or ill health depending on a complex of biological, psychological, and sociological forces affecting his behavior. These forces relate, so to speak, to the raw materials of which he is made, and to how these materials are shaped and molded through family and experiences, some of which impose critical stresses. In this view, everyone will at times experience psychological trouble, or feel troubled. The individual may successfully cope with these stresses, or fail to do so, in varying degree. Thus, we assumed, mental health springs not from avoiding all stress—always staying out of trouble—but from a capacity to accept normal amounts of stress, with some ability to rebound or to handle trouble. When he feels unable to do so through his own resources, the individual may or may not seek help from others—and he may or may not get it.

The lawmaker might now conclude that what we wished was a grass-roots poll on how Americans are behaving; the industrialist might construe the purpose as a market analysis of mental health "customers." The experts in public opinion surveys to whom we turned—mainly social psychologists—saw the need for an intensive interview survey.

We selected the University of Michigan's Survey Research Center, under the direction of Dr. Angus Campbell, to seek the answers to our questions. They used the same sort of scientifically proved techniques, based on probability sampling methods, that have been developed for assessing public opinion by the Survey Research Center and other groups in other social studies. The study group, headed by Drs. Gerald Gurin, Joseph Veroff, and Sheila Feld, the co-authors of *Americans View Their Mental Health,* interviewed 2460 Americans over the age of twenty-one living at home, selected so as to be representative of the total population in such characteristics as age, sex, education, income, occupation, and place of residence. Transients and all individuals in hospitals, prisons, or other institutions at the time were excluded. The interviewed group therefore constituted an accurately proportioned miniature of the "normal," stable, adult population of the United States.

We therefore are justified in drawing conclusions from this study about American attitudes in general within the small limits of error characterizing statistical methods, the variations of mutual understanding achieved between interviewer and interviewee, and any bias of the investigators in their interpretation of the data. But these limitations affect projections of exact numbers and percentages far more than they do the valid relationships, trends, and general truths that can be drawn from the study. As a matter of fact, the study receives added credibility—"face validity"—from the fact that it substantiates certain views that perceptive persons would surely have believed to be the case from general observation. On the other hand, the study reveals many facets of behavior that "come as news."

Interviews conducted by experienced interviewers were unusually long, ranging from one to four hours and averaging nearly two hours. Only 8 per cent of all persons approached refused to be interviewed—about the average for a public opinion survey. Furthermore, the majority of the respondents talked with remarkable frankness. Doubtless this is due partly to the skill of the interviewers and the careful manner in which questions were phrased so as to avoid the resistance that would be aroused by probing too deeply in sensitive areas; at the same time, the questions were designed to elicit responses suggestive in composite of the real nature of the respondents' feelings about themselves and others. We are struck by the cordial reception of the people in the sample to the survey and by their willingness to talk to total strangers in such intimate terms. But this is not an uncommon phenomenon. Given a neutral setting, individuals frequently like to tell their troubles to someone.

The kinds of questions asked by the survey fall into two general categories. The first deals with the way people feel they have adjusted to life—whether they think they are happy or unhappy, worried or unworried, the picture they have of themselves, and their attitudes toward the three most important areas of their lives—marriage, parenthood, and work.

The second group of questions follows from the first. How do people cope with problems? What motivates them to seek help and where do they turn for it? How effective do they think help has been? Why do some people fail to look for help, and how do they get along without it? The authors were particularly interested to discover if there is any connection between the attitudes that different kinds of people adopt toward themselves and the extent to which they seek help for their problems. The answer to this question has considerable significance in planning the most effective use of mental health resources, as we shall see later. Now what of the findings? What does this monograph tell us about the concerns of the American people?

Money and other material and economic considerations (or the lack of them) are one of the major sources of happiness and unhappiness, according to the study. Three out of ten say it is central to their happiness—or unhappiness. They see money, however, in the light of the material comforts, adequacy of living, and the security it can buy, rather than in terms of luxury.

On the other hand, roughly the same proportion of people regard their children as one of their primary sources of happiness. In addition, one out of five sees marriage as the wellspring of happiness, and approximately the same percentage look to their family in general.

One other interesting point can be made. Unlike the distress accompanying lack of material considerations, most people do not spontaneously mention family relationships as a source of distress.

All in all, it is clear that well over half the population finds its greatest happiness in the home, a state that is conditioned strongly by feelings of economic security.

It may come as a surprise to persons heavily involved in public affairs that international tensions, fear of atomic extinction, and the anxious atmosphere of a troubled world do not figure importantly among the things the American people say trouble them. Fewer than one in ten expressed an outstanding concern for community, national, or world problems. The reason for this finding is unclear. This indifference may be due partly to the fact that most of us are concerned with the realities of our immediate environments, and that the extent to which sources of worry and tension affect us decreases in proportion to their remoteness. It may also reflect a retreat from the realities of the larger world, a sense of helplessness in the face of events that the individual feels are beyond his ability to control. Or it could be a symptom of political immaturity combined with a persistent undercurrent of isolationism, resulting in a renunciation of social responsibility.

The meaning of happiness and unhappiness for Americans is not the same as the meaning of worries. That being happy does not imply an absence of worries can be seen by the fact that most people (about 90 per cent) say they are "very happy" or "pretty happy" rather than that they are "not too happy," but at the same time one out of four admits that he worries "a lot" or "all the time." Two out of five worriers blame money for their troubles.

Why is it that people who worry are not necessarily unhappy? Gurin and his collaborators note some interesting differences between these two states of mind. Unhappy people are pessimistic about the future and the possibilities of change; they are apathetic and have a deficit of psychological resources. The worrier, however, is likely to be more optimistic about the future; he believes things can change for the better and proceeds accordingly; he is active and positive in his approach to life.

Economic and material considerations are even greater sources of worrying (six out of ten) than of unhappiness. The focus of these concerns with material comfort and adequacy and their tie-in to aspirations is seen in the finding that people in the middle income group making from $3000 to $6000 a year report the most financial worries. They have adequacy, but not security, and therefore the strongest aspirations to higher incomes. Those in the low income brackets are more resigned and apathetic about the possibilities of raising their economic station in life.

A further contrast between happiness and worrying is seen in the comparison of people of different ages and educational backgrounds. Younger and better educated people are happier but worry more than those who are older or less educated. Younger people have their futures ahead of them and feel they have higher stakes in life. Along with the better educated, their aspirations and expectations are higher. Older people, conversely, have their lives largely behind them; they are unhappier, but worry less than the younger generation in spite of the association of economic insecurity with old age.

The greater unhappiness of those with less education may stem partly from their feelings of frustration in a society that places a high value on education as a tool for advancement.

These findings illustrate a point that is stressed throughout this monograph, that any evaluation of relative mental health of different groups depends upon the particular definition of mental health used. Thus, if the absence of worrying were taken as the criterion for mental health, a different set of people—the older and less educated—would be more "healthy" than if happiness were the criterion. In the latter case the younger, more educated people would have described themselves as most "healthy."

One of the most sensitive and difficult areas probed by the survey is the realm of self-perception. The problem was to get behind the façade that all of us present to the world to one degree or another, and to obtain some hint at least of the way people really feel about themselves. Any attempt at an analysis in depth was, of course, impossible in a two-hour interview. But it was possible to frame "end-run" questions in such a way that respondents could feel freer to reveal feelings about their strong and weak points without having to make difficult and soul-searching admissions.

Most people have no difficulty in identifying qualities in themselves of which they are proud, and very few explicitly state that they have none. More than two thirds believe that in some positive way they are different from other people. The strong points most people mention fall into the category of the stereotyped virtue; they regard themselves as good churchgoers, providers, housewives. In other words, they judge themselves in the light of their ability to come to terms with the external world rather than their ability to deal with their inner conflicts and personal problems. This suggests that most of us are preoccupied with conforming to accepted standards of behavior and that it is difficult for us to construct our own individual values and be guided by them when they differ from the expectations of our fellows.

Yet the answers to one oblique question designed to elicit feelings of weakness were puzzling. Respondents were asked: "If you had a son (daughter for women), how would you like him to be different from you?" More than two thirds said they wanted their child to be different, while only one out of ten expressed the opposite attitude.

It is interesting that the most educated groups are not only most prone to be self-critical but also when they are self-critical they are prone to refer to "deeper" personality characteristics. It would seem that the more educated are more attuned to their highly personal weaknesses—the kinds of inadequacies that often bring people to psychiatric resources.

The data on the way Americans view their functioning as husbands, wives, and parents point up some interesting differences between men and women, young people and old people, and the less educated and the more educated.

Earlier we found that most Americans look to the home for their greatest happiness and satisfaction. Upon closer questioning, it appears that for women the home also is a great source of distress, more so than for men; they are unhappier with marriage, more aware of problems with it. This holds true in their roles as parents as well as spouses; they feel more inadequate as parents and have more problems with their children. The greater distress of women is replicated in other parts of the study. Their outlook on life is more negative and passive, more introspective and inwardly turned; they are more sensitive about their personal relationships with other people. Being more introspective and aware of themselves they suffer some of the distress that usually accompanies self-analysis.

Without any independent assessment of the relative stresses and strains that men and women in modern American society are subjected to, the authors refrain from choosing among a number of plausible interpretations of these differences. It remains to be seen whether women are actually subject to greater stresses in our society or less able to cope with their troubles, whether they are more sensitive to their own and other people's feelings or are merely more willing to admit to distress and inadequacy than men.

Although men are less self-questioning than women, they are not without their feelings of inadequacy and distress. As fathers, men show an increasing concern over the tendency they see in themselves to neglect the emotional needs of their children; they feel some sense of failure in the amount of time they spend with their children. And in discussing their marital problems, they actually blame themselves more for marital difficulties than do women.

Older people seem to feel little self-doubt. Time rounds off the sharp corners. Things that appeared to be of vital importance to them when they were younger do not count so much as they grow older. Thus the survey found that older people give fewer negative self-appraisals; they are more satisfied about the way they have carried out their responsibilities as husbands, wives, and parents. It may be that, on the one hand, older husbands and wives have learned to compromise their differences; on the other, their influence over their children has probably waned, and they may feel less responsibility for them.

Yet older people do not feel happier with their marriages than younger people, and they evaluate their entire current life as less happy than do younger people. As in the findings that older people were generally more unhappy and yet worried less, these feelings toward marriage and parenthood seem to reflect a resignation, apathy, and passive acceptance of life and oneself.

The differences among people with differing levels of education once again point to the importance of considering several indicators of the ways people feel they have adjusted to life.

The more educated are more personally involved in marriage and parenthood, have higher expectations of their husbands or wives and children, and hence are presented with greater opportunities for both gratification and distress. They seem therefore to feel both happier with their marriages and yet more dissatisfied with the ways they have carried out their family responsibilities.

The attitudes of American men toward their jobs are conditioned by several factors, including the status their work carries with it, their income, their education, and their age.

As was expected, men with jobs that society regards as highly desirable also tend to be well-educated and to have high incomes. It is not surprising, therefore, that they say they get the most satisfaction from their work. But if their jobs are sources of considerable gratification to them, they are equally the source of greater worry and distress, because they attach more importance to their work and are more vulnerable to dissatisfaction or disappointment.

The authors discovered that the dissatisfaction expressed by men with less desirable jobs does not center on the lack of individuality, interest, or creativity in these jobs. Many observers believe that increasing automation and specialization in industry and office work have brought with them so much drudgery and alienation of the worker from his work that he presents special problems of psychological adjustment. Hence, many attempts have been made to provide these workers with other emotional outlets and to cater to their psychological deprivation. But men in lower job categories in the sample displayed less frustration and distress of this type than had been expected. Possibly their distress has found other outlets. Perhaps the industrial programs designed to meet their emotional needs are successful to some extent, or perhaps their aspirations in these areas are not as high as has been supposed and they are merely not as frustrated as has been thought. Or perhaps they have become resigned or adjusted to the lack of creative potential in their jobs.

In contrast to their general state of apathy, older men are both more satisfied and report fewer work problems with their jobs than younger men. The job may be an area where, rather than apathy, a sense of greater investment comes with increasing years. The people in the sample mentioned experiencing a variety of psychological and physical symptoms under stress. Women score high on all counts. Older people and the less educated are more preoccupied with their health; they score higher on a bodily symptom list, but they are prey to less psychological inertia. Incidentally, older women show more anxiety than younger women, whereas older and younger men do not differ in anxiety symptoms, an indication that the aging process may be harder on women psychologically, even though they tend to live longer. The fact that older people report more physical symptoms is apparently due, however, more to the increasing incidence of real illness that accompanies aging than it is to heightened distress. People with less education react to problems with physical symptoms, whereas the better educated show more stress in a psychological manner.

To the question, "Have you ever felt that you were going to have a nervous breakdown?" one out of five replied, "Yes." Definition of what he meant by "nervous breakdown" was left to the interviewee, the assumption being that a "nervous breakdown" was a popular label for a variety of severe mental disorders.

Two fifths of the people who said that they had experienced an emotional crisis of this magnitude blamed it on something external to themselves; the most frequently mentioned reason was death, illness, or separation involving a loved one; other reasons were tension connected with the job and financial or other external conditions. Another large group (one out of five) mentioned a physical illness. More psychological reasons given for the crisis included personality problems, and general tension and difficulties in relationships with others.

Evidence of the fact that many people are receptive to the idea of getting help with their problems shows up in the finding that almost half of those who felt they were going to have a breakdown consulted a professional source of help. Nearly nine out of ten of these reported seeing a doctor.

Up to this point it is clear that the way Americans view their mental health tends to be conditioned by their sex and age, the extent of their education, and the amount of money they make (a factor that is intimately connected with educational level). Is it possible that other differences, though less basic, are equally important to the mental health of the average American adult?

One example of these lesser differences taken by the survey is place of residence. The results are not at all clear-cut. The region in which various people lived did not seem to have any effect on their responses to the questions asked. The differences between farmers, city dwellers, and suburbanites leveled out, and the authors comment that "a young, educated, male farmer is more like a young, educated, male New Yorker than either is like his own father."

Male clerical workers and the wives of unskilled workers are most discontented and unhappy of all occupational groups. Managers, farmers, and salesmen worry most about their jobs, and the wives of professional men and salesmen complain most that their husbands' jobs interfere with their marriages.

Surprisingly, single women, proverbially frustrated in popular conception, are happier and more active in working out their problems than the supposedly carefree bachelors, although neither are as satisfied with life as married persons. Widows and widowers are especially unhappy.

People who attend church regularly report less distress than those who go to church infrequently, a finding that is perhaps related to both the religious commitment involved in frequent church attendance and its reflection of social integration in the community. People who come from homes disrupted by death or divorce in their childhood experience more distress than people from intact homes. Within this general difference, individuals whose fathers or mothers died while they were growing up are better able to deal with their problems than those whose homes were broken by divorce or separation; the latter have greater difficulty in working out their development and are less successful in their own marriages.

But by and large these more specific differences among Americans are not as striking as the similarities. The factors that appear most crucial to adjustment remain those over which adults have least control—sex, age, and education.

The second part of the study takes up the way Americans approach or fail to meet their problems.

Asked if he ever had a problem in which professional help would have been useful, nearly one in four said he had had such a problem. This problem occurred, as the interview was framed, sometime during life, and was not located as to time of occurrence.

One out of seven said he actually had sought help of some kind for past problems. This group that "went for help" was dominated by women, younger persons, and the better educated. These types, as we have observed, are inclined to be introspective, self-critical, and more concerned about themselves. In other words, they have a tendency to define their problems in psychological terms and to seek some form of psychological help.

Among those who sought help, 42 per cent reported their problems centered around their marriages, 18 per cent reported personal adjustment difficulties, and 12 per cent designated troubles involving their children.

Where did they go for help? Forty-two per cent consulted clergymen, 29 per cent physicians in general, 18 per cent psychiatrists or psychologists, and 10 per cent social agencies or marriage clinics.

People who saw their problems as arising from sources outside of themselves, such as marital troubles that they blamed on their partners, were less likely to go to psychiatrists than those who perceived the problem as a defect in themselves (or involving their children). In fact, two out of five who blamed themselves went to psychiatrists.

Similarly, we find that people with more education tended to use psychiatrists. These people, we have seen earlier, are more introspective and aware of their own inadequacies.

Despite the fact that it seems to take an unusual degree of insight for an individual to admit that he needs help with a mental or emotional problem, only about one fourth of those who sought assistance traced their problems back to their own inadequacies with any clarity. Most of them were looking for support and advice; few were prepared to be told that they must accept at least a share of the responsibility for their problems and that they must change themselves accordingly. This may be why so many chose the support of the clergyman and physician over the more searching, difficult, and prolonged therapy offered by the psychiatrist.

Fifty-eight per cent stated unequivocally that they were helped with their problems, while 14 per cent said they had received help, but with qualifications. One out of five reported that he received no help.

Marital problems and other troubles seen as arising from sources outside the individual fared worst; people with personal adjustment problems most often reported that the assistance they received was of value to them.

Sixty-five per cent of people who visited either clergymen or physicians said they were helped, while less than half (46 per cent) of those who went to psychiatrists felt it was worth while.

As implied by the nature of the most common troubles presented to them, clergymen and physicians are usually confronted with the more peripheral mental health problems. They appear more successful than psychiatrists in their efforts to tender support, and give advice, but they were not often seen as effecting "cures."

Psychiatrists, apparently, play a self-limiting role. Tending to regard support and comfort as secondary to therapy, they therefore may be restricted—in the amount of help they can give—to patients who have enough self-awareness to accept the necessity for exploration of their personalities and subsequent re-education. This may help to explain the large proportion of people who did not feel helped by their contact with a psychiatrist.

Only 28 per cent of the people who sought professional help spontaneously mentioned that someone else referred them to that source of help. The helping process seems to stop with the clergyman and physician in the majority of cases, and far more so with the clergyman than with the physician.

One in seven sought help, as indicated. An additional one out of ten who did not actually seek help recognized that he had a problem in the past that might have benefited from professional help. Among these latter persons, a fourth said they worked out their problems themselves. Another fifth said they didn't know where to go for help, and one out of seven gave a sense of shame or feeling of stigma connected with emotional problems as his reason for not seeking assistance.

These people who felt they could have used help often (three out of ten) did nothing about their problem or tried to work it out themselves (one out of four) or with the help of families or friends (one out of ten). A small number (3 per cent) said they resorted to prayer.

While the people who sought help were more educated, had higher incomes, and were from more urban areas than those who felt they could have used help but did not actually seek it, the differences between these two groups in the kinds of problems they faced, or the kinds of help they considered seeking actually were not striking. The latter were somewhat more vague about the nature of their difficulties and the possibilities for help and ended up by doing nothing or muddling through. The authors believe that a critical factor that led some to seek expert help was the availability of help and their awareness of it.

When psychiatric facilities were available in the community, they were used—predominantly and most effectively by people with better educations and higher incomes who thought in psychological terms, who were more aware of the presence and purpose of these facilities, and who could best afford them. The presence of mental health resources made it easier for people who were already disposed to look for this help to obtain it, rather than motivating people to seek assistance. These findings confirm on a national scale the conclusion of August B. Hollingshead and Frederick C. Redlich in *Social Class and Mental Illness* that psychiatric facilities in New Haven, Connecticut, were used mostly by the higher educational and income groups in that city.

One other major question was asked about the ways people handled their problems. What do they do about the day-to-day worries, or their periods of unhappiness that are not seen as requiring professional assistance? Many do nothing, or forget about it, essentially passive reactions that permit the situation to run its own course. Those who try to cope with their troubles on their own often turn to their spouses, other members of their families, or friends. Another sizable group prays. Sixteen per cent pray as a means of handling their daily worries and even more—a third—pray when faced with a critical unhappy period in their lives. Rarely did they put their faith in bartenders, taxi drivers, fortune tellers, or other supposedly popular but unorthodox confidants (or if they did, they didn't admit it to the interviewers).

The more active attempts to handle these situations—on one's own or with the aid of family and friends—are more common in men, younger people, the more educated and the higher income groups. Prayer and passive reactions are more common among women, the less educated, those with lower incomes, and older people. Thus the people who seek professional help when confronted with major personal problems—the better educated people with higher incomes—also take more initiative in trying to cope with less serious life problems.

What does the Survey Research Center's tremendously searching, methodologically precise study tell us by way of conclusions or implications? What, for example, does it suggest in sum about Americans' mental health?

First, it tends to support other observations that many persons are anxious and insecure. At the same time, it fails to document two other contentions: that Americans are luxury-oriented and that international tensions and the threat of nuclear war are a significant source of anxiety. Although our culture is highly materialistic, the data indicate that most people seek comfort and adequacy rather than luxury. And the sources of their anxiety, as people express them, appear to spring from their immediate environment.

Second, many men, perhaps reflecting the competition between home and job, feel unsure of themselves in their family relationships, on the one hand, and hard pressed on a ladder of status in their life work, on the other. Their wives, perhaps seeing themselves still cast in a secondary role, may be striving to achieve satisfactions that are not restricted to marriage and child-rearing. This is one possible source of their distress and unhappiness.

Third, older people are most consistently the ones in the culture who have achieved acceptance of themselves and have learned to live with their personal relationships, their work, and their fate. But this achievement occurs at the cost of resignation and apathy, and lower happiness and gratification.

Fourth, younger people, especially the well-educated, approach their lives, their relationships with others, and their careers with higher optimism and greater expectations. They possess greater potentials for satisfaction and also for frustration. This is seen in their greater happiness and satisfaction, accompanied by more problems and self-doubt.

What can be concluded from the study about the way Americans are facing their problems?

First, they have more chance for dealing with their troubles when they approach them subjectively, when they see them in internal, psychological, rather than external, physical terms, and at the same time wrestle with them actively instead of accepting them with apathy.

Second, their ability to adopt this attitude of "healthful worry" is more than any other factor dependent upon education. The higher their education, the greater their self-awareness, the greater their knowledge of channels for help, and, as a corollary to education, the more they can afford to spend on expert, effective help.

Third, most people have to rely on their own inner resources as they face their problems. When they do obtain help, it is usually informal, expedient, and temporary. Fourth, the problem of obtaining adequate professional help is particularly important in the lower status groups of the population. They have the least access to it, partly because they are less able to recognize their problems, and partly because they do not know where to look for this type of help, and also because it is not so readily available to them because of where they live and their low incomes. And not only professional help but their own resources are inadequate. The low use of psychiatric help by these groups has been found in other studies, like that by Hollingshead and Redlich. The present study adds the knowledge that these people also make less active use of other professional resources, their own resources, and of informal resources (family and friends). In addition, it is clear from the present study that lack of help-seeking in these groups does not stem simply from a lack of distress or motivation.

In general effect, the Gurin-Veroff-Feld monograph supports the community surveys showing a high prevalence of persons with various psychiatric or psychological illnesses or maladjustments as determined through psychiatric diagnosis of symptoms. For the more conventional questions, "How healthy do *we* think you are?" the present authors in effect substituted the question, "How healthy do *you* think you are?" With a "normal" rather than "sick" orientation, their interpretations lead us in another measure to the same impression. Nearly one in four adult Americans says that some time in life he has felt sufficiently troubled to need help. One in seven sought it.

This summation in itself indicates a rather high degree of self-perception and willingness for Americans to admit that they have weaknesses and problems, although they do not always identify the psychological aspects of their difficulty, and often see it as organic or external to themselves. Whether perceived as psychological problems or not, their troubles all appear to have a mental or emotional component, requiring understanding of the behavior of themselves and others.

The study additionally provides one of the first pieces, if not *the* first, of convincing evidence that public education in mental health principles during the present generation has increased general understanding of the human mind. It is still unclear what media and kinds of information are most effective, but it is clear that the younger, better educated group—the ones who have been exposed to the most mental health information in school or in their personal reading—have much greater recognition of the psychological nature of many of their problems and, hence, more appreciation of the mental health professions as a resource when help is needed. Indeed, *Americans View Their Mental Health* may stand as the most valuable research contribution yet made in the field of mental health education.

To reach this conclusion on the heels of George W. Albee's monograph, *Mental Health Manpower Trends,* can only serve further to disquiet us. Albee's work emphasized the continuing scarcity of professionally trained manpower.

Thus, these two monographs taken together underscore two of the most pressing problems in the field of mental health today. The present study indicates the potential value of attempts to reach more people and different classes of people with mental health education, whereas Albee begged the question of where we will get the manpower to meet the increased demand for mental health services. Here we have opposite sides of the same coin—the vast unmet need of the American people for help in recognizing and dealing with their mental and emotional troubles.

The shortage of trained mental health personnel works totally against the purposes of mental health education. Increased mental health education only serves to tax already inadequate mental health services. Inasmuch as present services tend to gravitate toward the best informed, it would appear that the psychologically rich get richer and the poor get poorer.

If our studies have raised social and economic as well as medical questions, we cannot duck them. We are forced into a position of finding solutions and pursuing them, or of admitting failure in both a professional and public responsibility.

JACK R. EWALT, M.D., DIRECTOR

Acknowledgments

THIS REPORT has been prepared by the Survey Research Center for the Joint Commission on Mental Illness and Health. At every step in the research, from the initial planning and design of the questionnaire to the final writing, we were indebted to the directors of both these organizations—Dr. Jack R. Ewalt, Director of the Commission, and Dr. Angus Campbell, Director of the Survey Research Center. Their support and encouragement, and their many valuable suggestions, have contributed immeasurably to the study.

Dr. Gordon W. Blackwell, in his association with the Commission, also provided considerable encouragement and assistance. To Mr. Greer Williams, Director of Information for the Commission, we are indebted for his helpful editorial comments.

In thinking through the problems investigated in this research, we consulted a variety of people. We should like to acknowledge especially the advice we received from our colleague at the Survey Research Center, Dr. Elizabeth M. Douvan, whose ability to highlight the pertinent theoretical problems was particularly helpful. At the beginning of this study Dr. William A. Scott, of the Department of Psychology, University of Colorado, did an admirable job of pulling together for us the pertinent research in mental health and pointing up those aspects of this research most relevant for conceptualization and measurement in a survey interview study. Drs. Alexander Leighton, Marvin K. Opler, Leo Srole, and Thomas Langner, all associated with the Midtown Study conducted at the Cornell Medical Center, very graciously gave us the benefit of their experience and advice and made available to us the data and the measures utilized in the interview part of their study. The late Dr. Allister MacMillan, in his role as research coordinator of the Stirling County study, took an active interest in the use of a symptom checklist in our study and provided us with most of the measures incorporated in the checklist that we utilized.

For carrying through the complex operations involved in a national survey, we are indebted to many of our colleagues in the Survey Research Center. Dr. Leslie Kish, head of the Sampling Section, and Miss Irene Hess supervised the design and selection of the sample. The field operations, complicated by the unusually personal nature of the content of the interview, were under the direction of Dr. Charles F. Cannell, head of the Center's field staff. Dr. Cannell, Dr. Morris Axelrod, and Mrs. Lois L. Davis supervised the training at the regional conferences set up to help the interviewers deal with the problems anticipated in the interview situation. The success of the field operations is due in large measure to their enthusiastic cooperation and the skill of their supervision and training. The coding of the interviews also involved special difficulties, which were overcome largely through the intelligence and conscientiousness of the coding staff and the efforts of Mrs. Charlotte C. Winter, head of the Coding Section, who combined unusual administrative efficiency with a refreshing eagerness to accept new and challenging problems.

To the interviewers for this study we owe a deep appreciation, for they handled a difficult assignment with dedication, enthusiasm, and unusual skill, succeeding in a task where many would have failed.

In the processing and analysis of the data, we were aided by Mr. C. Edwin Dean, head of the Statistical Analysis Section in the Center. Mr. William Smoke, a graduate student in mathematics at the University of Michigan, was particularly helpful in setting up special IBM 650 programming.

The preparation of this report has been facilitated by a research grant (M-2280) from the National Institutes of Mental Health, U.S. Public Health Service.

Finally, we should like to thank the four people who, more than any others, had to put up with the daily demands and share the tensions involved in processing a study such as this. Our research assistants, Mrs. Phyllis Hackett, Miss Elaine Hatfield, and Miss Patricia Hatfield, performed their many tasks with a conscientiousness and efficiency that served as models for our own work. The secretary for the project, Mrs. Joan Beatty, not only fulfilled what were often impossible demands but provided the good humor and general support that eased the pressures for all involved in this project.

GERALD GURIN
JOSEPH VEROFF
SHEILA FELD

Contents

	Page
Foreword	*v*
Staff Review	*ix*
Acknowledgments	*xxvii*

I. Introduction — 3
   Purpose and Content of the Study — 3
   The Methods — 8
   The Organization and Interpretation of the Report — 11

PART ONE. PROBLEMS OF ADJUSTMENT

II. General Adjustment — 19
   Present Feelings of Adjustment — 22
   Past Emotional Crises — 36
   Sex, Age, and Education Related to Measures of General Adjustment — 41
   Summary — 48

III. Perceptions of the Self — 52
   Interrelationships among Indices Pertaining to Self-Perception — 58

		Page
	Sex, Age, and Education Differences Related to Perceptions of the Self	65
	Summary	81
IV.	Marriage	84
	Orientation: Adjustment in Three Life Roles— Marriage, Parenthood, and Work	84
	Marriage	91
	Interrelationships among Three Measures of Marital Adjustment	92
	The Context for Judging Marital Adjustment	95
	Sex, Age, and Education Related to Marital Adjustment	101
	Summary	114
V.	Parenthood	117
	Interrelationships among Three Measures of Parental Adjustment	118
	The Context for Judging Parental Adjustment	120
	The Context Measures Related to the Self-Evaluations of Adjustment as Parents	124
	Sex, Age, and Education Related to Parental Role Adjustment	129
	Summary	140
VI.	The Job	143
	Interrelationships among Three Measures of Job Adjustment	144
	The Context for Judging Job Adjustment	148
	Context of Job Adjustment Related to Evaluations of Job Adjustment	150

CONTENTS

		Page
	Occupation, Age, and Education Related to Job Adjustment	*157*
	Summary	*171*
VII.	Symptom Patterns	*175*
	Factor Analysis of Symptom Items	*178*
	Interrelations among the Four Factor Scores	*185*
	Sex, Age, and Education Related to the Differential Prevalence of Symptom Factors	*187*
	Summary	*203*
VIII.	Selected Demographic Characteristics and Adjustment	206
	Sex	*208*
	Education	*210*
	Age	*212*
	Income	*215*
	Occupation	*223*
	Place of Residence	*228*
	Marital Status	*230*
	Religion and Church Attendance	*238*
	Broken Home Background	*246*
	Summary	*250*

PART TWO. SOLVING PROBLEMS OF ADJUSTMENT

IX.	The Readiness for Self-Referral	255
	Measuring Readiness for Self-Referral	*256*
	Relationship of Readiness for Self-Referral to Subjective Adjustment Measures	*260*

		Page
	Relationship of Readiness for Self-Referral to Demographic Characteristics	276
	Summary	298
X.	People Who Have Gone for Help	302
	Why People Go for Help	304
	Where People Go for Help	306
	How People Choose Help Resources	314
	Do People Feel They Are Helped?	317
	How People Feel They Are Helped	321
	Demographic Characteristics Related to Problems and Patterns of Help-Seeking	324
	Summary	341
XI.	A Critical Group	345
	Differences between People Going for Help and Those Who "Almost" Go	346
	Why People Do Not Go for Help	350
	How These People Handle Their Problems	359
	Summary	362
XII.	Personal and Informal Resources	364
	Methods of Handling Worries and Periods of Unhappiness	365
	Demographic Characteristics Related to Ways of Handling Worries and Periods of Unhappiness	369
	Summary	378
XIII.	Availability of Resources	381
	Over-all Relationships with Self-Referral Process	383
	Controlling for Education and Income	386
	Summary	394

	Page
PART THREE. SUMMARY AND CONCLUSIONS	
XIV. Implications	399

APPENDIXES

Appendix I
The Questionnaire — 409

Appendix II
Sample Design and Sampling Error — 425

Appendix III
Joint Commission on Mental Illness and Health. Participating Organizations, Members, Officers, and Staff — 433

References — 437

Index — 439

AMERICANS VIEW THEIR MENTAL HEALTH

I

Introduction

PURPOSE AND CONTENT OF THE STUDY

THIS MONOGRAPH is a report of a survey of the mental health of the nation, designed to investigate the level at which people are living with themselves—their fears and anxieties, their strengths and resources, the problems they face and the ways they cope with them. In order to gather systematic national information relevant to these aspects of the mental health of the general population, a total of 2,460 people, selected by methods of probability sampling to represent all American adults over twenty-one years of age living in private households, were interviewed by representatives of the Survey Research Center in the spring of 1957. Interviews ranged from one to four hours in length, averaging a little under two hours.

No special attempt was made to interview individuals who were obtaining or had ever obtained treatment for psychiatric disorders, although, in the course of obtaining a representative cross section of the population, a number of such persons were interviewed. Nor was any provision made to obtain data on the hospitalized population that is excluded in the usual national sample survey. Our interest was not in these people but in the general, "normal," stable population, the vast majority of whom never come into contact with any treatment resource.

The Area Investigated

Two broad areas were covered by the data collected in the interviews: (1) feelings of adjustment and (2) methods of handling emotional problems. In the area of feelings of adjustment, we wanted to explore some of the satisfactions and dissatisfactions people were deriving from life. We examined these feelings in a general sense and in several specific, critical areas: in three significant life roles (marriage, parenthood, and work); in attitudes toward the self (self-esteem, feelings of competence, identity, and the sense of self); and in psychosomatic and anxiety symptoms.

In connection with methods of handling emotional problems, we investigated several classes of variables. We were particularly interested in what we have termed the "readiness for self-referral," that is, a person's psychological readiness to turn to professional help with an emotional problem. To what extent is the use of such help a realistic alternative for people, something they see as relevant and appropriate for the problems they have encountered or might encounter within their life experience? We also explored the general approach people take in handling tensions and problems: Do they approach emotional and adjustment difficulties with apathy and resignation, with denial and displacement, with "coping" and resiliency, or with turning to God? And what are the sources of help to which people turn when faced with emotional and adjustment problems: Do they go to a psychiatrist, a social agency, a minister, their personal physician? Do they turn to family or friends?

Focus of the Analysis

In analyzing the data for this report, the major focus has been an epidemiological one, pointing up the relationships of measures of adjustment and methods of handling problems to such demographic characteristics as sex, age, education, income, rural-urban residence, religion, and occupational status. These findings should provide information that will help in assessing the ways in which various adjustment problems and characteristic modes of handling them are distributed in different subgroups of the population. We were concerned with questions of whether psychological and emotional stresses are experienced in some groups more than in others, and whether different subgroups in the population experience stress differently. Does stress tend to be experienced in some groups as physiological symptoms, in some as "unhappiness," in some as tension and "worrying," in some as self-doubt and inadequacy? In times of distress, which groups go to a psychiatrist, which to a minister, which turn to family and friends, which reject the use of any help and stress an ideology of "self-help?"

In addition to the descriptive information that this demographic analysis provides, it also serves an etiological function. Since variables such as sex, age, education, and "social class" define significant social roles and cultural subgroupings of the population, these demographic relationships provide clues to some of the cultural and social determinants of various adjustment problems and patterns of handling these problems. We shall point to etiological implications where they seem relevant.

Within this broader orientation to the data, we have done several other analyses, particularly in relating feelings of adjustment to the methods of handling problems. Our major question here was: Do different ways of experiencing and defining stress and problems have different implications for help-seeking solutions, particularly for referral to professional resources? In a sense, viewing these experiences of tensions and stress as potential symptoms for self-diagnosis, we were examining different "self-diagnosis–self-referral" patterns.

Relevance to Mental Health Criteria

In constructing the interview and analyzing the data, we focused on the "mental health" of this "normal" population as it is measurable in a national survey interview. Consequently, we have not attempted to utilize the interview material to classify the population in terms of standard diagnostic psychiatric categories. And, although we were interested in concepts of defensiveness and denial, in phrasing questions and analyzing data in such a way as to get beyond the more obvious conscious resistances, we did not, for the most part, attempt to probe for repressed material or to determine what people are "really like" beneath the level at which they think and feel in their daily functioning. Moreover, we have not tried to interpret our adjustment variables in terms of any conventional psychiatric definition of mental illness or health or to translate distributions on these variables into statements about the proportions of the population falling on different points of a "mental health–mental illness" continuum. In other words, we have viewed these measures as indices of "subjective need" rather than "need" as an expert psychiatrist might define it (although these two are undoubtedly related). We were exploring "self-diagnosis–self-referral" patterns rather than "diagnosis-referral" patterns. This does not represent an attempt to underplay the importance of the latter approach. We chose the former because it is especially appropriate to the sample survey interview technique and to the interest of the Joint Commission in studying a sampling of the "normal" population. In this population, behavior rarely takes the "acting-out" form that brings people to the attention of referral sources. Accessibility for help depends upon self-diagnosis and self-referral, and the investigation of the kinds of experiences and definitions of tensions and problems that will or will not bring people to the point of self-referral attains particular significance.

Although we do not attempt to use our measures of individual adjustment to diagnose people as "mentally healthy" or "ill," nevertheless we are somewhat concerned with the relevance of these measures to certain mental health criteria. Marie Jahoda (1958), in the first monograph in this series, pointed to the confusion and lack of consensus in the approaches to conceptualization and definition of mental health and mental illness. Many definitions have been used. In this study, we have dealt with variables which are relevant to several of these definitions. In the choice of specific variables to study, and in some of the approaches to measurement, we were influenced by considerations of relevance to some of the more common conceptualizations of mental illness and health. Feelings of well-being and unhappiness, attitudes toward the self (feelings of competence, sense of identity), maladjustment in central life roles—measured not only in terms of feelings of satisfaction and adequacy but in terms of "positive mental health" criteria (the breadth of gratification experienced in the role, the maximization of the possibilities afforded by the role) —are examples of variables in this study that represent concepts viewed in the psychiatric literature as relevant to definitions of mental illness and health. We also have included an anxiety and psychosomatic symptom list (discussed in Chapter VII); this not only has conceptual relevance but has some external validation against criteria groups differentiated by psychiatrists' diagnoses (although the validation was not done on a population comparable to the national sample we have studied).

Jahoda has pointed to the adequacies and inadequacies of these different sets of concepts and variables as criteria for mental illness and health, and they need not be repeated here. Despite their limitations, and their inadequacies as complete definitions, however, anxiety, feelings of unhappiness and frustration, a negative self-image, identity confusion, and maladjustment in important social areas of life would seem to be significant aspects of mental health, or at least, represent variables that have to be considered in any attempt at conceptualizing the problem. By providing data on some of the variables that have been used as criteria and by presenting relationships that give an idea of some of their different implications, the study may aid in the development of conceptualizations of mental health and in the evaluation of the place of different criteria in such conceptualizations.

In a certain sense, the approach in this study follows one of the suggestions offered in the Jahoda monograph—that a multiple criterion approach be utilized in studies of mental health. In pointing up some of the major research needs in this area, Jahoda emphasized the desirability of studies that would investigate the interrelationships of various measures of mental health and that would point up the distinctions and implications in the use of different criteria and indices. Although all the measures we deal with in this study relate to the problem of mental health from one limited point of view—that of the subjective evaluations of the people we interviewed—we have viewed these in terms of a multiplicity of criteria, stressing the many ways in which distress and well-being can be expressed. And our analysis of the data, which focuses on the examination of the interrelationships of several indices of mental health and their relationships to other variables, is a systematic attempt to investigate the implications of different mental health criteria.

As a contribution to the mental health literature, then, this study may be viewed as an empirical example of a multiple criterion approach, presenting data that may aid in evaluating the place of different criteria in a conceptualization of mental health. It should be reiterated, however, that any such contribution is secondary. The major significance of the study depends upon the assumption that the data collected in the study of tensions and problems as they are experienced, the distributions and variations of problems within certain subgroups of the population, and the differential implications of these problems for self-referral and problem-solving behavior are in themselves significant.

THE METHODS

The Interviewing Situation

In general, the procedures in this study followed the usual procedures of the Survey Research Center. However, because of the unusually personal nature of the content of the interview, we anticipated that there might be special problems in the interviewing situation, and certain steps were taken to solve these problems. In March 1957, immediately before the interviewing began, we held seven regional conferences throughout the country for the interviewers involved in the study. These conferences reviewed the problems that might be encountered in conducting interviews directed at this level of personal and emotional material. Special attention was given to ways of introducing the interview and establishing initial rapport and to problems of handling emotional disturbances that might be aroused in the interview.

In the actual interviewing situation, however, no special problems were encountered. The proportion of people who refused to be interviewed (8 per cent of those contacted) was not exceptionally high, and is comparable to the refusal rate usually obtained in the national studies conducted by the Survey Research Center. Moreover, in all except a few cases, these represented a refusal to be interviewed at all rather than a rejection of the content of the interview.

Rapport was generally good, as judged from the interviewers' impressions and from reading the interviews. These impressions were corroborated by the answers to a questionnaire sent to the respondents after their interviews had reached our office. These responses indicated no unusual criticism of the personal character of the questions and showed a generally favorable attitude to the interview experience.

Although there were apparently no special problems in obtaining the interviews, the question of the meaningfulness of the responses remains, specifically the question of the honesty of response. How freely did people talk to us about their problems and dissatisfactions, the things in life that were bothering them? This problem, it should be noted, although particularly pertinent here, is not qualitatively different from problems encountered in many other interview surveys that probe for information and attitudes in potentially sensitive areas. Success in meeting this problem depends to a large extent on the skill of the interviewers, who, through selection and training and experience, have the ability to enter a stranger's house and establish the kind of rapport that will allow the person to talk freely about private aspects of his life.

The problem of honesty of response is also dealt with in the construction of the interview schedule and the phrasing of the questions. Some of the techniques used may be illustrated by the handling of the questions on marriage (see Appendix I, questions 27 to 40). We first approached this potentially sensitive area by asking a question phrased in very general terms (question 27—"How is a woman's [man's] life changed by being married?"). We prefaced a question probing for the unsatisfying aspects of a marriage (question 32) with "Every marriage has its good points and bad points," and only after having allowed people to talk about the "nicest things" in their marriage did we ask about dissatisfactions. We allowed a person to express qualifications about his marriage by using the alternative "average" (question 34) instead of presenting him only with "happy" or "unhappy" alternatives.

It is difficult, of course, to assign a rating to the degree of success attained in meeting this problem in any given interview survey. Perhaps the most convincing evidence derives from a reading of the interviews; in this study, as in others, they reflect the surprising frankness with which people seem willing to talk to a survey interviewer about intimate aspects of their lives. But within a broader perspective, this question of honesty can be viewed as part of the general question of response validity, the ultimate test being the usability of the responses within the analysis framework of the study. In this connection, it might be noted, certain response problems have been minimized by the approaches we have emphasized in the analysis of the data. We have been mainly concerned with presenting *comparative* findings—for example, in comparing the responses of people in various demographic groups—and not with presenting absolute figures on the distribution of the population along the several indices of adjustment. Within such an analysis framework, the question is not whether or how much dishonesty of response was present, but whether there is any *systematic* bias, that is, whether dishonesty is more of a problem in certain groups than others.

Furthermore, only a particular type of systematic bias is a problem. We have not relied on a single measure of adjustment but have attempted to measure it in many different ways. For the most part, we focus on group differences in the ways of expressing problems. We do not ask the over-all question of whether one group expresses more problems or tensions than others. In general, then, we need not be concerned with the bias that might derive from certain groups being less willing *generally* to admit to problems, unhappiness, and tensions. For the most part, bias is an issue only to the extent that such hesitancy expresses itself systematically in response to *certain questions* but not to others.

One final problem with respect to the interviewing situation might be noted. In addition to problems posed by the nature of the content, there were special problems posed by the length of the interview. In an attempt to deal with this problem, three forms of the questionnaire were constructed, each one given to a randomly selected third of the interview population. Most of the questions—and all of those attacking the objectives of the study most directly—were asked on all three forms. Other questions, more exploratory and tangential to the major interests of the study, were asked on only two forms of the questionnaire, and, in some cases, on only one. In all except a few cases, the questions discussed in this report are those that were asked of the total population. The exceptions are noted when they appear in the report.

Sampling

Sampling presented no special problems in this study, since we were interested in the usual cross section sample and not in focusing on special groups. The sampling procedure restricts the survey to private households and excludes those people residing in military establishments, hospitals, religious and educational institutions, logging and lumber camps, penal institutions, hotels, and larger rooming houses. Thus our sample underestimates the transient, "anomic" segment of the population and that segment with severe "acting-out" behavioral symptoms. The sample is therefore probably biased in a conservative direction, one which tends to underestimate the extent of emotional disturbance in the population. A detailed description of the sampling procedure is given in Appendix II.

Coding

The coding of the interviews also followed the usual procedures of the Survey Research Center. Since translating the responses of a question into coding categories requires a good deal of inferential judgment, we tried to insure coding reliability by specifying in great detail what responses were to be considered under a given category. The code was unusually elaborate and necessitated considerable collapsing of categories before the data were usable for analysis purposes. However, it was felt that this procedure was desirable in this study, both as a way of obtaining high reliability and as a way of documenting the specific, detailed content of the categories ultimately utilized for analysis purposes.

THE ORGANIZATION AND INTERPRETATION OF THE REPORT

The analysis presented in this monograph is divided into two major parts, followed by a short concluding chapter. In Part One, we are concerned with the feelings of adjustment and the relation of these feelings to demographic characteristics. In Part Two, we are concerned with problem-handling—what people do about difficulties they have, what help they have sought to alleviate these difficulties. The appendixes to this book include a complete presentation of the interview schedule (Appendix I) and a detailed description of the sample design and sampling errors (Appendix II). A separate Tabular Supplement, available through the Survey Research Center,* contains three appendixes providing detailed tables of data that are just summarized in the present book. (All references in this volume to Appendixes A, B, or C relate to this Tabular Supplement.)

Part One describes some of the life satisfactions and dissatisfactions, tensions and concerns, and sources of happiness and strength that are experienced by a representative sample of the adult population of the United States. The separate chapters examine these experiences in several specific areas—in attitudes toward the self, in adjustment to three central life roles, in psychosomatic and anxiety symptoms.

Two general themes underlie much of the data throughout Part One, although we deal with many details specific to the particular topic under discussion. Some understanding of these themes may help in the integration of the discussions that follow.

The first theme is based on an exploration of some of the distinctions and interrelationships between two classes of variables: questions of gratification and satisfaction and questions of aspirations, involvement and investment in life. We are concerned not only with how positively or negatively a person evaluates different areas of his life—how "happy" he feels, how "satisfied" he is in his job, how positive or negative in his self-percept—but also in looking at these feelings in relation to the person's expectations and demands. In our descriptions of the various demographic groups, we try to distinguish the contentment that is a concomitant of limited aspirations and demands of life from the gratification that represents the realization of maximal expectations, to distinguish the dissatisfaction which represents a lack of gratification in life from the tensions and problems

* The *Tabular Supplement to Americans View Their Mental Health* may be obtained by writing to the Survey Research Center, University of Michigan, Ann Arbor, Michigan. Price: $1.50.

that do not reflect any unusual deprivation but are rather a natural consequence of an investment and involvement in life.

The general approach to measurement is consistent in most of the presentation in Part One, although the specific measures we have used to represent these two sets of variables differ according to the adjustment area investigated and vary somewhat from chapter to chapter. First of all, because of our interest in questions of aspiration and involvement as well as gratification, we not only ask about feelings of satisfaction and dissatisfaction but also explore the reasons for these feelings. Secondly, we attempt to evaluate feelings of well-being and distress with two types of questions, one phrased in terms of over-all evaluations of happiness or satisfaction and the other focused on more active feelings of distress—on the experience of tensions, problems, self-questioning—feelings that reflect some investment in life. In the following chapter, we see some of the implications of this distinction in the comparison we draw between the questions on "happiness" and "worries." Later chapters will distinguish between satisfaction or happiness on the one hand and the experience of problems and inadequacies on the other.

This distinction between satisfaction and involvement interests us because any evaluation of the meaning and implications of a person's feelings of well-being or distress would seem to require some understanding of the aspirations and expectations within which these feelings are experienced. The distinction is perhaps especially relevant in any attempt at evaluating these experiences in terms of criteria of mental health. In a sense, the two sets of variables reflect two dominant approaches to "positive mental health"—one stressing such concepts as adjustment and well-being, and the other stressing the fulfillment of potential, what Jahoda has referred to as "growth, development, and self-actualization." In examining the relationships between these two sets of variables, then, we may be able to point up some of the distinctions between the two approaches and demonstrate some of the different implications that follow from the use of each as a mental health criterion.

The second theme in Part One relates to a differentiation we draw as we examine the ways people describe the problems they face. In the areas of adjustment we have measured, we have attempted to distinguish between the internal and external structuring of problems. "Internal" refers to psychological definitions of problems, that is, definitions of problems that stress some personal or interpersonal malfunctioning, indicating some degree of introspection and self-questioning. "External," on the other hand, refers to problems seen in terms of external events or in terms of reactions to outside impersonal forces—job pressures, material deprivations, etc.—without involving any personal or interpersonal fault.

Our interest in distinguishing between these two approaches to problems stems mainly from our concern with exploring help-seeking patterns in the population. The ways a person experiences and defines the problems that he meets in life should bear certain obvious relationships to his ways of coping with these problems. And the extent to which he defines problems in internal or psychological terms should have special relevance in this connection, particularly in relation to his readiness to view these problems as requiring some outside professional help. The implications for help-seeking of these differential approaches to problems are investigated in Part Two.

The format in each chapter of Part One follows a general scheme. Each chapter begins with a discussion of the different ways people can define distress in the area under consideration, followed by a discussion of the differential meaning of these definitions: How much are they interrelated? What is their similar or differential content (e.g., what are the things people "worry" about as contrasted to what they feel "unhappy" about)? Then a detailed discussion of the relation of sex, age, and education to these different indices is presented. This is designed both to present descriptions of the three most important demographic groupings that merit detailed discussion and to gain some further insight into the indices we are discussing. After the detailed discussion of sex, age, and education, we will consider the other demographic variables—income, occupation, religion, rural-urban residence, and others—in a much more summary form, in a single chapter (Chapter VIII).

In Part Two, we are concerned with the ways in which distress and problems are handled. We pay some attention (in Chapter XII) to the use of informal personal and social resources—the turning to friends and family, the use of prayer, the tendencies to face problems with personal coping mechanisms or with passivity and resignation. But our major concern is with the use of professional help resources. Chapter X presents a detailed examination of those people in the population who at some time in their lives have actually used some professional resource for help with an emotional problem. Chapter XI tries to arrive at some understanding of the factors militating against the use of professional help, through study of a group that was "psychologically available" for such help but still did not make use of it. Chapter XIII will be concerned with patterns of use of professional resources in relation to the availability of mental health services in the community. In Chapter IX, we look at the question of the use of professional resources in a general sense, in terms of some of the factors related to the "readiness for self-referral," an index, it will be recalled, representing a person's psychological preparedness to turn to professional help with an emotional problem.

In studying the data in this monograph, one caution should be observed. They can most meaningfully be interpreted in terms of the comparative findings that are stressed in the report, and the absolute figures on the distribution to any question are to be interpreted with caution. In the analysis of the data we will be dealing, essentially, with *variables,* not with people. When one asks a person to assess a complex subjective state like "happiness," one should not give too literal an interpretation of the distributions of the responses. For example, in answer to Question 17 ("Taking things all together, how would you say things are these days—would you say you're very happy, pretty happy, or not too happy these days?"), 11 per cent of those interviewed said "not too happy." One should avoid interpreting this response as an absolute statement that "11 per cent of the American people are unhappy." We could have obtained a larger or smaller figure if the question had been worded differently.

The questions were worded as they were partly to obtain distributions, so that we could think of the responses as variables to relate to other variables. For example, since people are usually reluctant to admit to unhappiness in marriage, we introduced four alternative responses in the marital happiness question (Question 34—"very happy," "a little happier than average," "just about average," and "not too happy"). Many people who might not have said they were "not too happy" were able to say "just about average." But introducing this category meant that we got very few—only 2 per cent—in the "not too happy" category, and a statement that "only 2 per cent of the American people are unhappy in their marriages" would be misleading.

This limitation, it should be noted, applies more to Part One than to Part Two. In Part Two we can to some extent talk in terms of *people,* particularly with respect to Questions 91 and 92—how many people went for help, where they went, how many felt they were helped, how many had problems for which they feel they could have used help, but didn't go. Here, too, we will have to be cautious, and note that the figures were obtained in response to questions asked in a certain way. But the questions have more specific referents, especially where we ask about specific behavior, and the limitations engendered by the wording are probably less important here than in Part One.

NOTE

1. Memoranda describing the methods of study design, interviewing, coding, sampling, and analysis employed by the Survey Research Center are available on request. For a general statement of survey research methods, the reader is referred to the relevant chapters in Leon Festinger and Daniel Katz, Eds., *Research Methods in the Behavioral Sciences.* New York: Dryden Press, 1953.

PART ONE

Problems of Adjustment

II

General Adjustment

THIS PRESENT CHAPTER is concerned with our respondents' over-all evaluations of their emotional and psychological states. We explored these general attitudes and feelings in several ways, using the terminology that people themselves use in thinking about these things. In the most general sense, and in spite of the vagueness of the words, people tend to think of "happiness" and "unhappiness." A series of questions in the interview were structured in these terms. We not only asked people how happy they are but probed for the sources of happiness and unhappiness. In addition to concerning ourselves with the present, we attempted to provide some perspective to present feelings by asking about sources of past unhappiness and the anticipation of future happiness.

The questions were phrased as follows:

1. Why is this a happy time? How about the way things are today? What are some of the things you feel pretty happy about these days?
2. Everyone has things about his life he's not completely happy about. What are some of the things that you're not too happy about these days?
3. Thinking now of the way things were in the *past*, what do you think of as the most unhappy time in your life? Why do you think of that as an unhappy time?
4. Taking things all together, how would you say things are these days—would you say you're *very happy, pretty happy,* or *not too happy* these days?
5. Compared to your life today, how do you think things will be five or ten years from now—do you think things will be happier for you than they are now, not quite as happy, or what?

In addition to these general evaluations of happiness and unhappiness, we wished to probe for the specific tensions and problems that people were experiencing. Here the desire to use common terminology suggested the word "worry." We asked people what things they worried about most and how much they worried about such things. The questions were:

1. Everybody has some things he worries about more or less. What kinds of things do you worry about most?
2. Do you worry about such things a lot, or not very much?

In the questions on happiness and worries, we have some measure of the general feeling state of the individual, some of the primary tensions he is experiencing, and some of the major sources of his feelings of well-being. In addition, in the question probing for past unhappiness, we gain some historical perspective by obtaining information on what the individual feels to be the major emotional crises he has faced in his lifetime. However, we had a further interest in our exploration of past crises, an interest derived from our concern with what we have referred to as the "readiness for self-referral." We were interested not only in the critical emotional problems a person had faced but also in whether these had in any way been defined by the individual in "mental health" terms. We took two approaches to this question. In one, following the rationale of the use of words like "happiness" and "worries," we chose the term "nervous breakdown" as one of widespread common use, a phrase that many people use in describing a serious breakdown of psychic functioning. We asked the following questions of our respondents:

Have you ever felt that you were going to have a nervous breakdown? (If Yes) Could you tell me about when you felt this way? What was it about? What did you do about it?

We also approached this question of the "mental health" definition of a problem in another way. In one sense, an individual defines it as a "mental health" problem if he sees it as one he cannot handle by himself, one requiring the skill of some outside professional resource (just as feeling the need for a doctor may be viewed as an indication that an individual has defined himself as sick in a physical sense). Therefore, after a set of questions exploring what the respondents felt they would do if faced with a "personal" problem (defined as: "Sometimes . . . people are very unhappy, or nervous and irritable all the time. Sometimes there are problems in a marriage. . . . Or, sometimes it's a personal problem with a child or a job"), we then asked whether they ever had gone for help with such a problem, or whether they ever had had such a problem for which they felt outside help would have been relevant, even though they did not actually make use of it. The questions were worded as follows:

Sometimes when people have problems like this, they go someplace for help. Sometimes they go to a doctor or a minister. Sometimes they go to a special place for handling personal problems—like a psychiatrist or a marriage counselor, or social agency or clinic.

1. How about you—have you ever gone anywhere like that for advice and help with any personal problem? (If Yes) What was that about? Where did you go for help? How did you happen to go there? What did they do—how did they try to help you? How did it turn out—do you think it helped you in any way?

2. (If answered "No" to Question 1) Can you think of anything that's happened to you, any problems you've had in the past, where going to someone like this might have helped you in any way? (If Yes) What do you have in mind—what was it about? What did you do about it? Who do you think might have helped you with that? Why do you suppose that you didn't go for help?

Two things should be noted about these two questions. One is that we have defined professional resources in a broad sense to include medical doctors and ministers as well as individuals or agencies specifically relevant for handling mental health problems. The other is that we were interested not only in whether a person actually had gone for help with a personal problem but whether he felt he had ever had a problem for which the use of outside professional help was relevant, whether or not he had sought help.

In this chapter, we place the responses to these two questions in a single category, since our concern is with whether the individual has experienced a problem that he has defined in "mental health" terms, regardless of whether this was translated into an actual use of outside help. In Part Two of this monograph, where we are specifically concerned with the use of professional resources, we discuss some of the differences between people who, given the same definition of a personal problem as relevant to outside help, did or did not actually make use of such help.

The chapter has been divided into three parts. First we examine the material relating to present feelings—"happiness" and "worries." Then we look at the history of past emotional problems—sources of past unhappiness, the experience and content of "nervous breakdowns," and the experience of problems for which professional help was seen as relevant. Finally, we relate sex, age, and education to these experiences of happiness and distress.

PRESENT FEELINGS OF ADJUSTMENT

Experiences of Present Happiness and Unhappiness

Feelings of happiness were measured by responses to a question offering three alternative descriptions of their general feelings about "how things are these days." In answering this question, 35 per cent of the sample referred to themselves as "very happy," 54 per cent as "pretty happy," and 11 per cent as "not too happy." Absolute figures such as these are to be interpreted with caution, particularly for questions requiring people to make judgments on such a complex subjective state as happiness and to choose between such nebulous alternatives as "pretty happy" and "very happy." Our major interest in attempting to differentiate happy and unhappy groups lies not in determining the number of people in each group but rather in studying their comparative distributions among demographic groupings of the population and in analyzing the implications of this differentiation for problem-solving and help-seeking behavior.

Although we are not interested in the number of people falling into a given category of an adjustment variable like happiness, we *are* concerned with the question of the "meaning" of the categories. Before examining how people in the happy and unhappy groups differ in sex, age, and educational background, we should like to get some idea of what it means for a person to place himself in one of these two categories. What is a person thinking of when he describes

GENERAL ADJUSTMENT

himself as happy or unhappy? What are the connotations of these terms?

There are two approaches to the investigation of the meaning of the categories people choose for themselves. We will follow these two approachs in the analysis of the questions on happiness as well as in the investigation of the other adjustment measures explored in this monograph.

At the simplest level one can ask the respondent to tell you what he means. Thus, we asked people directly what things they are happy about and what things they are unhappy about. The other approach is more indirect and analytic. We can get some idea of what it means for persons to say they are "very happy" as contrasted to "not too happy" by relating these responses to their responses to other questions and seeing some of the ways that people in these two extremes differ. Using both approaches, for example, we can indicate that happiness means economic well-being not only by the fact that people tell us that they are happy for such reasons but also by our demonstration that people of higher income express greater happiness. Or, we can indicate that happiness is tied to a happy marital relationship not only because people very often mention marriage as a source of happiness but also because people spontaneously mentioning greater satisfaction from their marriages express greater happiness generally.

Although the reasons people give us directly constitute important data, particularly in a study that emphasizes a phenomenological approach, we rely chiefly on the meanings and connotations we can deduce from an analysis of interrelationships in the data. That is, in our analysis of the meanings and definitions that people give to different adjustment terms, we will emphasize these implicit definitions rather than those explicitly expressed. We are dealing in areas of life in which meanings and interpretations are not necessarily conscious or easily communicated and in which people cannot readily express the full ramifications of what they may mean. For example, when we note later that the expression of happiness implies optimism and faith in the future, this is a deduction from an analysis of the relationship between responses to the question concerning feelings of present happiness and responses to the one dealing with anticipation of future happiness. That is, the "very happy" group, when compared to the "not too happy" people, more often expect that things will be even happier in the future. This greater optimism was something that did not appear in the analysis of the reasons that people themselves gave for being happy, since it does not represent a concept that people spontaneously think or talk about when asked to tell why they are happy.

Let us turn now to the question of happiness, examining both its explicit and implicit meanings. The meaning of happiness is, of course, the subject of an ancient quest; the answer is not easily found in data and statistical analysis. Even having reduced the problem, as we have, to the question of how people themselves define the term (implicitly or explicitly), we are still faced with uniquenesses and nuances of meaning that do not readily translate into numbers on a coding sheet. Despite these limitations, however, there are certain communalities in these definitions that permit summarization and analysis; certain conclusions and generalizations can be drawn.

Table 2.1 presents the answers people gave to the questions asking for the things they feel happy and not happy about "these days." The table includes the first two reasons mentioned. Although some people

Table 2.1—Comparison of Sources of Happiness and Unhappiness (First Two Mentioned Reasons)

Reasons	Sources of Happiness	Sources of Unhappiness
Economic and material	29%	27%
Children	29	7
Marriage	17	5
Other interpersonal sources	16	3
Job	14	11
Respondent's health	9	7
Family's health	8	5
Independence; absence of burdens or restraints	8	—
Personal characteristics (and problems)	2	13
Community, national, and world problems	—	13
Miscellaneous	12	4
Not happy (unhappy) about anything	5	18
Not ascertained	2	2
Total	**	**
Number of people	(2460)	(2460)

** Here, and in following tables, this symbol (**) indicates that percentages total to more than 100 per cent because some respondents gave more than one response.

mentioned more than two codable reasons, it was felt that the first two would stress those that were primary in people's minds. The answers to these questions give, in a sense, the respondents' explicit definitions of happiness and unhappiness. They were combined into categories according to the area of life viewed as the source of happiness or unhappiness—economic and material things, the marriage relationship, the job, one's health or the health of others close to one, and so on.

Whenever possible, the happiness and unhappiness questions were summarized into parallel codes, but this could not be done in two instances. One of the unhappiness categories relates to impersonal problems—complaints about various aspects of community, national, or world affairs—an area that was not mentioned as a source of positive gratification. To the question of happiness, there were a number of responses coded as "independence; absence of burdens or restraints" —people who were happy because of their independence and freedom, the absence of worries, a lack of responsibility—a category without counterpart in the unhappiness area.

Looking at the findings presented in Table 2.1, we see that economic and material considerations represent the only category that is heavily mentioned both as a source of happiness and a source of unhappiness. Twenty-nine per cent of the people mentioned such considerations as one of the first two things they were happy about, and 27 per cent mentioned them in talking about the sources of their unhappiness. Contrary to the tendency of the romantic to depreciate the importance of money for happiness, people attach primary importance to economic and material considerations as they think about happiness and unhappiness. This is not necessarily a disagreement with the cultural admonition that "money can't buy happiness." The economic and material things that people talk about do not refer to wealth and luxury, and it is the necessity for great riches for happiness that some of the cultural ideals call into question. What people do emphasize, rather, is financial comfort and adequacy. Happiness is expressed in terms of having "enough" money, being free from debt, having a "nice" home. Similarly, the complaints are not of a lack of luxury, but refer to such things as debts, bills, and inadequate housing. People's economic and material aspirations are limited in scope, and happiness is defined in terms of comfort, not luxury.

The emphasis on health as a source of both happiness and unhappiness may also be viewed as reflecting a definition of happiness that stresses maintenance and comfort rather than the fulfillment of high aspirations. One would expect ill health to be a serious problem and an obvious cause for unhappiness. But it is somewhat surprising that 9 per cent of the population mention their own health and 8 per cent their family's health as major positive sources of happiness. These figures represent a sizable proportion of the population who define happiness in essentially negative rather than positive terms—"I can't complain, I've got my health." As we will note later, this response is predominant in the older age groups and reflects the generally lower level of aspiration and expectations in those groups.

Along with economic and material comforts, children are most often mentioned as a source of happiness, 29 per cent of the population pointing to their children or the relationship with their children in talking about the things that give them greatest happiness. Next in importance is the marriage relationship, mentioned by 17 per cent of the people, and "other interpersonal sources," mentioned by 16 per cent. The bulk of those who gave "other interpersonal sources" as a source of happiness mentioned pleasure in the family, a response including both children and husband or wife without distinguishing between them. Therefore these figures add up to well over half of the population for whom a major focus of happiness is in the broad area of marriage, children, and the family (even accounting for some overlap in responses, i.e., some people mentioning both marriage and children as sources of happiness).

It is interesting to note that children are mentioned more often than marriage as a source of happiness. To some extent, this is a function of the fact that a number of people with children—the widowed and divorced—are no longer married. But even if only those presently married are considered, the difference still remains. This suggests that the relationship with one's children, at least at the conscious level, may involve less ambivalence than the marriage relationship, an assumption conforming to some of the data to be discussed in the chapters devoted to marriage and parenthood (see Chapters IV and V).

Looking now at the sources of unhappiness, we see that marriage, children, and the family, compared to their salience as mainsprings of happiness, are much less often viewed as sources of distress. Five per cent of the population mentioned the spouse or some interpersonal aspect of the marriage as one of the major sources of unhappiness, and 7 per cent expressed unhappiness over some problem in the child or some aspect of the parent-child relationship.

These figures are much lower than the comparable ones listing these relationships as sources of happiness. On the other hand, in absolute figures, they do represent a large number of people finding some cause for unhappiness in what are the central life relationships. Although relatively rare as responses, unhappiness in these areas, particularly in the marriage relationship area, does have serious consequences in terms of over-all adjustment, as will be indicated in later discussions.

In addition to the relatively sparse mention of relationship problems as sources of unhappiness, there was also relatively little mention of what might be termed personal problems—conditions pointing to defects or inadequacies in the self. Although the 13 per cent of the population giving these responses represents a large number of people, it is much less than the proportion who saw the sources of their unhappiness outside the self.

In general, then, looking at the reasons people themselves give for their unhappiness, we see a great tendency for people to externalize their problems, to locate them in concrete, material things, or a job, or, if located in the self, to talk in terms of health rather than personal or interpersonal inadequacy. There is little introspection in these responses. It is, of course, interesting to speculate on how much this manner of defining unhappiness represents an externalization of really internal problems. There are suggestions, in the interviews, that, in some cases at least, this is true. But even if they reflect only defenses and externalizations, these data are significant, particularly in reference to their implications for help-seeking behavior. They point to the great tendency in the general population, whatever the "true" nature of their problems and unhappiness, to view unhappiness in nonpsychological terms, which would make it difficult for them to see the relevance of psychologically oriented help resources.

One final comment on the reasons for unhappiness may be of interest. Although most of the responses are not personal in the sense of involving self-questioning and self-blame, they do tend to be self-oriented. The causes for concern are, in most cases, limited to factors that have an immediate effect on the individual. Problems that have a community or national or world locus are mentioned by only 13 per cent of the population. Within this broader category, 4 per cent of our respondents expressed unhappiness over problems of world tension and the possibility of war, a figure that may seem small in the era of the hydrogen bomb and the cold war. This 4 per cent, it should be noted, is also the proportion of people mentioning such concerns in response to the question on what they worried about. In their day-to-day living, people are actively concerned with the things that affect them in immediate and tangible ways, and problems of broader and more general concern tend to sink beneath the level of immediate awareness.

Comparisons of Present Unhappiness and Worries

Over-all feelings of well-being and distress were measured not only in terms of happiness but also in terms of worries. In this section we examine some of the similarities and differences in the nature of the responses elicited by these two sets of questions.

Table 2.2 presents the interrelationship of the responses to the questions on how happy a person feels and how much he worries. We see that a strong relationship exists between these two measures: people who feel happier worry less; unhappy people worry more. For example, whereas 65 per cent of the people who are "very happy" say they worry "never" or "not very much," these answers are given by only 36 per cent of the "not too happy" group. The relationship between these measures is not surprising. What is of more interest, perhaps, is the fact that the relationship is not stronger than it is. There are many people who are very happy but still worry a good deal, and many in the unhappy groups who apparently meet their unhappi-

GENERAL ADJUSTMENT [29]

Table 2.2—Relationship between Evaluation of Happiness and Extent of Worries

Extent of Worries	EVALUATION OF PRESENT HAPPINESS		
	Very Happy	Pretty Happy	Not Too Happy
Never	13%	11%	5%
Not very much	52	44	31
Sometimes	6	8	3
A lot	22	28	44
All the time	2	4	14
Not ascertained	5	5	3
Total	100%	100%	100%
Number of people [a]	(849)	(1326)	(275)

[a] Does not include the 10 people whose response to the question on happiness was not ascertained.

ness with apathy and a low level of worry and concern. In looking at the explicit and implicit definitions of unhappiness and worries, then, we will explore some of the differences in the meanings that people attach to the two concepts.

Considering first the explicit definitions of these terms, we find in Table 2.3 a comparison of the responses to the question on sources of unhappiness with the responses to the question: "What kinds of things do you worry about most?" Again, only the first two mentioned reasons are tabulated. People point to similar kinds of things in talking about their worries and unhappiness. Three areas—the economic

Table 2.3—Sources of Unhappiness and Sources of Worries (First Two Mentioned Reasons)

Reasons	Sources of Unhappiness	Sources of Worries
Economic and material	27%	41%
Children	7	15
Marriage	5	2
Other interpersonal sources	3	7
Job	11	9
Respondent's health	7	10
Family's health	5	18
Personal characteristics (and problems)	13	5
Community, national, and world problems	13	11
Miscellaneous	4	5
Not unhappy (worried) about anything	18	10
Not ascertained	2	*
Total	**	**
Number of people	(2460)	(2460)

* Here, and in following tables, this symbol (*) indicates less than one-half of 1 per cent.

and material, family's health, and children—are somewhat more often mentioned as reasons for worrying than as reasons for unhappiness. All these are areas where a certain amount of tension and concern is possible even though the situation is not really unhappy at the present time. Thus, one can worry about something that is seen as only temporary and not serious or permanent enough to cause unhappiness. Personal problems and inadequacies, on the other hand, which are likely to be seen as more permanent and serious, are mentioned more often as sources of unhappiness than of worries. Also, worrying has a future reference, so that, particularly with respect to questions involving one's children, or money, or health, one can be concerned about things that might happen or responsibilities one will have to meet, even though the situation is at present under control. But these differences are relatively minor; as already indicated, the major impression from the data in Table 2.3 is one of similarity between the problem areas in people's definitions of unhappiness and worries.

If these explicit definitions of unhappiness and worries tend to be similar, what can we learn from some of the more implicit definitions, that is, from an examination of the relationship of feelings of unhappiness and worries to other questions? How similar or different are worrying and unhappiness in relation to other things? Are there certain things that go with worrying but not with unhappiness? Does worrying have implications that make it different from unhappiness?

When we examine these relationships we see that the feelings of worry and unhappiness do seem to differ in some of their implicit meanings. The question on worries seems to tap a life-involvement dimension, which, although related to the question of satisfaction and happiness, has additional elements as well. Worrying seems to imply an investment in life, the absence of worrying a lack of involvement and aspiration. We will illustrate this point in the discussion of findings to follow.

Having noted the sources of happiness, unhappiness, and worries, we now wish to consider whether these reasons are different for the happy and unhappy groups and for the worrying and nonworrying groups. Does feeling happy mean that one is deriving happiness from special kinds of things? Does rating oneself as "not too happy" mean a particular concern with certain areas of unhappiness and worries? And do the worriers differ from the unhappy people and the non-worriers from the happy people in the things they stress as sources of happiness, unhappiness and worries?

Looking first at the relationship between feelings of happiness and the sources of happiness, unhappiness, and worries, some interesting findings emerge. If we compare the reasons of the "very happy" people with the reasons of those who say they are "not too happy," the "very happy" much more often mention marriage and the family as sources of their happiness. Conversely, in looking at the sources of unhappiness, we find that marriage and children are much more often mentioned by the unhappy people. Thus, general feelings of happiness are clearly influenced by whether a person is satisfied or frustrated in his central life relationships—marriage and the family. When he is happy in these relationships he tends to be happy generally; when he is unhappy in these relationships he tends to be unhappy.

These findings are in contrast to the lack of relationship between feelings of happiness and the importance of economic and material factors as sources of happiness and unhappiness. If one corrects for the fact that very happy people tend to give more reasons for happiness, and that unhappy people tend to give more reasons for unhappiness, there is very little difference between the proportions in the "very happy" and "not too happy" groups mentioning economic and material reasons for happiness and unhappiness: people who mention economic and material factors as a major source of happiness are just as likely to say they are "not too happy" as they are to feel "very happy"; and those who mention these factors as a major source of unhappiness are just as likely to be "very happy" as they are to be "not too happy."

This does not mean that material considerations are unimportant for happiness. In our discussion of the relationships between adjustment measures and income (see Chapter VIII), we will see that material well-being does seem to be a significant variable in this area, separating people of different levels of happiness. Its effects, however, are apparently indirect. At the level of conscious awareness, although many people mention material and economic considerations in talking about happiness and unhappiness, these experiences of satisfaction or frustration in the economic and material area are not related to the distinction between feeling happy and unhappy. The involvement and concern with material matters appears to be less crucial as a determinant of happiness or unhappiness than is the involvement and concern with the interpersonal and familial aspects of life.

One other item in the relationship between feelings of happiness and the sources of happiness and unhappiness that might be briefly noted is that health emerges as an important consideration in the "not too happy" group. People in this group mention health more often, both as a source of happiness and as a source of unhappiness. This is related to the fact that there is a heavy concentration of older people in the "not too happy" category, and health is a vital consideration for them.

Thus, we see that a person's general, over-all feelings of happiness are closely tied to the particular content of his sources of gratification and distress. Satisfaction in the central life relationships—marriage and the family—is crucial. However, when we look at the relationship between how much a person *worries* and the sources of happiness, unhappiness, and worries, a different picture emerges. The difference is not in the reasons for unhappiness: greater worrying, like unhappiness, tends to be associated with stressing marriage, children, and health as sources of unhappiness. The difference is in the sources of happiness: unlike the people who were happier, people in the lower worrying categories do not find greater sources of satisfaction in the marriage and family areas.

To summarize, worrying and unhappiness both reflect a dissatisfaction with certain areas of one's life, particularly the basic relationships with husband, wife and children; gratification in these relationships, however, is associated with happiness but not with an absence of worrying. Unlike feelings of happiness, the absence of worry does not seem to be a reflection of any special gratifications.

Parallel to these findings on the *kinds* of reasons given for happi-

GENERAL ADJUSTMENT [33]

ness and unhappiness are the findings on the *number* of reasons given. As indicated in Table 2.4, happy people tend to give many more reasons for happiness and many fewer reasons for unhappiness than do the less happy groups. Seventy-four per cent of the "very happy" people mention two or more reasons for happiness as contrasted to 33 per cent of the "not too happy" group; and 21 per cent of the "very happy" people compared to 48 per cent of the "not too happy" group mention two or more reasons for unhappiness.

Table 2.4—Relationship of Feelings of Happiness and Worries to Number of Reasons Given for Unhappiness and Happiness

Two or More Reasons Mentioned for	EVALUATION OF PRESENT HAPPINESS		
	Very Happy	Pretty Happy	Not Too Happy
Happiness	74%	65%	33%
Unhappiness	21%	31%	48%
Number of people [a]	(849)	(1326)	(275)

Two or More Reasons Mentioned for	EXTENT OF WORRIES				
	Never Worry	Worry Not Very Much	Worry Sometimes	Worry a Lot	Worry All the Time
Happiness	62%	70%	69%	60%	49%
Unhappiness	14%	27%	34%	35%	44%
Number of people [b]	(271)	(1115)	(166)	(686)	(106)

[a] Does not include the 10 people whose response to the question on happiness was not ascertained.
[b] Does not include the 116 people whose response to the question on worries was not ascertained.

These findings are, of course, not surprising. What is of interest is that they do not parallel the findings on worries. The extent of worrying is very clearly related to the number of reasons given for unhappiness but not to the number of reasons given for happiness. Just as worrying was related to the kinds of unhappiness mentioned but not to the kinds of happiness stressed, it also reflects a greater *number* of sources of unhappiness but does not as clearly reflect any difference in number of sources of happiness. We may summarize these findings as follows: Unhappiness and worrying seem to be similar in reflecting a high number of frustrating and unhappy experiences as well as particular kinds of stresses. They differ, however, in that unhappiness also seems to reflect an absence of positive areas of satisfactions in life, whereas worrying does not seem to imply such a lack.

Another and related difference between the responses to the happiness and worries questions emerges when we compare them to the responses to the question on the anticipation of future happiness. As can be seen in Table 2.5, these two questions show opposite relation-

Table 2.5—Relationship of Extent of Present Worries and Happiness to Anticipation of Future Happiness

Anticipation of Future Happiness	EVALUATION OF PRESENT HAPPINESS		
	Very Happy	Pretty Happy	Not Too Happy
Happier	43%	43%	34%
About the same	38	29	17
Less happy	6	10	14
Don't know, won't be here	11	16	31
Not ascertained	2	2	4
Total	100%	100%	100%
Number of people [a]	(849)	(1326)	(275)

Anticipation of Future Happiness	EXTENT OF WORRIES				
	Never Worry	Worry Not Very Much	Worry Sometimes	Worry a Lot	Worry All the Time
Happier	27%	42%	48%	48%	40%
About the same	42	34	27	23	28
Less happy	8	9	8	11	7
Don't know, won't be here	20	13	16	18	17
Not ascertained	3	2	1	2	—
Total	100%	100%	100%	100%	100%
Number of people [b]	(271)	(1115)	(166)	(686)	(106)

[a] Does not include the 10 people whose response to the question on present happiness was not ascertained.
[b] Does not include the 116 people whose response to the question on worrying was not ascertained.

ships. People unhappy in the present are less optimistic about the future. Whereas 81 per cent of the "very happy" group feel that things will be the same or happier "five or ten years from now," such feelings are expressed by only 51 per cent of the "not too happy" group; the latter express both greater uncertainty and greater pessimism (14 per cent of them feel that things will be less happy, compared to 6 per cent of the "very happy" group who feel this way).

The pessimism, and particularly the uncertainty about the future, is to some extent a function of the fact that, as we will see later, the "not too happy" people are heavily represented in the oldest age groups. But even if we eliminate these oldest age groups from consideration, we still find an association between present unhappiness and pessimism or uncertainty about the future. Thus, if we examine the relationship between feelings of present happiness and anticipations of the future for persons under fifty-five years of age, we find the same tendency for those unhappier in the present to express greater pessimism and uncertainty about future prospects: 30 per cent of the "not too happy" compared to 12 per cent of the "very happy" feel either that things will be less happy in the future or that they do not know how things will be.

In contrast to the greater pessimism of the people who express distress in terms of unhappiness, worrying is associated with greater optimism. Of the people who say they worry "all the time," 48 per cent feel that things will be happier for them in the future, whereas only 27 per cent of the people in the "never worry" category feel this way. (It should be noted that this relationship is mainly a function of the difference between the extreme response of "I never worry" and all other responses, that express some worrying.)

One difference between unhappiness and worrying, then, may be seen in the perception of the changeability of things. Worrying implies to some extent a positive and hopeful view of life; unhappiness, a negative, passive view. Combined with the findings we have previously discussed, the differences may be summarized as follows: Unhappiness and worrying seem to be reflections of similar problems, tensions, and concerns. They differ, however, in that unhappiness also seems to reflect a lack of positive resources, whereas worrying does not necessarily imply such a lack. This lack of positive resources becomes associated, in unhappy people, with apathy and pessimism about the future; the worriers, not sharing this lack, are optimistic about the possibility of change.

These findings, then, illustrate the point we have made, that worrying, although related to unhappiness, also represents another dimension, one which cuts across the question of happiness. It appears to be a reflection not so much of whether or not one has problems as it is an attitude toward these problems and an orientation toward handling them. Worrying, for all its implications as to tensions, problems, and unhappiness, is, at least, not apathy, and seems to represent an investment in life, a view of life as changeable, and a commitment to change.

Thus, worrying and unhappiness differ in certain crucial ways as criteria of adjustment. We will see some implications of these differences when we examine the relationship of these two variables to sex, age, and educational background.

PAST EMOTIONAL CRISES

Past emotional crises, as we have indicated, were measured by three questions in the interview: one about the "most unhappy period of your life," one asking about a "nervous breakdown," and the third asking about personal problems for which professional help was seen as relevant. It is of interest to examine the specific content of the responses to the first of these questions in juxtaposition to those that were given as sources of present unhappiness. The responses to the question on past unhappiness may be viewed as a backdrop for the present tensions, for a look at the past gives some indication of the relative seriousness of present concerns, and suggests which of them will still seem critical in the years ahead.

Death of a loved one was the unhappiness most frequently recalled by people in talking of the past. More than one person in four mentioned the period in which a death occurred as the most unhappy time of their lives. About half of these responses referred to a parent or both parents, with death of a husband or wife, and death of a child, next in order of frequency. Since death affects only a limited proportion of a population at any given time, it was rarely mentioned as a source of present unhappiness, although there were some who spoke of the loneliness following a recent loss. The other reasons for past unhappiness, however, parallel the reasons mentioned for present unhappiness, and some of the comparative figures are of interest.

Economic and material things again receive prominent mention.

About one person in eight mentioned some crisis in this area as a major source of past unhappiness, compared with the one in four who mentioned such problems as sources of present unhappiness. Although such problems were mentioned less frequently for the past than for the present, the problems of the past were more serious than those of the present. The latter, as we have noted, were phrased mainly in terms of annoyances rather than crises, referring to such things as debts, bills, and inadequate housing. The economic problems recalled from the past, however, tended to be phrased in the stark terms of maintaining subsistence. Many of these problems related to difficulties during the depression of the early thirties. We would expect, then, that most of the economic concerns that bother people today will probably not seem significant in the future.

In addition to these economic and material problems, there were a number of other areas of concern, and these were mentioned with about the same frequency for the past as for the present. Thus, problems centering around the job, health of a loved one, one's own health, and the marriage relationship were each mentioned by almost the same proportion of the population (5 to 11 per cent) that gave these problems as sources of present unhappiness. It is not surprising that problems in marriage and a job should receive just as much emphasis in a long-range as in a narrower perspective, since they represent central areas of life. The emphasis on health may also have been expected. Serious sickness, particularly of a husband or wife, apparently has effects of long-range implication, not only in terms of the emotional reaction but also in terms of the total life dislocation it can cause.

One area that was rarely mentioned in the recall of past unhappiness, although it was of some importance in the present, concerned problems with children. About 7 per cent mentioned personal and interpersonal problems involving children as sources of present unhappiness, but only about one per cent recalled these problems as past emotional crises. It would appear that problems involving children, despite the concern they cause at the time they are occurring, are less disturbing in the long range than problems in other areas.

Although we have stressed the differences between present and past unhappiness, there was a similarity in one very important general sense, namely, that problems tended to be phrased as reactions to external events and were rarely viewed in the psychological sense of a breakdown in personality or interpersonal functioning.

We turn now to a consideration of those problems that were defined in mental health terms. Nineteen per cent of the people in the sample answered "Yes" to the question: "Have you ever felt that you were going to have a nervous breakdown?" And 23 per cent indicated that at some time they had had a personal problem for which some professional help might have been useful. (Fourteen per cent actually used such help and an additional 9 per cent thought they could have used professional help at some time.)

What kinds of problems do people have in mind when they say they once had felt they were about to have a "nervous breakdown" or could have used some help? And is there a relationship between those who define a problem as a nervous breakdown and those who see a problem as requiring professional help?

As expected, there is a clear relationship between these groups (Table 2.6). Forty-five per cent of the people who at some time had felt they were "going to have a nervous breakdown" also experienced a personal problem for which they thought professional help was relevant, whereas among the people who never had felt they were going to have a nervous breakdown only 18 per cent viewed past problems in help-relevant terms. What is perhaps of most interest is that an even stronger relationship was not revealed. Over half of the people who defined some problem in nervous breakdown terms

Table 2.6—Relationship of Feeling of Impending Nervous Breakdown to Perceptions of a Personal Problem as Relevant for Professional Help

Perception of Help-Relevant Problem	Felt Impending Nervous Breakdown	Did Not Feel Impending Nervous Breakdown
Had problem relevant for help	45%	18%
Did not have problem relevant for help	55	82
Not ascertained	*	*
Total	100%	100%
Number of people [a]	(464)	(1991)

[a] Does not include the five people whose responses to the "nervous breakdown" question were not ascertained.

did not see it as a problem for which professional help was relevant. Furthermore, if we percentage the data on which Table 2.6 is based in the horizontal rather than vertical direction, we find that of those who felt they had had a problem requiring professional help, over half (64 per cent) did not see this as a problem they would call a nervous breakdown.

An indication of why this relationship was not stronger can be gained from an examination of the specific problems discussed. Although the phrase "nervous breakdown" elicited a somewhat greater psychological response than did the question on unhappiness, the term still tended to be defined more often as an individual collapse in the face of some external stress than as a personality problem or a problem in interpersonal relationships (Table 2.7).

Table 2.7—Problems Mentioned in Feeling of Impending Nervous Breakdown (First-Mentioned Reasons Only)

External		39%
Death or illness of loved one; other separation	16%	
Work-related tension	14	
Financial or other circumstantial conditions	9	
Own physical illness or disability		18
Personality problems, general tensions		18
Interpersonal difficulties		16
Menopause		4
Not ascertained		5
Total		100%
Number of people		(464)

The external stresses were defined in several ways: 16 per cent of the people defined nervous breakdown as an extreme emotional reaction to ill health in someone close to them, or to death or some other externally induced separation (such as separation when the husband was in the army); 14 per cent defined it in terms of the strain from overwork and other job and business tensions; 9 per cent viewed it as an individual breakdown in the face of a deteriorating financial or other circumstantial condition. Eighteen per cent of the people defined their nervous breakdown as a reaction to their own physical illness or disability; although illness is "inside" the individual, it is "external" in the sense that it is something that happens "to" a person rather than something viewed as an outgrowth of his own personal or interpersonal malfunctioning.

Responses that might be viewed as more psychological in nature were given by only one person out of three who talked of a nervous breakdown. Eighteen per cent mentioned something that might be viewed as a personality problem, pointing to certain personality inadequacies, or speaking in terms of general personal disruptions or of feeling generally upset and worried and overwhelmed by things. Sixteen per cent spoke of defects in relationships—in marriage, with children, with others close to them.

These figures are in striking contrast to the responses to the question about problems requiring professional help (see Chapter XI, Table 11.1). The biggest difference is in the frequency with which problems in interpersonal relationships are mentioned. In contrast to the 16 per cent who mentioned such problems in talking of a nervous breakdown, they were mentioned by over 60 per cent of the people who talked of a personal problem requiring professional help. The biggest difference occurs with respect to marriage, mentioned as a problem by 8 per cent of the people who talked of a nervous breakdown, but by 45 per cent of those who spoke of personal problems needing professional help. Conversely, there was much less mention of problems phrased as emotional reactions to external stress. The job, physical illness, or concern over the health or death of a loved one, all received much less mention as personal problems needing professional help than as conditions precipitating a "nervous breakdown."

In the responses to the two questions there was not much difference in the extent to which people spoke in terms of personality adjustment problems in the self. But as we saw from the much greater focus on interrelationship problems and the much smaller focus on problems of "external" stress, people responded in much more psychologically pertinent terms to the question about problems for which professional help was seen as relevant than to the question on nervous breakdown (or the questions on past and present happiness). Some of the implications of this difference will be seen in the following sections, as we explore the relationship of these questions to the sex, age, and educational background of the respondents.

SEX, AGE, AND EDUCATION RELATED TO MEASURES OF GENERAL ADJUSTMENT

Sex, age, and education refer to significant social roles and cultural subgroups associated with different pressures, demands, areas of potential gratification, information, and values with regard to a psychological view of life. Sex and age, in addition, represent the complex interaction of physiological and cultural factors. All these factors presumably affect both the experiences of gratification and dissatisfaction and the readiness to admit to problems and distress.

Sex

Because the two sexes represent different social roles and cultural subgroups, are subject to different demands and expectations, and encouraged toward different avenues of self-expression and gratification, we should expect men and women to stress different things as the sources of their gratifications or of their tensions and discontent. The findings, in general, support this expectation. In talking of happiness, worries, and unhappiness, for instance, men more often stress the economic and material and the job, and women more often find both gratification and sources of concern in children and the family. These differences between men and women are not always very striking, but they are consistent and in the expected direction.

Turning to how much rather than what kinds of happiness, dissatisfaction, and tension the two sexes experience, we found, in general, that there was more expression of problems among women than among men (Table 2.8). Women expressed more worrying, more often felt they had experienced a nervous breakdown, and more often felt they had had a personal problem that could have benefited from professional help. To what extent these differences suggest that women in our society are subject to greater strains than are men and to what extent they reflect a greater willingness on the part of women to face these strains and to admit to difficulty in handling them cannot be deduced from the data. But whatever their ultimate meaning, the data do suggest that there is a greater conscious experience of tension among women, that women dwell on their problems

Table 2.8—Relationship between Sex and Measures of General Adjustment

Measures of General Adjustment	Men	Women
Extent of worries		
Never worry	14%	8%
Worry not too much	48	43
Worry sometimes	7	7
Worry a lot	24	31
Worry all the time	2	6
Not ascertained	5	5
Total	100%	100%
Evaluation of present happiness		
Very happy	33%	36%
Pretty happy	57	52
Not too happy	10	12
Not ascertained	*	*
Total	100%	100%
Feelings of impending nervous breakdown		
Felt impending nervous breakdown	12%	25%
Did not feel impending nervous breakdown	88	75
Not ascertained	*	*
Total	100%	100%
Experience of problem relevant for professional help		
Had problem relevant for help	18%	27%
Did not have problem relevant for help	81	73
Not ascertained	1	*
Total	100%	100%
Number of people	(1077)	(1383)

more, and more often view these problems in mental health terms. We will see these results duplicated in many other areas to be examined in the succeeding chapters, indicating a fairly general tendency for women to express more problems, tensions, and dissatisfactions.

It is of interest to note, in Table 2.8, that this difference between men and women did not appear in the question on the evaluation of one's over-all happiness. It was expected that women would express greater unhappiness, but no significant difference appeared. Apparently, the women's greater expression of tensions, problems, and dissatisfactions in specific areas is not reflected in the over-all evaluation of happiness. (It might also be noted that men and women did not differ in the anticipation of future happiness.) Possibly the

GENERAL ADJUSTMENT

ability of women to express tensions in worrying and specific areas of concern provides a certain amount of release, so that these tensions are less often expressed in their over-all feelings about their lives. Conversely, if men's lesser expression of problems and tensions involves an unwillingness to face up to problems that exist, it is possible that these problems and tensions, being unexpressed directly, more often find indirect expression in a lower sense of general well-being.

Age

The relationships between age and the measures of general adjustment are presented in Table 2.9, which indicates that the several measures of adjustment are differentially related to age.

Table 2.9—Relationship between Age and Measures of General Adjustment

	AGE			
Measures of General Adjustment	21–34	35–44	45–54	55 & over
Extent of worries				
Never worry	6%	10%	11%	17%
Worry not too much	51	46	46	39
Worry sometimes	8	9	6	4
Worry a lot	28	27	27	29
Worry all the time	3	5	4	5
Not ascertained	4	3	6	6
Total	100%	100%	100%	100%
Evaluation of present happiness				
Very happy	40%	38%	34%	27%
Pretty happy	55	52	52	55
Not too happy	5	10	13	18
Not ascertained	*	*	1	*
Total	100%	100%	100%	100%
Feelings of impending nervous breakdown				
Felt impending nervous breakdown	18%	22%	20%	16%
Did not feel impending nervous breakdown	82	78	80	84
Not ascertained	*	*	—	*
Total	100%	100%	100%	100%
Experience of problem relevant for professional help				
Had problem relevant for help	28%	29%	21%	14%
Did not have problem relevant for help	72	71	79	85
Not ascertained	—	*	*	1
Total	100%	100%	100%	100%
Number of people ᵃ	(759)	(548)	(459)	(681)

ᵃ Does not include the 13 people whose age was not ascertained.

Looking first at the findings on "happiness" and "worries," it is interesting to note that, although unhappy people tend to worry more (see Table 2.2), older people tend to be more unhappy but to worry less.

That older people tend to be less happy is not surprising—in a period of decline and growing limitation of gratification, we would expect to find less happiness. It is also consistent with other findings in the study. The older people view the future with much more pessimism, uncertainty, and resignation, and they show much more involvement with their health; they not only worry more often about health but also mention it much more often as a source of happiness, defining happiness in essentially negative terms, in terms of maintenance and survival rather than aspiration and positive gratification.

The younger people, on the other hand, are more involved in the active and participating aspects of life. They more often find their sources of happiness in such things as marriage and the job. Their sources of worry and unhappiness also indicate participation rather than withdrawal from life activities; in contrast to the older people's greater concern over health, younger people show more concern over such things as economic and material matters and the job.

From one point of view, it is not surprising that older people, in addition to being less happy, also tend to worry less, for this may be viewed as a reflection of lower aspiration and of withdrawal and resignation. As we have already pointed out, the presence of worries seems to be an indication of aspiration and investment in life, and we would expect to find this more often among younger people. In another sense, however, the findings with respect to worrying are surprising, for while worrying may reflect aspiration, it also reflects insecurity. Although old age is a period of lower aspiration, it has also been considered a time of great insecurity, especially economic insecurity, and in these terms we might have expected the older people to have evidenced a higher level of worrying. In this connection, the fact that older people worry less than younger people about economic and material things is rather striking: 41 per cent of the youngest age group (twenty-one to thirty-four years of age) give economic and material concerns as the first-mentioned source of worry, as contrasted with only 18 per cent of the people over fifty-five years of age (a difference that is, if anything, accentuated, when more than the first-mentioned reasons are considered). Without in any way minimizing the insecurities of old age, these findings do suggest that, at least if we view the population as a whole, for many older people economic insecurity may be less of a conscious problem than one might have imagined. With lower needs and aspirations in the material area, and living in an age where minimum security is guaranteed for most, their economic concerns apparently become less paramount. It is interesting to speculate on whether these findings represent a recent historical development and what we might have obtained in a survey conducted before the enactment of social security laws.

The relationships between age and the experience of emotional crises also present an interesting pattern. Despite the fact that older people, having lived longer, have had more opportunity to experience serious emotional crises, they do not mention such crises more often than do younger people. There is no difference between younger and older people in the experience of "nervous breakdowns." Younger people *more* often report problems for which they thought professional help was relevant.

Several possible explanations of these findings may be offered. It is possible, for example, that older people represent a "healthier" generation, one that was better able to cope with the problems they had to face or one that actually had fewer mental health problems. Or, these findings may indicate the minimization of these problems that comes with the perspective gained through the passing years. Looking back over the past, what once seemed a great emotional crisis may be viewed less seriously or even, in many cases, forgotten. Finally, we may view these findings as representing not a history of fewer tensions among the older generation, nor even less memory of tensions, but rather less tendency to view the tensions and problems they have felt in mental health terms. The findings support this view that the younger and older age groups in our society may represent very different cultural generations with respect to attitudes and values in the mental health area: Feelings of an impending "nervous breakdown," problems seen as reactions to "external" stress rather than as personality or interpersonal malfunctioning, are not experienced differentially by younger and older people; but the experience of problems requiring professional help, the more current "psychological" phrasing of such problems, is more often expressed among members of the younger generation. This is not surprising. The tendency to take a psychiatric view of serious emotional problems, to view them as illnesses rather than as defects of character, represents a recent development in our cultural history, and we would expect older and younger people to reflect this cultural change. We will return to these findings in Part Two of this monograph, where we will explore more fully the question of the "readiness for self-referral," and the factors related to this readiness.

Education

The relationships between education and the measures of general adjustment (Table 2.10) tend to parallel those discussed in connection with age; the more highly educated groups generally show a pattern of responses similar to that evidenced by the younger groups. Compared to people of grade-school education, people with some college education, like the younger people, tend to be happier but not less worried and to have experienced more problems seen as relevant for professional help but not more nervous breakdowns. In addition, like the younger groups, they are much more optimistic in their anticipation of future happiness, mention similar sources of happiness, unhappiness, and worries, and show greater involvement in the job, marriage, and the family; people of less education, like the older groups, show a greater involvement with their health.

The first question that arises is whether these parallel findings represent an artifact. There is a very strong relationship between age and education: older people tend to be much less educated. One may wonder whether these education findings merely reflect the age differences among the people in the several educational groupings. However, the relationships depicted in Table 2.10, and the others we have noted, remain even when age is "controlled," that is, when we look at education differences among people at similar age levels.

GENERAL ADJUSTMENT

Table 2.10—Relationship between Education and Measures of General Adjustment

	EDUCATION		
Measures of General Adjustment	Grade School	High School	College
Extent of worries			
Never worry	15%	8%	10%
Worry not too much	41	46	51
Worry sometimes	4	8	9
Worry a lot	31	28	23
Worry all the time	5	5	3
Not ascertained	4	5	4
Total	100%	100%	100%
Evaluation of present happiness			
Very happy	23%	39%	43%
Pretty happy	56	54	51
Not too happy	20	7	5
Not ascertained	1	*	1
Total	100%	100%	100%
Feelings of impending nervous breakdown			
Felt impending nervous breakdown	20%	19%	16%
Did not feel impending nervous breakdown	80	81	84
Not ascertained	*	*	—
Total	100%	100%	100%
Experience of problem relevant for professional help			
Had problem relevant for help	16%	25%	31%
Did not have problem relevant for help	83	75	69
Not ascertained	1	*	—
Total	100%	100%	100%
Number of people [a]	(802)	(1185)	(457)

[a] Does not include 16 people whose education was not ascertained.

The only exception to this generalization occurs with respect to the greater emphasis of people of less education on health when talking of the sources of their happiness and concern. This turns out to be largely a function of the age differences in the education groups, but, even here, some relationship with education does remain, over and above the age factor. We might note, incidentally, that the differences between the younger and older groups that were discussed above also remain when education is controlled: in short, the findings we have been discussing with respect to both variables are independent of each other.

If these parallel findings with respect to age and education represent independent relationships and are not an artifact, we may look to similar meanings of these variables to explain the similar results. The more highly educated people, like the younger groups, would appear to have greater aspirations and expectations in life. This would explain their greater happiness, optimism, involvement in such things as job and marriage rather than health; it would also account for the fact that, despite their higher level of gratification, they do not worry less than the less educated groups. (The slight relationship that does obtain between education and worrying is a curvilinear one: grade-school-educated people appear more frequently in both the "never worry" and high worrying categories.) We would also expect the most highly educated, as people most cognizant of and sympathetic to the latest intellectual developments in a culture, to share the younger generation's greater acceptance of a psychological view of emotional problems. This would explain their greater experience of emotional problems phrased in help-relevant terms and the lack of difference in the experience of problems phrased as a nervous breakdown.

SUMMARY

In this chapter we have looked at the responses to those questions in the interview which attempted to get the respondents to make some general, over-all evaluations of their emotional states. Following are some of the highlights of the analyses based on these evaluations.

Reasons for gratification and distress. When people talk about the things that satisfy or disturb them, two broad categories of reasons stand out. Heavy emphases are given to economic and material considerations, and to the central life relationships—marriage, children, and the family.

Although economic and material things are important as people talk of the sources of their happiness and distress, the emphasis tends to be on comfort and adequacy and limited aspirations, rather than luxury. Happiness is expressed in terms of having "enough" money, being free from debt, having a "nice" home. The complaints are of debts and bills and inadequate housing.

The importance of the person's central life relationships—marriage, children, and the family—is suggested both by the fact that over half of the respondents referred to this area when talking of things that gave them happiness in life, and by the finding that mention of this area as a source of happiness or unhappiness tends to be related to a person's general evaluation of his happiness. That is, when a person is happy in these relationships he tends to be happy generally; when unhappy in these relationships he tends to be unhappy otherwise.

In looking at the reasons people give for unhappiness and worries, one general point stands out. Interpersonal and personal problems are mentioned by only a minority of the population. People tend to externalize their problems, to locate them in "concrete" material things or a job, to see them as reactions to external events, not as problems in personal or interpersonal malfunctioning. Even in cases where this manner of defining unhappiness represents an externalization of what are really internal problems, these findings are significant, particularly in their implications for help-seeking behavior. They point to the tendency for people in the general population to phrase their unhappiness and concerns in nonpsychological terms, in ways not likely to bring them to the use of psychologically oriented help resources.

Distinctions among adjustment measures. We have emphasized the distinctions and different implications that follow from the particular ways in which adjustment, satisfaction, and distress are defined and measured. Two sets of distinctions especially noted in this chapter serve as integrating themes that will underlie much of the data analysis to be presented in this monograph.

One is the distinction between "satisfaction" and "involvement," a distinction evidenced in the differences between "happiness" and "worrying" as adjustment measures. Worrying, and unhappiness, were similar in reflecting similar tensions, problems, and concerns. But, whereas unhappiness reflects a lack of positive resources and an apathetic and pessimistic view of life, worrying seems to reflect an investment in life, a commitment to change, and an optimism about the possibility of change.

The second major distinction—between internal and external definitions of problems—was important in the reports of the respondents' past emotional crises. Where the question focused on psychological problems and the use of professional help with these problems, most of the respondents mentioned problems where the cause was located in personal and interpersonal processes. When asked about a "nervous breakdown," however, people who felt they had ever experienced (or come close to experiencing) one, more often defined it as an individual collapse in the face of some external stress—death of a loved one, the job, a physical illness—than as a personality or interpersonal problem.

Relationships with sex, age, and education. The importance of distinguishing different adjustment measures becomes evident in examining variations in adjustment patterns within different sex, age, and education groupings. In most instances, comparing the adjustment patterns in different subgroups of the population will involve statements not of "better" or "worse" adjustment, but rather of the different ways in which gratification and distress are experienced and defined. In most cases, population groups evidencing more distress in terms of certain criteria show less distress on others.

The age relationships presented in this chapter provide a good instance of this general point. Looking at adjustment in terms of feelings of happiness, we found that older people tend to be unhappier than younger people. Looking at the question on worries, however, older people show some tendency to worry *less* than younger people. These two findings may be viewed as a reflection of lower aspiration, withdrawal, or resignation. Even in the economic area, older people appear to worry less than do the younger. With other findings we will be discussing in later portions of the monograph, those presented in this chapter suggest that the problems of old age seem to be problems more of apathy than of anxiety and insecurity.

Age also relates differently to the two questions that focused on past psychological crises. Reports about a nervous breakdown—a problem seen as a reaction to external stress—are not different for younger and older people. But more psychological problems—personal and interpersonal problems for which professional help is needed—are much more often expressed by younger people. Age here seems to be a reflection of the cultural changes in the popular conception of causation of emotional problems. We have witnessed a movement away from an external and physical view toward a view of these problems as breakdowns in intrapsychic and interpersonal processes. As we would expect, the younger generation more often adopts the newer view.

The relationships between education and the measures of general adjustment tend to parallel those with respect to age. Like the younger people, the more highly educated tend to be happier but not less worried, and to have experienced more problems phrased in psychological terms but not more impending "nervous breakdowns." These and other parallel findings remain even when age is controlled. Education, like youth, seems to be associated with the investment of greater aspirations and expectations in life—an investment which brings greater gratification but not less tension and concern. And, like membership in the younger generation, education also brings a greater recognition of the latest intellectual developments in a culture, including a tendency to interpret problems in psychological terms.

The relationships between the adjustment measures and sex provide an interesting contrast to those involving age and education. The latter findings emphasized the importance of the particular definition of adjustment used. Men and women, however, seem to show a more general difference. Except for the question on the over-all evaluation of happiness, women generally seem to express more distress than men, regardless of the particular measure used. Although one cannot say from these data whether these findings mean that women are subject to greater strains in our society, or that they are more willing to face their difficulties in handling problems, it is clear that there is a greater experience of tension among women, evidencing itself in many different areas of distress. This finding is confirmed in future chapters.

III

Perceptions of the Self

THE SENSE of self is a man's strongest armor in his struggles to integrate the chaotic flows of events that engage his daily consciousness. The destruction that follows when this sense of self is weakened, when there is a lack of awareness of a self distinct from other people or things, is clearest in those who experience such confusion in certain psychotic states; but the incapacitating consequences of identity confusions have also been noted in certain neurotic conditions and in "normal" states as well.

This self-consciousness would seem to be a difficult psychological state to assess. A basic quality of self-perception is its apparent uniqueness for each individual. Because of this quality of uniqueness, it is difficult to think of self-perception in terms of a scientific analysis demanding the specification of dimensions by which all people can be measured. What things would one look for in measuring what people think of themselves? How could we compare people on this state of consciousness? It would seem that any attempts in this direction might do an injustice to those very qualities that make this self-awareness the cornerstone of consciousness. Finding common aspects in the self-perceptions of individuals destroys the richness of each idiosyncratic view of the self.

What follows in this chapter may be viewed, then, as only tentative beginnings in this area—an attempt to obtain some insight into the phenomenology of self-perceptions, what people think about themselves, their strong points and their weak points, their identities.

The discussions in this chapter are based on responses to three open-ended questions, asked in the order listed:

1. People are the same in many ways, but no two people are exactly alike. What are some of the ways in which you are different from other people?

2. If you had a son (daughter for women), how would you like him to be different from you?

3. How about your good points? What would you say were your strongest points?

We expected that responses to the first question would yield the respondents' general pictures of themselves. The neutral character of the question made it possible to respond by mentioning either strong points or weaknesses. These responses were coded in terms of the amount and direction—positive or negative—of affect associated with the self. By focusing on the notion of difference from others, we could also get some measure of the sense of uniqueness of the self; we were particularly interested in any respondents who explicitly said they are not different from most people.

The second question asks, *indirectly,* for a statement of weaknesses or shortcomings. Pretests had indicated that many people have difficulty in replying to a question that directly probes for their shortcomings; the indirect question threatens them less. In addition, by evoking identification with a son or daughter, we hoped to tap a level of emotional involvement not always obtained with more direct phrasing. We are interested in responses to this question primarily as a means of categorizing individuals according to the *content* of shortcomings they perceived in themselves. We are also interested, of course, in those respondents who do not report any shortcomings at all.

The third question asks directly for a person's perceived sources of strength. In addition to the kinds of strong points mentioned, we are particularly interested in the extreme, demoralized responses of those who feel that they have no strong points at all.

Several simple indices and two of a more complex nature seemed to have particular relevance for our analysis. In all, six indices were used, derived in the following ways:

1. *Perception of difference from others.* Frequent responses to the question "How are you different . . . ?" were, "I am not different," "I'm average," "I'm just like anyone else." These represent

significant rejections of the question. They are stronger than "I don't know," which was also frequent. By using the following categories we constructed an index representing a person's ability or willingness to see himself as different from others: those who explicitly said they were not different, those who said they did not know how they were different, and those who mentioned at least one way in which they were different from other people.

2. *Positiveness of Self-percept.* We judged those respondents who mentioned any differences in answer to the question "How are you different . . . ?" on their positive or negative orientation to the self. The rating scale ran from very positive ("I'm a very competent person") to very negative ("I'm the kind of person who can't get along with people") with two kinds of midpoints: "neutral," i.e., no indication of self-evaluation ("I'm a farmer") and "ambivalent," i.e., a combination of positive and negative self-descriptions with neither orientation predominating. Since the extreme negatives were not often given, the index was condensed into five categories: very positive, positive, neutral, ambivalent, and negative. This code was established on the first question rather than on all three questions for two reasons: to preserve *independent* measures of self-perception, and to obtain this kind of evaluation from a fairly neutral stimulus; the other two questions probe directly for positive and negative characteristics.

3. *Admission to shortcomings.* This index discloses whether the respondent was unwilling or unable to mention weaknesses in himself. Three groups were distinguished on the basis of their responses to the question on how they wanted their children to be different from them: those who answered with, "I don't want him to be different from me," those who described one or more desired changes, and those who said, "I don't know" or gave a desired change not clearly an indication of the respondent's own shortcomings.

4. *Sources of shortcomings.* This is a complex tabulation of the kinds of weaknesses mentioned in response to the second question. In arriving at our final set of categories, a good many inferences had to be made in placing many diverse responses into the same category. (A good example of the inferential quality of our final grouping,

made in order to put this code into some manageable form, is the category of social skills, which included such responses as "I would like my child to be more friendly," "more extroverted," "less sensitive," "have more personality." We assumed that any mention of characteristics potentially concerned with getting along with people could be coded together.) Despite the wide range of responses which necessarily had to be grouped under one heading, it was possible to arrive at a final set of categories representing concepts that were meaningful within the general theoretical orientations of the study. For example, the following are two of the conceptual guides we used in arriving at some of our classifications of shortcomings:

"External" failure vs. "Personality" shortcomings. Following our interest in distinguishing between the external and psychological definitions of problems, we differentiated between external and personality shortcomings. External shortcomings were those referring to visible status failures. Coded here were those responses relevant to wanting "better education," "more prosperity," an "easier financial life," and a "better occupation" for a child. In contrast, we established, as categories relevant to the personality domain, shortcomings that dealt with internal, personal, more probing characteristics. Some examples of these shortcomings were those related to lacks in "achievement traits," lacks in "adjustment," lacks in "anger control."

Interpersonal vs. noninterpersonal "Personality" shortcomings. Within personality shortcomings, we wanted to differentiate between traits that are related to social interaction and those that are not. We distinguished, therefore, between lacks in social skills and lacks in personal skills (various individual creative talents). For example, we viewed the category of achievement traits as irrelevant to interpersonal concerns and therefore placed it within the noninterpersonal grouping. In contrast, such things as "inability to control anger" or "lack of independence" are examples of personality shortcomings which we did view as relevant to social interaction.

5. *Denial of strong points.* An infrequent but striking response to the third question is a rejection of the idea of having any strong points. Since this response seems so rejecting of the self, we thought it important to isolate it as an index and to examine its relationship

with other variables. Again three groupings were used: those respondents who said they had no strong points; those who mentioned strong points; and those who said they did not know what their strong points were, or gave responses such as "you'll have to ask someone else."

6. *Sources of strong points.* The content of the responses to the question asking for strong points was another difficult area to code. We were able, by drawing a considerable number of inferences, to combine codes into a relatively small number of meaningful categories. Again, certain conceptual orientations influenced the process of categorization. As in our categorization of shortcomings and problem areas, we attempted to distinguish these positive responses along an external-internal dimension.

Two classes of "external" responses were isolated. First, there were responses which referred to any *social role,* the performance of which was viewed as a strong point—being a good husband (or wife), a good worker (or mention of a specific occupational task), a good parent, or a good housekeeper.

Second, among those responses referring to personality characteristics, we attempted to distinguish those more external and superficial from those seeming to indicate a more truly introspective view of the self. We made the assumption that a respondent who was not inclined to be introspective would mention highly stereotyped adjectives as strong points. We also assumed that they would tend to be stereotypes of a particular kind—those accenting a moralistic "goodness," virtues that can be viewed as universal cultural values rather than statements about the unique aspects of the self. Therefore, we included a category labeled "moral and virtuous stereotypes," consisting of *popular* adjectives which point to the moral worth of the individual. We presented the coder with a list of these adjectives that seemed to fall within this category. Some of these were "dependable," "thrifty," "sincere," "generous," "kind," "tolerant," "unselfish," "good," "upright," "truthful," "church-going." We anticipated that this category would reflect a lack of general introspective tendencies.

These moral and virtuous stereotypes were distinguished from personality strong points. The latter include what were viewed as the more introspective personality references. Within this general category, we further distinguished strong points that reflected personality traits dealing with social interaction and those that did not. The specific categories used here are identical to those used in the analysis of personality shortcomings.

In reviewing the construction of these six indices we have merely hinted at the potential meaning these measures may have. What does it mean for a respondent to feel no sense of uniqueness or difference from others; to reject the idea that his child should differ from him in any way; to say that he has no strong points? What does it mean to select positive, neutral, or negative characteristics in differentiating one's self from other people? What does it mean to select a particular trait as a shortcoming or as a strong point?

Relevant to all of these is the dimension of introspection—the person's ability or willingness to look inward at the self. We were interested in introspection as one aspect of what we have referred to as an "internal" or "psychological" orientation toward life and the problems life presents. As such, we viewed introspection as a psychological characteristic that would be related to the "readiness for self-referral." One would expect that people who introspect would take a more psychologically oriented view of emotional problems, would be more willing to see such problems in themselves, and more ready to utilize professional help resources in attempting to cope with them.

The relationship between introspection and some of the basic demographic characteristics investigated in this study is also of interest. It appears reasonable to hypothesize that certain social climates in this society foster introspection. For example, Miller and Swanson (1960) have pointed out how working-class children tend to be oriented to a *motoric* style of expression in their behavior, using their body in acting towards their world, while middle-class children are more oriented to a *conceptual* style of expression, to thinking abstractly about their behavior. Since this latter style includes the tendency to be introspective, we might expect a greater tendency toward introspection in the middle-class positions than in working-class positions. This would be reflected in relationships between introspection and several demographic variables—notably occupation, education, and income.

Introspection, then, was considered relevant to two of the central analyses of the study—the analysis of readiness for self-referral and the demographic analysis—and, as such, a potentially significant "intervening variable" helping to explain some of the relationships between demographic characteristics and help-seeking patterns.

All the indices developed for measuring self-perception reflect introspection in some way. People not inclined to introspection should tend to see themselves as not different from others and should be less willing to see strong points or weaknesses in themselves. Furthermore, if these people lacking in introspective orientations do mention differences from others and talk about strong points and weaknesses, their responses should be ones that are not deeply personal or indicative of intensive self-probing.

In addition to measuring tendencies toward introspection, these indices were designed to tap individual differences in the kinds of feelings and attitudes people have about themselves. We were particularly interested in the positive-negative dimension. Four of the indices—perception of difference from others, positiveness of self-percept, admission to shortcomings, and denial of strong points—have relevance to this dimension. The fact that each of these indices measures both a general tendency toward introspection and certain affective aspects of self-percept creates certain complexities, as we will see when we examine the interrelationships of these indices.

INTERRELATIONSHIPS AMONG INDICES PERTAINING TO SELF-PERCEPTION

Let us first examine the relationships among "perception of difference from others," "admission to shortcomings," and "denial of strong points." Each of these indices may be viewed as reflecting the acceptance or rejection of one of the three self-percept questions: acceptance or rejection of the idea that one is different from other people, acceptance or rejection of the suggestion that there are weaknesses in the self, acceptance or rejection of the suggestion that there are strong points in the self.

Looking at these indices as measures of introspection, we would expect that the less introspective people would tend to fall on the "rejection" ends of all three indices. If we consider introspection as the only factor operating, we would expect simple relationships among the three indices: people who said they were not different from others would also tend to say that they had no weak points or strong points; and, although it seems paradoxical, the latter two measures would also be related to each other—that is, people who denied having weaknesses would also deny having strengths.

But the three indices are also measuring affective aspects of self-percept. To reject the idea that one is in any way different from other people not only implies a lack of introspection but may also imply a negative evaluation of the self, reflecting an impoverished identity. To reject the idea that one has strong points also reflects a negative self-image. Rejection of the idea that one has shortcomings, on the other hand, has obvious implications for a *positive* view of the self. If we were to relate each of these indices to one another, then, *forgetting about the factor of introspection*, we would expect the following relationships: people who say they are not different from others should also say that they have no strong points (since both of these statements reflect a negative self-image); and both of these groups should say that they *do* have weaknesses. These expected relationships do not completely parallel those we anticipated when we viewed these indices as reflections of introspection. We will see the effects of this lack of parallelism as we examine the data on these relationships, presented in Tables 3.1 to 3.3.

Table 3.1 presents data on the relationship between perceiving the self as different from others and admitting to shortcomings. Looking at these two indices as measures of introspection, we might expect that people who see themselves as different from others would also say that they have some shortcomings, since both these responses represent the more introspective response. However, if we view these indices in terms of their implications for a positive or negative self-percept, we would expect the opposite relationship: people who see

Table 3.1—Relationship between Perception of Self as Different from Others and Admission to Shortcomings

	ADMISSION TO SHORTCOMINGS		
Perception of Self as Different	Explicitly Do Not Want Child Different	Explicitly Do Want Child Different [a]	Don't know; other [b]
Explicitly not different from others	18%	15%	15%
Don't know	15	14	18
Mention differences from others	67	71	66
Not ascertained	*	*	1
Total	100%	100%	100%
Number of people [c]	(255)	(1838)	(252)

* Here and in subsequent tables this symbol (*) indicates less than one-half of 1 per cent.

[a] Includes only respondents whose responses clearly referred to their own shortcomings.

[b] "Other" category includes respondents who suggested differences in the child, but these differences did not clearly refer to their own shortcomings.

[c] Does not include 115 people whose position on the "admission to shortcomings" index was not ascertained.

themselves as different (a more positive self-perception) should say they have *no* shortcomings. We might expect, then, that these two opposing predictions would tend to cancel each other out, resulting in little or no over-all relationship between these two indices. Table 3.1 indicates that this is the case: there is no relationship between the perception of the self as different from others and the readiness to admit to weaknesses in the self.

Table 3.2 presents data on the relationship between perceiving the

Table 3.2—Relationship between Perception of Self as Different from Others and Denial of Strong Points

	DENIAL OF STRONG POINTS		
Perception of Self as Different	Explicitly No Strong Points [a]	Don't Know [a]	Mention Strong Points [b]
Explicitly not different from others	30%	17%	15%
Don't know	24	30	12
Mention differences from others	44	51	72
Not ascertained	2	2	1
Total	100%	100%	100%
Number of people [c]	(84)	(244)	(2105)

[a] This category represents the initial response to the question on strong points. It includes respondents who mentioned strong points upon interviewer's probing.

[b] Consists of respondents who mentioned strong points in initial response to the question.

[c] Does not include the 27 people whose position on the "denial of strong points" index was not ascertained.

self as different from others and the denial of strong points in the self. In contrast to the relationship discussed above, we have here a relationship in which the prediction derived from viewing these indices as measures of introspection and that derived from a consideration of the affective self-orientation they represent reinforce rather than cancel each other. Those who see themselves as different should also see strong points in the self, since these two responses are both introspective and positive responses. And we see, in Table 3.2, that we do in fact obtain a strong relationship in the expected direction.

Table 3.3 presents the relationship between the admission to short-

Table 3.3—Relationship between Admission to Shortcomings and Denial of Strong Points

	ADMISSION TO SHORTCOMINGS		
Denial of Strong Points	Explicitly Do Not Want Child Different	Explicitly Do Want Child Different [a]	Don't Know; Other [b]
Explicitly no strong points	4%	3%	4%
Don't know	10	9	15
Mention strong points	85	87	79
Not ascertained	1	1	2
Total	100%	100%	100%
Number of people [c]	(255)	(1838)	(252)

[a] Includes only respondents whose responses clearly referred to their own shortcomings.
[b] "Other" category includes respondents who suggested differences in the child, but these differences did not clearly refer to their own shortcomings.
[c] Does not include the 115 people whose position on the "admission to shortcomings" index was not ascertained.

comings and the denial of strong points in the self. Here again we might expect a canceling out of opposing tendencies. Since both responses reflect a negative self-appraisal, we might expect that people who admit to shortcomings would more often deny strong points in the self. However, since admission to shortcomings represents an introspective response and denial of strong points a nonintrospective response, we might expect the reverse to hold true. The resultant, then, would be a lack of any relationship between these two indices, which turns out to be the case, as indicated in Table 3.3.

To summarize these findings, we may say that they seem to support some of the assumptions we have made in setting up the indices of self-perception. In particular, they support two of these assumptions: that the ability to differentiate the self—the sense of difference and uniqueness, the "sense of self"—is associated with a positive self-percept (Table 3.2); and that tendencies to perceive weaknesses and strengths in the self, although pointing in opposite affective directions, seem to share a common quality of introspection (Table 3.3). We will see further implications of these assumptions in some of the relationships we examine later in this chapter.

We have examined these relationships in some detail because they point to certain problems that appear when one looks at attitudes toward the self in terms of criteria of adjustment and mental health. Of particular interest is the apparent paradox presented by the complex relationship between introspection and the positive-negative percept of the self. Introspection, self-awareness—what Jahoda (1958) has referred to under the category "accessibility of the self to consciousness"—has been viewed as an index of positive mental health. However, these same introspective qualities involve recognition of the negative as well as the positive aspects of the self (as suggested in the findings of Table 3.3); hence they operate to reduce that positiveness of self-percept which has also been viewed as a healthy attribute.

From this apparent paradox arises the question of whether positiveness of the self-percept is in itself an adequate index of positive adjustment. This problem has been recognized in the mental health literature, where, as Jahoda has noted, theorists have stressed *acceptance* of the self rather than a completely positive self-picture in talking of healthy attitudes toward the self. Acceptance involves an attitude that is generally positive but can integrate within the self-picture the negative elements that exist. In a sense, self-acceptance combines positiveness and introspection.

It will be important to keep this in mind as we examine the findings on the positiveness of the self-percept, particularly in connection with the demographic relationships. The interpretation of these findings should always be made within the context of the findings on introspection. To characterize a population subgroup as positive in self-percept has certain implications if the group is also characterized as introspective and certain other implications if it is also characterized as nonintrospective. In one case the positive self-percept reflects an evaluation that has recognized and appraised the negative as well as the positive aspects of the self, implying a self-acceptance in the fuller sense of the term; in the other case it reflects an evaluation based on a limited self-awareness and hence a more limited self-acceptance.

Before examining the demographic relationships, some of the other interrelationships of the self-percept indices may be noted. In addition to the sets of interrelationships presented in Tables 3.1 to 3.3, the three indices represented in these tables were related to the other three indices of self-percept, and the latter in turn were related to each other. In most cases, no significant relationships were obtained. The feeling that one is different from other people is not associated with the particular kinds of strength or weakness that one sees in the self; to deny strong points in the self does not relate to the particular kinds of weaknesses that one stresses; the degree of self-acceptance is not related to the kinds of strengths that one sees in the self.

In three instances, however, significant relationships were obtained. They all involve the index called "positiveness of self-percept." This index, it will be recalled, represented the coder's judgment of the respondent's negative-positive orientation to the self, as indicated in the answers given to the first question in the series on self-percept (i.e., the question on how one is different from other people). The coders judged whether the responses to this question suggested a very positive, positive, neutral, ambivalent, or negative self-image. Making this judgment involved considerable inference on the part of the coder. One way of testing these inferences was to see whether this judgment of the response to the first question was related to the responses to the two other questions in the self-perception area.

We expected that the index on "positiveness of self-percept" would be related to the indices on "admission to shortcomings" and "denial of strong points," that the more negative a person was coded as being in his perception of himself, the more likely he would be to admit to shortcomings and deny strong points in himself. An examination of the interrelationships of these three indices confirms both of these expectations: compared with the people coded negative or ambivalent on the self-percept index, people with a positive self-image (particularly those coded very positive) more often say that they would not want their child to be different from them; and in response to the question asking them to list their strong points, those coded very positive in their self-percept, compared with all of the other groups, more often mention such strong points.

We see, then, that positiveness of self-percept is related to whether or not a person will see weaknesses or strengths in the self. But we were also interested in seeing whether it would be related to the particular *kinds* of weaknesses or strengths that a person would notice in the self. No relationship was obtained between the positiveness of self-percept and the kinds of strong points that a person sees in the self. But there was a relationship between this index and the kinds of shortcomings mentioned. People who were coded positive or very

Table 3.4—Relationship between Positiveness of Self-Percept and Perceived Sources of Shortcomings in the Self

Sources of Shortcomings [b]	POSITIVENESS OF SELF-PERCEPT [a]				
	Very Positive	Positive	Neutral	Ambivalent	Negative
Shortcomings in external achievement	32%	33%	28%	24%	21%
Occupation	5	3	3	3	2
Prosperity	5	5	4	8	3
Education	22	25	21	13	16
"Personality" shortcomings	30%	30%	35%	43%	50%
Achievement traits	4	6	5	7	3
Adjustment	9	7	7	13	13
Personal skills	2	3	4	1	6
Social skills	10	8	9	15	19
Anger control	4	3	5	5	5
Influence ability	1	3	5	2	4
Other shortcomings	13%	16%	16%	26%	20%
No shortcomings mentioned	21%	16%	15%	2%	9%
Not ascertained	4%	5%	6%	5%	*
Total	100%	100%	100%	100%	100%
Number of people	(81)	(1072)	(224)	(86)	(227)

[a] Does not include people who did not mention ways in which they were different from others and hence were not coded on "positiveness of self-percept."

[b] Excludes respondents who said they would like their child to be different, but these differences did not clearly refer to their own shortcomings.

positive most often describe shortcomings that are related to external achievement (occupation changes or better education for their children). The respondents who were coded negative and ambivalent more often emphasize the shortcomings dealing with internal personal adjustment (they would like their children to be more adjusted, get along better, have greater social skill and attributes, be more creative and talented). These results are summarized in Table 3.4. Apparently, then, a negative perception of the self reflects a discontent with the personal characteristics of the self, the attributes usually called personality traits. A positive conception of the self more often encompasses external characteristics as shortcomings, the attributes that are most visible to other people as status traits. These external characteristics seem to represent a less damaging self-criticism, a criticism of what one "does" rather than what one "is." Further implications of this distinction will be noted in some of the analyses which follow.

SEX, AGE, AND EDUCATION DIFFERENCES RELATED TO PERCEPTIONS OF THE SELF

Theoretical discussions of the concept of the self have stressed the significance of the groups of people among whom a person lives, grows up, and matures in the development of that person's self-perceptions. Many have viewed a person's self-perceptions as reflections of the perceptions that significant others have had and do have of him. The perceptions of him held by those with whom he associates serve as cues for the creation of his own self-image. Thus, the nature of the groups to which a person belongs, particularly those reference groups that are of psychological importance to him, should be critical influences in the development of his perceptions of himself. Because a person's sex, age, and education tend to be crucial determinants of the social groupings that are formed in our society and because they are also characteristics by which people tend to be differentially judged by others, we have considered them as the major characteristics to be examined in the demographic analysis of variations in self-perceptions.

Certain condensations in the presentation of data seemed advisable because we were dealing with relationships among six indices, two of which—"sources of shortcomings" and "sources of strong points"—we wished to examine in terms of the specific categories of the strengths and weaknesses mentioned. We have therefore presented only one set of tables, showing the data on all three demographic variables simultaneously; thus, the tables present the data for the total population divided into eighteen groups—men and women at three different age and education levels. Presenting the tables this way dictated another change: Inasmuch as it would have been confusing to attempt to present the total distributions of percentages on a given index for eighteen different groups in a single table, the tables present only single sets of percentages. That is, we present percentages only for a particular response within the index (for example, Table 3.5, showing the relationship of sex, age, and education to "perception of difference from others," presents only the percentages of those who perceive themselves as different, leaving out those who gave "not different" or "don't know" responses). Thus, these tables highlight certain data. The reader who may be interested in a more detailed description of the relationship of sex, age, and education to perceptions of the self, as measured by the indices of this study, is referred to Appendix A, where he will find tables with the complete sets of figures (Tables A.1 through A.6). (As noted in the Introduction, Appendix A, B, and C have been printed in a separate Tabular Supplement. See footnote, p. 12.)

Sex, Age, and Education Differences in (1) Perception of Difference from Others, (2) Admission to Shortcomings, and (3) Denial of Strong Points

The perception of oneself as different from others and the recognition of strengths and weaknesses in the self are viewed as measures of introspection with affective implications. Not to see oneself as different from others seems to connote a weak differentiation of the self, implying a negative self-image. Seeing shortcomings in the self also would seem to have certain obvious negative implications, while seeing strengths seems to imply a positive self-image. Therefore, in discussing how men and women at different age and educational levels differ on any one of these three indices, we must think of how these different groupings may vary along *two* dimensions: degree of introspectiveness and the negative-positive nature of their self-image.

Table 3.5 presents the sex, age, and education differences in the tendency to see oneself as different from others; Table 3.6 presents these differences in the admission to shortcomings; and Table 3.7 presents these differences in the admission to strong points.

Summarizing the data in Tables 3.5, 3.6, and 3.7, we can draw these conclusions from the comparisons:

1. Men and women do not differ systematically on any of the three indices. Women do not more often perceive themselves as dif-

Table 3.5—Relationship between Perception of Self as Different from Others and Sex, Educational Level, and Age of the Respondent [a]

Age	Education	Men	Women
21–34	Grade school	54	63
	High school	75	74
	College	84	73
35–54	Grade school	64	67
	High school	68	65
	College	67	66
55 and over	Grade school	68	73
	High school	71	65
	College	75	65

[a] Figures are the percentage of people in each group who perceive the self as different from others.

Table 3.6—Relationship between Admission to Shortcomings and Sex, Educational Level, and Age of the Respondent [a]

Age	Education	Men	Women
21–34	Grade school	79	89
	High school	91	90
	College	90	95
35–54	Grade school	80	75
	High school	86	83
	College	79	86
55 and over	Grade school	68	59
	High school	71	64
	College	75	82

[a] Figures are the percentage of people in each group who admit to shortcomings.

Table 3.7—Relationship between Admission to Strong Points and Sex, Educational Level, and Age of the Respondent [a]

Age	Education	Men	Women
21–34	Grade school	77	83
	High school	89	88
	College	93	91
35–54	Grade school	78	85
	High school	87	88
	College	91	89
55 and over	Grade school	78	83
	High school	87	80
	College	86	88

[a] Figures are the percentage of people in each group who perceive strong points in the self.

ferent, nor do they more often admit to strong points or weaknesses in the self. One might have expected women to demonstrate more introspection than men, and although there is some evidence for this in the indices we will examine later, it was not evident in these three indices.

2. The three age groups do not show any consistent differences in their tendency to perceive themselves as different from others or in their tendency to perceive strong points in themselves. There does seem to be a relationship, however, between age and the admission to shortcomings (Table 3.6): The older respondents are less likely to see shortcomings in themselves. Considering this result alone one might conclude either that younger people are more introspective than older people or that they are less integrated and more negative in their self-perceptions. One might expect a high introspective tendency and a negative self-image to reinforce each other, for self-searching entails a greater recognition of shortcomings in the self, which in turn may necessitate increased self-searching. However, other relationships we have discussed and will be discussing do not indicate any further age differences in introspection but do support the finding that older people seem to be more positive in their self-perceptions. Considered in this context, the difference in Table 3.6 probably reflects a difference in the positive nature of the self-images of older and younger people, rather than a difference in introspection.

3. In looking at the patterns of relationships in these three tables for the different educational levels, we find some clear results emerg-

ing. Although level of education is not clearly related to perception of difference from others (Table 3.5), Tables 3.6 and 3.7 indicate that respondents with higher education more often mention both shortcomings and strong points when asked to attend to these two aspects of self-perception. (The differences, though often small, are consistent.) Because the same education difference appears with respect to both strengths and weaknesses, the findings point to a difference in introspection rather than a difference in the positive or negative quality of the self-image. Respondents with less education tend to be less introspective about themselves—whether about strong points or shortcomings. This lack of introspection at the lower educational level emerges in connection with other findings to be discussed.

We may summarize the demographic findings discussed thus far as follows: Examining the tendencies to perceive differences, shortcomings, and strong points in the self-picture, we have no evidence of any differences between men and women in self-perception, some slight evidence that older respondents differ from younger respondents in being more positive about themselves, and some evidence that less educated respondents are less introspective about themselves than are more educated respondents. We will now examine the findings on the remaining indices of self-perception—"positiveness of self-percept," "sources of shortcomings," and "sources of strong points"—for further amplification or refinement of these tentative conclusions.

Sex, Age, and Education Differences in Positiveness of Self-Percept

In this section, we will discuss how men and women, older and younger respondents, and people of different educational backgrounds, may differ in "positiveness of self-percept" (the index derived from the coder's judgment of the affective orientation revealed in response to the first question in the series—that on ways of seeing the self as different from others). In Table 3.8, we have indicated the percentage of men and women at each age and educational level who answered this question with responses which were judged to be either predominantly negative and rejecting of the self or equally positive and negative ("ambivalent"). We combined both of these

Table 3.8—Relationship between Negative or Ambivalent Perception of Self and Sex, Educational Level, and Age of the Respondent [a]

Age	Education	Men	Women
21–34	Grade school	6	13
	High school	16	22
	College	16	26
35–54	Grade school	9	16
	High school	12	18
	College	18	12
55 and over	Grade school	8	12
	High school	5	9
	College	11	18

[a] Figures are the percentage in each group who were coded "negative" or "ambivalent" in the "positiveness of self-percept."

judgments for this table because the larger group gives a more reliable estimate of those people who gave any responses which were considered significantly self-rejecting.

We can conclude from Table 3.8 that all three variables—sex, age, and education—seem to be related to the positiveness of self-percept. The relationship is clearest with sex: In all but the middle-aged college group, more women than men are coded negative or ambivalent in self-percept. Although the differences are sometimes small they are consistent, showing the same tendency in eight out of nine possible comparisons.

The relationships are less clear with age and education: There is a slight tendency, consistent in five out of six possible comparisons, for younger respondents to be more negative or ambivalent in self-percept. And except for middle-aged women, college respondents, contrasted to the two other educational levels, are more often coded negative or ambivalent in self-percept. Again the differences are sometimes small, but are consistent in five out of six possible comparisons.

To be negative or ambivalent in one's self-picture seems to be associated with being a woman, being a young person, and being college-educated. In discussing the first three indices we pointed up only one aspect of this conclusion—that a negative self-image may be associated with difference in age: older people mentioned fewer shortcomings than younger people. The negative-positive aspect of the self-percept seems to emerge more clearly in the index on "positiveness of self-percept" than it did from the more extreme responses to the questions probing specifically for shortcomings and strong points (more extreme in the sense that relatively small proportions of people said that they had no shortcomings or strong points).

It appears, then, that sex, age, and education are related to the overall affective quality of the self-percept. To amplify the meaning of these relationships we will examine some of the differences in the *content* of the self-percepts associated with these demographic groups.

Sex, Age, and Education Differences in Sources of Shortcomings and Sources of Strong Points

In our discussion of the construction of the indices on "sources of shortcomings" and "sources of strong points," we noted some of the general conceptual orientations that guided the specification of categories within these indices. Under sources of shortcomings we distinguished between responses reflecting a concern with lack of external achievement (job, finances, education) and those reflecting a concern with flaws in personality dimensions. Further, within these personality dimensions we distinguished those shortcomings having an interpersonal orientation (not getting along with people in some way) from those having no such orientation (lacks in achievement qualities or personal skills). Under sources of strong points, we distinguished between strong points reflecting lack of introspection (defined in terms of social role behavior or mention of "moral or virtuous stereotypes") and strong points reflecting more introspective personality dimensions, divided into personality traits that were socially relevant and those that were not.

Many sex, age, and educational differences appear when we look at the self-perceptions of strengths and weaknesses within this classification scheme. We will discuss some of the more striking results to highlight the general findings. Tables 3.9 to 3.13 present the relationships between sex, age, and education and selected sources of shortcomings; Tables 3.14 to 3.17 present the relationship between sex, age, and education and selected sources of strong points. The

Table 3.9—Relationship between Mention of Lack of Education as a Shortcoming and Sex, Educational Level, and Age of Respondent [a]

Age	Education	Men	Women
21–34	Grade school	46	17
	High school	45	13
	College	18	8
35–54	Grade school	43	24
	High school	37	16
	College	17	4
55 and over	Grade school	30	16
	High school	31	8
	College	14	6

[a] Figures are percentages in each group who mention a shortcoming that was coded as a lack in education.

Table 3.10—Relationship between Mention of Lack of General Adjustment as a Shortcoming and Sex, Educational Level, and Age of Respondent [a]

Age	Education	Men	Women
21–34	Grade school	0	7
	High school	2	11
	College	14	12
35–54	Grade school	2	10
	High school	3	13
	College	6	18
55 and over	Grade school	2	8
	High school	2	10
	College	3	9

[a] Figures are percentages in each group who mention a shortcoming that was coded as a lack in general adjustment. (This category included such responses as "I want him to be more contented," "handle problems better.")

complete tabulations are presented in Appendix A of the Tabular Supplement (Tables A.5 and A.6).

We will summarize the results presented in these tables separately for each demographic characteristic.

SEX

Tables 3.9 to 3.17 depict a number of striking and consistent differences between men and women in their self-perceptions of strengths and weaknesses.

Table 3.11—Relationship between Mention of Lack of Social Skills as a Shortcoming and Sex, Educational Level, and Age of Respondent [a]

Age	Education	Men	Women
21–34	Grade school	0	9
	High school	3	19
	College	7	26
35–54	Grade school	1	8
	High school	3	11
	College	7	19
55 and over	Grade school	2	5
	High school	1	11
	College	14	23

[a] Figures are percentages in each group who mention a shortcoming that was coded as a lack in social skills. (This category included such responses as "more interested in people," "more tactful," "less easily hurt.")

Table 3.12—Relationship between Mention of Lack of Achievement Traits as a Shortcoming and Sex, Educational Level, and Age of Respondent [a]

Age	Education	Men	Women
21–34	Grade school	2	6
	High school	6	6
	College	15	9
35–54	Grade school	3	1
	High school	8	4
	College	12	1
55 and over	Grade school	5	2
	High school	7	3
	College	14	12

[a] Figures are percentages in each group who mention a shortcoming that was coded as a lack in achievement traits. (This category included such responses as "wish I were ambitious," "had more drive," "were more persistent.")

Looking first at the sources of shortcomings, we find the following:

1. *Lack of external achievement vs. personality deficiencies.* In talking of their shortcomings, men more than women stress their external failures, their lack of visible achievements. This is most dramatically illustrated by the very sharp difference between men and women in their report of lack of education as a shortcoming (Table 3.9).

Women, on the other hand, more often emphasize personality shortcomings. This is best illustrated by comparing the frequency

Table 3.13—Relationship between Mention of Physical Appearance as a Shortcoming and Sex, Educational Level, and Age of Respondent [a]

Age	Education	Men	Women
21–34	Grade school	0	9
	High school	4	8
	College	6	10
35–54	Grade school	1	7
	High school	1	8
	College	4	9
55 and over	Grade school	*	5
	High school	1	4
	College	5	17

[a] Figures are percentages in each group who mention a shortcoming that was coded as a lack in physical appearance. (This category included such responses as "desire to be more attractive," "more neat appearing.")

Table 3.14—Relationship between Mention of Moral or Virtuous Stereotypes as Strong Points and Sex, Educational Level, and Age of the Respondent [a]

Age	Education	Men	Women
21–34	Grade school	46	28
	High school	29	21
	College	30	28
35–54	Grade school	34	33
	High school	36	31
	College	29	23
55 and over	Grade school	45	41
	High school	40	40
	College	47	41

[a] Figures are percentages in each group who mention a strong point that was coded as a "moral or virtuous stereotype." (This category included such responses as "honest," "trustworthy," "loyal," "dependable," "religious," etc.)

of male and female responses dealing with general adjustment (being able to handle problems, having personal stability). At every age and education level (except the young, college educated) more women than men report characteristics of general adjustment as a shortcoming (Table 3.10).

2. *Interpersonal vs. non-interpersonal personality deficiencies.* Men and women also differ in the *kinds* of personality deficiencies they report. More women than men, in talking about personality flaws, think in terms of a personality deficiency in some way rele-

Table 3.15—Relationship between Mention of Personality Traits as Strong Points and Sex, Educational Level, and Age of the Respondent [a]

Age	Education	Men	Women
21–34	Grade school	24	24
	High school	49	48
	College	52	56
35–54	Grade school	30	40
	High school	41	52
	College	52	59
55 and over	Grade school	31	34
	High school	37	35
	College	36	48

[a] Figures are percentages in each group who mention a strong point that was coded as one of several personality traits: achievement characteristics, social characteristics, anger control, being independent, being well adjusted.

Table 3.16—Relationship between Mention of Nurturant Characteristics as Strong Points and Sex, Educational Level, and Age of the Respondent [a]

Age	Education	Men	Women
21–34	Grade school	4	7
	High school	4	7
	College	3	6
35–54	Grade school	4	14
	High school	6	11
	College	3	8
55 and over	Grade school	5	14
	High school	6	8
	College	0	12

[a] Figures are the percentage in each group who mention as strong points nurturant characteristics ("helpful," "kind to others," "take care of people").

vant to interpersonal concerns (deficiencies in social skills). There is also some indication (although slight) of the converse tendency for more men than women to mention shortcomings which are not directly relevant to interpersonal concerns—specifically, personality traits relevant to achievement strivings (being persistent, ambitious, having "more drive"). The women's greater focus on social shortcomings is reflected in Table 3.11, and the men's slightly greater focus on achievement shortcomings is presented in Table 3.12.

3. *Inadequate personal appearance.* Men and women differed in their concern over physical attractiveness, with women more often

Table 3.17—Relationship between Mention of Achievement Characteristics as Strong Points and Sex, Educational Level, and Age of the Respondent [a]

Age	Education	Men	Women
21–34	Grade school	2	0
	High school	14	7
	College	21	12
35–54	Grade school	4	7
	High school	8	10
	College	19	16
55 and over	Grade school	8	4
	High school	10	4
	College	8	12

[a] Figures are the percentages in each group who mention achievement characteristics as strong points ("work hard," "don't give up on things," "persistent," "doing one's best").

seeing a lack in attractiveness as a deficiency in the self (Table 3.13). Although concern over physical attractiveness does not fall within the conceptual distinctions that have been discussed, the male-female differences in this area can be integrated with the others we have noted, as will be indicated in a later discussion.

Turning now to a consideration of the sources of strong points, the following relationships stood out:

1. *Role characteristics.* As one would expect, men mentioned their occupational role performance as a source of strong points for them, whereas women refer to their housekeeping role performance as a strong point. If we compare the frequency with which men mention occupational strong points with the frequency with which women mention housekeeping strong points, there are no significant differences between them. There were also no significant differences in the extent to which men and women referred to the marital role and the parental role as sources of strong points. The latter findings are surprising, for it was expected that marriage and parenthood would appear as more central to the woman's identity and self-esteem.

2. *Moral and virtuous stereotypes.* Men are consistently (although not dramatically) higher than women in the frequency of mentioning strong points coded as "moral and virtuous stereotypes," a category we have viewed as suggesting lack of introspection (Table 3.14).

3. *Personality strong points.* Table 3.15 reveals a slight tendency for women to mention strong points related to personality characteristics more often than men do. When we examine individual personality traits, we find that in only one personality trait listed as a strong point is there any sharp difference between men and women —the mentioning of nurturant characteristics. Women more often mention such nurturant qualities as being kind to others, taking care of people, helping others (Table 3.16). It is interesting to note that men do not perceive achievement characteristics as a strong point more often than women do (Table 3.17) and that women do not perceive general social skills—getting along with people—as a strong point more often than men, whereas in discussing shortcomings, social skills defined an area that women listed as a deficiency, and there was some greater tendency for men to mention a lack in achievement traits. One wonders why these two areas which are so central to the cultural definition of the sex roles in our society—the social for women and achievement for men—show the sex differentiation in terms of inadequacies but not in strengths. It is possible that their very centrality creates a hesitation and modesty-conflict over indulging in self-praise in these areas.

How may we integrate this list of findings comparing men and women in the strengths and weaknesses that their self-percepts focus on? We have already suggested that women were more negative in their self-appraisals. These additional findings should help complete the picture by suggesting the qualities of self-perceptions that may underlie a more negative self-image in women.

Social theorists and observers of the contemporary scene, in their attempts to differentiate the male and female roles, to conceptualize the distinction between what it means to be a man and what it means to be a woman in our society, have pointed to distinctions which have pertinence to these findings. Margaret Mead (1949), for example, has pointed to the male role as an active *doing* role, in which his success and self-esteem depend upon his accomplishments, his effects on the world; in contrast, the female role has been pictured as a passive, *being* role, in which her self-esteem is dependent on her internal resources for gratification; gratification for the woman comes from responding to, rather than acting on, the world. One might expect, from this viewpoint, that as long as these cultural requirements for the male and female role persist women more than men will turn within themselves for identity anchors. A man looks for sources of self-esteem in external accomplishments, whereas a woman finds her sources of self-esteem in her internal responses and feelings. The woman's role fosters introspection. One might expect a woman, in thinking of her relation to the world, to be highly aware of the kind of *person* she is, rather than of her specific accomplishments. We would also expect her to stress the interpersonal in looking at her relation to the world, to structure interaction with the world in terms of mutual stimulation and response, to look at herself as an interacting person. A man, in thinking about his relation to the world, would be more likely to measure the things he has done or the failure to act and be recognized in the social system.

The results that have been presented highlighting the differences between men and women in the strengths and weaknesses stressed in the self conform to this interpretation of male and female roles in our society. Men seem to be less introspective about their strong points and shortcomings than women. Men more than women mention their shortcomings in external achievements, their "moral and virtuous" strong points. Both sets of characteristics can be considered as traits by which society can easily judge a person's merits. Women more often than men mention strong points and shortcomings that are less immediately visible to society, that are more inferential characteristics, more relevant to aspects of what is commonly called personality. When men do mention personality shortcomings they are more likely than women to talk of personality traits that are relevant to achieving.

Women's greater involvement with interpersonal interaction is evident in their greater concern over social inadequacies and their more frequent stressing of nurturant strong points. A woman seems to be concerned with how she is affecting others as a person rather than as a doer or accomplisher.

Another reflection of the fact that a woman tends to have greater awareness of herself as a person because of her passive role in life can be seen in women's greater concern with their physical appearance. It is interesting to note that this apparent narcissism in women emerges most strikingly in their appraisal of shortcomings but not in their appraisal of strong points. Again, as in the case of achievement for men and social skills for women, we may be dealing with an area of such basic importance for sex identity that self-praise becomes difficult.

AGE

Age does not appear to be as significant a factor as sex in the kinds of strengths and weaknesses stressed in self-perceptions. Younger respondents differ strikingly from older respondents in only one of the many categories of perceived shortcomings that were measured and in only one classification of strong points. In Table 3.9 we see that the younger men, more than older men, mention their lack of education as a shortcoming. And in Table 3.14, we see that the oldest groups (both men and women) generally report more "moral and virtuous stereotypes" in describing their strong points.

The difference in feelings about educational inadequacy is not surprising. The younger men, still struggling with their achievement aspirations, are more likely to be sensitive to areas of external failure such as a lack of education. Moreover, since education is a major path toward achievement in our society, lack of education not only is a deficiency in itself but blocks the younger men from other achievement gratifications. Older men, on the other hand, are more likely to have come to terms with this difficulty. In effect, one may conclude that older people probably come to terms with many aspects of themselves which might have concerned them as younger people. This is reflected not only specifically in the education finding but also in the findings we noted previously suggesting that older people are generally more positive in their self-perceptions than are the younger groups.

The differences between the age groups in mentioning "moral and virtuous stereotypes" offer greater complexities in attempts at interpretation. Although we have viewed this category as a measure of introspection, it does not seem appropriate to interpret the higher frequency of this response among older people as an indication of less introspection among the older groups, since "education" was also viewed as a nonintrospective response, and, as we have seen, it was the younger people who showed the greater concern there. Rather than showing a difference in introspection, this response seems to indicate that people at different age levels differ in the areas in which they get involved, as they turn away from looking directly at the self. Younger people get involved in achievement; older people are apparently more involved in considerations of morality, ethics, virtue.

We may interpret the older people's greater concern in such matters in several ways. It may reflect a cultural difference between the generations, the older groups representing a generation that was more concerned with moral issues, that tended more to evaluate people in moral and ethical terms, in terms of the "old virtues" that have disappeared. Or it may be a concern that comes with increasing age. As one grows older, with the lowering of striving and aspiration, there may come a lowering in the desire for personal uniqueness, and self-aspirations may turn from a desire for uniqueness and achievement to satisfaction in being a moral, "good" person. Or these findings may have religious implications. As people age, they become more concerned about death and what it means for them as individuals. It would seem likely that a consequence of this greater concern with death would be an increased interest in religious interpretations of death and in moral self-evaluations.

EDUCATION

Turning to the kinds of strong points and shortcomings that are associated with different educational levels, we find a common theme: the more highly educated respondents refer to personality characteristics more often than do the less educated respondents. Evidence for this general interpretation comes from the following sources:

In sources of shortcomings, more highly educated respondents more often mentioned deficiencies in achievement characteristics (Table 3.12), deficiencies in social skills (Table 3.11), and deficiencies in general adjustment (Table 3.10). Less educated respondents more frequently mentioned lacks in external achievement. As one would expect, this result is best exemplified in Table 3.9, which shows that less educated respondents more often report lack of education as a shortcoming.

In sources of strong points, more highly educated respondents more often mention personality traits (Table 3.15). This stress on personality traits is especially evident in the frequency with which achievement personality traits are mentioned (Table 3.17).

What these findings seem to represent is a heightened self-probing —both for strengths and weaknesses—that can and evidently does result from increased education. These findings are consistent with those noted in a previous section, which pointed to the greater introspection in more highly educated groups, as measured by their greater ability to see both strong points and weaknesses in the self. What the present findings indicate is not only that the less educated are less inclined to see strengths and weaknesses in the self but that, when they do see such strengths and weaknesses, they are less likely to emerge with self-evaluations relevant to their more intimate personal lives.

SUMMARY

Examining certain aspects of self-attitudes, particularly introspection and the positive-negative orientation to the self, we found that the relationship between these two dimensions involves many complexities: Although introspective self-awareness and a positive self-percept have both been viewed as components of a "healthy" orientation to the self, in some ways they appear to be contradictory. Introspection tends to heighten a sensitivity to the negative as well as the positive aspects of the self and consequently works to reduce the positiveness of the self-percept.

Sex, age, and education all appear to be crucial variables in understanding a person's orientation to the self. A brief summary highlights these relationships:

Sex. Women are both more negative in their self-image and more introspective. Whereas men put more emphasis on their shortcomings in external achievements, women stress their personality and interpersonal weaknesses and strengths. These findings are consistent with differences in the cultural definitions of the sex roles. The man's role is one of acting and *doing,* with success and self-esteem dependent upon his accomplishments, while the woman's is a more passive, *being* role, with the sources of self-esteem found in internal responses and feelings.

Age. Older people are more positive in their self-image: they see fewer shortcomings in the self and are rated higher in their general self-acceptance. With age, people seem to come to terms with self. However, there is no apparent relationship between age and introspection. Rather than differing in introspection, older and younger people seem to differ in the areas in which they get involved. As they turn away from looking at the self they focus on characteristics of the self appropriate to their life stages: younger people are more involved in achievement, and older people more involved in considerations of the "moral" and the "good."

Education. The more highly educated, like women, are both more negative in their self-image and more introspective. Education seems to bring a heightened self-awareness, evidenced in these data by the fact that the more highly educated see both more shortcomings and more strong points in the self and by the fact that they focus on personality shortcomings. But with this heightened self-awareness comes a greater self-criticism, for we saw that more of the highly educated people were rated as negative or ambivalent in their percept of the self.

The education and sex relationships point up what has already been noted in the examination of the interrelationships among the self-percept indices: greater introspection is associated with a more negative self-image, a tendency to view the self critically. What are the mental health implications of the variations in self-percept that we have observed within the different sex and education groupings? The acceptance of the self that has been viewed in the literature as indicative of a healthy attitude toward the self involves a self-awareness that recognizes negative elements in the self but permits an over-all positive self-evaluation. But none of the sex or education subgroups meet both of these criteria. Rather, the findings suggest that the social and cultural conditions that lead to introspection and a heightened self-awareness may also lead not only to a realistic self-criticism but to a generally negative self-percept. Thus, groups more positively adjusted in terms of one component are less adjusted in terms of the other.

IV

Marriage

In this and the following two chapters we examine the experiences of adjustment in three major life roles—marriage, parenthood, and work. Each role is discussed within the same conceptual framework, although the specification of the concepts varies from one role area to another. Before proceeding to the separate discussions it may be helpful to delineate this conceptual framework and to indicate how it will be applied, so that these chapters will be seen as facets of general theoretical problems rather than as disparate investigations of three life areas.

ORIENTATION: ADJUSTMENT IN THREE LIFE ROLES—MARRIAGE, PARENTHOOD, AND WORK

Adjustment to any one of these life roles is a complicated human experience involving highly elaborate behavior patterns and emotional reactions. Only a few of the many possible dimensions of role adjustment were selected for consideration in this study. These are not necessarily the most refined dimensions of role adjustment, but we felt that they were significant and that they were appropriate for the data obtainable in a survey interview.

The most readily apparent dimension to consider is the amount of satisfaction or dissatisfaction that a person feels the role and its attendant behaviors hold for him. Does he enjoy being a parent, being married, doing the kind of work he does? Although data of this sort might seem at first glance simple enough to assess (one has only to ask a person how happy he is in his marriage, as a parent, or in his work) certain difficulties become apparent as one attempts to deal with the question systematically.

One difficulty in conceptualizing and measuring role *satisfaction* lies in the fact that gratification in a role is not a single dimension but a composite of several factors. A person who is satisfied in a role and generally content about the experiences in it may also sense dissatisfaction or be aware of certain problems that he finds in that role. A person may feel happy about a marriage even though at times he may have feelings of difficulty—either in the demands the role places on him or in the feelings of inadequacies that performance of the role may engender. Unhappiness, the sense of inadequacy in role performance, and the sense of problems may be either highly related or independent.

Three aspects of role adjustment were singled out for study. Two of them, feelings of *gratification* and the experience of major difficulties and *problems,* parallel our concern with "happiness" and "worries" in the investigation of general adjustment (see Chapter II); the experience of problems, like worrying, was viewed as indicative of some degree of expectations, investment, and involvement. The third aspect of role adjustment studied, feelings of *adequacy* in the role, is central to the understanding of some of the crucial dynamics of role adjustment. Theorists concerned with the study of role and the problems of an individual's adjustment to a role have placed particular emphasis on the demands that a role places on an individual and on the problems he faces in meeting the demands. These are key problems because role demands tend to be internalized and tied to the self-image, so that not meeting them leads to feelings of inadequacy and self-blame.

We would expect all three of these adjustment measures—gratification, problems, and adequacy—to be related to each other but also to differ in certain ways. Gratification in a role would appear to be a function mainly of the *opportunities* that a role offers an individual, the chance it gives him to express and maximize certain of his needs. Adequacy, on the other hand, is a function mainly of the *demands* that the role places on him and his ability to meet these demands. Problems and difficulties experienced can refer either to frustration and lack of gratification or to tensions springing from an inability to meet demands, or to other sources. With a consideration of all three measures we have a more complete picture of adjustment in the role than could be obtained from any single measure.

This brings us to another difficulty in examining the concept of role satisfaction: a consideration of satisfaction should take account of the *context* of the judgment being made, whether one thinks in terms of one, three, or any number of adjustment measures. Two people who both say that they are "very happy" in their marriages or who "often" feel inadequate as a husband or wife, or who have had a "problem" in their marriages, may be defining these terms in completely different ways. It is not enough to ask people to place themselves along continua measuring happiness or feelings of adequacy or the experience of problems. A similar problem was faced in the preceding chapters when we explored the explicit and implicit "definitions" of happiness, worries, strong points, and so on.

In order to evaluate the context of role satisfactions, in order to understand the meaning of feelings of satisfaction or adequacy or problems, we have tried to take account of the *degree of personal involvement* in the role, the degree to which the person's "self" is invested in it, how important it is in a person's life. This matter of involvement has implications for identifying how much and what kind of gratification a person expects from the role: a high degree of personal involvement implies that he expects to gain from it an expression of the self and the satisfaction of personality and interpersonal needs. For example, satisfaction in a job that is seen as a major outlet of creativity and a source of major life gratifications is quite different from satisfaction in a job that is defined as the place one spends the day and earns the money necessary to find basic gratifications in other areas of life. The degree of personal involvement implies how limited or broad is the person's conception of the role, how limited or broad are the gratifications derived from it. In this sense, a high degree of personal involvement has sometimes been viewed as reflecting a "healthy" adjustment, an indication that one is getting "more" out of the role.

The degree of involvement further suggests the extent to which a person seeks to validate the self in the role, the extent to which the role serves as an identity anchor, the extent to which inadequacies and problems in the role are experienced as ego blows. A woman who finds her major validation as a woman in her performance as a wife and who expresses feelings of adequacy or feels she has no problems in this role is different from one who expresses similar feelings within a context in which the marital role is much less central. In the latter case, lack of self-doubt may merely reflect lack of involvement, interest, and aspiration in the marital role.

Our interest in the degree of personal involvement in a role also stemmed from an anticipation that it would be related to the help-seeking patterns utilized in handling problems. Problems arising in a role in which the individual has deep personal involvement should more often be experienced as problems of the "self" and lead to the use of outside help resources. This question is dealt with in Part Two of the monograph.

The specific ways in which we conceptualized and measured this involvement dimension varied according to the role and the particular adjustment variable being investigated. In general, the measures of involvement derive from the *sources* of gratification, inadequacy, and problems mentioned by the individual. These sources were coded mainly in terms of a distinction between "intrinsic" and "external" aspects of the role. For instance, in our example above, the man satisfied with the job because it gives him financial security was coded as seeking external gratification; the man who is satisfied because of the self-expression that the work allows was coded as seeking ego or intrinsic gratification. Or, to cite another example, problems in a marriage can be seen as arising from situational difficulties the couple have faced (economic hurdles, illness, in-law interference) or from the intimate marriage relationship itself; the latter would be viewed as suggestive of a higher degree of personal involvement in the role.

Measures of Role Adjustment

Before proceeding to the discussion of the three role areas, it may be helpful to present an overview of the questions used to derive the adjustment and context measures.

General feelings of satisfaction. This aspect of adjustment had to be approached differently in the three role areas. The question about marriage satisfaction was phrased in terms of happiness because this seemed to be the concept most popularly used in considering satisfaction in marriage:

Taking things all together, how would you describe your marriage—would you say your marriage was *very happy, a little happier than average, just about average,* or *not too happy?*

But the concept of happiness could not be used directly in questions on parenthood and the job. As far as parenthood is concerned, too much stigma is attached to the person who is unable to find gratification in that role. To admit to unhappiness as a parent, even to admit lack of satisfaction as a parent, is an admission that few parents in our society would be willing to make, for there are too many implications for self-blame in such an admission. The prevailing attitudes in this culture would seem to place almost full responsibility on the parent himself for lack of gratification in his role. The child is molded by the parent—"a problem child is a problem parent." Although lack of satisfaction in marriage can be readily attributed to faults in the spouse or to exigencies of certain unfavorable situations, this attribution of blame to another is not so readily available in parenthood. In a pretest of the questionnaire used in this study, we asked respondents to tell us about the things they were not too happy about as a parent and also to evaluate their satisfaction as a parent. Although people could talk of "problems" with children, the responses were uniformly rejecting of the possibility that they might in any way feel "unhappy" about the role. In the final questionnaire, therefore, we attempted to approximate the self-evaluation of satisfaction as a parent in the following *indirect* question:

First, thinking about a man's (woman's) life, how is a man's (woman's) life changed by having children?

We attempted to derive the person's positive-negative orientation to children by coding the responses to this open-ended question according to whether he saw children as bringing positive, neutral, or negative changes in his life. Because of the indirectness of the question, its usefulness as a conscious self-evaluation measure is limited, and its results will be interpreted with caution.

Because one usually speaks of "satisfaction" rather than "happiness" in a job, we asked the following question to assess the general feelings of satisfaction on a job:

Taking into consideration all the things about your job, how satisfied or dissatisfied are you with it?

We coded this open-ended question for degree of expressed satisfaction. Unlike the marriage question, there were no fixed alternatives for the respondents. Generally, we prefer this kind of question because the respondent can use his own words to express qualitative and quantitative distinctions. We used fixed alternatives for the marriage question because the pretest results suggested that an open-ended question would elicit very few negative responses. By presenting fixed alternatives, including "average" rather than a more negative word, we were able to obtain a good distribution of responses to the marriage question.

Feelings of inadequacy. Feelings of inadequacy in marriage and parenthood were measured by parallel questions. For the marriage role, the question was:

Many men (women) feel that they're not as good husbands (wives) as they would like to be. Have you ever felt this way? (If Yes) Do you feel this way a lot of times, or only once in a while?

For the parent role, the question was:

Many men (women) feel that they're not as good fathers (mothers) as they would like to be. Have you ever felt this way? (If Yes) Have you felt this way a lot of times, or only once in a while?

Since inadequacy seems to have a specific meaning for role performance on a job (skill or ability at the work), we phrased the question about feelings of inadequacy at work in terms of skill or how good a job a person felt he was doing.

> How good would you say you are at doing this kind of work—would you say you were *very good, a little better than average, just average,* or *not very good?*

Here again we used alternatives, including an "average" alternative to maximize the possibility of getting a good distribution of responses.

Experience of problems. The experience of problems in marriage, in bringing up children, and in the job were measured in slightly different ways in the three role areas. For marriage, we structured what we meant by a problem in the question:

> Even in cases where married people are happy there have often been times in the past when they weren't too happy—when they had problems getting along with each other. Has this ever been true for you?

For the occupational role, the definition of a problem was even more structured, in order to get the respondent to focus on emotional rather than skill-relevant problems:

> Have you ever had any problems with your work—times when you couldn't work or weren't getting along on the job, or didn't know what kind of work you wanted to do?

For the parent role, because of the hesitancy in admitting to negative aspects of parenthood, we structured the question so as to make it difficult for the respondent not to report problems in that area. We did this by pointing to the problems "most parents" have. (Wording the question in this way does raise the danger of making the question so "easy" that everyone reports problems. However, this was not the case here. We still find about one quarter of our respondents saying they have never had such problems.) The question was phrased as follows:

> Most parents have had some problems in raising their children. What are the main problems you've had in raising your children?

Here we left open to the respondent how a "problem" should be defined.

Measures of Degree of Personal Involvement in Roles

We are concerned not only with measuring an individual's judgment of his adjustment in the three roles, but in the experiential context of these judgments. To do this, we have used the obvious approach: We asked the respondents directly about the sources of their judgment.

Married respondents were asked what were the "nicest things" about their marriage, what things about their marriage were "not as nice" as they "would like them to be," what kinds of things have made them feel inadequate and what kinds of problems they have faced in marriage. Similarly, we asked parents to tell us the "nicest thing about having children," the kinds of things that have made them feel inadequate as parents, and the kinds of problems they have had in raising their children. We did not ask them for sources of unhappiness as a parent since this question tended to be rejected by the respondents in the pretest. And finally, in the work area, we asked the respondents what kinds of things on their job particularly satisfied them, what kinds of things dissatisfied them and what kinds of problems they had faced on the job. Since the question of inadequacy in the job was structured specifically in terms of ability and skill, there was no need to probe for specific sources of inadequacy in the work role.

Plan of Analysis in the Role Areas

In general, the analysis conforms to the procedure developed in the preceding two chapters, and proceeds in the following steps: (1) the interrelationships among the three indices of adjustment; (2) the "meaning" of these indices described by relating them to the "context" measures; and (3) the relationship of sex, age, and education (and occupation in Chapter VI) to both the indices of adjustment and the "context" of these measures.

MARRIAGE

Marriage represents for most people a central life adjustment area. Scientific theorists and inspirational leaders have often looked to the institution of marriage for keys to general feelings of well-being and the roots of discontent; similarly, they have looked for extreme psychological problems in the status of the person deprived of the marriage role.

There is good reason for exploring this life role in the study of general adjustment. Being married or not married is an all-pervasive life condition which sets up certain requirements for human conduct, certain channels for the gratification of important human needs, and certain inevitable blocks to these needs. Furthermore, the marriage role can, in a sense, set the pace of other important life roles—friendship, parenthood, work. It is for these reasons that we are exploring marriage in some detail.

INTERRELATIONSHIPS AMONG THREE MEASURES OF MARITAL ADJUSTMENT

The three subjective indices of marital adjustment investigated in this study centered around the concepts of happiness, adequacy, and problems. We examined the interrelationships among these indices, to see the extent to which they were tapping similar or different aspects of adjustment to the marriage role. These interrelationships are presented in Tables 4.1, 4.2, and 4.3.

Table 4.1 presents the relationship between feelings of marital happiness and the frequency of feelings of inadequacy as a husband or wife. In general, there is only a slight relationship between the

Table 4.1—Relationship between Evaluation of Marital Happiness and Frequency of Feelings of Inadequacy as Spouse

Frequency of Feeling Inadequate	EVALUATION OF MARITAL HAPPINESS			
	Very Happy	Above Average	Average	Not Too Happy
A lot of times; often	9%	12%	15%	22%
Once in a while; once or twice	44	43	40	18
Never	44	42	42	54
Not ascertained	3	3	3	6
Total	100%	100%	100%	100%
Number of people [a]	(870)	(399)	(546)	(50)

[a] Does not include seven married people whose evaluation of marital happiness was not ascertained.

two variables—i.e., greater happiness in marriage shows a slight association with fewer feelings of inadequacy in the marital relationship. However, it is interesting to look at the "not too happy" group in contrast to the other three; respondents in this group tend to answer at either extreme of the adequacy question—either admitting to a good deal of inadequacy or asserting that they "never" feel inadequate. Although based on only a small number of cases (50 people), this finding may suggest a dual tendency in a marriage that is perceived as unhappy. Persons may either assume a great deal of guilt (greater feelings of inadequacy) or take a position avoiding guilt feelings completely (never feeling inadequate), perhaps blaming the partner or situational difficulties for the problem.

Is there any tendency for feelings of inadequacy as a spouse to be translated into a personal problem in marriage? Table 4.2 suggests

Table 4.2—Relationship between Frequency of Feelings of Inadequacy as Spouse and the Report of Personal Problems in Marriage

Report of Marriage Problem	FREQUENCY OF FEELING INADEQUATE		
	A Lot of Times; Often	Once in a While; Once or Twice	Never
Had problems	59%	45%	31%
No problems	34	48	62
Inapplicable [a]	4	1	3
Not ascertained	3	6	4
Total	100%	100%	100%
Number of people [b]	(213)	(782)	(811)

[a] Refers to 50 married people who evaluated their marriage as "not too happy" and therefore were not asked whether they ever had any marriage problems.
[b] Does not include 66 married people whose frequency of feeling inadequate as a spouse was not ascertained.

that this is so—that admission to inadequacy is part of the pattern of perceiving problems in marriage. The fact that there is not a stronger relationship between the two variables suggests that, for some respondents, inadequacy in the marriage relationship is held apart from thinking of a "problem" in the marriage; for them, self-doubt and the things causing self-doubt are not necessarily a "problem." However, for the majority of respondents, to be sensitive to one's inadequacy also means that one is sensitive to problems in the marriage.

In Table 4.3—the relationship between marital happiness and the report of problems in marriage—we do not include those respondents who said their marriage was "not very happy." We assumed that people who said that their marriages were not very happy were facing personal problems in their marriages, and we therefore did not ask them a further question about whether they had any problems; thus the relationship between these two variables is reported for the remaining groups of respondents. As indicated in the table, a distinct relationship appears. The respondents reporting happier marriages are less likely to report ever having experienced a personal

Table 4.3—Relationship between Evaluation of Marital Happiness and the Report of Personal Problems in Marriage

	EVALUATION OF MARITAL HAPPINESS		
Report of Marriage Problems	Very Happy	Above Average	Average
Had problems	32%	50%	51%
No problems	65	47	41
Not ascertained	3	3	8
Total	100%	100%	100%
Number of people [a]	(870)	(399)	(546)

[a] Does not include 50 married people who evaluated their marriages as "not too happy" and therefore were not asked whether or not they ever had marriage problems; does not include 7 married people whose evaluation of marital happiness was not ascertained.

problem in their marriages. It is interesting, however, that the relationship is not an even more dramatic one. Feeling happiness in one's marriage does not preclude the possibility of having perceived a problem in the marriage. Indeed, later results will show that this is a common pattern for certain demographic groupings.

We may summarize the pattern of findings in Tables 4.1, 4.2, and 4.3 in the following way: Happiness and feelings of adequacy in marriage show little relationship to each other, suggesting both that happiness in marriage does not preclude the possibility of self-questioning and self-doubt, and, conversely, that unhappiness in marriage does not necessarily turn into self-blame. However, although not related to each other, both happiness in marriage and the frequency of feelings of inadequacy relate to the report of personal problems in marriage. It would seem that there are two distinguishable components in defining a marriage problem—one related to general felt distress and the other related to feelings of inadequacy.

THE CONTEXT FOR JUDGING MARITAL ADJUSTMENT

We have assumed that to be involved in a marriage is to have a great deal of energy invested in the marital *relationship* itself. Married people undoubtedly differ in the investment they have in each other as people, in how much they depend on the interpersonal aspects of the marriage for sources of gratification in their lives. And we would expect these differences to be reflected in the standards they set for their behavior as husbands and wives and in the problems they experience in the marriage.

Some marriage partners *coexist,* each performing the culturally prescribed role requirements of a husband or wife, providing or keeping house, attending to each other's physical needs, without too much attention to the subtleties of potentially intimate relationships. Stresses on this kind of marriage can depend largely on external factors such as financial ups and downs, the children's stage of development, and the physical environment.

Other marital partners have a more personal impact on each other, are more aware of each other's subtle personal needs, look to the marriage for deep personal gratification, interact as persons in the relationship. Stresses on this kind of marriage can depend largely on relationship difficulties—lack of consideration for each other, an alien need in the spouse that cannot be integrated into a functioning marriage, lack of adjustment in the self.

The general focus of the context measures, then, will be on whether or not there is a concern with the qualities of the interpersonal relationship in the marriage. We will look at expressions of marital happiness, feelings of inadequacy, and experiences of problems in the marriage within the context of whether or not there is such a concern.

The context measures were derived from the questions on the sources of happiness, unhappiness, inadequacies, and problems in the marriage. The sources of happiness and unhappiness were measured in the following two questions in the interview:

1. We've talked a little about marriage in general. Now, thinking about your own marriage, what would you say were the nicest things about it?
2. Every marriage has its good points and bad points. What things about your marriage are not quite as nice as you would like them to be?

For the sources of inadequacy, we followed the question on feelings of inadequacy with this probe: "What kinds of things make you feel this way?" Similarly, people who reported a problem in the marriage were asked: "What was that about?"

The responses to these four context questions were coded mainly for their emphasis on the *relationship* aspect of marriage. Four major categories were distinguished for both sources of problems and sources of unhappiness:

Difficulty in the relationship: "We just don't get along." "We fight." "My husband and I don't share the same interests." "We don't love each other."
Difficulty in the self: "I haven't been able to earn enough." "I'm not a good cook." "I get angry too quickly."
Difficulty in the spouse: "My husband drinks too much." "My wife is too extravagant." "My husband doesn't spend enough time home."
Difficulty in the situation: "During the depression." "When the children took up so much time." "My in-laws nag us."

Sources of happiness in marriage were similarly coded:

Relationship sources: "We're happy being together." "The companionship." "We get along." "My husband and I love each other."
Spouse sources: "He's a good provider." "She keeps the house running smoothly." "He's very kind to me." "He doesn't drink." "He's a very responsible person."
Situational sources: "We have a nice house." "The children." "We don't have to worry about money."

Sources of inadequacy were divided into two categories:

Inadequacy in protective trait. This category includes those replies most relevant to the relationship: "I don't spend time talking with my wife." "I'm not considerate enough."
Role functioning inadequacies: poor housekeeper, poor provider, poor parent.

Table 4.4—Relationship between Evaluation of Marital Happiness and Sources of Happiness (First-Mentioned Reasons)

Sources of Happiness	EVALUATION OF MARITAL HAPPINESS			
	Very Happy	Above Average	Average	Not Too Happy
Relationship	47%	42%	35%	18%
Spouse	21	24	19	26
Situation	22	25	36	40
Other	8	7	6	2
Not happy about anything	—	—	—	8
Not ascertained	2	2	4	6
Total	100%	100%	100%	100%
Number of people [a]	(870)	(399)	(546)	(50)

[a] Does not include seven people whose evaluation of marital happiness was not ascertained.

Table 4.5—Relationship between Evaluation of Marital Happiness and Sources of Unhappiness (First-Mentioned Reasons of Respondents Giving Any Reason for Unhappiness)

Sources of Unhappiness	EVALUATION OF MARITAL HAPPINESS			
	Very Happy	Above Average	Average	Not Too Happy
Relationship	12%	15%	16%	23%
Spouse	19	23	27	50
Self	9	8	8	—
Situation	50	46	37	23
Other	—	—	*	2
Not ascertained	10	8	12	2
Total	100%	100%	100%	100%
Number of people [a]	(518)	(306)	(440)	(48)

* Here and in all subsequent tables this symbol (*) indicates less than one-half of 1 per cent.
[a] Does not include seven married people whose evaluation of marital happiness was not ascertained or the 553 married people who said there was nothing about their marriage that was not quite as nice as they would like it to be.

We will now turn to the relationships between the adjustment and context measures. Table 4.4 presents the relationship between a person's evaluation of his marital happiness and the kinds of happiness he finds in the marriage; Table 4.5 presents the relationship between the evaluation of happiness and the sources of unhappiness in the marriage. We are interested in looking at these tables with the following questions in mind: Are the kinds of happiness experienced by people who call their marriage "happy" different from the kinds of happiness experienced by those people who say that their marriage is "average" or "not too happy"? Conversely, does being unhappy in marriage imply an involvement with certain kinds of stresses in marriage different from those which concern the people who evaluate their marriage in more positive terms?

Tables 4.4 and 4.5 indicate that there is a very clear relationship between one's over-all feelings of happiness in the marriage and the kinds of things one is happy and unhappy about. People who report very happy marriages are more likely to concentrate on relationship sources of happiness, while those reporting less happiness in marriage tend to concentrate on the situational aspects of marriage (home, children, social life) as sources of their marital happiness (Table 4.4). Conversely, in the association with sources of unhappiness, we see that those happier in marriage—when they give any reasons for unhappiness—tend to focus on situational sources, while the less happy stress difficulties in the relationship (or the spouse). Thus, feelings of happiness in marriage bear a clear relationship with the extent to which a person is satisfied or frustrated in the relationship aspects of his marriage. When he is happy with the relationship aspects of the marriage he tends to feel generally happy in the marriage; when unhappy with this aspect of the marriage, he tends to be unhappy. This association is clearer on the positive side than it is on the negative. That is, focusing on relationship sources of happiness is more markedly related to feeling happy in marriage than focusing on relationship sources of distress is related to feeling unhappy in marriage. A good deal of unhappiness in marriage seems to get expressed in complaints against the spouse rather than the relationship. But even with this qualification, Tables 4.4 and 4.5 indicate that to a considerable extent happiness in marriage implies happiness in the *relationship*.

The relationship between the frequency of feelings of inadequacy and the content of these feelings is presented in Table 4.6. Since people who said they never felt inadequate could not be questioned as to the sources of inadequacy, the table includes only those who admitted to some inadequacy. But, within this group, we can compare people who differed in the extent of their inadequacy feelings. Table 4.6 indicates that there is no relationship between the degree of one's feelings of inadequacy and the content of inadequacy. Those people who feel inadequate most frequently tend to speak of the

MARRIAGE

Table 4.6—Relationship between Frequency of Feelings of Inadequacy as a Spouse and Sources of Inadequacies (First-Mentioned Reasons)

	FREQUENCY OF FEELING INADEQUATE	
Sources of Inadequacies	A Lot of Times; Often	Once in a While; Once or Twice
Role functioning		
Poor provider	23%	22%
Poor housekeeper	21	19
Poor parent	1	1
Relationship with spouse		
Inadequacy in protective trait	15	18
Too dominant	4	8
Other characteristics		
Drinking	3	1
Physical health	4	2
Sex	3	1
Others	24	24
Not ascertained	2	4
Total	100%	100%
Number of people [a]	(213)	(782)

[a] Does not include 811 people who said they "never" felt inadequate or 65 people whose frequency of feeling inadequate was not ascertained.

same kinds of inadequacies as those who do not often feel inadequate. This suggests that strong feelings of inadequacy can come equally from many sources. It is also possible that this lack of relationship between the degree and the content of inadequacy feelings means either that the particular content areas we have chosen are irrelevant to the strength of inadequacy feelings, or that the crucial distinction in terms of the context variables is not how strong are one's feelings of inadequacy but rather whether or not one feels inadequate at all. There is a suggestion from some of the findings we will examine later, particularly the relationships with education discussed in the following section (Table 4.10), that the latter interpretation may be the correct one.

We cannot relate the experience of problems to the particular context of the problem, since people who did not experience a problem could not be asked for the content of problems and people who did experience a marriage problem were not further asked about the seriousness of the problem. However, we may examine the question of the context of problems by comparing the areas of stress mentioned in response to the question on problems with those mentioned in response to the question on sources of unhappiness. This comparison is presented in Table 4.7.

Table 4.7—Comparison of the Sources of Unhappiness in Marriage with the Sources of Personal Problems in Marriage (First-Mentioned Reasons)

Sources Mentioned	Unhappiness	Problems
Relationship difficulty	14%	31%
Difficulty in spouse	24	21
Difficulty in respondent	8	10
Situational difficulty	44	28
Other	*	—
Not ascertained	10	10
Total	100%	100%
Number of people [a]	(1318)	(844)

[a] Includes only respondents who report some marital unhappiness or some personal problem in marriage.

As indicated in Table 4.7, sources of unhappiness show a higher concentration on situational difficulties—material problems, financial difficulties, the job interfering with the marriage. Sources of problems, on the other hand, show a higher concentration on relationship difficulties with the marriage partner. This difference suggests that the question on unhappiness elicits more of the on-going annoyances that occur day to day, whereas the problems question probes for a more serious, introspective evaluation of the long-term marriage relationship. This is probably partly a function of the different phrasing of the questions ("problems" pointing more to the relationship itself), and partly a function of the fact that the unhappiness question refers to the present, whereas the problems question takes in the whole marriage history.

To summarize briefly then, happiness is related to the extent to which a person is satisfied or frustrated in the *relationship* aspects of the marriage; the extent of one's inadequacy feelings is not related to stressing inadequacies most relevant to the relationship aspects of the marriage; and "problems," more than "unhappiness," imply relationship stresses. The implications of these findings become clearer in the demographic relationships to be examined below.

SEX, AGE, AND EDUCATION RELATED TO MARITAL ADJUSTMENT

In this section, we will be concerned with whether differences in sex, age, and education are relevant for distinguishing different ways of responding on the measures of marital adjustment. We will first consider the relationships with the adjustment indices and then elaborate their meaning by considering relationships with the context measures.

Sex

Since the role requirements of marriage are quite disparate for men and women, one might expect striking differences between the sexes in response to the questions dealing with evaluations of marital adjustment. Such was not the case. There were differences, but none were dramatic.

In Table 4.8 we observe that men and women are alike in the frequency of feeling inadequate; but men say they are happier and have had fewer personal problems in their marriages. Some of these differences are slight but they are consistent with the findings in other areas of the interview, indicating a general tendency for women to express more problems and stress.

Do men and women differ in the context of these evaluations? Examination of relationships between sex and the context questions indicates no differences between men and women in their tendency to stress the relationship aspect of marriage. However, there is an interesting difference in the extent to which sources of marital stress are seen as arising from the self. Although there was no difference between men and women in their statements of how often they felt inadequate, examination of the context questions suggests that there may be a greater degree of self-blame among the men than there is among the women. For example, in the responses to the question on sources of unhappiness in marriage, 24 per cent of the women blamed the husband for some negative aspect of the marriage, while only 10 per cent of the men directed any blame towards their wives

Table 4.8—Relationship between Sex of Respondent and Marital Adjustment Indices

Marital Adjustment Indices	Men	Women
Evaluation of marital happiness		
Very happy	48%	45%
Above average	23	20
Average	26	32
Not too happy	2	3
Not ascertained	1	—
Total	100%	100%
Frequency of feeling inadequate		
A lot of times; often	11%	12%
Once in a while; once or twice	41	42
Never	45	42
Not ascertained	3	4
Total	100%	100%
Report of marriage problems		
Had problems	36%	45%
No problems	56	49
Inapplicable [a]	2	3
Not ascertained	6	3
Total	100%	100%
Number of people	(908)	(964)

[a] Refers to 50 people who evaluated their marital happiness as "not too happy" and therefore were not asked whether or not they ever had personal problems in their marriage.

Parallel results are obtained in examining the differences between men and women in their responses to the kinds of problems they have faced. The pattern which seems to emerge from these results is that although feelings of inadequacy occur just as frequently in men as they do in women, when men do feel inadequate there is a more pervasive self-accusation. Furthermore, this self-accusation extends into the perception of problems they actually *have* faced in marriage. We will discuss some possible explanations of this finding later in this chapter.

Age

In Table 4.9, the measures of marital adjustment are compared for different age groups. The most striking finding is that feelings of inadequacy and problems progressively decrease with age. One might suspect that over time there tends to be an increasing adaptation to the marital partner and to the distresses in the marriage. This adapta-

Table 4.9—Relationship between Age of Respondent and Marital Adjustment Indices

Marital Adjustment Indices	Age Groups					
	21–24	25–34	35–44	45–54	55–64	65 and over
Evaluation of marital happiness						
Very happy	52%	48%	48%	43%	40%	46%
Above average	20	22	23	22	20	18
Average	26	28	26	31	34	34
Not too happy	2	2	2	4	5	2
Not ascertained	—	—	1	—	1	—
Total	100%	100%	100%	100%	100%	100%
Frequency of feeling inadequate						
A lot of times; often	15%	14%	11%	8%	8%	11%
Once in a while; once or twice	51	47	42	38	37	24
Never	31	36	43	50	51	59
Not ascertained	3	3	4	4	4	6
Total	100%	100%	100%	100%	100%	100%
Report of marriage problems						
Had problems	45%	50%	42%	38%	31%	19%
No problems	53	44	51	54	58	71
Inapplicable [a]	2	2	2	4	5	2
Not ascertained	—	4	5	4	6	8
Total	100%	100%	100%	100%	100%	100%
Number of people [b]	(132)	(509)	(472)	(366)	(228)	(160)

[a] Refers to 50 people who evaluated their marriage as "not too happy" and were therefore not asked whether or not they had marriage problems.
[b] Does not include five married people whose age was not ascertained.

tion, for economy of operation of the marriage, may involve minimization, denial, or gradual working through of problems. A problem, in retrospect, may appear not to have been a problem at all. Furthermore, it should be expected that, with advancing years, the marriage relationship becomes more and more an integral part of the self-picture of the respondents. Any threats to the perception of smooth functioning in this identity—that is, introspections about problems or inadequacies—might be greater to an older marriage than to a younger marriage.

These findings are reminiscent of those discussed in Chapter II, where we noted that older people, although less generally happy, also showed some tendency to worry less than younger people. In the marriage area we now find that older people are again, if anything, less happy, but also see fewer problems. Increasing age seems to bring increasing acceptance of one's lot rather than increasing positive gratifications.

Examination of the context variable for the different age groups indicates that there is no distinctive difference in the sources of happiness and unhappiness. Furthermore, when people at different age levels admit to inadequacies or problems, the kinds of problems and inadequacies they feel do not generally differ.

Thus, it appears that age has an important bearing on the initial admission to distress in marriage, but that once distress is admitted, older and younger married respondents are generally alike in the kinds of distress they feel. The lack of difference in the kinds of stresses accented may indicate, in a way, the permanence of the concern with relationship aspects of marriage. The failure in the relationship, the desire for companionship, may be basic, permanent aspects of marriage, transcending even so significant a variable as age.

Education

Table 4.10 summarizes the comparison of respondents at three educational levels in their responses to the three marital adjustment questions. Some dramatic educational differences are evident in this table. Marital happiness is related rather strongly to the educational level of the respondents, with those at higher educational levels reporting greater marital happiness. Furthermore, there are strong relationships between educational level and feelings of inadequacy and problems in the marriage; the more educated, although happier, admit to more inadequacies and problems in the marriage. (It should be noted that this last result—the relationship between level of education and admission of problems in the marriage—does not persist when age is controlled.)

How may we explain these apparently contradictory findings—that more highly educated people are happier in marriage, but experience greater feelings of inadequacy? Some clue may be found in an examination of the responses that the different educational groups give to the questions on sources of happiness and unhappiness in marriage. As we noted, these responses were grouped according to their pertinence to some aspect of the marriage relationship—i.e., whether the

Table 4.10—Relationship between Education and Marital Adjustment Indices

Marital Adjustment Indices	Grade School	High School	College
Evaluation of marital happiness			
Very happy	38%	46%	60%
Above average	16	25	22
Average	41	27	17
Not too happy	5	2	1
Not ascertained	—	—	—
Total	100%	100%	100%
Frequency of feeling inadequate			
A lot of times; often	10%	13%	10%
Once in a while; once or twice	34	42	53
Never	53	42	33
Not ascertained	3	3	4
Total	100%	100%	100%
Report of marriage problem			
Had problems	33%	44%	45%
No problems	56	50	51
Inapplicable [a]	5	2	1
Not ascertained	6	4	3
Total	100%	100%	100%
Number of people [b]	(553)	(950)	(362)

[a] Refers to 50 people who evaluated their marriage as "not too happy" and therefore were not asked whether or not they ever had problems.
[b] Does not include seven married people whose educational level was not ascertained.

happiness (or unhappiness) stemmed from some aspect of the husband-wife interaction. The differences among groups of different educational levels are particularly striking in the happiness question: 32 per cent of the grade-school group, 41 per cent of the high-school group, and 55 per cent of the college group saw their marital happiness as deriving from some aspect of the marriage relationship. Although not as striking, the question on sources of marital distress yielded similar results, with the college-educated respondents again mentioning more relationship aspects of the marriage: 15 per cent of the latter compared to 8 per cent of the grade-school group and 9 per cent of the high-school group.

When we look at the kinds of problems and the sources of feelings of inadequacies mentioned by respondents at different educational levels, we find a similar relationship between education and a stressing of the relationship aspects of the marriage. Higher education is associated with a greater reference to relationship difficulties in talking about marriage problems and difficulties. Furthermore, higher education is associated with more frequent mention of inadequacies concerned with the intimate relationship to the spouse (not being considerate enough, being too bossy, etc.). These results, based on only those respondents who mention having had a problem or having felt inadequate, are presented in Table 4.11.

Table 4.11—Relationship between Education of Respondent and the Mention of Relationship Characteristics as Marital Problems and Inadequacies (First-Mentioned Reasons Only) [a]

Education	Relationship Problem	Relationship Inadequacy
Grade school	26%	14%
High school	29	27
College	44	27

[a] Figures are the percentage of married respondents in each educational group who mentioned relationship sources of problems or feelings of inadequacy.

It would seem, then, that an effect of education might be to increase the salience of the more internal, intrinsic aspects of marriage, making marriage, in a sense, more central in one's life. This greater centrality might explain the finding that the more highly educated, although happier in marriage, also feel more inadequacy and self-questioning. Greater centrality might mean both a greater potential for happiness on the one hand (recalling the strong relationship between happiness and the stress on the relationship aspects of the marriage, Table 4.4) and on the other hand greater expectations and demands for what marriage should be. The greater amplitude of such demands may lead to feelings of inadequacy when the demands are not completely fulfilled.

Indices of Marital Adjustment Related Jointly to Sex, Age, and Education

Because we might expect sex, age, and education to interact with each other in complex ways in their influence on adjustment to the marital role, we have examined how these three variables operate simultaneously in this area. The respondents were divided into 18 groups (two sex groups subdivided into three age groups, then further subdivided into three educational levels). Tables 4.12 through

Table 4.12—Relationship between Evaluation of Marital Happiness as "Average" or "Not Too Happy" and Sex, Educational Level, and Age of Respondent [a]

Age	Education	Men	Women
21–34	Grade school	46	59
	High school	25	33
	College	15	18
35–54	Grade school	39	47
	High school	27	31
	College	16	23
55 and over	Grade school	41	52
	High school	21	35
	College	13 [b]	— [c]

[a] Figures are the percentage of married respondents in each group who evaluate their marital happiness as "average" or "not too happy."
[b] Sample size is between 15 and 30.
[c] Figure is omitted; sample size is less than 15.

Table 4.13—Relationship between Mentioning Some Aspect of the Marital Relationship as a Source of Marital Happiness and Sex, Educational Level, and Age of Respondent (First-Mentioned Reason) [a]

Age	Education	Men	Women
21–34	Grade school	32	38
	High school	34	45
	College	53	52
35–54	Grade school	30	30
	High school	41	42
	College	54	62
55 and over	Grade school	38	33
	High school	39	40
	College	50 [b]	— [c]

[a] Figures are the percentage of married respondents in each group who mention some aspect of the marital relationship as the nicest thing about their marriage (first-mentioned reason).
[b] Sample size is between 15 and 30.
[c] Figure is omitted; sample size is less than 15.

4.20 present the distribution of responses on each of the indices of marital adjustment among these 18 groups.

These tables present some refinement of our previous discussion in this chapter of sex, age, and education as separate variables. The findings from these tables, together with those from the previous discussion, are summarized in the following pages.

Table 4.14—Relationship between Reporting Feelings of Inadequacy in Marriage and Sex, Educational Level, and Age of Respondent [a]

Age	Education	Men	Women
21–34	Grade school	44	57
	High school	65	62
	College	65	78
35–54	Grade school	55	37
	High school	45	55
	College	58	60
55 and over	Grade school	43	32
	High school	42	38
	College	50 [b]	— [c]

[a] Figures are the percentage of married respondents in each group who say they have felt inadequate as a husband or wife.
[b] Sample size is between 15 and 30.
[c] Figure is omitted; sample size is less than 15.

Table 4.15—Relationship between Mentioning Role Functioning as a Source of Inadequacy and Sex, Educational Level, and Age of Respondent (First-Mentioned Reason) [a]

Age	Education	Men	Women
21–34	Grade school	83 [b]	47 [b]
	High school	49	45
	College	37	54
35–54	Grade school	53	32
	High school	44	28
	College	40	29
55 and over	Grade school	51	31
	High school	59 [b]	33 [b]
	College	— [c]	— [c]

[a] Figures are the percentage of married respondents in each group who admit to feelings of inadequacy *and* also mention an aspect of providing (for men) or housekeeping (for women) as a source of feelings of inadequacy (first-mentioned reason).
[b] Sample size is between 15 and 30.
[c] Figure is omitted; sample size is less than 15.

MALE-FEMALE DIFFERENCES IN MARITAL ADJUSTMENT

1. Women report that they are less happy in their marriages than men (Table 4.12), but they do not differ in the mention of relationship sources of marital happiness (Table 4.13).

2. Men and women do not differ in their reports of how often they feel inadequate (Table 4.14). Men generally feel more inadequate

Table 4.16—Relationship between Mentioning Lack of Protectiveness and Consideration for the Spouse as a Source of Inadequacy and Sex, Educational Level, and Age of Respondent (First-Mentioned Reason) [a]

Age	Education	Men	Women
21–34	Grade school	—	16[b]
	High school	31	24
	College	37	15
35–54	Grade school	11	11
	High school	28	34
	College	29	27
55 and over	Grade school	19	38
	High school	21[b]	22[b]
	College	—[c]	—[c]

[a] Figures are the percentage of married respondents in each group who admit to feelings of inadequacy *and* also mention their own lack of protectiveness or consideration as a source of these feelings (first-mentioned reason).
[b] Sample size is between 15 and 30.
[c] Figure is omitted; sample size is less than 15.

Table 4.17—Relationship between Reporting Having Had Personal Problems in Marriage and Sex, Educational Level, and Age of Respondent [a]

Age	Education	Men	Women
21–34	Grade school	34	59
	High school	57	53
	College	50	62
35–54	Grade school	50	49
	High school	45	49
	College	45	51
55 and over	Grade school	32	45
	High school	37	40
	College	33[c]	—[b]

[a] Figures are the percentage of married respondents in each group who report having had personal problems in marriage.
[b] Figure is omitted; sample size is less than 15.
[c] Sample size is between 15 and 30.

about their central role function (providing vs. housekeeping) (Table 4.15). The one reversal that occurs is among college-educated young men and women. In this group, women feel more inadequate in this area.

3. At most educational and age levels, more women than men report having had a problem in their marriages (Table 4.17). When

Table 4.18—Relationship between Mentioning a Characteristic of the Self as Creating a Marital Problem and Sex, Educational Level, and Age of Respondent (First-Mentioned Reason) [a]

Age	Education	Men	Women
21–34	Grade school	—[b]	11[c]
	High school	16	6
	College	14	12
35–54	Grade school	19	2
	High school	10	10
	College	10	13
55 and over	Grade school	15[c]	7[c]
	High school	14[c]	—[b]
	College	—[b]	—[b]

[a] Figures are the percentage of married respondents in each group who report personal problem in marriage *and* also mention some fault in themselves as causing the problem (first-mentioned reason).

[b] Figure is omitted; sample size is less than 15.

[c] Sample size is between 15 and 30.

Table 4.19—Relationship between Mentioning a Characteristic of the Spouse as Creating a Marital Problem and Sex, Educational Level, and Age of Respondent (First-Mentioned Reason) [a]

Age	Education	Men	Women
21–34	Grade school	—[b]	50[c]
	High school	9	28
	College	11	19
35–54	Grade school	17	22
	High school	18	40
	College	16	20
55 and over	Grade school	11[c]	50[c]
	High school	10[c]	—[b]
	College	—[b]	—[b]

[a] Figures are the percentage of married respondents in each group who admit to a personal problem in marriage *and* also mention some fault of the spouse as causing the problem (first-mentioned reason).

[b] Figure is omitted; sample size is less than 15.

[c] Sample size is between 15 and 30.

men do report marriage problems, they are less likely to attribute the cause of these problems to their wives than women are to attribute these problems to their husbands (Table 4.19).

We may interpret these findings, again, in terms of the centrality of the marriage role. Although it was not evidenced in the measure

Table 4.20—Relationship between Mentioning Some Aspect of the Marital Relationship as Creating Problems in Marriage and Sex, Educational Level, and Age of Respondent (First-Mentioned Reason) [a]

Age	Education	Men	Women
21–34	Grade school	—[b]	22[c]
	High school	36	34
	College	52	43
35–54	Grade school	27	41
	High school	39	26
	College	45	49
55 and over	Grade school	26[c]	29[c]
	High school	24[c]	—[b]
	College	—[b]	—[b]

[a] Figures are the percentage of married respondents in each group who admit to personal problem in marriage *and* also mention some aspect of the marital relationship as causing the problem (first-mentioned reason).

[b] Figure is omitted; sample size is less than 15.

[c] Sample size is between 15 and 30.

of role involvement utilized in this study, it is likely that women have more invested in their marriages, that marriage and home are more central to the woman's life. With greater centrality come greater expectations and demands. Women's greater sensitivity to problems might be viewed as a reflection of greater expectations, and their lower degree of happiness an indication that, to some extent, these expectations are not fulfilled.

The greater tendency for women to blame the husband for marriage problems is somewhat contradictory to the other findings. One would expect that greater centrality would lead to greater self-questioning in the women, but it does not. Men, with less investment in the marriage, may be freer to admit to things about themselves that have led to disruptions in the marriage. For women, the greater investment in the marriage might make such self-blame much more threatening.

However, we may interpret the sex difference in the assignment of blame from another point of view, one which we noted in our discussion of sex differences in self-perception (Chapter III). If we think of the usual male-female role distinctions for marriage—the man as initiator and the woman as supporter—it is, in a way, "easier" to think of problems occurring in the active as opposed to the passive role. It is easier to pinpoint a man's lack of material support than the more tenuous emotional support that is a major contribution of the woman to marriage. "Drinking" and "running around with other women," the wife's frequent complaints, may also be seen as a concomitant of man's more active role in our society, with no such obvious comparable failings springing from the more passive feminine orientation.

AGE DIFFERENCES ON INDICES OF MARITAL ADJUSTMENT

1. Young, middle-aged, and old respondents generally report the same levels of marital happiness (Table 4.12) and do not differ in their mention of relationship sources of happiness (Table 4.13).

2. There is a marked tendency, although irregular at some educational levels, for the older respondents to report fewer feelings of inadequacy than are reported by the younger respondents. This tendency appears stronger for women than men (Table 4.14). There is also some relationship between age and the *source* of inadequacy, particularly in the "deficiency as a provider" or "housekeeper" category, which older people less often see as a source of inadequacy (Table 4.15).

3. Except for grade-school educated men, personal problems in the marriage are reported more often by younger than by older men and women (Table 4.17). There is no relationship between the age of the respondent and the *kinds* of problems they report having faced (Tables 4.18–4.20).

It would appear from these findings that although the level of happiness in a marriage does not increase with age, there is a softening of the difficulties. The perspective on problems and inadequacies narrows with older marriages. Difficulties are probably minimized by older people in order to maintain the anchor of identity that marriage provides for them. The longer the investment in the marriage, the more important it would be to avoid thoughts or situations that would bring difficulty. Furthermore, older people would be expected to have gradually worked through many problems and feelings of guilt, so that these are no longer perceived as difficulties. This may represent merely an adaptation to a problem, so that a former difficulty is no longer seen as a problem. But it is likely that not only time, but motivation to maintain personal identity in marriage should foster such adaptation.

LEVEL OF EDUCATION AND MARITAL ADJUSTMENT INDICES

1. For both men and women in all age groups, marital happiness increases with increased educational level: college-educated people report greater marital happiness than do the high-school educated, and they, in turn, report greater marital happiness than do the grade-school people (Table 4.12). Furthermore, education is related to reporting some aspect of the relationship as being the nicest thing about the marriage. The college-educated men and women, at all age levels, stress this most often (Table 4.13).

2. For women, educational level has a pronounced effect on feelings of inadequacy in the marriage. At each age level, the college-educated women report feeling inadequate most often, and the grade-school-educated women report feeling inadequate least often, with the high-school-educated women falling in between. This relationship does not obtain as strongly for the men (Table 4.14). Education bears on the kinds of inadequacies mentioned in only one instance: There is some tendency for the more educated men to report more inadequacies due to insufficient protectiveness or consideration of the spouse (Table 4.16).

3. There is no consistent relationship between education and the experience of problems in the marriage (Table 4.17). College-educated men, however, refer to more relationship problems—problems of adjusting to the wife, "getting along," "fighting." This relationship between education and reporting relationship problems also holds for women, but not as clearly as for men (Table 4.20).

In general, then, the findings with respect to education suggest that the more educated respondents are more sensitive to both the positive and negative aspects of the marriage relationship. Their greater sensitivity to the positive aspects is reflected in the fact that expressed marital happiness increases progressively with increasing education. This finding is undoubtedly a reflection of many factors: the increased involvement in the more "intrinsic" interpersonal aspects of marriage in the more educated groups; the lesser economic strains on the marriage that one might expect in these groups; perhaps a greater concern with "happiness" as an ideal in marriage.

The fact that educated respondents are more ready to report the negative aspects of their marriage is demonstrated differently for men and women. Educated women seem to be particularly attuned to perceive their own inadequacies in marriage. For educated men, the sensitivity to negative aspects is evidenced in their greater stress on relationship problems and inadequacies.

Education for women in this society represents a training for living which is often looked upon as incompatible with the standard feminine housewife role. This perceived incompatibility probably engenders in educated women a greater potentiality for seeing some inadequacy in their roles as wives. Why education should be an important factor in producing a heightened awareness of "relationship" problems in marriage for men but not for women is another question needing comment. There has been some speculation that one of the effects of education on men may be to sensitize them to what might be called the more "feminine" value orientations. One of these supposed values is a concern for social and interpersonal relationships. It might be hypothesized that women, regardless of education, are trained to be concerned with the interpersonal aspects of their significant social relationships. If these assumptions are correct, they would help to explain the finding that education clearly increases the sensitivity to relationship problems for men but not for women.

SUMMARY

We have been concerned in this chapter with questions of *gratification* in the marriage role, feelings of *adequacy* in meeting requirements for this role, and the experience of *problems* in this role. Interrelating these three measures of adjustment yielded the following pattern of results: Unhappiness and feelings of inadequacy in marriage showed little relationship to each other, but both were related to the experience of problems in marriage. Unhappiness in marriage does not necessarily lead to feelings of inadequacy and self-blame; nor, conversely, does self-questioning in a marriage necessarily imply unhappiness. But both unhappiness and inadequacy appear to be components of what is defined as a marriage problem.

In marriage, as in the other role areas, we have attempted to elaborate on the meaning of the indices of adjustment by considering the context in which these judgments of adjustment were made. One general dimension of "context" was used—the degree of personal involvement in the role. This refers to the centrality of the role in a person's life, the extent to which the person's self is invested in the role. It has been measured by the extent to which a person focuses on "intrinsic" rather than "external" aspects of the role in talking of the sources of his gratification, dissatisfaction, and problems. In the marriage area, this was seen as evidenced by the investment of energy in the marital *relationship* itself, as measured by the extent to which relationship reasons were emphasized when a person talked about the sources of happiness, inadequacy, or problems in the marriage.

The interpretation that these relationship reasons do reflect the "centrality" of marriage to a person is supported by the finding that a person, when happy in the relationship aspects of marriage, tends to be generally happier in the marriage; when unhappy with the relationship, he tends to be generally unhappier with the marriage.

The sex, age, and education results in this chapter tend to be consistent with those we have already noted in the previous chapters, although one or two exceptions occur.

With respect to *sex,* the tendency for women to express more dissatisfaction and distress is evidenced in the marriage area in their greater experience of unhappiness and problems, but not in the findings on feelings of inadequacy. Women do not express greater feelings of inadequacy in marriage. Moreover, women are not only not intrapunitive in the marriage area, if anything, they are more extrapunitive than are the men. Much more often than men blame their wives, women blame their husbands for marital unhappiness. This seems to reflect what has often been observed in American marriages—that the women demand more of their husbands than the men demand of their wives. It was further suggested that this finding might be related to the male-female role distinction for marriage, with failures in the more active male role being less tenuous and more easily pinpointed than failures in the female's more passive and supportive role.

The findings with respect to *age* are also consistent with those we have examined in previous chapters. Older people, although not evidencing any greater happiness in marriage, do express fewer problems and fewer feelings of inadequacy. With age and a lengthening investment in the marriage, people seem to attain some perspective on the difficulties that have been experienced, and problems and guilt feelings get worked through. In marriage, as in the other life areas we have examined, aging brings adaptation, acceptance, and a minimization of stress.

The *education* findings present a particularly interesting pattern. The more highly educated people seem to show a greater investment and involvement in their marriages that bring with them a greater sensitivity to both the positive and negative aspects. The greater involvement of the more highly educated people is evidenced in their greater focusing on the relationship aspects of the marriage when they talk of the sources of their gratification, dissatisfaction, problems, and inadequacy. Their greater sensitivity to the positive aspects of marriage is reflected in their much greater expression of marital happiness than that of people of less education. But with this greater happiness there is also an increase in certain stressful aspects of the marriage: the more highly educated people are more self-questioning, they express more feelings of inadequacy.

These education findings illustrate a theme which recurs frequently throughout this monograph: Heightened involvement and expectations in a life area—found more often in highly educated groups—bring with them a greater potential not only for gratification but also for tensions and distress—gratification when the expectations are fulfilled, discomfort when they are not fulfilled.

V

Parenthood

MARRIAGE in America tends to focus on the children. The pleasures, the problems, the responsibilities that go along with the rearing of children are intimately involved in the perception of what marriage entails. Indeed, it would almost appear that these two roles—marriage and parenthood—are inextricably linked for most people. And, in the same way that marriage becomes a status one has to achieve in order to enjoy the trademark of a full-fledged adult, to be a parent is also a necessary status for the truly responsible adult. This perceived necessity for being a parent in our society is probably more marked for women than for men. The energy that a woman is expected to direct toward motherhood is comparable to the energy that a man is expected to direct toward his work. Nevertheless, the essentially demanding force of the parent role in determining one's adult identity is applicable to both men and women. Those people who are childless—whether men or women, married or single—are viewed with compassion; they are seen as people who have missed the full richness of adult experiences.

This perception of the parent role probably has been more exaggerated in the past decade than it has in any other period of this country's history. The developmental orientation that personality theorists have assumed in the twentieth century, greatly extended by the general absorption of Freud's thinking, has become a part of the popular ideology. The beliefs that "the child is father of the man" and that parents have a great deal of control in determination of the child's character are now fairly commonly held. Being a parent, then, has a new facet; theories of modern psychology point out that parents, in their own behavior toward their children, possess a powerful weapon for reshaping the society, for creating a brave new world. The parent role has become more central in our perception of society's functioning.

The heavy accent placed on parenthood has led us to consider this role in some detail in the present study. What is the impact of this role on adults in our society? What are the difficulties experienced in attempting to fulfill it adequately? What are the sources of its satisfactions and dissatisfactions? These are some of the questions that concern us in this chapter. As always, we are considering a person's own evaluation of his functioning in this role. And, as in the other chapters, we will first present the self-evaluation indices and their interrelations, then view these within the context of the judgments made, and finally examine their relationships to sex, age, and education.

INTERRELATIONSHIPS AMONG THREE MEASURES OF PARENTAL ADJUSTMENT

In assessing the respondents' own evaluations of their adjustment to the parental role, we relied on three sets of questions, one to measure the feeling of satisfaction as a parent, the second to measure the feeling of inadequacy as a parent, and the third to measure the perception of problems in raising children. These measures and the questions used to assess them are listed below:

1. *Satisfaction as a parent:* Thinking about a man's (woman's) life, how is a man's (woman's) life changed by having children?

2. *Problems as a parent:* Most parents have had some problems in raising their children. What are the main problems you've had in raising your children?

3. *Inadequacy as a parent:* Many men (women) feel they're not as good fathers (mothers) as they would like to be. Have you ever felt this way? (If "Yes") Have you felt this way a lot of times or only once in a while?

We assessed the feeling of satisfaction as a parent with an indirect measure because answers to the more direct measures in the pretest tended to be uniformly "happy." But when we asked people to describe the changes that children bring to a man's or woman's life, we were able to code the responses on a positive-negative dimension that we felt would approximate their feelings of satisfaction in the parental role. Although this index does imply a coding judgment on our part, and as such is not directly comparable to the respondent's self-evaluation of marital happiness or job satisfaction, we attempted to code only the manifest content of the replies. Typical reported changes coded as negative were "you're too busy"; "you have to work much harder"; "you have more worries"; "you can't do the things you want to do." Reported changes coded as neutral included such responses as "you settle down"; "you have different things to do"; "it changes you." Replies that were coded as positive included a wider variety of content. Some of these were: "they make you happier"; "you have someone to love"; "it brings you closer together to your husband (wife)"; "you become mature." Because this is not a direct self-evaluation, we will not focus on this index of parental satisfaction as much as on the indices involving more direct self-evaluation.

How do these three aspects of adjustment as a parent relate to each other? We find no relationship between the estimate of satisfaction derived from the indirect question and the two direct indices of parental distress, expressed either as having had problems in raising one's children or as feelings of inadequacy. Why should this be the case? It is possible that over-all happiness as a parent bears no relation to self-questioning and the experience of problems in the parental role. But it is also possible that the lack of relationship results from the indirect phrasing of the satisfaction question, so that this lack of relationship should be interpreted with caution.

What, then, is the relationship between the two evaluations of adjustment that do probe directly for the respondent's feelings and experiences as a parent? From Table 5.1, which presents the relationship between these two indices, we can see that people who say that they "never had any problems in raising their children" are more likely to say they have never questioned themselves as parents than are people who report having had such problems. Thus, it seems that to deny both problems and inadequacies reflects a common orientation toward the parent role. There are indications that the

Table 5.1—Frequency of Feelings of Inadequacy as a Parent and the Report of Problems in Raising Children

Frequency of Feelings of Inadequacy	Report No Problems	Mention Problems
Never	67%	44%
Once in a while; once or twice	8	19
A lot of times; often	24	34
Not ascertained	1	3
Total	100%	100%
Number of people [a]	(310)	(954)

[a] Includes only respondents who answered Forms A or C of the interview. Does not include 21 people whose reports of problems in raising children were not ascertained.

general orientation which leads to such responses stems from a lack of introspection about the parental role rather than from an unusually positive adjustment to the role. We will come back to this interpretation later in this chapter.

THE CONTEXT FOR JUDGING PARENTAL ADJUSTMENT

Parenthood is a role that carries enormous responsibilities. We were concerned with measuring the potentially different ways that parents approached these responsibilities, viewing these general orientations toward parenthood as the context within which judgments of adjustment are made.

Just as with the marital role, the degree of personal involvement in the parenthood role is the general dimension we established to consider the context of respondents' judgments of their adjustment to the role. We viewed personal involvement in marriage and parenthood in parallel ways because both these roles center around the relationship to another person. Just as in marriage there can be more or less concern with the intrinsic marital relationship, so mothers and fathers can be more or less involved in their personal relationships with their children.

There are parents who, although they have a great deal invested in their children, do not necessarily concern themselves with their personal relationship with the children. These parents may focus their energy on providing the necessities and comforts of life or the environmental supports that they feel will enrich their children's experience—a "good education," a "nice home," stimulating cultural experiences. And still, they may not be concerned about what effects they themselves as people are having on their children or how their children are responding to them as people. We want to distinguish those people whose evaluations of themselves as parents are made in a context of concern with parent-child interactions from those whose evaluations are made in other contexts.

To measure the dimension of personal involvement in the parental role we coded three sets of responses: the sources of gratification derived from children, the sources of parental inadequacies, and the content of the problems perceived in raising children. The first measure, the sources of gratification, based on responses to the question, "What would you say was the nicest thing about having children?" did not materialize as a context variable, because practically all the replies could be construed to imply a concern with parent-child relationships, although some indicated more involvement than others (e.g., "there is someone to love," or "you have good times together"). In itself, this is an interesting finding. Unlike the reports on the nicest thing about marriage, the responses on the nicest things about having children deal almost exclusively with some aspect of an interpersonal relationship with the children. When respondents talk about the nice things about a marriage, they are able to mention situational factors that are extrinsic to the actual marital relationship (a nice house, a job, financial security, the children). This is apparently not as possible when a parent thinks of the nice things about having children, and gratifications become more completely focused in the relationship itself.

The other two context measures were based on the questions asking for the content of feelings of inadequacy and the problems perceived in raising children. In the parallel codes established for these questions we made one major distinction—responses which indicated a direct concern with the parent-child relationship as opposed to responses which did not. Further distinctions were made within each of these two broad categories. Under the category "concern with parent-child relationship," we distinguished three subcategories: *concern with parent-child affiliation* ("we aren't close enough," "there isn't enough love," "I don't spend enough time with them"); *concern with parental intolerance for child's behavior* ("I lose my temper with them too easily," "I'm impatient," "I'm not understanding with them"); *concern with obedience, discipline* ("getting them to listen," "they are disobedient," "I don't know how to discipline them," "I am too strict with them," "I'm too easygoing with them"). As evidence of concern with parent-child relationships, these three categories are not conceptually distinct. For example, concern with obedience can involve concern both with lack of a close, understanding relationship and with a parent's lack of tolerance for the child's behavior. Nevertheless, we maintained these distinctions because at least one of them, concern with obedience problems, can be seen as a weaker statement of a parent's concern with the intrinsic parent-child relationship. To worry about obedience can mean that the parent is concerned about the child's behavior independent of the child's relationship to the parent. Thus, this category may be midway between the response that exhibits a concern with the parent-child interaction and the response that does not.

Within the major coding category of "lack of concern with the parent-child relationship" we distinguished two types of responses: *physical care and material provision* and *child's non-family adjustment*. Typical responses included in the former category were: "there was too little money or food," "I could not provide them with a good education," "they were sick a lot," "it was hard to take care of them," "there wasn't enough time to watch over them." The other subcategory included a variety of responses having to do with the child's behavior or characteristics outside of the home: "they didn't have any friends," "he was very shy," "he had a run-in with the law," "when she was having trouble at school," "they fought a lot." These responses indicating "lack of concern with the parent-child relationship" predominated in the descriptions of the problems faced in raising children; the responses coded as indicating concern with parent-child relationships predominated in the descriptions of why the

Table 5.2—Comparison of Kinds of Problems Reported in Raising Children and Sources of Feelings of Inadequacy as a Parent (First-Mentioned Reasons)

Content of Problems or Feelings of Inadequacy	Problems	Inadequacies
Physical care, material provisions	35%	22%
Child's nonfamily adjustment	17	*
Obedience, discipline	24	10
Parent-child affiliative relationship	8	25
Lack of tolerance for child's behavior	—	21
Other	13	17
Not ascertained	3	5
Total	100%	100%
Number of people	(1470)	(649) [a]

* Here and in subsequent tables this symbol (*) indicates less than one half of 1 per cent.
[a] Includes only parents who answered Interview Forms A or C.

respondents felt inadequate as parents. In Table 5.2 we present this comparison.

It would appear from Table 5.2 that defects in the relationship with the child are more often phrased as the parent's inadequacy than as a problem in raising the child; problems, in turn, are more often phrased as defects in the child or as stresses created by factors such as sickness and material needs, which are pressures outside the relationship or either party in the relationship. One exception to this generalization occurs with respect to the category "obedience and discipline." Although discipline problems refer to some defect in the relationship between parent and child, they tend to be more often viewed as problems than as parental inadequacies.

It is interesting to look at these comparative findings from the point of view of parental self-blame. The problems considered in Table 5.2 may be viewed as difficulties in which responsibility tends to be assigned either to the child or to external events. The inadequacies, on the other hand, represent difficulties which the parent views as reflections of his own problems. Thus, for example, it would appear that problems of obedience and discipline are usually not seen as the parent's fault, but rather as a problem "in" the child. A defect in the affiliative relationship, on the other hand, a lack of closeness between parent and child, does appear to be something for which, in our society, the parent tends to blame himself.

THE CONTEXT MEASURES RELATED TO THE SELF-EVALUATIONS OF ADJUSTMENT AS PARENTS

In this section, we will explore some of the implications of the two context measures in an attempt to obtain a more coherent picture of the bases of self-evaluations of adjustment in the parent role.

Relationships between frequency of feelings of inadequacy as a parent and the context measures. There is surprisingly little difference between the kinds of inadequacies reported by parents who say they feel inadequate "a lot of times" or "often" and those reported by parents who say they feel inadequate "once in awhile" or "once or twice." One distinction does occur: 33 per cent of the former group mention the parent-child affiliative relationship as a reason for their feelings of inadequacy, while only 22 per cent of the latter group mention this reason. One may take this finding to mean that reporting a higher frequency of feelings of inadequacy as a parent reflects slightly more involvement with the parent-child relationship. But the over-all lack of relationship between feelings of inadequacy and the context for this judgment implies that these are two fairly disparate indices. Consequently, in our further analysis of feelings of inadequacy in the parent role we will have to consider both the reported frequency of these feelings and the sources of these judgments as two distinct measures, each having different implications. In admission to feelings of inadequacy we have a significant variable, probably reflecting an introspective orientation to the parental role. But the content of these feelings of inadequacies seems to be determined by other factors in addition to the introspective orientation to the role. These factors are probably tied to the particular role requirements for the individual and the way he or she carries out these requirements. This view is substantiated by sex differences in the content of these feelings of inadequacy which we will report later in this chapter.

Perhaps one of the factors which may determine the *intensity* of feelings of parental inadequacy is the nature of the perceived problems encountered as a parent. There is a slight relationship between the respondents' reported frequency of feelings of inadequacy as parents and the kinds of problems that they have perceived in the course of raising their children (Table 5.3). The report of more frequent feelings of inadequacy as a parent seems to be associated with the perception of obedience problems, suggesting that parents with tendencies toward self-questioning and self-doubt as parents may be particularly vulnerable to the present cultural ambivalence about discipline. There is also some support for the idea that denial of feelings

Table 5.3—Frequency of Feelings of Inadequacy Related to First-Mentioned Problems in Raising Children

Kinds of Problems	FREQUENCY OF FEELINGS OF INADEQUACY		
	A Lot of Times; Often	Once in a While; Once or Twice	Never
Physical care, material provisions	32%	31%	38%
Child's nonfamily adjustment	17	17	19
Obedience, discipline	32	25	21
Parent-child affiliative relationships	9	10	5
Other	8	16	15
Not ascertained	2	1	2
Total	100%	100%	100%
Number of people [a]	(182)	(323)	(430)

[a] Includes only parents who answered Interview Forms A or C. Does not include 40 parents whose frequency of feeling inadequate was not ascertained.

of inadequacy indicates a lower degree of introspection about parenthood in general: Respondents who did not admit feelings of inadequacy more often mentioned physical care or material problems, responses which we interpret as a lower degree of personal involvement in the parent-child relationship. Although the relationship is only a slight one, it is consistent with others we will be reporting.

Relationship between experience of problems in raising children and the context measures. The only way we can directly investigate the context of the respondents' judgment of the presence or absence of problems in raising their children is to compare people who did and did not admit to problems in the sources of feelings of inadequacy that they report. (We could not compare them on the sources of problems, since people who said they had no problems would obviously not be asked for the content of problems.) Table 5.4 summarizes this comparison.

Table 5.4—Relationship between the Report of Problems in Raising Children and First-Mentioned Sources of Feelings of Inadequacy as a Parent

Inadequacies	Report No Problems	Mention Problems
Physical care, material provisions	24%	22%
Obedience, discipline	5	12
Parent-child affiliative relationship	30	25
Lack of tolerance for child's behavior	22	21
Other	14	17
Not ascertained	5	3
Total	100%	100%
Number of people [a]	(104)	(531)

[a] Includes only parents who answered Interview Forms A or C. Does not include 14 parents whose report of problems in raising children was not ascertained.

Here we find a result consistent with one mentioned above. Those who report problems tend to mention inadequacies related to obedience difficulties more often than those who do not admit to problems. We have already found that there is a tendency for those who report frequent feelings of inadequacy to report more problems related to obedience and discipline than those who report infrequent feelings of inadequacy as a parent. These two results seem to indicate that obedience difficulties with a child may serve as a significant conditioner for admitting both to feelings of inadequacy and to having had problems in raising one's children.

Relationship between satisfaction in the parent role and the context measures. We found no significant associations between the measure of satisfaction in parenthood and the kinds of problems respondents said they experienced with their children. Furthermore, there was no direct association between the measure of satisfaction in parenthood and the kinds of inadequacies that were mentioned. But when we look at this latter association separately for men and women, we find that two interesting relationships emerge, one peculiar to the fathers and the other peculiar to the mothers. When mothers and fathers were considered together, these associations were not evident. Table 5.5 reports the relationship between satisfaction (measured indirectly, it will be recalled, by asking the respondent to describe the life changes that children bring) and the kinds of inadequacies that respondents mentioned. This relationship is presented separately for mothers and fathers.

Table 5.5—Relationship between Satisfaction as Parent (Affective Orientation of First-Mentioned Life Change Accompanying Parenthood) and Sources of Feelings of Inadequacy (Sex of Respondent Controlled)

Sources of Feelings of Inadequacy	SATISFACTION AS PARENT					
	Men			Women		
	Positive	Neutral	Negative	Positive	Neutral	Negative
Physical care, material provisions	30%	21%	23%	18%	20%	16%
Obedience, discipline	8	10	15	10	10	15
Parent-child affiliative relationship	32	42	42	24	17	13
Lack of tolerance for child's behavior	14	12	4	25	24	35
Other	11	11	8	18	26	15
Not ascertained	5	4	8	5	3	6
Total	100%	100%	100%	100%	100%	100%
Number of people [a]	(132)	(90)	(26)	(176)	(130)	(87)

[a] Includes only parents who answered Interview Forms A or C. Does not include eight parents whose affective orientation was not ascertained.

If we consider only those men whose orientations are positive or neutral—only a small number of fathers reported negative life changes accompanying parenthood—two differences appear in this table. The men who were coded "positive" are more likely to mention inadequacies pertaining to physical care or material provisions and less likely to mention inadequacies related to parent-child affiliative difficulties than are the men coded "neutral." On the other hand, women who are more positively oriented to parenthood mention affiliative inadequacies with their children *more often* than women who are negatively oriented to parenthood. Mothers who are negatively oriented to parenthood mention more frequently than other women their lack of tolerance for their child's behavior.

How do we explain these differences? How do we explain the fact that among parents who have more positive feelings about their roles, fathers are *less* likely, and mothers *more* likely to mention the affiliative aspects of their role as sources of inadequacy? And furthermore, why is it that the negatively oriented women emphasize more than other women their lack of tolerance of the child, while positively oriented men more than other men emphasize their lack of material provision?

Some explanation for these findings may be derived if we look at the content of inadequacy as a reflection of role demands and draw a distinction between the more traditional and the more recently emphasized aspects of the parental role. What are the traditional role requirements for mothers and fathers? Men spend less time with their children than women do; men are generally gone a good part of the day while performing their major function as family breadwinner; women are generally in intimate contact with their children and provide them with day-to-day attention. Traditionally, then, the parental role has demanded material provision from men and some aspects of the affiliative relationship from women. Other factors that parents talk about when asked for the sources of parental inadequacy —for a man, spending time with his children and establishing a close relationship with them; for a woman, showing tolerance for her children's behavior—may be viewed as more recent additions to the parental role requirements. Although possibly present in the past, they have received greater emphasis in recent years.

Looking at the findings in Table 5.5 in terms of this distinction, we find that when parents who have good feelings about their roles feel inadequate they emphasize the most traditional aspect of the role—material provision for men and some aspect of the affiliative relationship for women. And those parents who are more negative in their feelings about parenthood highlight the more recently established role requirements when they talk about their inadequacies— failure in establishing a warm parent-child relationship for the men, and insufficient tolerance for the women. Apparently, the increased self-consciousness about the parental role that seems to characterize the current American scene and the kinds of role demands that are a product of this self-consciousness bring with them a greater sensitivity to the burdens and limitations that parenthood can impose.

In summary, we can derive three major conclusions from these series of interrelationships of adjustment and context measures: First, the extent of parental satisfaction is not related to either problems or inadequacies. Second, parents who see themselves in a traditional parental role tend to find positive satisfactions in children, whereas those who evaluate their adequacy in terms of the newer parental role—e.g., interpersonal warmth or tolerance—tend to express negative or neutral parental satisfaction. Third, although problems and inadequacy go together, the context for each differs. Problems tend to be seen as arising from external sources and imply less self-blame; inadequacy is usually stated in terms of personal weaknesses and self-doubts. As we shall see, the social characteristics associated with these indices further reflect both this distinction and the distinction made earlier between a self-questioning orientation to parenthood and the kinds of things on which this self-questioning is focused.

SEX, AGE, AND EDUCATION RELATED TO PARENTAL ROLE ADJUSTMENT

In this section we are interested in the relationship between our indices of parental role adjustment—both evaluations of adjustment and the contexts for judging these evaluations—and a respondent's sex, education, and age. We will consider each of these demographic characteristics separately and then integrate the findings from them.

Sex

In Table 5.6, we see that more women than men are negative about parenthood. Apparently, women are more bothered by the burdens of parenthood, especially by the restrictions that come from their greater interaction with children and the feeling of being "tied" to the house.

Within the group of parents who view the life changes accompanying parenthood as positive, men and women differ in the kinds of satisfactions they mention (Table 5.7). Although not large, these differences conform to an expected pattern. Men differ from women in more often stressing satisfactions that come from influencing their

Table 5.6—Relationship between Sex of Respondent and Satisfaction as a Parent (Affective Orientation of First-Mentioned Life Change Accompanying Parenthood)

Satisfaction as a Parent	Men	Women
Positive	50%	43%
Neutral	37	33
Negative	10	22
Not ascertained	3	2
Total	100%	100%
Number of people	(845)	(1102)

Table 5.7—Relationship between Sex of Respondent and Positive Changes Accompanying Parenthood

Positive Life Changes Accompanying parenthood	Men	Women
General happiness	18%	23%
Children are stimulating	6	7
Children are a necessity for growth	18	24
Spouse-related changes	9	6
Affiliation-related changes	16	27
Influence-related changes	10	3
Achievement-related changes	8	2
Other changes	15	8
Total	100%	100%
Number of people [a]	(418)	(470)

[a] Includes only parents whose first-mentioned life change accompanying parenthood was coded "positive" in orientation.

children or the satisfactions involving achievement, ambitions, and accomplishments. Women are more concerned with the global satisfactions and with the affiliative satisfactions stemming from the parent-child relationship—the increased love, affection, and companionship available. Women also view children as more essential to their growth as a person, to their stability and maturity, and to the focusing of their life, giving such responses as: "children provide a goal in life," "they are a fulfillment," "having children is what women are made for," "you become more mature," "you really grow up."

Turning now to our major indices of parental role functioning, we find in Table 5.8 that women indicate somewhat more difficulties than men; 78 per cent of the women as contrasted with 70 per cent of the men mention problems encountered in raising their children; 51 per cent of the women have at some time felt inadequate as parents, whereas only 41 per cent of the men reported feeling this way. These findings are not unexpected. In discussing self-perception in Chapter III, we noted that women were both more introspective about themselves and more negative about themselves than men. Furthermore, parenthood is a more central life role for women than for men, and we have seen in other findings that self-questioning and sensitivity to problems seem to be associated with greater involvement in a role.

Table 5.8—Sex of Respondent and Indices of Parental Role Adjustment

Indices of Parental Role Adjustment	Men	Women
Report of problems in raising children		
Mention problems	70%	78%
No problems	29	21
Not ascertained	1	1
Total	100%	100%
Number of people	(845)	(1102)
Frequency of feelings of inadequacy [a]		
A lot of times; often	14%	18%
Once in a while; once or twice	27	33
Never	55	46
Not ascertained	4	3
Total	100%	100%
Number of people	(551)	(734)

[a] This question was asked only on Interview Forms A and C.

Although the differences between men and women in reported inadequacies and problems are not as striking as we might have surmised, these differences exist at all educational levels and for all age groups (Tables 5.9 and 5.10). We find that at most educational and age levels the percentage of women mentioning problems or feelings of inadequacy is greater, and that the greatest differences occur between college-educated men and women, and in the age group between twenty-one and thirty-four.

Table 5.9—Relationship between Reporting Problems in Raising Children and Sex, Educational Level, and Age of Respondent [a]

Age	Education	Men	Women
	Grade school	62[b]	85
21–34	High school	71	84
	College	68	80
	Grade school	78	78
35–54	High school	72	78
	College	71	85
	Grade school	65	65
55 and over	High school	62	74
	College	60[b]	—[c]

[a] Figures are the percentage of parents in each group who reported having had problems in raising their children.
[b] Sample size is between 15 and 30.
[c] Figure is omitted; sample size is less than 15.

Table 5.10—Relationship between Having Felt Inadequate as a Parent and Sex, Educational Level, and Age of Respondent [a]

Age	Education	Men	Women
21–34	Grade school	—[b]	—[b]
	High school	41	63
	College	38[c]	63[c]
35–54	Grade school	32[c]	42
	High school	46	56
	College	60	73
55 and over	Grade school	37	39
	High school	40[c]	29[c]
	College	—[b]	—[b]

[a] Figures are the percentage of parents in each group who reported having felt inadequate as parents.
[b] Figure is omitted; sample size is less than 15.
[c] Sample size is between 15 and 30.

Do men and women also differ in the context for judging their problems or inadequacies, in the kinds of problems or inadequacies they describe? Interestingly, they do not differ in the kinds of problems they report but they do differ in the sources of their feelings of inadequacy (Table 5.11).

Men are more sensitive to inadequacies in their major role function—physical and material provision. We might expect a similar sensitivity for women in the affiliative realm. However, the data do

Table 5.11—Sex of Respondent Related to Kinds of Problems Reported in Raising Children and Sources of Feelings of Inadequacy as a Parent (First-Mentioned Reasons)

Content of Problems or Feelings of Inadequacy	INADEQUACIES[a]		PROBLEMS	
	Men	Women	Men	Women
Physical care, material provisions	26%	19%	35%	34%
Child's nonfamily adjustment	—	—	16	18
Obedience, discipline	10	11	26	24
Parent-child affiliative relationship	36	19	8	7
Lack of tolerance for child's behavior	12	27	—	—
Other	10	20	12	15
Not ascertained	6	4	3	2
Total	100%	100%	100%	100%
Number of people	(250)	(399)	(602)	(868)

[a] This question was asked only on Interview Forms A and C.

not support this expectation. Rather, what appears is a difference in the *way* affiliative inadequacies are expressed. Women, spending a lot of time with children, get concerned and guilty not over lack of an affiliative relationship but over their exasperation and loss of temper from too much interaction. Men, not spending much time with their children, are guilty over the lack of a warm relationship ("I don't spend enough time with them").

Although these differences are understandable, it is still interesting that, if we add the affiliative and lack of tolerance categories together, women do not express more inadequacy in this general area than men, as one might expect if it were more central to the mother than the father role. This probably reflects an important cultural change now in process, where affiliation is becoming a central part of the father's role, and "I don't spend enough time with them," a major source of the father's guilt.

We might explain the lack of differentiation in the kinds of problems reported by men and women by referring to our interpretation of what it means to report problems with children. These problems do not seem to be personally tied to the parent's self-image and do seem to be determined by objective, day-to-day events. Women, in greater day-to-day contact with their children, experience more problems, but not necessarily different problems, than men do. Experiencing problems and perceiving the sources of these problems may actually be determined in a large part by realistic, objective factors that respondents have faced in raising their children. On the other hand, the perception of inadequacies and their sources—both of which are related to sex—may be determined by more personal involvements in the role, by the way the role has been internalized and tied to the self-image, and may be less susceptible to objective circumstances.

One way we could find indirect support for these assumptions was to compare parents with smaller families to parents with larger families. One would suppose that the more children parents had, the more they had faced *objective* situations that could determine a perceived problem. And we do find this to be so. Sixty per cent of the parents with one child, 75 per cent of the parents with two children, and 80 per cent of the parents with three or more children mention problems. But, as we also expected, there is no relationship between number of children the respondents have and their feelings of inadequacy—a variable which, according to our hypothesis, should be related more closely to internal than to external factors.

Education

Differences in educational level can be viewed from several perspectives. Greater education implies generally higher social status, both in its own right and in its association with higher income and higher job status, and the material and psychological concomitants of such status. Stemming more directly from the educational process, differences in education also imply differences in values, goals, ways of thought, and philosophy of child-rearing. These two perspectives on educational differences should be kept in mind in our discussion of the relationships between education and our indices of parental role functioning.

Although responses to other questions suggest differences in the expectations and perceived requirements of the parental role for persons of differing educational levels, differences do not appear in the replies to our question concerning the changes that come when one has children. No differences appear among the three educational levels with respect to either their affective orientation to parenthood or the content of the changes they feel accompany parenthood.

When we turn to our indices of parental role distress, we do find indications of such differences. As can be seen in Table 5.12, feelings of inadequacy are strongly related to educational level. The more educated person is more likely to feel inadequate. And, referring back to Table 5.10, we see that this relationship is maintained when sex and age are controlled. This is the same relationship we found in general self-perceptions and in the marriage area. It will be recalled that the more educated respondents are more willing or able to think of shortcomings in the self than are less educated respondents; and more educated respondents are more likely to feel inadequate as spouses than are less educated people.

We see no significant relationship, however, between education and the report of problems (Table 5.12). Once again we see that

Table 5.12—Education of Respondent and Indices of Parental Adjustment

Indices of Parental Adjustment	Grade School	High School	College
Report of problems in raising children			
Mention problems	71%	76%	75%
No problems	27	23	24
Not ascertained	2	1	1
Total	100%	100%	100%
Number of people [a]	(646)	(955)	(337)
Frequency of feelings of inadequacy [b]			
A lot of times; often	15%	16%	19%
Once in a while; once or twice	22	33	40
Never	60	47	37
Not ascertained	3	4	4
Total	100%	100%	100%
Number of people [a]	(424)	(632)	(224)

[a] Does not include nine parents whose educational level was not ascertained.
[b] This question was asked only on Interview Forms A and C.

the report of problems and feelings of inadequacy are differently related to social characteristics.

This difference between problems and inadequacies is less evident with respect to the context of evaluating difficulties—sources of problems and sources of inadequacy. In Table 5.13, we see that for both indices, more education implies less concern over the provision of adequate physical care and material goods. (This is true for both men and women, at all age levels.) For both indices we also find

Table 5.13—Education of Respondent Related to Kinds of Problems Reported in Raising Children and Sources of Inadequacy (First-Mentioned Reasons)

Content of Problems or Feelings of Inadequacy	INADEQUACIES [a]			PROBLEMS		
	Grade School	High School	College	Grade School	High School	College
Physical care, material provisions	38%	17%	11%	44%	31%	26%
Child's nonfamily adjustment	—	—	—	21	15	19
Obedience, discipline	8	12	10	15	29	27
Parent-child affiliative relationship	16	26	36	5	8	11
Lack of tolerance for child's behavior	10	25	25	—	—	—
Other	20	16	14	11	15	15
Not ascertained	8	4	4	4	2	2
Total	100%	100%	100%	100%	100%	100%
Number of people [b]	(172)	(332)	(141)	(470)	(730)	(256)

[a] This question was asked only on Interview Forms A and C.
[b] Does not include four parents whose educational level was not ascertained.

that the parents with higher education show more concern over difficulties in their relationship with the child—expressed in the greater frequency with which they mention inadequacies of affiliation and lack of tolerance and obedience problems. These relationships are probably a function of the association of higher education with both higher economic status and greater introspection about personal shortcomings. (The relationship between education and obedience problems tends to be confirmed for both men and women at each age level. Regarding sources of feelings of inadequacy, the relationship between education and affiliative difficulties is greater for men, while the relationship between education and lack of tolerance for the child's behavior is greater for women.)

It is interesting that parents with higher education stress these relationship difficulties. If we view confusion over discipline values, concern over the affiliative relationship, and guilt over being angry with a child as major concomitants of the changing cultural ideology with respect to parent-child interaction, we would expect the more highly educated, as the people most attuned to the latest intellectual trends in the culture, to show the greatest reflection of these confusions and concerns. It is also interesting that the sex difference—that the relationship between education and affiliation difficulties is greater for men—also reflects the cultural trends. To spend more time with the child is a recent cultural admonition directed toward the men, and it is the most highly educated men especially who express this type of inadequacy.

Age of Respondent

The older a person is, the more positive is his general orientation to the life changes accompanying parenthood (Table 5.14). When the respondent is directly asked to consider his life as a parent and point out the main problems he encountered in raising his children, we also find that fewer older people report having experienced problems (Table 5.15). Referring back to Table 5.9, we see that the relationship between age of respondent and the report of problems in parenthood tends to be sustained when sex and educational level of respondent are controlled. This finding parallels that in the marriage

Table 5.14—Age of Respondent Related to Satisfaction as a Parent (Affective Orientation of First-Mentioned Life Change Accompanying Parenthood)

Satisfaction as a Parent	AGE OF RESPONDENT			
	21–34	35–44	45–54	55 and Over
Positive	40%	42%	54%	51%
Neutral	38	39	30	30
Negative	21	17	14	14
Not ascertained	1	2	2	5
Total	100%	100%	100%	100%
Number of people [a]	(579)	(466)	(361)	(533)

[a] Does not include eight parents whose age was not ascertained.

Table 5.15—Age of Respondent and Indices of Parental Role Adjustment

Indices of Parental Role Adjustment	AGE OF RESPONDENT			
	21–34	35–44	45–54	55 and Over
Report of problems in raising children				
Mention problems	78%	76%	78%	67%
No problems	21	23	21	32
Not ascertained	1	1	1	1
Total	100%	100%	100%	100%
Number of people [a]	(579)	(466)	(361)	(533)
Frequency of feelings of inadequacy [b]				
A lot of times; often	16%	20%	17%	12%
Once in a while; once or twice	34	32	27	29
Never	47	44	50	57
Not ascertained	3	4	6	2
Total	100%	100%	100%	100%
Number of people [a]	(373)	(313)	(245)	(351)

[a] Does not include parents whose age was not ascertained.
[b] This question was asked only on Interview Forms A and C.

area, where older people also reported having experienced fewer problems.

Older people also have experienced less inadequacy (Table 5.15). However, the relationship between age of respondent and feelings of inadequacy as a parent is not sustained over sex and educational levels (Table 5.10). It appears that educational level and sex of respondent —more permanent characteristics of the person—not age, account for the major sources of variance in feelings of inadequacy as a parent.

This is consistent with our assumption that feelings of inadequacy indicate more general personality characteristics than does the report of problems in raising children.

Looking at the sources of feelings of inadequacy or problems in raising children, we find quite parallel relationships with age for both indices (Table 5.16). The older person is more concerned with inadequacies and problems in physical care and material provision; the younger person is more concerned with the central interpersonal sources of difficulties, lack of tolerance for the child's behavior in the inadequacy realm, and obedience and discipline problems. (If we look at these relationships with sex and educational level of the respondents controlled, we find once again that systematic differences still occur in the areas most salient to the respondent; for men, both physical care inadequacies and problems relate to age even with educational level controlled; for women, lack of tolerance for the child's behavior is related to age with educational level controlled; for both men and women, concern with obedience and discipline problems decreases with increasing age despite controls on educational level.)

It is difficult to say what the implications of these relationships are. Two quite distinct explanations are possible. Age can be viewed as a cultural variable, with differences in attitudes and feelings related to differences in generations. There is probably more emphasis on interpersonal aspects of parenthood today than there was thirty or forty years ago; with the increased literature on child-rearing and its potential pitfalls, these difficulties in being a parent may be more salient and more admissible than in earlier generations.

Age can also be viewed as indicative of different parental role requirements. Age of respondent and age range of the respondent's children are closely associated. The parents of younger children are in more intimate contact with them than are parents of older children, and parenthood might be more central to their life functioning. In particular, the interpersonal problems and inadequacies might be more salient to younger parents than to older parents. Younger parents may more often mention difficulties relating to discipline and anger control because these are the problems most important to them

Table 5.16—Age of Respondent Related to Kinds of Problems Reported in Raising Children and Sources of Feelings of Inadequacy (First-Mentioned Reasons)

Content of Problems or Sources of Feelings of Inadequacy	INADEQUACIES[a]				PROBLEMS			
	21–34	35–44	45–54	55 and Over	21–34	35–44	45–54	55 and Over
Physical care, material provisions	17%	18%	25%	29%	30%	31%	32%	45%
Child's nonfamily adjustment	—	—	11	—	10	18	28	18
Obedience, discipline	12	10	28	9	33	25	25	13
Parent-child affiliative relationship	20	30	14	25	9	10	6	5
Lack of tolerance for child's behavior	37	18	17	9	—	—	—	—
Other	11	19	5	20	16	14	7	14
Not ascertained	3	5	—	8	2	2	2	5
Total	100%	100%	100%	100%	100%	100%	100%	100%
Number of people[b]	(198)	(175)	(123)	(150)	(457)	(360)	(284)	(363)

[a] This question was asked only on Interview Forms A and C.
[b] Does not include eight parents whose age was not ascertained.

as parents of young and growing children; that the older parents fail to mention these things may not mean that they lacked experience with these problems and feelings of inadequacy when they were younger, but rather that these are so irrelevant to them now that they have been forgotten.

SUMMARY

In this investigation of adjustment in the parental role, we have been mainly concerned with two questions—the experience of problems in parenthood and feelings of inadequacy. These measures were related to each other, but also differed in certain ways. The experience of problems does not necessarily imply self-blame as the admission of inadequacy does. Problems are more often attributed to sources outside of the self—defects in the child, or stresses created by such external factors as sickness or material needs.

The relationships between parental adjustment and sex, age, and education are analogous to those observed in the other life areas. Women again express more feelings of distress than do men—the mothers more often see some of the negative aspects of parenthood, they sense more feelings of inadequacy as parents, they perceive more problems in raising their children.

The educational levels differ in their approach to parenthood just as they seemed to differ in self-perception and in evaluations of marital adjustment. Parents of a higher educational level seem to be more involved in the parental role, as measured by their greater concern with the parent-child relationship. With this involvement comes more introspection about their parental adjustment, evidenced, as in the marriage area, in their greater sense of inadequacy in the role.

The age findings are also consistent with previous results, pointing to a growing adaptation that comes with age. Older parents have a more positive picture of the parental role, and they report having experienced fewer problems as parents. In one set of results, however, the findings diverge from those we have previously examined. Whereas older and younger people showed no differences in introspectiveness, or in the sources of inadequacies and problems in marriage, they do differ in these areas as parents. The older parents seem to be less involved in the personal relationships with the child and less introspective about their roles as parents than are the younger parents. We have suggested two interpretations of these findings, one pertaining to the life cycle stages of older and younger parents and the other pertaining to differences in attitudes and values with respect to parent-child interactions from one generation to the next.

Special emphasis has been given to some of the broader cultural implications of the data in this chapter because the parental role seems to represent an area where cultural values have undergone considerable change in recent years. The data in this study seem to reflect these changes, especially as regards the importance of the parent-child *relationship* to the parental role. As people question what kinds of parents they have been, as they list the sources of their inadequacies as parents, they appear much more concerned with failures in their relationship with the child than in their failures as providers or in caring for the child. Although there are no comparable data available on parents of one or two generations ago, it is likely that this concern over the relationship with the child represents a recent cultural emphasis, a change in American values. Indirect evidence to support such a hypothesis comes from the fact that these relationship problems and inadequacies are emphasized by both more highly educated and younger people, whom we would expect to reflect the current cultural ideology in a period of change.

Although we would expect the relationship with the child to be the mother's special province and material provision the father's major concern, relationship concerns are mentioned as frequently by men as by women. But mothers and fathers do differ in the way relationship inadequacies are expressed. Women, concerned over their reactions to their constant interaction with the child, get guilty about their anger and loss of temper with the child. Fathers, on the other hand, seem to be reacting to a lack of a warm relationship, and feel guilty about emotional neglect of the child. Again, we would expect that this concern over the relationship with the child is a more prominent aspect of the father's role today than it was a generation or two ago, and that in their expression of this concern, the fathers in our sample are reflecting what are recent cultural emphases in this area.

These cultural implications of the data have special relevance in a phenomenological study of mental health. The findings that problems experienced in the parental role are becoming increasingly defined in psychologically relevant terms and increasingly experienced as psychological stress should be reflected in the help-seeking process, particularly in the content of the problems brought for help. Therefore, we might expect to see problems around parenthood becoming increasingly important as areas to be dealt with by mental health practitioners.

VI

The Job

Much of a man's life is spent at his job. Potentially, a man's work may be the focus of his identity, his social status and prestige, his feelings of masculinity, worth, and competence. Life without work—in states of unemployment or retirement—is often a struggle against demoralization and anomie.

Because of the importance of work in a man's life, one would expect to find his job adjustment to be a crucial indicator of his general adjustment in life. Yet, there is some question whether this is necessarily true, particularly in light of the great changes—both technological and organizational—that have occurred in recent years in the industries and professions. With the alienation from the job that occurs with industrialization and increasing automation, with the shortening of the work day and concomitant expanding opportunity for a life outside the job that this allows, the job tends to lose its central position in a man's life. More energy is channeled into life outside the work, and the possibility arises for nonjob areas of life to provide the meaning and identity anchors that the job once provided.

We may view the job as an area of potentially great importance in a man's life, but one where there are more possibilities for withdrawal and separation of the self from the role than there are, for example, in the marriage role. Because the centrality of the job cannot be assumed, it is important in this discussion, even more than was the case in the examination of the other roles, to concern ourselves with more than expressions of satisfaction or problems. We will pay particular attention to *sources* of satisfaction and problems and we will view expressions of job adjustment within the context of the meaning that the job has in a man's life.

INTERRELATIONSHIPS AMONG THREE MEASURES OF JOB ADJUSTMENT

In the job area, as with marriage, we were concerned with three measures of adjustment—satisfaction (phrased as "happiness" in the marriage area), feelings of adequacy, and the experience of problems. In this section we will discuss the measures used and examine their interrelationships and then proceed in the following sections to examine their relationship with other factors.

Satisfaction with the job was measured in an open-ended question: Taking into consideration all the things about your job, how satisfied or dissatisfied are you with it? The answers to this question were coded into one of six categories ranging from "very satisfied" to "very dissatisfied." Both the two middle categories—"ambivalent" and "neutral"—are neither predominantly positive nor negative, but ambivalence indicates an affective reaction and involvement in the job, whereas neutrality suggests withdrawal and disengagement.

Problems in the work area were measured by the following question: Have you ever had any problems with your work—times when you couldn't work or weren't getting along on the job, or didn't know what kind of work you wanted to do? This question is more specific than the ones for eliciting the history of problems in marriage and parenthood because it was felt that allowing the respondent to define completely what he meant by "problem" would be a more difficult task in the job area; a disproportionate number of comments relating to technical or extrinsic aspects of a job (such as the working conditions on a given job) might be elicited to the neglect of more personal problems. An attempt was made, therefore, to structure the question in terms of problems that might have such personal relevance—work blocks, inability to get along on the job, problems over vocational choice.

Adequacy in the job was measured in a series of questions which were concerned not only with how adequate the respondent felt but also with his perception of how much the job demands. Problems with respect to feelings of inadequacy in the job relate to judgments not only of the self but also of the job as a test of one's competence. Thus we started by asking the respondents:

1. What does it take to do a really good job at the kind of work you do?
2. How much ability do you think it takes to do the kind of work you do?

We then proceeded to the specific adequacy measure:'

2. How much ability do you think it takes to do the kind of thing you do? say you were *very good, a little better than average, just average,* or *not very good?*

Again, this question is more structured than the comparable one for marriage and parenthood. It was felt that adequacy in the marital and parental roles can be defined in many ways, and the questions were left unstructured enough to enable the respondent to give them his own interpretation. With respect to the job, however, it was felt that adequacy referred primarily to competence and skill at handling the work, and that a question phrased in unstructured terms would only be confusing. Thus, the question was phrased so as to elicit a self-judgment of competence and skill. Also, since it was felt that adequacy had a specific common meaning, no attempt was made to get at different *sources* of inadequacy.

In view of these considerations, one would expect that feelings of inadequacy in the job would be different from the comparable feelings assessed in marital and parental relationships. Specifically, there are clearer and more objective measures for judging adequacy on a job than for judging adequacy as a parent or husband or wife. Consequently, one might expect that self-judgment in the job is not so strong an indication of a general introspection and self-questioning as it seems to be in the marriage and parenthood areas. We shall see reflections of these differences when we examine some of the relationships involving adequacy in the job area and compare them with the parallel relationships in the marriage and parental roles.

Two further points should be noted. First, because we viewed responses to the question on job adequacy as less determined by personality than the responses to the comparable questions in the other roles, we considered this a less crucial measure of adjustment and therefore asked the question on only one form of the interview. This means that the findings involving this variable apply to only one third of the sample. Second, the data presented and discussed here are confined to employed men. It was felt that this represented the most relevant group, since most women are not employed outside the home (only a quarter of our female sample had full-time jobs), and even among the minority that do work, the job rarely assumes the importance that it does for men.

Let us now turn to an examination of the interrelationships among these measures of job adjustment. To what extent do our questions on job satisfaction, adequacy, and problems measure similar or different aspects of adjustment on the job? The relationships between job satisfaction and the report of work problems, between job satisfaction and feelings of adequacy on the job, and between the report of work problems and feelings of adequacy on the job are presented in Tables 6.1, 6.2, and 6.3.

An interesting pattern of relationships appears in these three tables. Job satisfaction shows a clear relationship to the experience of problems (Table 6.1) and adequacy (Table 6.2), but the latter two measures are only minimally related to each other (Table 6.3). The positive relationships are not surprising, for one would expect dissatisfied people to experience more work problems and to feel less ade-

Table 6.1—Relationship between Job Satisfaction and the Report of Work Problems (among Employed Men)

JOB SATISFACTION

Report of Work Problems	Very Satisfied	Satisfied	Neutral	Ambivalent	Dissatisfied [a]
Had problems	23%	27%	29%	37%	49%
Had no problems	77	73	71	62	51
Not ascertained	*	—	—	1	—
Total	100%	100%	100%	100%	100%
Number of men [b]	(255)	(444)	(49)	(87)	(76)

* Here and in subsequent tables this symbol (*) indicates less than one half of 1 per cent.

[a] Because of the small number of men coded as "very dissatisfied" with the job, these are included with the "dissatisfied" group in this and subsequent tables.

[b] Does not include the 14 employed men whose job satisfaction was not ascertained.

Table 6.2—Relationship between Job Satisfaction and Feelings of Adequacy on the Job (among Employed Men)

	JOB SATISFACTION		
Feelings of adequacy on Job	Very Satisfied	Satisfied	Neutral, Ambivalent, Dissatisfied [a]
Very good	39%	28%	20%
Little better than average	40	41	47
Just average; not very good	19	30	33
Not ascertained	2	1	—
Total	100%	100%	100%
Number of men [b]	(100)	(153)	(54)

[a] Categories are combined because of low frequencies.
[b] Includes only employed male respondents who answered Form C of the interview schedule. Does not include the six employed men on Form C whose job satisfaction was not ascertained.

Table 6.3—Relationship between the Report of Work Problems and Feelings of Adequacy on the Job (among Employed Men)

	REPORT OF WORK PROBLEMS	
Feelings of Adequacy on Job	Had Problems	Had No Problems
Very good	26%	32%
Little better than average	48	39
Just average or not very good	26	27
Not ascertained	—	2
Total	100%	100%
Number of men [a]	(97)	(214)

[a] Includes only employed male respondents who answered Form C of the interview schedule. Does not include the two employed men on Form C whose report of work problems was not ascertained.

quate and competent than satisfied people. And these findings do indicate that dissatisfaction is a significant component of a person's definition of a work problem and is also tied to feelings of lower adequacy and competence.

What is of interest is the low relationship between the adequacy and problems measures, indicating that people apparently do not translate feelings of lower adequacy and competence into what they define as a work problem. This contrasts with the findings in the marriage and parenthood areas, where feelings of inadequacy were clearly related to the experience of problems (see Chapter IV, Table 4.2, and Chapter V, Table 5.1). The lack of relationship between these measures in the job area may reflect the factor that we noted above, namely, that adequacy in the job has a much clearer objective referent than in the marital and parental roles and may therefore be less related to the general introspection or self-questioning that is represented in recognizing problems in a role.

THE CONTEXT FOR JUDGING JOB ADJUSTMENT

What is the context within which a man says he is "satisfied" or "dissatisfied" with his work, that he has had "problems" in his work, that he is "very good" or "not very good" at what he is doing? Again, by context we refer to the degree of personal involvement in the role.

We have considered personal involvement in the job as the extent to which an individual seeks some expression and actualization of the self in his work as opposed to his making the job ego-alien, divorced from ego gratifications. Although this distinction parallels those we have drawn in the marriage and parenthood areas, it has particular relevance to mental health in the job area. Questions of job involvement and alienation have received considerable attention among those who have studied job adjustment in terms of its mental health implications. Some comments about the relevance of this distinction to a concept of mental health are therefore appropriate here.

Alienation from the job, the inability to find a creative outlet for the self in a job, has usually been viewed as an unhealthy development involving considerable personal impoverishment. The problem, however, has tended to be viewed as an environmental rather than personal problem, as an unhealthy situation rather than as a reflection of lack of personal resources in the individual. Many jobs just do not offer creative and self-actualizing possibilities. Moreover, the choice of such a job is not necessarily viewed as indicative of personality problems, for choice in the job area is limited—by considerations of status, circumstance, ability. In these respects, attitudes toward the job differ from those on marriage or parenthood, roles that are assumed to have broad possibilities that any "healthy" individual should be able to maximize. This difference is implicitly recognized in the fact that personal therapy is more often recommended as a solution to problems and dissatisfactions in marital and parent-child relationships than it is with respect to problems and dissatisfactions in the job. In areas of job problems, one tends to seek solutions by changes in the job situation rather than changes in the dissatisfied individual. Very often even the job situation is not seen as changeable, for there is a certain inevitability in some of the processes that have led to many job problems and dissatisfactions, particularly those of alienation and lack of fulfillment in a job. The inevitability of certain of these problems may be seen in many of the remedial programs proposed for industrial organizations, in the great emphasis that is placed on the supervisor and his "human relations" skills. These programs are oriented toward teaching the supervisor somehow to "give" the worker the feeling of significance that the work itself cannot provide.

The implications of these comments led us, in light of the data to be discussed below, to accentuate some of the precautions we noted in the introductory chapter about the problems of translating such concepts as adjustment and satisfaction into indices of mental health. In particular, Jahoda (1958) has cautioned that such feelings of well-being are dependent on environmental vicissitudes, and the environment is not always subject to individual control and personal determination. Because such control and determination are probably less possible in the job than in the other life roles that we have examined, dissatisfaction with a job and a limited "extrinsic" definition of gratification in the role are to be viewed even less as indices of *personal* maladjustment than are the comparable concepts in the marriage and parenthood areas. We will return to some of the mental health implications of these data later in this chapter. But regardless of their relevance for formal definitions of mental health, we are interested in delineating dissatisfactions, inadequacies and problems as they are experienced, in following through their contextual meanings, their distributions within significant subgroups of the population, and, in Part Two of this monograph, their implications for help-seeking behavior.

Our most direct measure of job involvement and alienation was derived from the respondents' replies about the things they liked and did not like about the job. These replies were coded according to a distinction between "ego" and "extrinsic" satisfactions (or dissatisfactions). Under the ego category we coded responses presumed to represent a personal involvement in the job—some expression of the self in the job. These responses indicated satisfaction or dissatisfaction with the *kind* of work one does, its interest, variety, and the skills involved; the opportunities that the job grants for the expression of responsibility, independence, competence; the potential that it offers for the gratification of interpersonal and friendship needs. Examples of extrinsic reasons are those stressing such things as money, job security, and working conditions. In making this distinction, there is no attempt to minimize the importance of these latter reasons; the crucial consideration is not whether a person is concerned with such things as money and security, but whether his concern with such matters excludes consideration of the ego factors. Only under the latter circumstance can one speak of alienation from the job.

CONTEXT OF JOB ADJUSTMENT RELATED TO EVALUATIONS OF JOB ADJUSTMENT

What is the contextual meaning of the measures of adjustment in terms of this distinction between ego and extrinsic gratifications? To what extent do dissatisfaction, experience of problems, and inadequacy reflect similar or different degrees of involvement in or alienation from the job? What are the implications of differential satisfaction, adequacy, and experience of problems as we have measured them? We may approach these questions by comparing the sources of job gratification and frustration for people of varying degrees of satisfaction, adequacy, and problems; that is, we may ask whether the satisfied job holder tends to get a special kind of gratification from the job that is much less often experienced by the dissatisfied job holder, and whether there are special kinds of frustrations that tend to be associated with feelings of dissatisfaction or problems or inadequacy.

Context for Judging Satisfaction in the Job

Let us first examine the implications of this distinction between ego and extrinsic satisfactions in terms of the degree of satisfaction that a person derives from the job. On the basis of our hypothesis that

THE JOB [151]

a greater and fuller satisfaction derives from what we have termed ego satisfactions and that a more limited and less intense satisfaction derives when gratification comes mainly from extrinsic aspects of the job, we would expect to find a relationship between the degree of satisfaction with the job and the sources of satisfaction derived, with those people who experience greater satisfaction more often mentioning ego gratifications. Table 6.4 corroborates this hypothesis. All the reasons given for liking the job were summarized according to whether the respondent mentioned only ego satisfactions, only extrinsic satisfactions, or both. Whereas 62 per cent of the men who

Table 6.4—Relationship between Extent and Sources of Satisfaction with the Job (among Employed Men)

	JOB SATISFACTION				
Sources of Job Satisfaction	Very Satisfied	Satisfied	Neutral	Ambivalent	Dissatisfied
Mention only ego satisfactions	62%	54%	33%	65%	42%
Mention both ego and extrinsic satisfactions	29	25	33	15	16
Mention only extrinsic satisfactions	6	17	24	16	28
Mention no reasons for liking job	—	1	10	2	10
Not ascertained	3	3	—	2	4
Total	100%	100%	100%	100%	100%
Number of men [a]	(255)	(444)	(49)	(87)	(76)

[a] Does not include the 14 employed men whose job satisfaction was not ascertained.

were very satisfied with their job gave exclusively ego reasons for their satisfaction, these reasons were given by only 42 per cent of those who were generally dissatisfied with the job; conversely, exclusively extrinsic reasons for liking the job were given by 28 per cent of the dissatisfied and only 6 per cent of the very satisfied group. Greatest satisfaction in a job tends to be associated with a fulfillment of ego needs; gratification in the job only in extrinsic terms occurs disproportionately among those who are generally dissatisfied with the job.

A similar relationship was *not* obtained to the same extent between the degree of job satisfaction and sources of *dissatisfaction* with the job (Table 6.5). Since job satisfaction was associated with ego gratification, it was expected that job dissatisfaction would be associated with the frustration of ego needs. That this is true to some extent is

Table 6.5—Relationship between Job Satisfaction and Sources of Dissatisfaction with the Job (among Employed Men)

JOB SATISFACTION

Sources of Job Dissatisfaction	Very Satisfied	Satisfied	Neutral	Ambivalent	Dissatisfied
Mention only ego dissatisfactions	15%	18%	25%	32%	29%
Mention both ego and extrinsic dissatisfactions	8	8	12	11	26
Mention only extrinsic dissatisfactions	37	48	43	47	41
Mention no reasons for disliking job	38	25	18	8	—
Not ascertained	2	1	2	2	4
Total	100%	100%	100%	100%	100%
Number of men [a]	(255)	(444)	(49)	(87)	(76)

[a] Does not include the 14 employed men whose job satisfaction was not ascertained.

indicated by the fact that ego factors are mentioned exclusively as a source of dissatisfaction with the job by 29 per cent of the dissatisfied group and only 15 per cent of the very satisfied group. However, this difference is largely due to the fact that dissatisfied workers give more reasons generally for disliking the job, since there is no comparable tendency for the very satisfied group to give an undue proportion of exclusively extrinsic reasons. Extrinsic reasons are important sources of dissatisfaction for both satisfied and dissatisfied workers.

This finding underscores our point that the association of greater job satisfaction with ego gratifications does not imply that extrinsic factors such as money are unimportant. In conscious experience, however, these extrinsic factors seem to be more important as deficiencies than as sources of gratification. Exclusively extrinsic reasons appear as dissatisfactions as prominently among the complaints of the dissatisfied people as among the complaints of the satisfied groups (Table 6.5); but extrinsic gratifications are not experienced as a great source of satisfaction in a job (Table 6.4). Exclusive mention of them as sources of job satisfaction occurs more often among the dissatisfied groups, suggesting that when they are the only job gratifications experienced, there is a lack of a fuller and greater gratification.

Moreover, ego factors are mentioned much more as positive than as negative characteristics of the job, and extrinsic considerations are much more noted as complaints than as sources of satisfaction. Whereas 55 per cent of the men gave exclusively ego satisfactions as a source of satisfaction on the job, only 19 per cent gave exclusively ego dissatisfactions in listing their complaints; conversely, 15 per cent mentioned exclusively extrinsic factors in listing their sources of gratification, whereas 42 per cent mentioned such factors exclusively in listing the things with which they were dissatisfied.

Thus, extrinsic factors are more often experienced and salient in consciousness as deficiencies than as positive factors. Such factors as money seem to act as necessities whose absence causes pain but whose presence tends to be taken for granted. In addition, ego satisfactions are more often experienced as a positive factor than the lack of ego satisfactions is experienced as a deficiency. This suggests two possible interpretations: people either are finding more ego gratification in their jobs than many observers of the contemporary scene have hypothesized or are adjusting to job situations that provide limited opportunity for self-expression, so that the limitations are not consciously experienced as deficiencies. In any event, this finding suggests that there is relatively little introspection in analyzing the sources of distress on the job—that complaints tend to be externalized rather than cast in personality terms. We will return to this question when we consider this distinction between ego and extrinsic sources of gratification in relation to the individual's occupational status.

One further finding in Table 6.4 that is of some interest is the comparison between the sources of job satisfaction of the ambivalent and neutral groups. Exclusively ego sources of gratification are mentioned much less frequently by the neutral (33 per cent) than the ambivalent group (65 per cent). Because the crucial distinction between these two groups lies in the degree of involvement in the job, ambivalence representing involvement and neutrality representing a certain amount of alienation and withdrawal, these findings may be viewed as evidence of the validity of our assumption in setting up the code, that ego satisfactions reflect a greater centrality and involvement in the job than extrinsic factors.

Context for Judging a Problem on the Job

What does a man mean when he says that he has had a problem on his job? What is the context of meanings and definitions and aspirations on the job, within which problems are experienced? Do people who do and do not report having had such problems differ in what they look for in a job? Before attempting to answer these broad questions, by looking at the experience of problems in relation to the kinds of gratifications and frustrations experienced in the job, let us examine the content of the problems that the respondents experienced in their job history. Because the question on job problems was structured in terms of personal problems, we cannot consider the responses as a systematic context variable. However, an examination of the kinds of problems that people do mention when asked about personal problems encountered in their job history helps to clarify what the question meant to them.

That we were successful in pushing toward a personal definition of problems is suggested by the fact that only about one third of the men who said that they had had a problem defined these problems in impersonal terms—problems in working because of health or physical disability, loss of work at some period in their lives because of external uncontrollable factors like the depression or a company closing, unhappiness on some job because of extrinsic factors (money, work conditions, or the like). This is a relatively small proportion compared to the responses to the general, unstructured question on sources of dissatisfaction, which elicited impersonal causes of complaint from a large majority of the respondents (Table 6.5).

Two thirds of those who mentioned having had some problem (about one out of five of the total employed male sample) talked in terms of some kind of personal problem. The problem most often mentioned was one of vocational choice—either some difficulty or conflict or uncertainty in deciding what kind of work to go into, or some past or present unhappiness with the kind of work the respondent was doing. Two other kinds of problems were frequently mentioned: one involved an interpersonal problem on a job (usually a problem in getting along with the supervisor or boss); the other

THE JOB

involved some history of inadequacy on a job, such as inability to handle a given job or problems during the learning period on a job. It should be noted that, whereas all of these are referred to as personal problems, they do not necessarily reflect any problem in personality functioning or mental health. They do, however, represent the areas where personality problems might be expected to manifest themselves.

We now turn to the broader context question to see whether there is a difference in the degree of personal involvement between those who said they had a job problem and those who said they never had a job problem (personal involvement as measured by the choice of ego rather than extrinsic sources of job satisfaction and dissatisfaction). We saw in the discussion on marriage in Chapter IV that there was some indication that the perception of problems was associated with a greater investment in marriage, with greater demands and expectations, with greater centrality of the marriage relationship in the person's life. We might expect to find a similar association between the perception of some problem in one's job history and an orientation toward the job stressing ego rather than extrinsic gratifications and frustrations. Tables 6.6 and 6.7 indicate that this expectation is borne out.

Those who have had some personal problem in their work history much more often criticize their job for its frustration of ego needs than do those who report no work problems (Table 6.6). And furthermore, in Table 6.7 there is a slight relationship between the admission of problems and the tendency to find ego *gratification* in

Table 6.6—Relationship between the Report of Work Problems and Sources of Dissatisfaction with the Job (among Employed Men)

Sources of Job Dissatisfaction	Had Problems	Had No Problems
Mention only ego dissatisfactions	26%	17%
Mention both ego and extrinsic dissatisfactions	16	7
Mention only extrinsic dissatisfactions	41	45
Mention no reason for disliking job	14	29
Not ascertained	3	2
Total	100%	100%
Number of men [a]	(267)	(654)

[a] Does not include the four employed men whose report of work problems was not ascertained.

Table 6.7—Relationship between the Report of Work Problems and Sources of Satisfaction with the Job (among Employed Men)

Sources of Job Satisfaction	Had Problems	Had No Problems
Mention only ego satisfactions	60%	53%
Mention both ego and extrinsic satisfactions	22	26
Mention only extrinsic satisfactions	15	16
Mention no reasons for liking job	1	2
Not ascertained	2	3
Total	100%	100%
Number of men [a]	(267)	(654)

[a] Does not include the four employed men whose report of work problems was not ascertained.

the job: 60 per cent of the men with some job problem find exclusively ego satisfactions in the job, as contrasted with 53 per cent of those who report no work problems. Although this difference is not large, it is particularly interesting in that it runs counter to what one might have expected from the fact that people with problems tend to be less satisfied with the job (see Table 6.1) and less satisfied people tend to find extrinsic rather than ego gratification in the job (Table 6.4). The findings in Tables 6.6 and 6.7 suggest that problems on the job have a special relevance to the distinction we have drawn between ego and extrinsic orientations to the job. The report of problems tends to occur within an orientation toward the job that maximizes involvements, expectations, and demands; lack of problems becomes, to some extent, a function of the fact that the job is less central to the individual, a source of less ego gratification as well as less ego frustration, an area in which the individual tends to minimize expectations and demands.

Context for Judging Adequacy on a Job

Unlike the relationships obtained with the experience of problems on the job, the choice of ego as opposed to extrinsic reasons for liking or not liking the job is not significantly related to feelings of adequacy on the job. As we have measured them, feelings of inadequacy on the job are not significantly related to a more central and intrinsic orientation to the role. This does not necessarily contradict our assumption that introspection and self-questioning spring from a greater involvement in a role. As we have pointed out, feelings of adequacy in the job area have a relatively clear objective referent for self-judgments, and thus should reflect less of these broader personality and attitudinal tendencies.

In summary, of the three adjustment measures, the expression of problems on the job would seem to be most clearly related to stressing the job as an area central to the individual, one in which there is an attempt to attain some expression of the self. An admission to work problems implies the clearest concern with ego gratifications both in the sources of gratification and in the sources of frustration on the job.

Job dissatisfaction, like the experience of problems, is tied to the frustration of ego needs, suggesting that the expression of dissatisfaction occurs more readily when the job has some centrality. This relationship, however, is not a very striking one and, unlike the absence of problems, satisfaction is not tied to a lack of involvement in the work. Whereas those people who experience problems seem to be most involved in their work, it is the satisfied men rather than the dissatisfied ones who have the greater involvement.

In contrast to both of the other measures, feelings of adequacy on the job are unrelated to the choice of either sources of job satisfaction or dissatisfaction. Feelings of adequacy seem to be more determined by objective skill and status referents than by such psychological characteristics as a person's orientation to his job.

OCCUPATION, AGE, AND EDUCATION RELATED TO JOB ADJUSTMENT

In this section, we will examine the relationship between the measures of job adjustment and three relevant demographic variables: age, education, and occupational status. We will not consider sex as a variable since we have been concerned only with men.

Occupational Status

How does a man's adjustment on his job relate to the particular kind of job he has? How do the status and prestige of a given occupation, the kind of work involved, its meaning within the social structure relate to a man's satisfaction with it, the problems he has experienced, his ego involvement in his work, his experiences of adequacy and inadequacy? To explore some of these questions, we will examine the relationship between occupational status and our measures of job adustment.

We have used a traditional occupational status code to classify jobs. Among the highest status jobs we have distinguished two categories: *professionals-technicians,* including such groups as doctors, lawyers, accountants, engineers, and *managers-proprietors,* including self-employed businessmen and various levels of managerial personnel. Among those usually referred to as the white-collar group, two other categories were distinguished: *clerical workers* including such occupations as cashiers, bookkeepers, office workers, and *sales workers* including all categories of sales workers. In the blue-collar occupations, we have separated three categories: *skilled, semiskilled,* and *unskilled workers. Farmers* constitute the final category.

These eight occupational categories do not represent a single continuum, for they vary along many quantitative and qualitative dimensions—prestige, income, the nature of the work involved, the "way of life" represented in a given occupation. We will discuss some of the broader implications of occupation in our analyses of the relationships between occupational status and measures of adjustment in areas beyond the job (see Chapter VIII). In the present analysis, we will be mainly concerned with occupation in terms of the kind of work involved, particularly the opportunities that the work allows for the satisfaction of ego needs, although in some instances we will also look to the broader social implications of a man's occupation in our attempts to explain some of the findings.

Because the adjustment on a job seems to be critically related to the centrality of the job to the individual and to the types of gratifications sought and derived from the work, we will first look at the relationships between occupational status and the types of gratifications and frustrations found in the work (Tables 6.8 and 6.9). Table 6.8, presenting the relationship between occupational status and the responses to the question on what things are liked most in the job, shows par-

Table 6.8—Relationship between Occupational Status and Sources of Satisfaction with the Job (among Employed Men)

OCCUPATIONAL STATUS

Sources of Job Satisfaction	Professionals, Technicians	Managers, Proprietors	Clerical Workers	Sales Workers	Skilled Workers	Semi-skilled Workers	Unskilled Workers	Farmers
Mention only ego satisfactions	80%	68%	39%	60%	54%	40%	29%	58%
Mention both ego and extrinsic satisfactions	16	20	35	29	28	31	26	17
Mention only extrinsic satisfactions	2	9	24	7	14	24	29	17
Mention no reasons for liking job	—	—	2	2	2	3	8	1
Not ascertained	2	3	—	2	2	2	8	7
Total	100%	100%	100%	100%	100%	100%	100%	100%
Number of men [a]	(119)	(127)	(46)	(55)	(202)	(152)	(84)	(77)

[a] Does not include the 63 employed men whose occupations were not codable into one of the eight categories.

ticularly striking results. Except for farmers, whose position tends to be ambiguous, we have ordered the occupational categories in a rough ranking of their social status or prestige, from the professional group on one end to the unskilled laborers on the other. The clerical and sales groups, although listed separately in Table 6.8, might perhaps best be considered together as a broad lower-middle-class or white-collar category.

Viewing this order, we see a very strong relationship between the social status of the occupation and the tendency to find ego gratifications in the work: whereas 80 per cent of the professional group reported exclusively ego satisfactions in the work, this type of satisfaction was the exclusive source of gratification for only 29 per cent of the unskilled workers, with the other occupations tending to fall into a consistent progression between the two extremes. The one exception is the clerical group, who gave an unusually low proportion of ego-satisfaction responses, a finding consistent with what we will be reporting later on the state of high dissatisfaction in this group.

When we look at the relationship between occupational status and the kinds of dissatisfactions found in the work, a further interesting result appears. Because lower status jobs would seem to be particularly frustrating of ego needs, one might expect people in these jobs to express greater ego dissatisfaction. However, the findings presented in Table 6.9 indicate that the relationship, although small, tends to go in the opposite direction. It is the people in the higher status jobs who, despite their much greater ego gratification in the work, also express a greater degree of frustration of ego needs.

It appears that people in higher status jobs not only get more ego gratification in their work but seek such gratifications more, with consequently greater frustration experienced when these needs are felt to be unsatisfied. This finding has interesting implications as one considers the possible effects of the automation and separation of the self from the work involved in lower status, less skilled blue-collar jobs. It would appear from Table 6.9 that most of these less skilled blue-collar workers either come into the job situation with minimal ego-fulfillment aspirations or begin with aspirations but become adjusted to the lack of ego fulfillment in the job. In either case, the

Table 6.9—Relationship between Occupational Status and Sources of Dissatisfaction with the Job (among Employed Men)

OCCUPATIONAL STATUS

Sources of Job Dissatisfaction	Professionals, Technicians	Managers, Proprietors	Clerical Workers	Sales Workers	Skilled Workers	Semi-skilled Workers	Unskilled Workers	Farmers
Mention only ego dissatisfactions	25%	26%	26%	22%	20%	13%	16%	13%
Mention both ego and extrinsic dissatisfactions	15	9	13	18	6	8	7	8
Mention only extrinsic dissatisfactions	31	39	37	40	46	52	46	56
Mention no reasons for disliking job	26	24	20	11	26	26	30	23
Not ascertained	3	2	4	9	2	1	1	—
Total	100%	100%	100%	100%	100%	100%	100%	100%
Number of men [a]	(119)	(127)	(46)	(55)	(202)	(152)	(84)	(77)

[a] Does not include the 63 employed men whose occupations were not codable into one of the eight categories.

minimal opportunities for fulfillment are apparently not experienced by them as a lack or frustration, at least at the conscious level.

Occupational status, then, is strongly related both to the amount of ego gratification found in the work and to the importance of such gratifications as expectations in a job. And we have already seen that the gratification of ego needs in a job was related not only to greater job satisfaction but also to the experience of greater job problems. We should expect, therefore, that those in the higher status occupations, as groups for whom ego needs are both relevant and gratified, would express greater satisfaction with the job but also experience greater problems. That this expectation is borne out is indicated in the relationships presented in Table 6.10. The proportion of people very satisfied with their work ranges from 42 per cent of the professional category to 13 per cent of the unskilled group. The experience of problems, on the other hand, although only slightly related to occupational status, does vary, as expected, in the opposite direction: more people in the middle-class occupational categories than in the blue-collar categories admit to the experience of problems.

In juxtaposing the findings on satisfaction and problems, we see that the lower middle-class white-collar categories of clerical and sales show a particularly interesting pattern. More of the men in these groups express dissatisfaction than do the men in any other occupational category except the unskilled group; and 37 to 38 per cent in these white-collar groups have experienced problems, contrasted to only 21 per cent in the unskilled category who mention such experiences. Thus, these white-collar categories are the only groups that are high in both dissatisfaction and the expression of problems. If we view the experience of problems as an indication of ego involvement and aspiration in the job, we may say that these white-collar categories maximize the frustration that derives from the nonfulfillment of high ego involvement and aspiration.

Frustration in these groups, particularly in the clerical category, is evident in the responses to another question, intended to measure this mixture of dissatisfaction and aspiration. The respondents were asked: "Regardless of how much you like your job, is there any other kind of work you'd rather be doing?" It was felt that the desire

Table 6.10—Relationship between Occupational Status and Job Adjustment Measures (among Employed Men)

OCCUPATIONAL STATUS

Job Adjustment Measures	Professionals, Technicians	Managers, Proprietors	Clerical Workers	Sales Workers	Skilled Workers	Semi-skilled Workers	Unskilled Workers	Farmers
Job satisfaction								
Very satisfied	42%	38%	22%	24%	22%	27%	13%	22%
Satisfied	41	42	39	44	54	48	52	58
Neutral	1	6	9	5	6	9	6	4
Ambivalent	10	6	13	9	10	9	13	9
Dissatisfied	3	6	17	16	7	6	16	7
Not ascertained	3	2	—	2	1	1	—	—
Total	100%	100%	100%	100%	100%	100%	100%	100%
Number of men [a]	(119)	(127)	(46)	(55)	(202)	(152)	(84)	(77)
Report of work problems								
Had problems	36%	33%	37%	38%	25%	29%	21%	25%
Had no problems	64	66	63	62	75	71	78	75
Not ascertained	—	1	—	—	—	—	1	—
Total	100%	100%	100%	100%	100%	100%	100%	100%
Number of men [a]	(119)	(127)	(46)	(55)	(202)	(152)	(84)	(77)
Feelings of adequacy on job								
Very good	37%	37%	33%	32%	24%	22%	27%	24%
Little better than average	46	42	42	37	45	44	31	45
Just average or not very good	13	21	25	31	29	34	38	31
Not ascertained	4	—	—	—	2	—	4	—
Total	100%	100%	100%	100%	100%	100%	100%	100%
Number of men [b]	(46)	(43)	(12)	(19)	(66)	(50)	(26)	(29)

[a] Does not include the 63 employed men whose occupations were not codable into one of the eight categories.

[b] Includes only employed male respondents who answered Form C of the interview schedule. Does not include 22 of these men whose occupations were not codable into one of the eight categories.

for some other kind of work not only reflects a certain degree of dissatisfaction with one's present work but also implies a certain degree of involvement and aspiration in the work area, since aspiration gives an impetus to the exploration of alternatives. Fifty-seven per cent of the clerical group expressed a wish for some other kind of work, a figure at least 10 per cent higher than that obtained in any other occupational category. This finding, together with those presented in Table 6.10, is consistent with the usual picture of the lower-middle-class white-collar group—mobility oriented, high in aspiration, involved in the job area, and frustrated. Evidences of this frustration in other areas of their life will be further discussed in Chapter VIII.

In singling out groups of particular interest, the farmers might also be briefly noted, particularly since they are difficult to place on the status dimension we have been discussing. Farmers as a group seem to derive a good deal of ego gratification from their work (Table 6.8), are not unusually satisfied or dissatisfied (Table 6.10), and are relatively low in the experience of work problems (Table 6.10). This indicates that farmers are a fairly satisfied, complacent group. As for the desire for other work, only 16 per cent of the farmers say that they would rather be doing some other kind of work, a figure 15 per cent lower than that obtained in any other occupational category. This suggests that, in the midst of the movement away from the farm, those who remain tend to be generally satisfied with the work aspects of farm life.

In concluding this discussion of occupational status, we turn to the findings on adequacy in the job (Table 6.10). Although the number of people in some categories is small (because the adequacy question was asked on only one form of the interview), there appears to be a clear relationship between occupational status and the perception of one's ability on the job. This relationship is particularly clear in the "just average or not very good" category; 13 per cent of the professional category compared with 38 per cent of the unskilled workers judge their job competence in those terms.

This association between lower status and greater feelings of inadequacy is interesting, especially compared with the education findings in the preceding two chapters, which showed that *higher* rather than lower status (in this case educational status) was associated with greater feelings of inadequacy. The findings in Table 6.10 suggest that self-judgment of one's skill and competence in a given line of work is not only based on skill and competence but on general status considerations as well. That is, the general social status accorded a given line of work appears to operate as a frame of reference within which people evaluate and judge their own performance. Even a highly competent unskilled laborer, in judging his ability to do his work, would be affected by an underlying feeling of inadequacy springing from the generally low status of the job.

In certain ways, these findings may be seen as consistent with those previously reported on the relationship between educational status and feelings of inadequacy as a parent, husband or wife. Less educated people, although feeling less inadequate generally, expressed much more inadequacy for material (as opposed to psychological) reasons. The less educated men in particular felt their failure to make an adequate contribution to the material well-being of their wives and children. To the extent that feelings of inadequacy that spring from holding a lower status job reflect a feeling of failure in the material rather than personal area, the greater incidence of these inadequacy feelings among people in the lower status jobs is consistent with the findings on inadequacy in the marriage and parenthood roles.

Education

The relationships between educational status and job adjustment follow closely those we have noted with respect to occupational status. As in the case of occupational status, the focal relationship may be viewed as that between education and ego involvement in the job. For the more highly educated men, as for those of higher occupational status, the job is more central and tied to the self and is an area in which one seeks the gratification of ego needs. This is evidenced in Tables 6.11 and 6.12, where we see that the college-educated men more often find both ego gratifications and the frustration of ego needs in their jobs.

Again paralleling the report on occupational status, the relation-

Table 6.11—Relationship between Education and Sources of Satisfaction with the Job (among Employed Men)

Sources of Job Satisfaction	Grade School	High School	College
Mention only ego satisfactions	46%	54%	68%
Mention both ego and extrinsic satisfactions	25	26	21
Mention only extrinsic satisfactions	19	17	8
Mention no reasons for liking job	5	1	—
Not ascertained	5	2	3
Total	100% [a]	100%	100%
Number of men [a]	(282)	(423)	(214)

[a] Does not include the six employed men whose education was not ascertained.

Table 6.12—Relationship between Education and Sources of Dissatisfaction with the Job (among Employed Men)

Sources of Job Dissatisfaction	Grade School	High School	College
Mention only ego dissatisfactions	15%	19%	28%
Mention both ego and extrinsic dissatisfactions	6	10	15
Mention only extrinsic dissatisfactions	49	45	34
Mention no reasons for disliking job	30	23	19
Not ascertained	*	3	4
Total	100%	100%	100%
Number of men [a]	(282)	(423)	(214)

[a] Does not include the six employed men whose education was not ascertained.

ships between education and satisfaction on the job and experience of problems follow from these findings on ego involvement. We would expect that the more highly educated men, for whom ego needs are both more relevant and more often gratified in the job, would express both greater satisfaction and more problems in the work area. This expectation is supported by the findings in Table 6.13. Thirty-six per cent of the college-educated men in the sample were very satisfied with the job, contrasted to only 21 per cent of those with grade-school education. At the same time, as a reflection of their greater involvement in the job, the college-educated men also reported more problems in the work area: 37 per cent of the college-educated group reported some such problem, as contrasted to only 21 per cent of those with grade-school education.

Since education is the path to better jobs in our society, and education and occupational status are highly related, it is not surprising that the relationships between education and job adjustment should parallel those obtained with occupational status. The greater job

Table 6.13—Relationship between Education and Job Adjustment Measures (among Employed Men)

Job Adjustment Measures	Grade School	High School	College
Job satisfaction			
Very satisfied	21%	28%	36%
Satisfied	60	43	41
Neutral	7	6	3
Ambivalent	5	11	11
Dissatisfied	6	10	7
Not ascertained	1	2	2
Total	100%	100%	100%
Number of men ª	(282)	(423)	(214)
Report of work problems			
Had problems	21%	30%	37%
Had no problems	79	70	63
Not ascertained	*	*	—
Total	100%	100%	100%
Number of men ª	(282)	(423)	(214)
Feelings of adequacy on job			
Very good	31%	28%	35%
Little better than average	34	41	54
Just average or not very good	34	30	8
Not ascertained	1	1	3
Total	100%	100%	100%
Number of men ᵇ	(100)	(137)	(74)

ª Does not include the six employed men whose education was not ascertained.
ᵇ Includes only employed male respondents who answered Form C of the interview schedule. Does not include two of these men whose education was not ascertained.

involvement of the more highly educated groups is undoubtedly largely a reflection of the fact that they tend to occupy the higher occupational status categories. But we might expect education to have an effect even beyond its congruence with occupational status. We would expect the broadening of perspectives and expectations that comes with education to sensitize an individual to the broader need-fulfilling aspects of a job, to accentuate the importance of the job as a vehicle for self-expression. It is interesting in this connection to note that education was related not only to whether or not a work problem was experienced but also to the particular *type* of work problem. In particular, those problems most clearly reflecting an orientation to a job as a vehicle for self-expression—problems in arriving at a vocational choice or of being in an unsuitable job that was not need-satisfying—were much more often mentioned by the more highly educated groups. Looking only at the first-mentioned work problems, these two types of problems were mentioned by 43 per cent of the college-educated men who reported work problems as contrasted to 32 per cent of the high-school and 13 per cent of the grade-school groups.

Finally, we note in Table 6.13 the high relationship between education and feelings of adequacy on the job. Men of college education perceive themselves as more competent in their work than do those of lower education, a relationship again paralleling findings presented with respect to occupational status. This relationship, it may again be noted, runs counter to the tendency observed in the marriage and parenthood areas, where higher education was associated with greater feelings of inadequacy and reflects the greater influence of objective criteria in determining self-judgments in the job area.

Age

Differences in age reflect differences in aspirations, experience, education, commitment to a type of work, and therefore are relevant to adjustment on the job. Yet because of the multiple concomitants of age we might expect a somewhat less clear or integrated picture of relationships than those we have observed with respect to education and occupational status. And when we look at the relationship between age and ego involvement in the job, we see, in Tables 6.14 and 6.15, that there is no tendency for the choice of either ego satisfactions or ego dissatisfactions to vary systematically according to age.

Table 6.14—Relationship between Age and Sources of Satisfaction with the Job (among Employed Men)

	AGE			
Sources of Job Satisfaction	21–34	35–44	45–54	55 and Over
Mention only ego satisfactions	52%	55%	58%	56%
Mention both ego and extrinsic satisfactions	26	23	22	27
Mention only extrinsic satisfactions	17	16	14	13
Mention no reasons for liking job	2	3	3	1
Not ascertained	3	3	3	3
Total	100%	100%	100%	100%
Number of men [a]	(292)	(237)	(208)	(185)

[a] Does not include the three employed men whose age was not ascertained.

Table 6.15—Relationship between Age and Sources of Dissatisfaction with the Job (among Employed Men)

Sources of Job Dissatisfaction	AGE			
	21–34	35–44	45–54	55 and Over
Mention only ego dissatisfactions	21%	24%	17%	16%
Mention both ego and extrinsic dissatisfactions	15	10	8	5
Mention only extrinsic dissatisfactions	43	45	45	41
Mention no reasons for disliking job	19	18	28	36
Not ascertained	2	3	2	2
Total	100%	100%	100%	100%
Number of men ª	(292)	(237)	(208)	(185)

ª Does not include the three employed men whose age was not ascertained.

This lack of relationship between age and ego involvement in the work may possibly be viewed as the result of the canceling out of contradictory tendencies—the higher education and aspirations and demands that are a concomitant of the younger years being counterbalanced by the greater investment and commitment to a given job and type of work that comes with age.

Age is related, however, to other aspects of job adjustment (Table 6.16). We see, for instance, that age seems to bring both an increase in satisfaction and a diminution of problems in the work area. This relationship between age and problems, which we have observed in the marriage and parenthood areas and which may be interpreted in the same terms, suggests that age brings a growing adaptation to a role, a minimization of aspirations and self-demand, an increasing ability to reconcile aspiration and accomplishment. Of special interest is the fact that this adaptation in connection with the job apparently also brings an increase in the over-all satisfaction with the job. Although increasing age was associated with a slightly *lower* satisfaction in marriage, the older men appear to be slightly more satisfied with the job. This difference may reflect the feeling that taking a job does not represent the commitment involved in getting married. A job, particularly for the young person, tends to be a tentative choice, and many years may be spent in testing out different possibilities. We would expect this tentativeness to give a somewhat unsettled quality to the younger person's relation to his work, with a certain amount of tension, dissatisfaction, and ambivalence.

Table 6.16—Relationship between Age and Job Adjustment Measures (among Employed Men)

Job Adjustment Measures	21–34	35–44	45–54	55 and Over
Job satisfaction				
Very satisfied	26%	26%	29%	31%
Satisfied	44	46	49	56
Neutral	4	7	6	4
Ambivalent	13	11	8	4
Dissatisfied	11	8	6	5
Not ascertained	2	2	2	—
Total	100%	100%	100%	100%
Number of men [a]	(292)	(237)	(208)	(185)
Report of work problems				
Had problems	38%	33%	23%	17%
Had no problems	61	67	77	83
Not ascertained	—	—	*	—
Total	100%	100%	100%	100%
Number of men [a]	(292)	(237)	(208)	(185)
Feelings of adequacy on job				
Very good	28%	30%	35%	31%
Little better than average	43	44	41	38
Just average or not very good	28	25	22	29
Not ascertained	1	1	2	2
Total	100%	100%	100%	100%
Number of men [b]	(87)	(95)	(68)	(61)

[a] Does not include the three employed men whose age was not ascertained.
[b] Includes only employed male respondents who answered Form C of the interview schedule. Does not include two of these men whose age was not ascertained.

Two other findings tend to illustrate this difference in commitment. The first is a very strong relationship between age and the responses to the question on whether or not one would rather be doing some other kind of work. Whereas 52 per cent of the youngest group, twenty-one to thirty-four years of age, express a desire for some other kind of work, this desire is expressed by only 25 per cent of the oldest group (fifty-five years and over). The second finding relates to the differences in the nature of the work problems discussed by the several age groups. Not only do young people mention work problems more often but the kinds of problems they mention are different from those discussed by the older men. The younger men more often mention problems indicative of the unsettled nature of their work choice—problems in vocational choice, dissatisfaction with a job that is not need-satisfying, problems in meeting the demands of a job. The older workers, on the other hand, more often refer to problems that do not reflect on the work itself or on the particular choice they have made. Thus, they speak in terms of such things as failures in health, dissatisfaction with certain extrinsic aspects of a job, problems that arose because of external factors (such as losing a job when the company closed).

Finally, we may note in Table 6.16 the lack of any relationship between age and feelings of adequacy on the job. Since we observed previously that feelings of adequacy were related to education, and young people tend to be more highly educated, we might have expected to find greater feelings of adequacy in the younger groups. It is likely, however, that the better training and greater energy of the younger groups are counterbalanced by the greater experience and commitment of the older men, so that no over-all relationship obtains.

SUMMARY

As in the other roles we investigated, feelings of adjustment in the job were measured in terms of satisfaction, feelings of adequacy, and the history of problems (in this case only for employed men). Unlike the marriage and parenthood areas, little relationship was found between feelings of inadequacy and problems in the job, although both were related to job dissatisfaction. There seem to be clearer objective standards for measuring job adequacy than for evaluating one's adequacy as a spouse or a parent and therefore judgments of adequacy in the work seem to reflect less of a general personality tendency toward introspection than was true in marriage and parenthood.

These different implications of admission to inadequacy are reflected in differential relationships with education. Higher education was related to greater feelings of inadequacy in marriage and parenthood, but in the job area, higher education (as well as higher occupational status) was related to *lower* feelings of inadequacy.

As before, we examined the person's evaluation of his job adjustment within the context of his personal involvement in the role, in order to determine the extent to which some expression and actualization of the self is sought in his work. This was measured by a person's choice of ego rather than extrinsic factors in talking of the sources of satisfaction and dissatisfaction on the job. A pattern of results paralleling one that we have previously observed was obtained: involvement in the job is related both to job satisfaction and to the experience of job problems. People who look for some expression of the self in the job experience a higher degree of job satisfaction (when these expectations are gratified) than is experienced by those people who get from the job only material and other extrinsic gratifications. But these greater ego expectations, even when gratified, also lead to the experience of problems on the job. The experience of problems on the job, as in marriage, is a reflection not so much of dissatisfaction as of higher involvements, expectations, and demands.

These interrelationships among job involvement, satisfaction, and problems are reflected in the demographic findings. Education and occupational status operate in similar fashions: the higher educational and higher status occupational groups express greater ego involvement in the job and, following from this greater involvement, greater satisfaction in the job on the one hand, but more work problems on the other.

Age, which is not related to job involvement, showed a different pattern of results. Older men are more likely to be satisfied with their job, and to report *no* work problems. This lower experience of problems parallels the findings in the other roles, pointing again to the growing adaptation to a role that seems to come with age. The greater satisfaction of the older workers, however, is not consistent with most of the other findings we have examined. The lower experience of tensions that comes with age is apparently a function of lower involvement and expectations and is usually accompanied by lower rather than greater gratification; older people tend, if anything, to express less general and marital happiness. That older people are more satisfied with their jobs may reflect certain special aspects of the job role in relation to age. Commitment to the job takes a longer time to develop than commitment to marriage or to being a parent.

Early choices tend to be more tentative, and the younger person's lower satisfaction may reflect some of the uncertainty of a "testing-out" period.

Concern has been expressed over mental health implications of the increasing alienation of the self from the job that seems to be a concomitant of increasing industrialization, specialization, and automation. The lack of ego gratifications that can be derived from many jobs today, particularly those in the lower-skilled blue-collar categories, has also caused concern. The present findings seem to suggest that the lack of self-fulfillment in lower status jobs is less often experienced as a problem than one might have expected it to be. Ego frustrations are mentioned much less often than extrinsic factors as reasons for dissatisfaction with a job; when they are mentioned, they are noted more often by people in higher status rather than lower status jobs. Although higher status jobs offer more opportunity for self-fulfillment, and people in these jobs much more often mention ego satisfactions on the job, they also express a greater degree of frustration of ego needs. Apparently, these people not only receive more ego gratification in their work but also seek such gratifications more, and consequently experience frustration when they feel these needs are not satisfied. Conversely, people in lower status jobs less often experience the lack of ego gratifications on the job as a frustration either because they come to these jobs originally with lower expectations and desires for self-fulfillment, or because they become adjusted to the lack of opportunities for such fulfillment.

These findings parallel those observed in the analysis of the marriage and parenthood data, where we also noted that the higher status groups—in these cases the higher educated—although having a greater intrinsic involvement in the role and deriving greater satisfaction from it, also experience more tensions and self-questioning. The lower educated groups, with their lower involvement in the intrinsic aspects of the role and their lower gratification, also seemed to have less conscious distress in the role.

These findings have particular interest because in those conceptions of mental health which stress self-actualization as a criterion of positive mental health the broadening of the sources of gratification derived from a role, the gratification of deeper personal needs, and the expression of the self in the role, have often been viewed as indications that a person's adjustment to his role is a "healthier" one. Our data point out that the use of such a criterion of positive mental health tends to define the more highly educated, higher status groups as "healthier"—i.e., as more self-actualizing. Furthermore, it is a criterion in which the definition by the expert observer that a mental health problem exists differs from the self-definitions of the lower status, less self-actualizing groups, who do not tend to experience this as a problem.

Taken together, these findings underscore the middle class values implicit in the self-actualizing definition. This does not necessarily imply that the definition is incorrect. All definitions of mental health are made within some value framework, and usually a middle class one. But it is important to recognize these values and their implications in order to understand and properly evaluate any given criterion. In some cases, explication of values and their implications may lead to the re-evaluation of the appropriateness of any given criterion. In pointing up the empirical implications of different mental health definitions, as we are attempting to do in this monograph, we hope to aid in such possible clarifications and re-evaluations.

VII

Symptom Patterns

SPECIFIC PSYCHOLOGICAL, physical, or psychosomatic symptoms have often been used as critical diagnostic indices of psychological distress, both in research on mental disturbance and in actual clinical settings. Not only do symptoms have a certain amount of face validity as diagnostic criteria, but the use of a symptom list has the great advantage of administrative simplicity. However, the lack of a developed conceptual and theoretical framework for this technique limits its appeal.

Frequently, in the research and clinical use of symptom lists, conceptual and theoretical questions are neglected in favor of the grossest kind of "cookbook" empiricism. To a considerable extent, symptom lists have been useful as screening instruments, and there has been relatively little concern with the conceptual ramifications of the measures. But in the long run this lack of concern with theoretical considerations limits the practical usefulness of these measures because of the intimate interrelationship of theoretical and practical knowledge. In our analysis and discussion of the symptom checklist, therefore, we will attempt to stress some of these theoretical concerns.

The list of 20 symptom items presented in Table 7.1 was taken from a checklist and from other questions of the questionnaire and forms the basis of the analysis presented in this chapter. The items not starred were prepared specifically for this study; the starred items were taken from the survey interviews of two community studies, Stirling County (Macmillan, 1957) and Midtown (Rennie, 1953), and they differentiate respondents diagnosed by psychiatrists as having psychological difficulty from respondents diagnosed as not having

[176] PROBLEMS OF ADJUSTMENT

such difficulty. For the Stirling County study, the diagnoses were based on short interviews conducted by the psychiatrists with each respondent; in the Midtown study, the judgments of the psychiatrists were based on their appraisal of the responses to the total survey interview including the symptom items. In the present study, the first 16

Table 7.1—List of Twenty Symptom Items

Items	Alternatives
* 1. Do you ever have any trouble getting to sleep or staying asleep?	Nearly all the time. Pretty often. Not very much. Never.
** 2. Have you ever been bothered by nervousness, feeling fidgety or tense?	Nearly all the time. Pretty often. Not very much. Never.
3. Are you ever troubled by headaches or pains in the head?	Nearly all the time. Pretty often. Not very much. Never.
* 4. Do you have loss of appetite?	Nearly all the time. Pretty often. Not very much. Never.
* 5. How often are you bothered by having an upset stomach?	Nearly all the time. Pretty often. Not very much. Never.
6. Do you find it difficult to get up in the morning?	Nearly all the time. Pretty often. Not very much. Never.
* 7. Has any ill health affected the amount of work you do?	Many times. Sometimes. Hardly ever. Never.
* 8. Have you ever been bothered by shortness of breath when you were not exercising or working hard?	Many times. Sometimes. Hardly ever. Never.
* 9. Have you ever been bothered by your heart beating hard?	Many times. Sometimes. Hardly ever. Never.
10. Do you ever drink more than you should?	Many times. Sometimes. Hardly ever. Never.
* 11. Have you ever had spells of dizziness?	Many times. Sometimes. Hardly ever. Never.
** 12. Are you ever bothered by nightmares?	Many times. Sometimes. Hardly ever. Never.
** 13. Do you tend to lose weight when you have something important bothering you?	Many times. Sometimes. Hardly ever. Never.
* 14. Do your hands ever tremble enough to bother you?	Many times. Sometimes. Hardly ever. Never.
** 15. Are you troubled by your hands sweating so that you feel damp and clammy?	Many times. Sometimes. Hardly ever. Never.
16. Have there ever been times when you couldn't take care of things because you just couldn't get going?	Many times. Sometimes. Hardly ever. Never.
* 17. Do you feel you are bothered by all sorts of pains and ailments in different parts of your body?	Yes. No.
* 18. For the most part, do you feel healthy enough to carry out the things you would like to do?	Yes. No.
* 19. Have you ever felt that you were going to have a nervous breakdown?	Yes. No.
* 20. Do you have any particular physical or health problem?	Yes. No.

* Items used in Stirling County (MacMillan, 1957) and/or Midtown Study (Rennie, 1953).
** Based on items used in Stirling County and/or Midtown Study; slight revisions in wording made in consultation with A. Macmillan.

items in Table 7.1 were presented as a checklist which the interviewers were instructed to give the respondent to fill in himself. Where respondents were not able to read—because of illiteracy, poor eyesight, or other reasons—the interviewer read each item and the alternative replies.

What do these items mean collectively or individually? Because symptom items usually have been viewed within a practical rather than theoretical context, previous work in this area throws little light on the theoretical meanings of these items. Nor can we use the symptom list as a screening device, for the populations on which the items were validated are not comparable to a national population. We will attempt to view these symptoms, then, as we have viewed the other adjustment measures we have examined in this study, as different ways of expressing emotional stress and disturbance. And, as with the other measures, we will attempt to show what these items mean by studying their relationships with each other and with other variables explored in the study.

In order to decide what index or indices to build from the collection of responses to these symptom items, the most reasonable first approach seemed to be to examine the results of a *factor analysis* of all the items. A factor analysis is a statistical treatment of data, used to uncover fundamental theoretical dimensions (factors) underlying the pattern of responses on a series of separate and specific measures. This treatment of data is based on the supposition that there are basic factors (abilities, traits, general characteristics of people) which determine how people respond to a series of attitudinal, ability, or personality measures and how these measures are intercorrelated. Therefore, if one starts not with the factors but with the intercorrelations of measures, one can abstract the underlying factors. This is the method of factor analysis: going from an intercorrelation matrix to hypothetical factors determining this matrix.

With this in mind, the symptom items were intercorrelated,[1] and the intercorrelation matrix was factored. This factor analysis was used as the basis for constructing symptom indices; these, in turn, were related to the other variables in this study.

FACTOR ANALYSIS OF SYMPTOM ITEMS

Because we were studying symptoms on a nationwide sample, the first decision we had to make was whether to consider all respondents together or to consider them separately in a number of significant population groups. On the one hand, it seemed desirable to express our findings in a way which could be used across all demographic groupings. In order to describe what groups in the population most often exhibit the symptoms, or to what other variable in the study the symptoms are related, everyone in the population had to be measured on the same indices. On the other hand, previous studies have indicated very large relationships between symptom scores and such demographic variables as sex, age, and education and a single factor analysis did not seem appropriate. Therefore, separate tables of intercorrelations were obtained for significant groups, separate factor analyses were run for these groups, and then we looked for communality in structure *after* the analysis, rather than assuming it by doing our factor analysis for the whole sample at once.

Originally, we chose age and sex as variables to define significant groups, but the factor analyses of the different age groups varied according to no discernible pattern and were too complicated to be of practical use. Therefore we have considered only the factor analyses run for men and women. The measures we use in this chapter are based on these two factor analyses and reflect factor structures which are *common* to both men and women.

Table 7.2 and 7.3 present the intercorrelations of all symptom items for men and women separately, based on only those subjects who responded to all questions. Table 7.4 presents the resulting factor structure of these matrices for men and women.[2]

This factor-analytic procedure tells us that in the group of 20 items, four striking factors emerged to account for the response patterns of both males and females. The numbers in Table 7.4 represent the "factor loadings" of each item on each of the four factors. The "factor loading" indicates the extent to which the responses to the item are a reflection of the factor. Factor loadings range theoretically

Table 7.2—Intercorrelation Matrix for Symptom Checklist (Men Only)[a]

Symptom Items	1	2	3	4	5	6	7	8	9	10	11	12	13	14	15	16	17	18	19	20
1. Trouble sleeping																				
2. Nervousness	.51[b]																			
3. Headaches	28	34																		
4. Loss of appetite	28	26	24																	
5. Upset stomach	28	28	27	32																
6. Difficult getting up	22	16	15	19	14															
7. Ill health interferes with work	12	31	24	30	22	07														
8. Shortness of breath	30	32	19	24	17	06	42													
9. Heart beats hard	24	34	17	18	14	06	37	52												
10. Drinking	04	08	03	05	06	15	—04	—02	07											
11. Dizziness	26	26	32	30	22	06	36	36	36	01										
12. Nightmares	23	21	20	21	19	10	16	16	10	15	27									
13. Losing weight	16	20	10	28	16	14	17	14	03	17	18	16								
14. Hands tremble	28	39	22	27	19	11	27	27	31	08	26	26	17							
15. Hands sweat	16	36	20	20	25	16	22	21	19	20	18	21	24	37						
16. Can't get going	22	35	25	21	23	19	27	28	37	29	20	30	25	33	20					
17. Pains and ailments	18	24	24	24	15	09	17	30	36	—03	24	19	09	29	19	32				
18. Healthy enough to do things	19	18	15	13	11	11	12	—03	—01	—07	19	12	00	24	17	18	18			
19. Nervous breakdown	19	19	30	14	14	14	20	15	06	06	15	30	16	18	12	14	23	20		
20. Health trouble	20	25	24	22	20	19	24	22	25	—08	26	36	16	29	15	28	11	15	20	

[a] Correlations are based on 956 men who answered all 20 symptom items.
[b] Figures in table are product-moment correlations. Decimal points are omitted in all other figures. All correlations are positive unless otherwise indicated.

Table 7.3—Intercorrelation Matrix for Symptom Checklist (Women Only)[a]

SYMPTOM ITEMS

Symptom Items	1	2	3	4	5	6	7	8	9	10	11	12	13	14	15	16	17	18	19	20
1. Trouble sleeping		.46[b]	30	26	22	03	34	25	26	04	32	18	15	23	15	26	24	17	22	29
2. Nervousness			36	26	29	20	39	32	36	11	38	24	24	33	27	34	28	17	34	30
3. Headaches				27	25	12	28	28	28	07	37	17	12	19	18	27	24	14	18	22
4. Loss of appetite					24	13	24	21	21	07	28	09	25	19	21	27	17	11	17	14
5. Upset stomach						17	29	23	25	05	29	21	15	21	20	26	21	11	16	19
6. Difficult getting up							09	05	09	21	10	16	10	14	17	24	05	01	09	—01
7. Ill health interferes with work								48	41	00	42	20	17	30	21	47	33	39	29	50
8. Shortness of breath									57	01	39	17	08	30	19	34	28	29	23	33
9. Heart beats hard										05	44	19	13	29	27	35	29	21	28	29
10. Drinking											06	11	11	12	15	09	01	—07	08	—03
11. Dizziness												20	19	34	30	42	27	16	31	34
12. Nightmares													19	22	16	20	17	06	14	13
13. Losing weight														18	22	20	12	05	17	06
14. Hands tremble															33	30	20	17	19	19
15. Hands sweat																32	19	09	24	12
16. Can't get going																	26	24	31	28
17. Pains and ailments																		29	19	30
18. Healthy enough to do things																			14	33
19. Nervous breakdown																				23
20. Health trouble																				

[a] Correlations are based on 1221 women who answered all 20 symptom items.
[b] Figures in table are product-moment correlations. Decimal points are omitted in all other figures. All correlations are positive unless otherwise indicated.

Table 7.4—Factor Loadings from Normalized Varimax Rotations[a]

Symptom Items	Factor 1		Factor 2		Factor 3		Factor 4		h^2 [b]	
	Men	Women	Men	Women	Men	Women	Men	Women	Men	Women
1. Trouble sleeping	.57[c]	57	17	19	08	06	14	07	38	37
2. Nervousness	64	60	12	20	23	27	24	12	53	49
3. Headaches	38	48	25	17	20	13	02	16	24	30
4. Loss of appetite	34	40	29	17	32	20	−05	−08	31	23
5. Upset stomach	36	33	21	18	23	24	−09	10	23	21
6. Difficult getting up	08	05	−04	02	51	48	−02	06	27	24
7. Ill health interferes with work	20	34	66	63	19	11	18	13	54	54
8. Shortness of breath	15	24	46	48	13	11	52	49	52	55
9. Heart beats hard	22	31	28	41	09	19	61	43	51	48
10. Drinking	13	05	−20	−09	19	36	12	02	11	14
11. Dizziness	38	49	38	34	11	21	20	15	34	42
12. Nightmares	42	22	07	09	16	30	09	14	22	17
13. Losing weight	27	24	10	11	25	33	00	−20	15	22
14. Hands trembling	37	22	15	26	32	39	24	16	31	29
15. Hands sweating	25	19	03	21	53	46	16	−02	37	29
16. Can't get going	20	27	24	45	47	38	21	03	36	43
17. Pains and ailments	23	25	48	42	04	09	10	10	29	26
18. Healthy enough to do things	09	06	51	56	−02	−02	14	03	29	32
19. Nervous breakdown	34	30	10	28	08	22	13	−02	15	22
20. Health problem	22	32	58	54	04	08	10	09	39	40

[a] These factor loadings are derived from intercorrelation matrices based on samples of 956 men and 1221 women. All respondents who omitted one or more of these 20 questions were omitted from the factor analysis.
[b] h^2 is equal to the communality of the item, a figure which indicates the degree to which these factors account for the responses to these items.
[c] Decimal point is omitted from all other figures in Table 7.4. All factor loadings are positive unless otherwise indicated.

from plus one to minus one. A high positive factor loading indicates that the item reflects the factor to a large extent, and that the relationship between the item and the factor is a positive one, i.e., people high on the factor will tend to be *high* on the item. A high negative factor loading also indicates that the item reflects the factor to a large extent, but the relationship between the item and the factor is a negative one, i.e., people high on the factor will tend to be *low* on the item. And a factor loading around zero indicates that the responses to the item have little relation to people's positions on the factor.

A comparison of the factors that emerged for men and women reveals striking similarities for the most part. That is, the 20 items show generally similar patterns of factor loadings for men and women. There are some differences, but it is apparent that items that have high factor loadings on a given factor for men tend to have high loadings on that factor for women; and items that have low factor loadings on a given factor for men tend to have low loadings on that factor for women. This meant that we could reasonably use identical factor scores for men and women.

The next step was to derive indices based on selected symptom items that would adequately describe the nature of each factor for both men and women. What criteria could be used to derive such factor scores? What criteria could we use for selecting certain symptom items rather than others as representative of a factor? Let us first examine possible mathematical criteria and save for later the question of what psychological constructs may be offered to identify these factors.

First of all, the size of the factor loadings of each item on a given factor aided our selection of items for factor scores. We selected arbitrarily a loading of .40 or higher as the lower limit of items to consider. It may be noted that this is an extremely conservative limit to establish, since, with a sample the size of the male and female populations in this analysis, a much lower figure would be considered a stable factor loading.

Then we considered only those items which were highly loaded *only* on the factor in question and ignored those items which had a high loading (over .30) on more than one factor, so that the emerging factor scores would be relatively independent of one another.

Both criteria were used in examining the factor loadings of males and females at the same time. If an item met the criterion for the males but not for the females, it was not used.

With this procedure we were able to extract two items for each of three factors, as can readily be seen by consulting Table 7.4.

> Factor 1: Do you ever have any trouble getting to sleep or staying asleep? (Item 1)
> Have you ever been bothered by nervousness, feeling fidgety and tense? (Item 2)
> Factor 2: Do you feel you are bothered by all sorts of pains and ailments in different parts of your body? (Item 17)
> For the most part, do you feel healthy enough to carry out the things you would like to do? (Item 18)
> Factor 3: Do you find it difficult to get up in the morning? (Item 6)
> Are you troubled by your hands sweating so that you feel damp and clammy? (Item 15)

It was impossible to obtain any item that would fulfill both these criteria for Factor 4. We therefore applied only the first criterion, selecting items that had high factor loadings, although they were also high on Factor 2. Therefore, our measure of Factor 4 is impure; when it is important to differentiate relationships between Factor 4 and other variables from the relationships obtained between Factor 2 and these variables, we will control on Factor 2.

> Factor 4: Have you ever been bothered by shortness of breath when you were not exercising or working hard? (Item 8)
> Have you ever been bothered by your heart beating hard? (Item 9)

Factor scores were computed by adding together the responses to the two items selected for each symptom factor (weighting the responses as indicated in Note 1).

From the clustering of high and low factor loadings for each factor, and especially from an examination of the items that we have selected for factor scores, how can we best label the factors conceptually? Below are our tentative suggestions. How meaningful these suggestions are—their "construct validity"—can best be judged when we examine the relationships of these factor scores to other variables in the study.

Factor 1: *Psychological Anxiety.* The items highly loaded on this factor—trouble sleeping, nervousness, loss of appetite, dizziness, etc.—seem to have a common thread of a conscious distress state without, for the most part, a specific localization in the body. Having headaches is the major exception to this statement, but this is perhaps the most common somatization of psychological distress.

Factor 2: *Physical Health.* Ill health or bodily complaints characterize the items highly loaded on this factor—interference of ill health with work, shortness of breath, pains and ailments, healthy enough to do things.

Factor 3: *Immobilization.* This is our most tentative label for a factor. The two items selected to measure this factor seemed widely discrepant, and we are more guided by one of them—difficulty getting up in the morning—rather than by the other—hands sweating. The "immobilization" label also fits the item with the next highest loadings on this factor—Item 16: "Have there ever been times when you couldn't take care of things because you just couldn't get going?"

Factor 4: *Physical Anxiety.* There are only two items with high loadings on this factor—shortness of breath and heart beats hard—both of them selected for the factor scores. These two have physical references, which is not surprising considering the fact, as we noted previously, that they are also highly loaded on Factor 2 (Physical Health). However, they differ from most of the other items involving physical symptoms in being extreme symptoms, often noticed to be part of intense anxiety.

It is possible to look at Factors 1 and 3 simultaneously, as different manifestations of psychological dysfunction of which the respondent has some degree of awareness. His symptoms, in these two factors, have an immediacy for him as a psychological incapacity—in Factor 1 a kind of free-floating anxiety, and in Factor 3 a psychological inertia involving tension. In both these symptom syndromes the respondent would be expected to feel his incapacity and to recognize his lack of psychological integration.

In contrast to these two factors, Factors 2 and 4 represent a somatization of ills—physical disease, organic disorder, or a psychological malfunctioning reflected in bodily reactions. Whatever the source,

SYMPTOM PATTERNS

one can assume that there is some psychological distress involved in the reaction to these physical symptoms; but we cannot assume that these physical symptoms necessarily reflect a *response* to psychological distress. We would have to control for the degree of medically diagnosed organic involvement to establish that these syndromes have this meaning. The only diagnosis of physical health that we have is a self-diagnosis, which is not trustworthy enough to be used as a systematic control. Because of this qualification, our interpretations of the relationships involving Factors 2 and 4 should be viewed as tentative formulations.

INTERRELATIONS AMONG THE FOUR FACTOR SCORES

The purpose of a factor analysis is to emerge with "orthogonal" factors, that is, with factors independent of each other. The four factor scores that we have derived would be unrelated to each other if they were "pure" measures of the factors, i.e., if the items making up a given factor score had zero factor loadings on all of the other factors. We know from Table 7.4 that this is not completely true. We would expect, therefore, some relationship among the four factor scores.

In Table 7.5 we present the intercorrelations of the four factor

Table 7.5—Intercorrelations of Symptom Factor Scores

Factors Correlated	Men	Women
1. Psychological Anxiety:		
and 2. Physical Health	+.27[a]	32
3. Immobilization	29	24
4. Physical Anxiety	39	39
2. Physical Health:		
and 3. Immobilization	08	12
4. Physical Anxiety	38	38
3. Immobilization:		
and 4. Physical Anxiety	19	22
Number of people [b]	(1036)	(1332)

[a] Figures are product-moment correlations. Plus sign and decimal point are omitted in the rest of the table.
[b] Does not include 41 men and 51 women whose answers to one or more questions used in computing the factor scores were not ascertained.

scores for 1036 men and 1332 women, and, as expected, these factor scores are all significantly related to one another.

The pattern of intercorrelations in Table 7.5 may be viewed as a measure of the extent to which the four scores we have derived depart from the ideal of "independence." However, it may also be viewed as reflecting what we would expect to find when we look at people's functioning in terms of a standard symptom list—that any given symptom item does in fact reflect more than one factor. Thus, the relationship between the scores on Factor 2 (Physical Health) and Factor 4 (Physical Anxiety) suggests that symptom items with a high somatic component tend to reflect both of the "somatic" factors. The high relationship between Factor 1 (Psychological Anxiety) and Factor 4 suggests that anxiety symptoms tend to have both physical and psychological components, that for many people these two manifestations of anxiety—physical and psychological distress—go hand in hand. On the other hand, the fact that the score on Factor 3 (Immobilization) represents the lowest contributor to the table of intercorrelations suggests that symptoms reflecting this factor tend to have very few somatic or anxiety overtones.

Although we have stressed the relationships among the four factor scores, it should be noted that much of the variance is still unaccounted for by these relationships. There are individuals who have somatic complaints without conscious anxiety, others who have conscious anxiety without somatic involvement, still others who have somatic anxiety without tying it to a health condition—all indicating that individuals have great capacities for isolating different aspects of malfunctioning.

It is because of this capacity that these separate factors emerge from the factor analysis. When looking at the relationships of these factors to other variables, therefore, we will expect to find certain differences in their relationship patterns. We will particularly expect to find differences between the relationships involving Factor 1 (Psychological Anxiety) and Factor 3 (Immobilization) and those involving Factor 2 (Physical Health) and Factor 4 (Physical Anxiety); e.g., because Factors 1 and 3 involve a more psychological expression of distress than either Factor 2 or Factor 4, we might expect them to have different implications for help-seeking behavior.

SEX, AGE, AND EDUCATION RELATED TO THE DIFFERENTIAL PREVALENCE OF SYMPTOM FACTORS

A national sample survey gives us a rich opportunity to examine the incidence of these symptoms in various social groupings, such as sex, age, and education. Do men and women, younger and older respondents, more educated and less educated respondents report different patterns of symptoms?

Sex

What kinds of male-female differences in experienced behavioral symptoms can one predict? Again, as in other areas, prediction is difficult. In addition to differences stemming from biological differences, there are those that derive from the ramifications of the sex roles in present-day society. In spite of significant attempts to describe these ramifications in a simplified manner, one must always cope with the highly complicated fabric of American social structure in considering the social roles of men and women. For example, social class differences in the expectations of men and women have been only casually explored. The research in this area is minimal, restricted to selected subpopulations in our society. Consequently, it is difficult to arrive at a simple theoretical prediction of the differences between men and women in the prevalence of psychological symptomatology; we can, however, formulate several general hypotheses.

For instance, there has been a good deal of general speculation about different psychological reactions in men and women, and these may be helpful in looking at our data. It has often been advanced that men and women orient themselves to their bodies differently, that the significance of the body for men lies in activity or in initiating potential gratification. It might be suggested, then, that bodily reactions to psychological distress may be more prevalent in women than in men, since men, habituated to act, may be more likely to do something to remove psychological distress. Since there is a heavy loading of the somatic aspect of psychological distress in our symptom checklist, we might expect that women would score higher than men, generally speaking.

It is also frequently pointed out that the female role in our culture, affected by recent socio-historic changes, is no longer so clearly defined as the male role and is more subject to conflict. This conflict and lack of clarity may generate active anxiety that is translated into symptoms.

There is also the factor, previously noted, of the differential readiness of men and women to admit to the same symptoms, which is also a question of differential role expectations. Thinking in terms of readiness to admit to weakness in the self, one might expect that women would find this easier to do, having been granted greater freedom to do so by a society which distinguishes between the "stronger" and "weaker" sexes.[3]

Turning to the data (Table 7.6), we find that consistent sex differences in the incidence of these symptom factors do occur. Women score "higher" than men on each of the symptom factor scores. Thus women express more psychological distress not only in the broad adjustment areas we have considered in the preceding chapters but also in specific, somatic symptomatology.

Age

In examining the data for potential age and education differences in the prevalence of the symptom factors, we will look at the relationships separately for men and women, because of the strong sex differences.

Age (Tables 7.7–7.10) by itself seems to play an important role in the determination of the responses to the symptom items in the factor syndromes. Only for men on Factor 1 (Psychological Anxiety) is there an unclear picture with age. In all the other instances, there are striking relationships between age and factor scores for both men and women. In the cases of men and women on Factors 2 (Physical Health) and 4 (Physical Anxiety) and in the case of women on Factor 1 (Psychological Anxiety), the older age groups show higher

Table 7.6—Relationship between Symptom Factor Scores and Sex of Respondent

Factors	Scores	Men	Women
1. Psychological Anxiety	7–8	3%	8%
	6	7	12
	5	12	20
	4	28	27
	3	25	21
	2	23	11
	NA*	2	1
Total		100%	100%
2. Physical Health	8	5%	7%
	6	14	19
	4	80	73
	NA	1	1
Total		100%	100%
3. Immobilization	7–8	3%	5%
	6	5	5
	5	12	16
	4	15	19
	3	24	23
	2	40	31
	NA	1	1
Total		100%	100%
4. Physical Anxiety	7–8	3%	6%
	6	5	8
	5	6	7
	4	14	19
	3	14	13
	2	56	45
	NA	2	2
Total		100%	100%
Number of people		(1077)	(1383)

*Refers to people whose replies to these questions were not ascertained.

incidence of symptoms. The findings with respect to Factor 1 are not so clear for men. Extreme Psychological Anxiety is admitted more often by older men, but the relationship breaks down when the entire distribution is considered.

Factor 3 (Immobilization) is of special interest because the relationship with age is the reverse of those obtained for the other three factors: with both men and women, it is the *younger* groups which show the markedly higher incidence of symptoms.

Reviewing the evidence that more older than younger people report symptoms of Physical Health and Physical Anxiety, these results

Table 7.7—Relationship between Scores on Symptom Factor 1 (Psychological Anxiety) and Age and Sex of Respondent

	AGE GROUPS					
Scores	21–24	25–34	35–44	45–54	55–64	65 and over
Men						
7–8	—%	1%	2%	3%	9%	5%
6	5	5	6	8	5	12
5	17	10	17	9	13	10
4	32	34	30	29	23	22
3	21	27	28	20	22	24
2	25	22	15	28	26	25
NA	—	1	2	3	2	2
Total	100%	100%	100%	100%	100%	100%
Number of men [a]	(65)	(252)	(241)	(209)	(146)	(161)
Women						
7–8	1%	5%	7%	7%	13%	15%
6	9	9	10	13	16	19
5	22	20	22	21	16	17
4	28	29	28	29	28	23
3	31	25	22	17	17	14
2	9	12	11	12	8	11
NA	—	—	—	1	2	1
Total	100%	100%	100%	100%	100%	100%
Number of women [a]	(98)	(344)	(307)	(250)	(183)	(191)

[a] Does not include three men and ten women whose age was not ascertained.

Table 7.8—Relationship between Scores on Symptom Factor 2 (Physical Health) and Age and Sex of Respondent

	AGE GROUPS					
Scores	21–24	25–34	35–44	45–54	55–64	65 and over
Men						
8	2%	1%	2%	4%	11%	12%
6	6	7	16	14	11	28
4	92	92	81	82	78	59
NA	—	—	1	—	—	1
Total	100%	100%	100%	100%	100%	100%
Number of men [a]	(65)	(252)	(241)	(209)	(146)	(161)
Women						
8	4%	2%	3%	8%	11%	16%
6	8	15	16	17	25	32
4	88	82	81	74	63	51
NA	—	1	—	1	1	1
Total	100%	100%	100%	100%	100%	100%
Number of women [a]	(98)	(344)	(307)	(250)	(183)	(191)

[a] Does not include three men and ten women whose age was not ascertained.

Table 7.9—Relationship between Scores on Symptom Factor 3 (Immobilization) and Age and Sex of Respondent

	AGE GROUPS					
Scores	21–24	25–34	35–44	45–54	55–64	65 and over
Men						
7–8	8%	5%	3%	—%	1%	1%
6	14	5	7	3	—	1
5	15	15	14	11	9	9
4	17	23	16	14	10	5
3	26	28	24	23	22	15
2	20	23	34	46	56	67
NA	—	1	2	3	2	2
Total	100%	100%	100%	100%	100%	100%
Number of men [a]	(65)	(252)	(241)	(209)	(146)	(161)
Women						
7–8	8%	8%	5%	2%	2%	3%
6	6	7	7	4	3	1
5	23	22	20	14	8	6
4	28	20	24	17	15	12
3	20	25	20	26	30	18
2	13	17	23	35	41	58
NA	2	1	1	2	1	2
Total	100%	100%	100%	100%	100%	100%
Number of women [a]	(98)	(344)	(307)	(250)	(183)	(191)

[a] Does not include three men and ten women whose age was not ascertained.

seem self-evident. With increased age, physical health becomes a much more realistic problem area. Since the body is more vulnerable in older people, one might expect more physical reactions to anxiety by them than by younger people, even in cases where there is in reality no physical impairment.

The fact that Immobilization seems to be a younger person's syndrome of psychological dysfunctioning is an interesting result. Immobilization, ennui, and lack of energy are all psychological states that suggest lack of integration, rather than an insurmountable, immediate psychological difficulty. In a life situation, where one is caught among different pressures for integration of the self—pressures that may operate at cross-purposes (such as the "achievement vs. housewife" conflict for some women) or pressures that are so varied that they are not all attainable at the same time—one may frequently experience a lack of integration. Such pressures are more likely to occur early in life and then gradually diminish as patterns

Table 7.10—Relationship between Scores on Symptom Factor 4 (Physical Anxiety) and Age and Sex of Respondent

Scores	AGE GROUPS					
	21–24	25–34	35–44	45–54	55–64	65 and over
Men						
7–8	—%	—%	—%	3%	6%	8%
6	3	4	4	5	7	9
5	3	3	7	11	5	11
4	12	8	18	15	16	12
3	15	14	15	11	14	16
2	67	70	56	53	49	41
NA	—	1	—	2	3	3
Total	100%	100%	100%	100%	100%	100%
Number of men [a]	(65)	(252)	(241)	(209)	(146)	(161)
Women						
7–8	3%	3%	3%	6%	10%	14%
6	5	6	7	8	7	14
5	6	8	7	7	10	8
4	15	19	20	19	23	18
3	13	12	15	13	12	9
2	58	51	47	45	35	35
NA	—	1	1	2	3	2
Total	100%	100%	100%	100%	100%	100%
Number of women [a]	(98)	(344)	(307)	(250)	(183)	(191)

[a] Does not include three men and ten women whose age was not ascertained.

of integration are chosen. Until such integration occurs, however, one might expect that a common reaction to these cross-pressures which are too divergent or too numerous to handle would be withdrawal, with its concomitant restlessness and disruption. Since this problem is more often encountered by the young adults, perhaps this is one reason that young people are prone to symptoms of the Immobilization type.

Certain physiological changes that accompany aging are also relevant here. A progressive atrophy of skin with increasing age reduces the sweat secretion, and very old people commonly have extremely dry skin; this could affect the responses on the "hand sweating" symptom in Factor 3. With increasing age, people also require less sleep, and this would make "getting up in the morning" (the other symptom in Factor 3) less of a problem for them. These physiological facts may in themselves account for the relationship between Immobilization (Factor 3) and age. However, in view of the relationship between education and the Immobilization factor when age

SYMPTOM PATTERNS

of respondent is controlled, to be reported more fully later in this chapter, we suspect that this physiological explanation is not sufficient in itself.

Factor 1 (Psychological Anxiety) shows a clear relationship with age for women—older women experience this syndrome more often than younger women—but an unclear one for men—only extreme scores show this same relationship. The implications for life functions inherent in the aging process probably have a greater significance for women than for men, which should contribute to a mounting anxiety that is greater for women than for men. The threat of decreased physical, and hence, social desirability is probably a more realistic social image for older women than it is for older men. The anticipation and realization of this problem should lead to the generation of greater Psychological Anxiety for aging women than for aging men.

Table 7.11—Relationship between Scores on Symptom Factor 1 (Psychological Anxiety) and Education and Sex of Respondent

Scores	HIGHEST EDUCATIONAL LEVEL ATTAINED		
	Grade School	High School	College
Men			
7–8	6%	3%	1%
6	8	7	5
5	11	11	16
4	25	28	37
3	28	28	26
2	20	23	15
NA	2	—	*
Total	100%	100%	100%
Number of men [a]	(367)	(461)	(242)
Women			
7–8	12%	6%	3%
6	18	10	10
5	16	21	23
4	24	30	30
3	16	23	23
2	13	9	11
NA	1	1	*
Total	100%	100%	100%
Number of women [a]	(435)	(724)	(215)

* Here and in all subsequent tables this symbol (*) indicates less than one-half of 1 per cent.
[a] Does not include seven men and nine women whose educational level was not ascertained.

There is another way of looking at this result. Energy mobilized by most women during early adulthood to meet the greater demands of family living in a sense takes time away from the concerns that may generate Psychological Anxiety. This great expenditure of energy is easily perceived as fulfillment at the moment. But the relinquishing of nurturant ties to children, the gradual moving away of the children from the home into other circles, and other signs of breakup of the family may cause women to suffer from the reduced opportunity for fulfillment through their families. For men, the later life stages may increase their life fulfillment at least until retirement: for example, the meaning of their work can become clearer or at least more stable as they grow older. Thus, aging would have less anxiety-inducing implications for men than for women.

Education

Our findings as to the prevalence of symptoms at different educational levels (grade-school, high-school, and college-educated groups) parallel our results from the different age levels. In general, less educated groups show symptom patterns that are similar to those in older age groups. In particular, the Physical Health and Physical Anxiety symptoms that we observed to be more prevalent among older respondents are also more prevalent at lower educational levels for both men and women, as indicated in Tables 7.12 and 7.14. These two factors are most prevalent among people with grade-school education in both male and female groups. These people differ markedly from the high-school groups, who in turn show a slightly higher frequency of these physical symptoms than do the college groups.

We are probably confronted here with a strong combined effect of age and education, since there are many more older people in the lower educational groups. Beyond that, with respect to Factors 2 and 4, we can also assume that the lower educational groups have not only fewer resources for physical care but also less information that might forestall, prevent, or cure physical ailments. Furthermore, one might expect that the body itself is a more salient consideration for the less educated respondents, especially for the men; their work,

Table 7.12—Relationship between Scores on Symptom Factor 2 (Physical Health) and Education and Sex of Respondent

Scores	HIGHEST EDUCATIONAL LEVEL ATTAINED		
	Grade School	High School	College
Men			
8	11%	2%	2%
6	19	11	10
4	69	86	88
NA	1	1	*
Total	100%	100%	100%
Number of men [a]	(367)	(461)	(242)
Women			
8	14%	4%	1%
6	24	17	13
4	61	78	85
NA	1	1	1
Total	100%	100%	100%
Number of women [a]	(435)	(724)	(215)

[a] Does not include seven men and nine women whose educational level was not ascertained.

Table 7.13—Relationship between Scores on Symptom Factor 3 (Immobilization) and Education and Sex of Respondent

Scores	HIGHEST EDUCATIONAL LEVEL ATTAINED		
	Grade School	High School	College
Men			
7–8	3%	2%	3%
6	3	6	5
5	11	12	16
4	10	15	21
3	18	23	31
2	52	41	23
NA	3	1	1
Total	100%	100%	100%
Number of men [a]	(367)	(461)	(242)
Women			
7–8	3%	5%	6%
6	4	6	5
5	11	18	18
4	17	20	20
3	22	24	27
2	41	26	24
NA	2	1	—
Total	100%	100%	100%
Number of women [a]	(435)	(724)	(215)

[a] Does not include seven men and nine women whose educational level was not ascertained.

Table 7.14—Relationship between Symptom Factor 4 (Physical Anxiety) and Education and Sex of Respondent

	HIGHEST EDUCATIONAL LEVEL ATTAINED		
Scores	Grade School	High School	College
Men			
7–8	5%	2%	1%
6	7	4	3
5	8	5	8
4	16	12	12
3	13	15	14
2	48	61	60
NA	3	1	2
Total	100%	100%	100%
Number of men [a]	(367)	(461)	(242)
Women			
7–8	11%	4%	3%
6	9	6	10
5	9	7	6
4	18	21	16
3	12	14	10
2	39	47	54
NA	2	1	1
Total	100%	100%	100%
Number of women [a]	(435)	(724)	(215)

[a] Does not include seven men and nine women whose educational level was not ascertained.

at this educational level, is more likely to involve a heavy expenditure of physical effort.

A general tendency for a higher prevalence of the factor syndrome of Immobilization (Factor 3) to appear in the more educated groups of both men and women is shown in Table 7.13. We may interpret this difference in light of our discussion of Immobilization as it pertains to age; if Immobilization reflects a withdrawal in the face of a complexity of demands, we may surmise that the life patterns associated with higher education in our culture represent greater and more complex psychological and social demands on the individual.

It is interesting to note that marked differences between educational groups on Factor 3 appear at different points for men and women: for men, the major difference holds between college and the other two educational levels, whereas for women the difference is noteworthy only between the grade school and the two more educated groups. Assuming again a connection between immobilizing symptoms and the complexity or extent of demands, one might hypothesize that the life patterns of high-school- and college-educated men are more widely disparate than the patterns of high-school- and college-educated women.

Why should this be so? Perhaps the investment of energy for women of both high-school and college education is made along similar channels—the family, the neighborhood, the immediate social environment. College-educated men, however, face many more diverse demands than do high-school-educated men; the pressures for achievement at home, as parent and husband, and commitment to work, are probably stronger for the better educated group.

Another effect of college education more profound on men than on women is exposure to a new value system. It has often been noted, for instance, that during their college careers men become interested in traditionally feminine concerns and activities to a greater extent than women become interested in masculine concerns. Perhaps the college experience leads to more conflict about sexual identity for men than for women. Immobilization stemming from this conflict may be especially pronounced for college-educated men.

While Immobilization can be considered a concomitant of college experiences for both men and women, we would still expect the effects to be stronger in men; higher education is more related to a man's future life experiences—the complexities, the conflicts, the pressures he will have to meet.

Psychological Anxiety symptoms (Factor 1) do not seem to be clearly associated with educational levels among men, but are related to education in women. The biggest difference appearing in Table 7.11 is among women between the grade-school and the other educational levels. To the extent that this factor reflects lack of fulfillment, either potential or actual, one may understand why it occurs at the lowest educational levels for women. The other groups, however, show no consistent differences.

Interrelationships among Sex, Age, and Education

We noted above that the findings with respect to age paralleled those with respect to education, with younger age groups showing a similar symptom picture to higher education groupings, and older people paralleling the less educated groups. Because of the strong inverse relationship between age and education—the youngest group is the most highly educated—the question arises as to whether these results represent two independent sets of relationships or are in fact a contamination of one relationship. It is important, then, to examine the relationship of age to the symptom factors when education is controlled and also to observe what happens to the education findings when age is controlled.

In order to make these comparisons, we combined the scores on each symptom factor into three groups—high, medium, and low scores. These groupings, shown in Table 7.15, were based on the distributions of the scores among both men and women; the groups were divided as nearly as possible into equal thirds. Using these

Table 7.15—Distribution of Summary Symptom Factor Scores in Men and Women

			DISTRIBUTIONS OF SCORES	
Factor	Summary Scores	Original Scores	Men	Women
1. Psychological Anxiety	High	5–8	22%	40%
	Medium	4	28	27
	Low	2–3	48	32
	NA		2	1
	Total		100%	100%
2. Physical Health	High	8	5%	7%
	Medium	6	14	19
	Low	4	80	73
	NA		1	1
	Total		100%	100%
3. Immobilization	High	5–8	20%	26%
	Medium	3–4	39	42
	Low	2	40	31
	NA		1	1
	Total		100%	100%
4. Physical Anxiety	High	5–8	14%	21%
	Medium	3–4	28	32
	Low	2	56	45
	NA		2	2
	Total		100%	100%
	Number of people		(1077)	(1383)

summary scores, we compared men and women, dividing each into three age groups—age 21–34; 35–54; 55 and over—and then subdividing each age group into three educational levels—grade school, high school, and college. These refined comparisons, in general, substantiated the results reported earlier in our discussions of the separate relationships of sex, age, and education to the symptom factor scores.

These refined comparisons have been summarized in Tables 7.16–7.19. In order to facilitate presentation in these tables, we have reported only the relationship between the extreme scores—either high or low—and these social characteristics.[4] From these figures, one can see at what age group the strongest educational differences occur on the various factors or at what educational level the most dramatic age differences appear, or at what age and educational level the greatest sex differences occur.

As a final recapitulation, we present below a summary of the relationships between sex, age, and education and each of the four symptom factor scores.

PSYCHOLOGICAL ANXIETY FACTOR RELATED TO SEX, AGE, AND EDUCATION (TABLE 7.16).

1. Men have lower scores on Psychological Anxiety than women do at every age and educational level.

Table 7.16—Relationship between Scoring Low on Factor 1 (Psychological Anxiety) and Sex, Educational Level and Age of Respondent [a]

Age	Education	Men	Women
	Grade school	60	37
21–34	High school	48	38
	College	42	38
	Grade school	45	30
35–54	High school	51	31
	College	41	34
	Grade school	50	27
55 and	High school	53	23
over	College	39	24

[a] Figures are the percentage of men and women in each group who scored low on Factor 1. See Table 7.15 for definition of a "low" score.

2. For men, there is no consistent relationship (across educational levels) between age and scores on Psychological Anxiety. For women, there is a consistent relationship; older women at each educational level report more symptoms in this factor than younger women.

3. College-educated men tend to have fewer low scores on this factor than do the other two male educational groups. There is no consistent difference as a function of education for women.

PHYSICAL HEALTH FACTOR RELATED TO SEX, AGE,
AND EDUCATION (TABLE 7.17).

1. Women in general report a higher incidence of Physical Health symptoms; this sex difference is minimal for college-educated respondents at each age level.

2. For both men and women, at every educational level, older respondents score higher on this symptom factor than do younger respondents.

3. At every age level, for both men and women, grade-school-educated respondents are outstandingly high on this symptom factor. The distinction between high-school- and college-educated men is not clear on this factor, but high-school-educated women report more of these symptoms than do college-educated women.

Table 7.17—Relationship between Scoring Low on Factor 2 (Physical Health) and Sex, Educational Level, and Age of Respondent [a]

Age	Education	Men	Women
	Grade school	85	74
21–34	High school	94	84
	College	94	90
	Grade school	75	70
35–54	High school	85	79
	College	87	89
	Grade school	63	51
55 and	High school	79	66
over	College	73	74

[a] Figures are the percentage of men and women in each group who scored low on Factor 2. See Table 7.15 for definition of a "low" score.

SYMPTOM PATTERNS

IMMOBILIZATION FACTOR RELATED TO SEX, AGE,
AND EDUCATION (TABLE 7.18).

1. Middle-aged men, and to some extent older men, have lower scores on the Immobilization factor than do women of comparable age; no consistent sex difference is apparent in younger men and women.

2. Age presents the clearest demographic relationship with this factor. For both men and women, younger respondents at every educational level report more of these symptoms than do older respondents.

3. Although not so consistent as the relationship with age, the relationship of education to Immobilization also persists; higher educated groups score higher on this factor, except among the oldest women.[5]

Table 7.18—Relationship between Scoring Low on Factor 3 (Immobilization) and Sex, Educational Level, and Age of Respondent [a]

Age	Education	Men	Women
	Grade school	31	34
21–34	High school	25	15
	College	13	12
	Grade school	50	33
35–54	High school	42	27
	College	26	24
	Grade school	62	49
55 and	High school	72	54
over	College	47	50

[a] Figures are the percentage of men and women in each group who scored low on Factor 3. See Table 7.15 for definition of a "low" score.

PHYSICAL ANXIETY FACTOR RELATED TO SEX, AGE,
AND EDUCATION (TABLE 7.19).

1. Women again report higher scores on this symptom factor.

2. Older respondents of both sexes report more of these symptoms at all educational levels.

3. Education is not clearly related to this factor. There is, how-

ever, a trend for the less educated groups to report more extreme scores on these symptoms than the more educated respondents (grade-school respondents compared to the other two educational levels combined). This trend disappears, however, when scores on Factor 2 (Physical Health) are controlled.

Table 7.19—Relationship between Scoring High on Factor 4 (Physical Anxiety) and Sex, Educational Level, and Age of Respondent [a]

Age	Education	Men	Women
21–34	Grade school	11	24
	High school	4	16
	College	9	15
35–54	Grade school	16	24
	High school	14	15
	College	14	21
55 and over	Grade school	27	37
	High school	19	25
	College	18	26

[a] Figures are the percentage of men and women who scored high on Factor 4. See Table 7.15 for definition of a "high" score.

In general, considering the relationships to symptom syndromes of sex, age, and education simultaneously, we find similar results to those we have noted in the separate consideration of each variable. The sex differences remain the clearest and most consistent—women express more symptoms on all four symptom factors. Age remains clearly related to the three factors which showed relationships when age was considered without the educational control—younger people express fewer of the physical symptoms (Factor 2 and 4) and have higher scores on Factor 3 (Immobilization). The relationships between education and scores on these three factors are not so clear when age is controlled, although there is still a clear tendency for the more highly educated, like the younger groups, to express fewer physical symptoms (particularly in Factor 2) and higher scores on Immobilization (Factor 3).

One interesting aspect of these findings is that the Immobilization factor on the one hand and the Physical Anxiety and Physical Health factors on the other, although positively related to each other, relate differently to age and education. Older people and less educated people score higher on the physical factors but lower on Factor 3. Using education as a rough index of social class, these findings conform to speculations and observations that bodily symptoms are more common to the working class, and psychological symptoms are more characteristic of the middle class.

Although the findings in Tables 7.16 to 7.19 generally confirm the results obtained when age and education were considered separately, certain interesting exceptions appear, particularly in the cases where general relationships are not duplicated in all sex-age-education groups. One especially interesting finding that appears when the age and education controls are instituted occurs with relation to Factor 1 (Psychological Anxiety). As may be observed in Table 7.16, there is no relationship between education and Psychological Anxiety for women, but one does appear for men: in general, more highly educated men seem to experience more Psychological Anxiety. In terms of some of the speculations offered previously, it would appear that education plays a more crucial role in the lives of men than of women, that it is more related to the life-patterns they will form and the extent and complexity of the demands and the tensions that they will experience. Thus, with respect to the induction of Psychological Anxiety, education may have a parallel function for men that aging has for women—since Table 7.16 confirms the previously discussed finding that age brings greater Psychological Anxiety for women but not for men.

SUMMARY

In this chapter, we have examined the responses to the type of symptom checklist that has often been used as a rough diagnostic screening instrument. We viewed these symptoms not as diagnostic criteria, but as different ways of expressing emotional disturbance and we were concerned not with a total symptom score, but with analyzing the dimensions that underlie the responses to a symptom list. A factor analysis of the responses to the symptom list yielded four such dimensions or "factors." Two of these seem to represent "psychological" expressions of dysfunction, where symptoms are experienced as a psychological incapacity—in one (Psychological Anxiety) a kind of free-floating anxiety, in the other (Immobilization) a psychological inertia. The other two factors (Physical Health and Physical Anxiety) seem to represent a somatization of distress.

In looking at the relationships between scores on these factors and demographic characteristics, we were particularly interested in the extent to which the relationships with the psychological and physical symptoms paralleled those we have observed between demographic characteristics and tendencies to experience distress in psychological as opposed to external terms. We found consistent differences between men and women: women expressed more symptoms on all four of the symptom factors. This parallels the results noted in the preceding chapters, and again documents the tendency for women to express more distress in all areas.

In the relationships with *age,* a distinction occurs between the psychological and physical symptom factors. Older people express more physical symptoms on both the Physical Health and Physical Anxiety factors. But on the psychological factor of Immobilization, the relationship is reversed: the young people express more symptoms. And on Psychological Anxiety no clear pattern emerges: older women express more symptoms of Psychological Anxiety, but no clear relationship appears for men. This last difference suggests that the aging process in our culture may have more traumatic implications for women than for men.

That more older than younger people report symptoms of Physical Health and Physical Anxiety is not surprising since increasing physical vulnerability comes with increasing age. What is of interest is that older age is not similarly associated with an increase in scores on the psychological factors. This points up the importance of the physical element in explaining the findings from previous research that total symptom scores increase with increasing age. Such relationships do not necessarily mean that older people are psychologically "sicker," but seem rather to reflect the fact that a symptom list has a strong physical component, and older people tend to express the distress that they do experience in physical terms.

The relationships between *education* and symptom factor scores were similar to those obtained with age. The less educated, like the older age groups, showed higher scores on the physical factors (particularly Physical Health) and lower scores on Immobilization. These relationships, though less clear than those obtained with age, remain even when age is controlled, suggesting that the results are not merely a reflection of physiological concomitants of the aging process. Using education as a rough index of social class, these findings conform to observations that have previously been made about bodily symptoms being more common to the working class, and psychological symptoms being a more characteristic middle-class mode of expression. These education relationships are also consistent with other findings from this study which have shown that the higher educated more often manifest psychological rather than external expressions of distress.

NOTES

1. Scale values for the responses were arbitrarily assigned 1, 2, 3, 4 for items with four alternatives, and 2 and 4 for items with two alternatives.
2. The factors were extracted by the Centroid method. The method of rotation is one programed for IBM 650 operation in the Normalized Varimax program.
3. An attempt was made to mitigate the effects of this problem—at least to some extent—by having the respondents check the symptom lists themselves rather than give their replies to the interviewer.
4. The decision as to which end of the scale to present—either high or low scores—was based on the distribution of these scores in the entire sample. In the case of Factors 1 and 3, the "low" scores came closest to including one third of the entire sample; for Factor 4 the "high" scores met this criterion; for Factor 2 the "low" scores were used by default, there being too few "high" scores to warrant their presentation. We have included the complete tables in Appendix A of the Tabular Supplement for the interested reader (Tables A.7-A.10).
5. This finding is of particular interest in view of the physiological facts of aging cited in our earlier discussion of age and Immobilization. The fact that educational differences are sustained in all except our oldest group lends support to the interpretation of these symptoms as indicative of psychological as well as purely physiological differences.

VIII

Selected Demographic Characteristics and Adjustment

THE MAJOR purpose of this chapter is to describe various demographic groupings in our society according to their perceptions of the satisfactions and the problems they experience. Primarily, we wish to discover whether, and in what ways, city dwellers' feelings are different from those of country people, how Protestants differ from Catholics, how the rich differ from the poor, and so on.

The demographic variables we use for classifying people can be thought of both as contemporary characteristics indicative of current life-adjustment patterns and as enduring characteristics that have helped to shape these patterns. In some of our speculations and interpretations we shall draw upon both these meanings to help integrate the findings. But we have kept such speculation to a minimum, for these data may be viewed within many theoretical contexts and approaches, and it is beyond the scope of this study to attempt a systematic theoretical integration. The present state of epidemiological knowledge in this area would make any such systematic attempt premature. The interpretations that we do suggest and the etiological implications that we draw are thus to be viewed as tentative formulations. As descriptive facts, however, as assessments of the ways in which various adjustment problems are experienced in different subgroups of the population, the findings have meaning regardless of the validity of any interpretation.

The variables discussed in this chapter are independent neither of one another nor of other important social characteristics. Although we have controlled some variables while studying the effects of others in certain crucial instances, time limitations and considerations of analysis priorities have not enabled us to do this in all relevant instances. In addition, an inferential analysis pointed at isolating the effects of each variable would, in many cases, require the kinds of extensive controls more fruitfully established by selective sampling of certain subgroups than by a representative national sampling.

The preceding chapters have delved into relationships within each of three demographic categories: sex, age, and education. In this chapter, we shall first present a summary of these findings, pointing up the male-female differences, age differences, and education differences that have appeared *across* the different areas of adjustment that have been investigated. We will then comment upon whatever striking differences have appeared in analyses of other demographic characteristics in the relationships to adjustment areas. A section will be devoted to each of the following: income, occupation, present place of residence (rural-urban), marital status, religion and church attendance, and broken home background.

These variables were selected because each of them, in some respect, has been considered relevant in the area of adjustment. We eliminated others with this qualification (region, generation, ethnicity, family size) because preliminary analyses indicated only minimal relationships with the type of adjustment indices measured in this study. Although our list is fairly inclusive, it admittedly neglects facets of the social world that may be meaningful for the adjustment of certain select groups.

"Broken home background," it should be noted, was included even though it is not a demographic variable. This index records whether or not an individual lived with both of his real parents until he was sixteen years of age. This kind of information is the clearest direct measure in the study of an early, formative, social environment of potentially crucial relevance for adjustment. It is included because it measures directly the influence of early social background, an influence which we are often interested in deducing from demographic findings, but which such findings can only suggest.

We related each demographic characteristic to the same variables that we studied in relation to sex, age, and education: indices of general adjustment, self-perception, symptoms, and feelings of adjustment in marriage, parenthood, and work. Because space considerations prevent the presentation of tabulations of all the relationships, we shall list only those results in which responses differed noticeably within the demographic category under consideration. In the interest of succinctness, we have omitted negative results and have commented only on consistent relationships. Our brief considerations of each variable are suggestive, not definitive, and should not be taken as intensive appraisals of relationships to adjustment patterns.

Certain areas of adjustment showed few significant relationships with any of the selected social characteristics, beyond the sex, age, and education relationships already discussed. For example, no systematic relationships obtained between demographic variables and our measures of self-perception or our measures of adjustment to parental and occupational roles. Consequently, these areas are largely omitted in the following discussions, except in infrequent instances where a finding fitted into a general pattern of relationships with other adjustment areas.

Because a large amount of data has been summarized in this chapter, and because we have chosen a descriptive level of presentation, all related tables have been placed in Appendix B of the Tabular Supplement (see footnote p. 12). For the benefit of the interested reader, these tables are referred to, by number, wherever appropriate. Tables relevant to findings on sex, age, and education can be found in previous chapters of Part I.

SEX

Numerous differences between men and women have been reported in earlier chapters, and in reviewing these findings, several persistent themes appear. The most consistent sex difference in our data is the greater experience of distress reported by women as compared to men in all areas of adjustment with which we have dealt. It occurs in some evaluations of general adjustment, in the attitudes toward the self, in the evaluations of functioning in the marital and parental roles, and in the specific symptom patterns reported by men and women; women are more worried, more unhappy in their marriages, more aware of problems in their marriages, more likely to have felt that they had experienced a nervous breakdown. They also feel more inadequate in the parental role and are less accepting of themselves in the self-image they present. These experiences of distress are clearly manifest in the more frequent reports of all types of psychosomatic and anxiety symptoms.

What is the meaning of this? The simplest explanation would appear to be that women in our society are subject to greater stress than men. Margaret Mead (1949) has been particularly concerned with this problem and has pointed out that with the increasing flexibility in the feminine role in modern society there occurs a concomitant increase in uncertainty and stress in a woman's life. Although we have no way to assess the "actual" stresses and strains faced by our respondents, and thus cannot directly test this interpretation, we can with our data make some evaluation of its importance. If this interpretation does operate, it would be expected that the greatest difference in the experience of distress occurs among the younger respondents, where these cultural changes have had the greatest impact. There is some evidence for this in the fact that differences in the reports of difficulties in the marital and parental roles and in the incidence of negative self-evaluations are more apparent in the comparisons between younger men and women than in the comparisons between older men and women. We find no indication of greater differences in symptom patterns for younger than older men and women, however, so that the evidence bearing on the relevance of this interpretation of our data remains uncertain. What alternative interpretations can we offer?

We have already pointed to the possibility that these findings may reflect a greater readiness to admit distress rather than an actual difference in the stresses and strains encountered by men and women. The existence of such a difference between men and women in our society would not be surprising. The male role is closely linked to an active, coping interaction with the world, and a man's masculine identity is closely linked to his success in coping with his environment, to his strength in the face of difficulties. It would not be surprising, then, if a man defended against feelings that attested to his failure in this respect, and not only experienced such feelings less often than women but also was less likely to report them if they were experienced. Women, on the other hand, commonly viewed as the "weaker" sex, would be less subject to identity problems linked to the experience and admission of difficulties and suffering.

Another frequently noted aspect of the feminine role in our society appears to be intimately related to the *experience* of distress: woman's role is viewed as more closely related to the maintenance of the solidarity of the family and larger social groupings of which she is a part. Fulfillment of this role would require sensitivity to the socio-emotional climate. Such sensitivity, involving a responsiveness to personal qualities in other people as well as in the self, could readily be manifest in our subjective measures of adjustment. A greater awareness of the "feeling" aspect of behavior, that is, a greater introspectiveness on the part of women, could account for many of our findings, not only those related to feelings of distress. We saw in Chapter III, for example, that women are more likely to report interpersonal or personality sources of shortcomings. In many realms of adjustment, women can be expected to be more attuned than men to the psychological facets of experience.

EDUCATION

Two important themes run through the differential responses of persons at varying educational levels. First, people with more education seem to be more introspective about themselves, more concerned about the personal and interpersonal aspects of their lives. Secondly, more educated people seem to have, coupled with this introspectiveness, a greater sense of well-being and satisfaction.

Their introspectiveness is reflected in the greater prevalence among the more educated respondents of (1) feelings of inadequacy both as a parent and as a husband or wife, (2) reports of *both* shortcomings and strong points in the self, and (3) more of the psychological immobilization symptoms.

In addition to these indications of introspectiveness, the context within which these more highly educated respondents evaluate their adjustment reflects a greater awareness of the potential for gratification or frustration of emotional needs in various aspects of their life functioning; they are more likely than the less highly educated respondents to report interpersonal sources of present happiness, personality and interpersonal sources of strengths and weaknesses in the self, the marital relationship itself as a source of both marital happiness and unhappiness, interpersonal sources of parental role inadequacies, and ego-relevant sources of both job satisfaction and dissatisfaction. This theme is quite parallel to one that we commented on in our discussion of sex differences. It appears as if greater education implies a more "feminine" life orientation.

However, the second theme that is characteristic of our higher educational group—the greater sense of well-being—is quite "unfeminine." The woman's greater introspectiveness seems to be reflected only in a greater sensitivity to the *stressful* aspects of her life. The more highly educated respondents, both men and women, on the other hand, seem to be more aware of *both* the positive and the negative aspects of their lives. They are happier—in their over-all evaluations of their current happiness, in their marriages, and in their jobs—and are more optimistic about the future than the less educated respondents.

These two themes which appear so clearly in our data seem to point to education as broadening one's perspective and raising one's aspiration level—which leads to both an increased realization of problems and unfulfilled expectations, and a greater awareness of life satisfactions. It is interesting to note that these educational differences are maintained even when another important aspect of social status, income level, is held constant (see later section of this chapter and Tables B.12 through B.17 in the Tabular Supplement). Thus, the findings on the greater satisfactions associated with higher education cannot be viewed merely as a reflection of the greater material advantages that also tend to come with higher education.

AGE

Although the age-pattern data show a good deal of similarity to our education findings, as might be expected in view of the relationship between these two demographic variables, there are interesting differences between the two sets of results. The most consistent difference we obtained between young and old people was the minimization of both self-doubt and the perception of problems among the older respondents. Older people reported worrying less often, fewer feelings of inadequacy in marriage, fewer problems in marriage, in raising children, and in the job, and a more positive self-image coupled with fewer perceived shortcomings in the self. These results are similar to those reported for the lower educational levels. They are of particular interest here, however, when one considers that older people have had a greater opportunity to experience problems in their lives than younger people. If, when asked to consider their entire married life, or job history, for example, older respondents had been *more* likely to report having had problems in these areas than younger people, we would have been faced with a dilemma in interpretation. The fact that, despite this "methodological" difficulty in comparing the reports of older and younger people, the older respondents report having had *fewer* problems and *fewer* feelings of self-doubt than the younger respondents makes these findings especially significant. What does this lack of perceived difficulties mean?

Two alternatives are immediately apparent. On the one hand, we may be seeing the effects of a greater perspective that comes with the passage of time—what appears as a problem or inadequacy at the moment of involvement in an issue may seem much less serious, may even be forgotten, with the passage of time. More recent events may seem to be of greater consequence than remote ones. On the other hand, our older respondents may have experienced fewer problems throughout their lifetime. For we have here not only differences in age but also generational differences, in which may be reflected a cultural change in tendencies toward introspectiveness.

It is difficult to choose between these two alternatives, and it is likely that both contribute to the findings we obtained. We find some support for both views in our data. For example, in the discussion of shortcomings in the self, we saw that younger men are more concerned about their lack of education—a concern very relevant to a man in the early phase of establishing his status in society —and older men are more concerned with what we have called "moral and virtuous stereotypes"—a concern with the moral worth that may be related, we suggested, to the greater salience of death to the older person. In other areas, however, we do find differences that may well reflect cultural changes; we find that while age is not related to the report of experiencing a nervous breakdown—a disruption defined largely in nonintrospective terms—age *is* related to the experience of a personal problem for which help is seen as relevant —a disruption defined largely in personality and relationship terms. In this latter case, older people report fewer such problems than do younger people.

What about the more positive aspect of feelings of adjustment? Do older people, who see fewer difficulties in life, also feel more gratified? Yes, but only partially so. Older men are more satisfied with their job than younger men (we have suggested that this may reflect a greater commitment to their job on the part of older men). Older men and women are more satisfied as parents than younger men and women (we suggested that this was a reflection of the older parents' remoteness from the restrictions placed on parents by young children). There was no relationship, however, between the evaluation of marital happiness and age. And despite these indications of lack of problems and of high feelings of satisfaction in specific areas of life, older respondents, when asked to give a *general* evaluation of their current life satisfactions, report that they are *less* happy than the younger persons.

In an attempt to explain this pattern of findings, it is interesting to recall that the reasons the older person gives for both his current happiness and unhappiness are frequently related to health. The great salience of health for the older person, and the obvious decline in health that comes with old age, serve to explain why, even though in his major life roles the older person is as happy as or happier than the younger person, he is "in general" not very happy. This overriding importance of health and physical decline is also reflected in the psychosomatic and anxiety symptoms the older people report. Older men and women report more symptoms having to do with their physical well-being—Physical Health and Physical Anxiety symptoms—but they do not differ consistently in their report of Psychological Anxiety symptoms, and they report *fewer* symptoms of Immobilization. Again, it is in the realm of health that the older respondents indicate *less* well-being.

What can we conclude from these patterns of relationships? Age differences seem most of all to reflect differences in the current level of aspiration in older and younger people. Older people are on the whole not dissatisfied or troubled about most aspects of their lives—either because of a lowering of aspirations and expectations as a result of a positive adaptation to the realistic possibilities in their life situation or as a result of a more passive resignation to their life situation. But neither are they particularly happy or optimistic about their lives. Their satisfactions seem to be based on limited expectations and a passive acceptance of their status. (This passivity will be pointed up again in Part Two when we report the findings on the way younger and older people handle their problems.) Only in one area of their lives does there seem to be much investment of energy—in their concern with their health and general physical well-being.

Younger people, on the other hand, are actively involved in the numerous aspects of their lives—their families, their jobs, their friends—and express greater self-questioning about their behavior in these realms and sometimes greater dissatisfactions about their lives. This self-questioning and dissatisfaction seem to be a reflection of greater involvement, however, rather than greater malfunctioning. These differences in involvement are probably a reflection not only of changes which accompany the aging process but also of cultural changes that have occurred, particularly with respect to the degree of personal involvement in the marriage and parenthood roles.

INCOME

The question of the relationship between money and happiness has a certain fascination in our culture. Only a few would offer a simple answer—that everyone would be happy if he had enough money or that happiness is in no way dependent upon financial resources. Most Americans are probably ambivalent on this score; they would *like* to think they could be happy without money, but so many "good things in life" seem inaccessible without it. It is the ambivalence of the fox and the "sour grapes." This attempt to deprecate the importance of money while underneath feeling it to be important is reflected in many common adages which begin by suggesting the unimportance of money and end with a sardonic twist: "I've been poor, and I've been rich, and believe me—rich is better," or "Money can't buy happiness—but it helps."

It seems probable that the kind of relationship between income and contentment that an individual accepts as being a true one will affect any number of his other attitudes toward life and will help to shape his social, religious, and political ideologies. It was with a very broad and general interest, therefore, that we categorized respondents by income level and compared their responses to questions measuring feelings of adjustment. These relationships may have indirect bearing upon the kinds of economic considerations that should be included—or at least understood—in policy decisions aimed at alleviating psychological stresses in the population.

General Adjustment and Symptom Patterns

What does someone's economic condition have to do with the things that trouble him? Does the absence of financial security nurture a concern expressed by worrying? Is it related to the *kinds* of worries—particularly economic—that a person has? A direct connection between income and financial or material worries does not appear in our data (Table B.1). The relationship, rather, is curvilinear; those who mention financial worries most frequently fall into the *middle-income* range—from three to six thousand dollars annually. This finding seems to reflect the importance of aspirations as well as the actual economic situation. The low-income groups' relative lack of concern over material matters may reflect a lower aspiration level. Maximal concern over money is concentrated in the middle-income groups, where we would expect to find the highest concentrations of people with high aspirations not yet attained.

This explanation in terms of aspiration may also account for the fact that people earning higher incomes more often report job worries. These worries evidently are not related to economic instability of the job so much as to a general psychological investment usually demanded by occupations that offer high financial rewards.

An indication of an individual's general well-being may be inferred from reports on the extent of his worries and his happiness. However, these two estimates of well-being do *not* parallel each other exactly. Although income is related to both these variables—higher income is associated with fewer worries and greater happiness—we find that the degree of association is much stronger for the "happiness" measure than for the "worries" measure (Table B.1).

Another index of well-being is the individual's attitude toward the future. We find that people in higher-income brackets not only report greater present happiness than people with lower incomes but they also more frequently anticipate *increased* happiness in the future. The most optimistic of all groups are those in the middle-income range—the same groups, it will be recalled, who report the most extensive worries about financial matters. To the extent that these worries reflect the discrepancy between aspiration and attainment, as we have surmised, people in these groups appear to be hopeful of the possibilities for attainment in the future.

It appears that somehow the well-being attendant upon financial stability contributes more to positive feelings of happiness than it does to relative absence of worries. What is more, this well-being cannot simply be a function of feeling more economically secure, because although individuals with higher incomes worry less in general, there is *no* linear relationship between income and financial or economic worries, as we have already pointed out. To account for this lack of relationship and for the fact that income does not relate more highly to the absence of worries, we may again point to the possible effects of differential aspiration.

In Chapter II we saw that worrying indicates an aspiring, striving person who copes actively with life, trying to realize what he wants from it rather than resigning himself to whatever it brings him. This interpretation of worries stemmed especially from comparisons of the incidence of worries among various age groups. We concluded from these facts that younger respondents report more worries because they try to cope with problems they encounter, while older respondents, reporting fewer worries, are likely to have become resigned to a lower level of gratification. If to be worried, then, implies something more than a simple response to economic deprivation and its consequences, if it connotes an orientation toward personal fulfillment and gratification of ego needs, we may thus explain its minimal relationship to income level.

Respondents grouped by level of income show clear differences in reporting specific psychological, physical, and psychosomatic symptoms, as summarized in Table 8.1.

The findings in Table 8.1 present a pattern of both expected and somewhat unexpected results. The association between low income

Table 8.1—Summary Descriptions of Relationships between Symptom Factor Scores and Income Level: Men and Women

Symptom Factor Score	Men	Women
1. Psychological Anxiety	The highest scores are obtained by men with high and low incomes; the incidence of high scores decreases gradually as middle incomes are approached (Table B.2).	The nature of the relationship is the same as for men.
2. Physical Health	Low-income groups (under $3,000) have a high incidence of high scores; all other income levels show little variation (Table B.3).	There is a gradual decrease in the incidence of high scores as income increases.
3. Immobilization	There is a gradual increase of high and medium scores as income increases (Table B.4).	The nature of the relationship is the same as for men, although the association is not as strong.
4. Physical Anxiety	Very low income is associated with high scores; the lowest scores occur at middle-income levels (Table B.5).	There is a gradual decrease in the incidence of high scores as income increases.

and the physical expression of symptoms (Physical Health and Physical Anxiety) conforms to expectations about symptom expression in lower status groups. The findings with respect to Psychological Anxiety, however, are somewhat surprising. These symptoms appear more often in both income extremes, with the middle-income groups expressing the least Psychological Anxiety. It may be that Psychological Anxiety symptoms reflect blocking and consequent indirect expression of energy. In both high- and low-income groups, this blocking of energy and inability to find direct outlets may derive from an inability to give it direct expression in one's interaction with the world, specifically, in this instance, in efforts directed toward bringing about concrete environmental changes that have visible effects on one's status. For the economically deprived groups, this inability would spring from overwhelming environmental blocks; for the economically privileged group it would spring from the fact that many concrete aspirations were already fulfilled. Thus, under highly dissimilar conditions, these two groups may experience similar problems.

The relationships between income and Immobilization follow those reported with respect to education in the preceding chapter: the higher income groups, like the more educated, have higher scores on this factor. As we will note at a later point, the relationship with income disappears when education is controlled, so we may take this finding to be a reflection of education.

In summary, high income is associated with greater happiness, fewer worries, more frequent anticipation of future happiness, fewer physical symptoms, and more symptoms of energy immobilization. Low income implies current unhappiness and worries, a lack of confidence in the future, and the expression of anxiety through physical symptoms. Middle-income groups, who worry the most about money matters, are least likely to show symptoms of Psychological Anxiety and are most optimistic about the future.

Adjustment in the Marriage Role

How much does economic position contribute to the feelings of adjustment in a marriage? Is a person facing economic handicaps as happy in marriage as one who is free from economic pressures?

There is a clear relationship between high family income and feelings of happiness in marriage (Table B.6). Our two indices of marital distress, however, bear very little relationship to income level and, if anything, go in the other direction: feelings of inadequacy and the experience of problems in marriage are likely to be reported *more* frequently at higher income levels. The apparent paradox of greater happiness in marriage reported by the same group that most often reports problems and feelings of inadequacy has been discussed earlier. It has been interpreted as indicating a greater involvement in marriage, leading both to greater satisfaction in marriage and to a self-questioning that springs from greater expectations. A couple faced with economic privations is likely to direct its energy toward overcoming them or at least toward learning to "make do"; but these efforts may deplete their investment in the marital relationship itself, an investment which would have led both to efforts to achieve greater marital satisfaction and attempts to acknowledge and cope with personal problems or inadequacies.

Further evidence of this difference in involvement among income groups may be found in relationships between *sources* of inadequacy feelings and income. There is a high concentration of concern with economic provision among people with low incomes, but a focus on inadequacies manifest in the marital relationship (particularly those we coded "protective traits"—inconsiderateness, impatience, etc.) among those at the higher income levels (Table B.7). A similar distribution of emphasis is found in relationships between income level and sources of both current dissatisfactions and past problems in marriage.

Adjustment in the Parental Role

Income is one of the few demographic variables that shows any consistent relationship with indices of parental role adjustment, and even these relationships are of a very special variety. They do not exist between income and either the extent of inadequacy feelings as a parent or the frequency of reporting problems in raising children. They arise, rather, in reports of the *kinds* of problems and inadequacies mentioned by the parents.

Parents with low incomes emphasize concern with the provision of food, shelter, and other physical requirements as problems they have encountered in raising children and as the basis for feelings of inadequacy (Tables B.8 and B.9). Parents from high-income homes seem especially concerned with problems and their own inadequacies in the relationship aspects of parent-child interaction: how they get along with their children, whether they are understanding enough, show them enough attention, spend enough time with them. Evidently, financial security removes the concern over the basic parental responsibility of keeping a child physically comfortable, permitting the parent to shift toward more psychological aspects of the parent-child relationship. This interpretation parallels the one made above from similar information on adjustment to the marital role.

Adjustment in the Job Role

The picture that emerges in this area of life functioning is similar to the one we have seen before. Higher income level is associated with both greater job satisfaction and more frequent reports of job problems (Table B.10). In this realm, we have fairly direct evidence for the interpretation that this combination of greater satisfaction and greater experience of problems derives from a greater involvement in the role; for higher income is associated with more frequent mention of ego sources of both job satisfactions and dissatisfactions —that is, with the kinds of satisfactions and dissatisfactions we have interpreted as indicative of high personal involvement—and less frequent reports of extrinsic satisfaction and dissatisfaction. (If we merely had found that low-income respondents reported more extrinsic job *dissatisfactions*—mainly monetary dissatisfactions—we could not conclude that their personal involvement in their jobs was low, since they are in fact receiving few such monetary rewards. But they also more frequently report extrinsic sources of job *satisfaction* as well as job dissatisfaction; this is not in keeping with their low level of extrinsic rewards.)

That the higher income groups feel more adequate in the fulfillment of job responsibilities is consistent with other data reported in

Chapter VI. We saw there that the perception of job adequacy is connected to "objective" criteria—the job's status and its economic rewards—that do not exist for self-judgments of adequacy as a parent or spouse.

Income, Education, and Adjustment

In our review of the relationships between income level and adjustment in several areas of functioning, we have so far seen a great many indications of strong associations with measures of satisfaction, inadequacy, and problems, and the context in which these self-evaluations are made. This relationship pattern is very similar to that between educational level and these measures of feelings of adjustment. In view of the close association between income and educational level, it therefore seemed appropriate to investigate whether the relationships we have reported between income level and measures of adjustment can be explained by the relationship between income and educational level, i.e., to see whether these relationships remain when education is controlled.

To keep our education groups—grade school, high school, and college—large enough for analysis, we broke income into only two groups, close to the median income level: the "low" income group earns less than $5,000 a year, the "high" income group earns $5,000 a year or more. With these new groupings, we can re-explore some of the *linear* relationships existing with income level alone, keeping this question in mind: Do any of the previously reported differences between income levels disappear when education level is controlled? The results of the new analyses are summarized below.

1. GENERAL ADJUSTMENT AND SYMPTOM PATTERNS (TABLES B.12 AND B.13)

a) High- and low-income groups at each educational level still differ in their evaluations of current happiness: greater income is associated with greater happiness.

b) Low-income groups still show higher scores on the Physical Health symptom factor. This relationship is stronger for women than for men and is strongest for both men and women at the grade-school educational level.

c) Physical Anxiety symptom scores are related to income only for women when education is controlled; even this relationship is weak, with women from low-income groups reporting somewhat more symptoms than women from high-income groups.

d) Immobilization symptom scores are unrelated to income when education is controlled.

2. ADJUSTMENT IN THE MARITAL ROLE (TABLE B.14)

a) In evaluating the happiness of their marriages, high-income respondents at every educational level report happier marriages than low-income respondents. However, frequency of inadequacy feelings as a spouse and report of marriage problems do not relate to income when education is controlled.

b) The greater concern with economic inadequacies in low-income groups is most evident for people of grade-school education. Concern with housekeeping inadequacy—another noninterpersonal problem—differentiates low-income groups when education is controlled.

3. ADJUSTMENT IN THE PARENTAL ROLE (TABLE B.15)

Low-income parents still report more physical or material problems in raising children, and inadequacies in material provisions as a parent; they report few affiliative problems or inadequacies, especially if they are highly educated.

4. ADJUSTMENT IN THE OCCUPATIONAL ROLE
(TABLES B.16 AND B.17)

a) High-income groups report slightly more job satisfaction, and, among grade-school-educated men, slightly more job problems than lower-income groups. Reports of job adequacy are still decidedly higher for high-income groups, particularly among grade-school- and high-school-educated men.

b) High- and low-income groups still differ as to the context in which they judge job satisfactions when education is controlled;

in judging job dissatisfactions, only high-school-educated men differ according to income; both sets of differences have high-income groups showing more ego and fewer extrinsic sources of satisfaction and dissatisfaction.

In conclusion, we see that the low-income groups who experience some economic deprivation focus on the material aspects of their marriage, parenthood, or job in discussing both their positive or their negative feelings; the economic necessity consumes all their thoughts and energies. Interpersonal and personal sources of satisfaction assume prominence only when the basic material requisites for living are no longer in doubt, as in the economically comfortable groups. The relationship between income level and happiness has subtle elements; greater happiness stems not only from economic security but from the increased awareness of other than economic or material sources of gratifications when economic security is present.

OCCUPATION

In Chapter VI we discussed the relationships between occupational status and feelings of adjustment in the job area. But occupation is also a potential factor in a man's general adjustment to life, and his own adjustment, in turn, affects the adjustment of his family. The job has consequences for a man's relationships with others and his acceptance of himself. His job has a certain status in the community, provides opportunities for the fulfillment of physical and ego needs, and has considerable influence on the establishment of living patterns outside of the job setting. In classifying people according to their occupation, then, we are, in a rough sense, also classifying them along other social and behavioral dimensions as well—social status, opportunity for need fulfillment, impingement of the job on other aspects of living. We will draw on some of these latter implications of occupation in discussing the relationships presented in this section.

Because of the relationships between feelings of adjustment and

[224] PROBLEMS OF ADJUSTMENT

two other indices of social status—education and income—we expected to find some general over-all relationships between feelings of adjustment and the occupational categories viewed along a "quantitative" status dimension. This turned out to be true, but only to a minimal extent. The distinctions between "high" and "low" occupations are by no means as clear or consistent as those between high- and low-income or high- and low-education groups. In terms of the adjustment patterns we have measured in this study, the qualitative distinctions among the occupation categories seem to be at least as important as their differences along a quantitative status dimension. Any attempt to observe the influence of occupation in this area demands careful attention to each of the occupational categories.

Table 8.2 summarizes the findings that characterize the eight

Table 8.2—Summary Descriptions of Adjustment Patterns Peculiar to Various Occupational Groups

Husbands	Wives
Professional men and technicians have a more differentiated self-percept than any other group except the clerical workers (B.22). They are relatively high in their positive evaluations of their own marriages (B.28). At the same time, they are more likely than any other occupational group to recall inadequacies they have felt in carrying out their roles as spouse and parent (B.29 and B.33). Their pattern of symptoms is distinctive only in a relatively high incidence of Psychological Anxiety symptoms (B.24).	*Wives of professional men and technicians*, as part of a general relationship between high occupational status and happiness, report the highest level of general happiness (B.18). This group is more likely to perceive their husbands' jobs as interfering with their marital happiness than any other group except the wives of salesmen (B.32). They are quicker to admit to inadequacies they have felt in marriage and parenthood than many other groups (B.29 and B.33) and to attribute the source of past marital problems to themselves (B.31). Except for farmers' wives, they have the most negative self-image of all women (B.23). These women also report family health as a major source of worries more often than any of the other women do (B.21).
Managers and proprietors tend to speak about their jobs when general adjustment is discussed. A high proportion of this group worry about their jobs, as do salesmen and farmers (B.21). They also report, more than other groups, that their jobs interfere with their marriages (B.32). Their evaluations of their general happi-	*Wives of managers and proprietors* complain about their husbands' inadequacies in connection with marital unhappiness. They share this complaint with wives of unskilled workers (B.32). This group of women reports the lowest incidence of feelings of an imminent nervous breakdown (B.20).

Note: Numbers in parentheses refer to tables in Appendix B of the Tabular Supplement. The findings described are based on 738 men and 814 women.

Table 8.2—continued

Husbands

ness (B.18) and their happiness in marriage (B.28) are both high in relation to most other groups.

Along with other white-collar workers, these men are likely to recall feelings of inadequacy as a parent (B.33).

These men are more likely than any other occupational group to describe themselves as not different from other people (B.22).

Their symptom pattern is distinctive in the low frequency of high scores on the Immobilization factor (B.26).

Clerical workers seem to be most consciously depressed about the state of their lives. More than any other group, they report:
1. Greater general unhappiness (B.18).
2. Many worries (B.19).
3. Less strong happiness in their marriages (B.28).
4. Problems in their marriages (B.30).
5. Ambivalent self-images (B.23).

As sources of general worries, they are more likely to mention economic or material causes than other white-collar workers (B.21). As sources of problems in marriage, they are more likely than other groups to report troubles in the marriage relationship itself (B.31 and B.32).

They are among the lowest groups in reporting feelings of inadequacy as husbands (B.29), and as parents (B.33).

Salesmen, like managers, report high feelings of general happiness (B.18). They do, however (along with farmers), report a high incidence of feelings of an impending breakdown (B.20).

Like the manager-proprietor group, their sources of worry are frequently their jobs (B.21).

Like professional men, they report happy marriages on the one hand (B.28), and frequent feelings of inadequacy as husbands (B.29) and fathers (B.33) on the other.

Another similarity to professional men is their high report of Immobilization symptoms (B.26).

Skilled workers have few distinguishing characteristics except that they are the least likely to admit to having any worries at all

Wives

Wives of clerical workers, unlike their husbands, evaluate their marriages as happy—happier, indeed, than any other group but the wives of salesmen or professionals (B.28).

Like their husbands, however, they mention economic or material deprivations as sources of worry more often than other wives (B.21). This reason is also mentioned frequently as the source of past marriage problems (B.31) and of marital unhappiness (B.32).

They again are like their husbands in being one of the groups least likely to report feelings of inadequacy as a parent (B.33).

Wives of salesmen are distinctively high in their reports of happy marriages, making sales people an occupational group in which husbands and wives report similar levels of happiness (B.28).

These wives also report, like wives of professional men, that their husbands' jobs interfere with their marriages (B.32).

As sources of worry, these women mention the state of their family's health more frequently than almost any other group (B.21).

Wives of skilled workers do not stand out as distinctive in any way.

Table 8.2—continued

Husbands	Wives
(B.19) or to feelings of inadequacy as a spouse (B.29).	
Semiskilled workers have no distinguishing characteristics. Along with other blue-collar workers, they are not especially happy either in general (B.18) or in their marriages (B.28).	*Wives of semiskilled workers*, like the wives of unskilled workers and farmers, report relatively negative evaluations of their marital (B.28) and general (B.18) happiness. This group is also high in reported feelings of imminent nervous breakdowns, similar to the wives of unskilled workers (B.20).
Unskilled workers report more general unhappiness (B.18), and have a more negative self-image (B.23), than any other group. Unskilled workers cite their own inadequacies as providers and parents when discussing the negative aspects of their marriages (B.32) and emphasize material sources of past marriage problems (B.31). Along with farmers, they are high in their report of Physical Health symptoms (B.25).	*Wives of unskilled workers*, compared to other groups, feel unhappy in their marriages (B.28) and blame their husbands' inadequacies for this unhappiness (B.31 and B.32). More than any other group, they claim never to have felt inadequate themselves as wives (B.29) or mothers (B.33). Like their husbands, these women report more general unhappiness than other groups (B.18). Their sources of worries are more likely to be economic than they are for other groups (B.21). As previously noted, they feel as if they were going to have a nervous breakdown relatively frequently (B.20). They report fewer Immobilization symptoms than any other group (B.26).
Farmers are one of the least happy groups (B.18), and one of the groups with a high report of feelings of an imminent nervous breakdown (B.20). Like managers and sales personnel, they worry about their jobs more than other groups (B.21). Their self-image is the least differentiated (B.22) and the most negative (B.23) of any group. With unskilled workers, they are high in their report of Physical Health symptoms (B.25) and are distinctively high on Physical Anxiety symptoms (B.27). They are least likely of any group to report past problems in their marriages (B.30).	*Wives of farmers* report relatively unhappy marriages (B.28), but at the same time, like their husbands, are least likely to mention having had problems in their marriages (B.30). They attribute their marital unhappiness less often to relationship and more often to material sources than other groups (B.32). In contrast to their lack of feelings of inadequacy, they have a more negative self-image than any other group (B.23). They are relatively high on symptom scores, especially with respect to Psychological Anxiety (B.24, B.25, B.27).

occupational classifications and lists adjustment patterns peculiar to each. These summaries were based on Tables B.18 to B.33 in Appendix B of the Tabular Supplement. (In order to focus consistently on the impact of a man's occupation on himself and on his family, we have limited our analysis to married people only.)

There are some striking results when we look at the distinctive aspects of the occupational groupings. Certain occupational groups particularly stand out: for men, the clerical group, and for women, the wives of unskilled workers. Of all groups, these two seem to be experiencing the most heightened sense of unhappiness and discontent. Both of these seem to be groups with maximal frustrations and minimal avenues of expression.

A man with a clerical job engages in a particularly inactive, unmasculine activity. Considering the fact that there are few other men who share his position, a clerical worker can obtain little assurance of his masculinity. It is interesting to note that this group of men seems to be struggling with marriage as a crucial problem; perhaps the challenge to his masculinity on the job may be transferring to the challenge in his marriage. Since the wives of these men are happy in their marriages, it is possible that there is a personal, autistic basis for the disruption perceived by the men. This disruption may very well stem from the disquieting effect of his occupation on his perception of himself.

The wives of unskilled workers are perhaps the most deprived of all women. To realize that their husbands will probably always be at "the bottom of the barrel" in the occupational world may fill them with a pervasive sense of frustration. An additional difficulty for them is that their channels of expression are, for the most part, limited to their homes. At least their husbands have their jobs to provide another focus for their lives, although unskilled workers themselves also score at the low end of the happiness scale.

Although farmers' wives may also be thought of as an economically deprived group, their psychological deprivations may not be as great as those of unskilled workers' wives. The acquaintances of a farmer's wife are likely to be a homogeneous group, living in conditions very similar to her own. The wife of an unskilled worker, in contrast, is exposed to a good many opportunities for immediate social comparisons, from which she inevitably emerges feeling inferior.

Another finding which might be highlighted pertains to the higher frequency, for some occupations, of spontaneously mentioning the job itself in connection with general adjustment. The groups of men most likely to mention their jobs as a source of worries are managers, salesmen, and farmers. These three occupations have in common an entrepreneurial focus and a dimension of self-direction which doubtless make these occupations a more salient concern for the men who work at them.

That wives of both professional men and salesmen complain about the interference of their husbands' jobs with their marriages may reflect a realistic problem. Both groups of men may invest a good deal of time and energy in their work for purposes of self-fulfillment; their wives must adjust to the intense devotion professionals and salesmen are likely to lavish upon their jobs.

In general, these findings point to occupation as a variable significantly associated with adjustment patterns. However, the complex operation of this variable and the importance of the qualitative as well as quantitative status distinctions suggest the need for more intensive examination of this variable than was possible in a broad national survey. In this area, then, even more than in others, the caution about the suggestive rather than conclusive nature of the findings is particularly appropriate.

PLACE OF RESIDENCE

Any attempt to predict relationships between place of residence and feelings of adjustment raises questions of great complexity. Hypotheses abound, but they are derived from folklore as much as from systematic theoretical considerations. To a large extent, we are dealing in this area with stereotypes—the independent farmer, the anomic, driven city-dweller, the utopia of the small town, the frantic other-directedness of suburban life.

But, when we look at this variable systematically, it becomes apparent that place of residence is a complex of many dimensions, varying in their implications for relationships with our adjustment measures. Further complications are introduced by the fact that place of residence can be viewed not only as a situational determinant of adjustment but also as a reflection, or end-result, of various adjustments. Undoubtedly, some individuals have consciously selected a residential location compatible with previously formed personal preferences, whether by the decision to migrate to a metropolitan area, to remain on a farm or in a small town, to move to a small town, and so on. However, regardless of theoretical problems, place of residence represents a variable of particular descriptive interest in a national study of adjustment patterns.

The five residential groupings used in this analysis were:

1. Metropolitan areas (e.g., New York, Chicago, Los Angeles, etc.)
2. Suburbs of metropolitan areas.
3. Small cities (populations over 50,000).
4. Small towns (populations under 50,000).
5. Rural areas.

Of all the relationships examined, only four sets of findings suggested enough of a relationship for inclusion in tables, and these are far from striking (see Tables B.34 to B.37 in the Tabular Supplement). These tables indicate that people living in metropolitan areas seem to show different reactions from the other groups—particularly the rural—but these differences do not form any consistent pattern. In the area of general adjustment, people in metropolitan areas express more worrying and less happiness than do the other groups (Table B.34). But in the evaluation of marital adjustment (Table B.37) the relationships tend to go in the opposite direction, with people from metropolitan areas expressing greater happiness and fewer feelings of inadequacy.

There is a possibly interesting sex difference in the expression of symptoms. More Physical Health and Immobilization symptoms are reported by men in rural areas, whereas their female counterparts report more symptoms of Physical and Psychological Anxiety (Tables B.35 and B.36). Although this may be a chance difference, it may reflect a difference in the meaning attached to rural life by men and women—that men experience problems connected with the inhibition of work (either physically or psychologically) while rural women react to more generalized conflicts, expressed in physical or psychological anxiety.

All these differences are slight, however, and the general picture that emerges is one of minimal relationship between place of residence and the kinds of feelings of adjustment that we have measured. Furthermore, regional differences (South, Northeast, Midwest, Far West) also did not emerge in the data, whereas large differences were obtained with such variables as sex, age, education, and income. What seems to be crucial for feelings of adjustment are the kinds of demographic variables representing clear differences in life stages or concrete rewards and gratifications derived from life or clear cultural differences in expectations, demands, and gratifications sought from life. Regional distinctions and place-of-residence considerations apparently reflect such cultural and level-of-gratification differences minimally. In terms of the variables we have measured, a young, educated, male farmer is more like a young, educated, male New Yorker than either of these people is like his own father. Although cultural subgroupings based on geographic distinctions may have had meanings in the past, before the mass media and the transportation revolutions, they are probably becoming less critical today.

MARITAL STATUS

Living alone represents a psychological problem that is, for many adults in our society, the most stressful life situation they have to face. Single men and women, widows, widowers, and divorced persons all face the same problem in one form or another. Although certain aspects of solitary living probably have common effects on people in all these positions, it is likely that each of these "solitary" statuses also operates uniquely in some ways, producing differential effects on the adjustments of individuals. Therefore, we will examine generally what it means to be not married as opposed to married, and more specifically, what it means to be single rather than widowed or widowed as opposed to divorced or separated.

Although there is little organized theory or empirical background to fall back on for a definitive direction to the analysis of these problems, several aspects of the solitary statuses lead us to expect reports of unhappiness, distress, or anxiety among occupants of these roles.

The fact of being alone is itself probably the greatest source of stress. We have seen that interpersonal sources of gratification are associated with feelings of well-being. These gratifications are severely limited for people in our society who are not married, leading to frustration and feelings of loneliness.

Aside from the fact of being alone and its accompanying loneliness, not being married means the lack of an anchor point central to most people. Marriage not only is itself potentially gratifying but has ramifications in many other life areas. The unmarried individual occupies a position in society generally considered by social theorists as dysfunctional in the societal structure, a position that is out of step with the normative pattern of living. Furthermore, these atypical roles in society are not associated with clear requirements for behavior. In the case of married people, society has defined more clearly the ramifications of the demands attached to a position occupied by a majority of its adults. The roles for solitary statuses may be delineated more or less clearly, to some extent depending on how many people occupy each role, but the general lack of clarity of role requirements for the solitary statuses perhaps forces the role occupants to define their positions for themselves. We might expect this ambiguity to generate adjustment problems.

We have assumed that these minority positions, in addition to lacking clear role requirements, are undesirable positions which are not held voluntarily. The possibility exists, however, that members of two of these solitary groups may have deliberately, positively chosen their roles as being most compatible with their own desires. Some single people probably belong in this group, as well as others who have tried marriage, found the role unsatisfactory, and chosen to return to single status through divorce or separation. We can assume that in most cases, however, not being married is viewed as undesirable or, at best, the lesser of two evils, and that, even when desired, these people still have to grapple with problems of ambiguous role requirements.

We shall be interested, in our examinations of the data, in whether discomfort and distress are more prevalent among unmarried members of our society. We shall also be interested in differences among the various solitary statuses. The variability we may discover in responses from men and women in the different statuses may give us a clue as to which positions offer more accessible adjustment patterns.

Married vs. Unmarried Statuses

How do married men and women differ from individuals who are not married? The most striking finding is that married respondents report feeling happier than those who are unmarried, and the difference is a sharp one for both men and women (Table B.38). Moreover, from the reports of sources of happiness we find that marriage itself is the greatest source of happiness for 12 per cent of the married men and 16 per cent of the married women. Of course, this source of happiness is unavailable to unmarried respondents, but the very occurrence of these responses for the married group is noteworthy; apparently marriage is not taken completely for granted by married people.

In contrast, there is no parallel difference between married respondents and others on the reported amount of worrying; on the contrary, *fewer* married respondents report that they "never" worry. (This is especially clear for men.) Moreover, when we consider sources of worry or unhappiness, married men are more distressed about economic and material matters than any of the unmarried male groups (Table B.40). This difference is probably indicative of the greater responsibility attached to the married status.

Combined, these two sets of results suggest that married respondents' greater happiness can be interpreted as indicative of a greater involvement in their current lives—involvement expressed both as happiness and as a recognition of the responsibilities of marriage.

Anticipating some findings to be reported in Part Two, we note that married men and women more frequently turn to another person for help during unhappy periods (47 per cent of the married men and 37 per cent of the married women, contrasted with at most 20 per cent and 28 per cent of the men and women not currently married, gave this response). Since the spouse is named as the helpful person by a high percentage of married people, the differences between the two groups are not surprising. Nevertheless, there are many other possible outside sources of solace aside from a spouse, such as friends and relatives of all descriptions and levels of intimacy. When one considers the low percentage of unmarried respondents who depend upon *anyone* in times of stress, it seems clear that a close associate other than a marital partner is not considered as appropriate a resource for help as a spouse, and that other relationships cannot completely substitute for the marital one.

There are no other striking differences among the indices we have considered for married and unmarried groups. Variation in response to the symptom checklist was slight, as it was to the question of whether respondents had ever felt they were going to have a nervous breakdown, and the degree and extent of anticipated future happiness. Since questions about adjustment in the marriage and parental roles were asked only of those people presently married, we cannot compare the several marital statuses in these areas.

To recapitulate, the findings seem to reflect an emotional investment made by married people in the relationship with their spouses, an investment offering them general support and happiness as well as comfort during unhappy periods. At the same time, however, this investment may awaken concern, particularly about material problems which must be reasonably solved in order to fulfill the responsibilities of the relationship.

The Unmarried Statuses—Single

It appears that adjustments attendant to a single status are dramatically different for the sexes. Generally, single women apparently experience less discomfort than do single men; they report greater happiness, are more active in their working through of the problems they face, and appear in most ways stronger in meeting the challenges of their positions than men.

The specific differences found between single men and women are outlined below:

1. Single women are happier and worry more than single men.

This association of happiness and worries has occurred before and has been interpreted as indicative of a greater active involvement in one's life (Table B.38).

2. Single women report having experienced an approaching nervous breakdown less often than other women, whereas single men do not differ from other men in this respect. In fact, although there is in general a large difference between men and women in the experience of a nervous breakdown (women experiencing them more often), this difference is minimized when single men and single women are considered (Table B.38).

3. On the Immobilization factor score, we find that single women are slightly lower than single men, whereas for other marital statuses, women are considerably higher on this factor than men. Furthermore, single men score higher on this symptom factor than any other group of men; among women, it is the married people who report these symptoms most often (Table B.39).

These results were contrary to the popular stereotypes of the frustrated old maid and the free and unencumbered bachelor life, and we suspected some further source of difference between the single men and single women in our sample. One possibility was that the men were older and that older men are more demoralized than younger men (or women). We did find a fairly strong age difference between the two groups, but the difference is that single men tend to be somewhat *younger* than single women: 53 per cent of the single men were under thirty-five years of age, and only 37 per cent of the single women were this young. This was surprising because this age difference would lead one to expect differences in the opposite direction from those actually obtained. For example, younger people worry more and are slightly more happy than older people; yet single men, although younger, are *less* happy and worry *less* than single women.

One exception, where the age bias may indeed be operating, is the Immobilization factor score. Single women checked fewer Immobilization responses than did single men; this follows the finding that older respondents score lower on the Immobilization symptom factor than do younger respondents. In this instance, therefore, it is possible that single status and age are confounded to produce the results.

In terms of the stereotype of single men and women, one other differentiation is often made. Women are seen as more able to form or to maintain other than marital attachments; their ties to the family and friends can be very strong. The story of the single aunt who assumes the role of a doting mother-figure to her nieces and nephews is not uncommon. For a single man, however, in addition to the stereotype stressing freedom and independence, there is also the picture of the lonely, anomic, rootless man, living out his life in single rooms. Perhaps it is in an ability to form and maintain meaningful personal attachments that we may find a clue to these differences we have seen—that single women are less distressed than single men.

The Unmarried Statuses—Divorced or Separated

Divorce or separation—the disrupted marriage, whether voluntary or involuntary—may be considered a reflection of the defective adjustments of the marital partners. The social consequences of divorce or separation can also create problems in those social groups where divorce is not condoned. The problem presented to the individual's adjustment by this situation is further complicated by another factor that applies to widows as well: the married status, with its accompanying role requirements, has been experienced, and a change to a solitary status involves the removal of what was a central anchor and identity focus.

Comparing the effects of divorce or separation on men and women, we find noticeably different reactions for the two sexes, and, for women, reactions different from the other solitary statuses (Tables B.38 and B.39).

1. Divorced or separated women report worrying "all the time" much more frequently than the men in the corresponding groups; they share with widows the highest frequency for this response. Although they are only slightly less happy than men in the same

position, for all other marital status groups women are happier than men.

2. Divorced or separated women report having felt an impending nervous breakdown more often than their male counterparts and more often than any other group, male or female. This is in keeping with the general pattern of the experience of a nervous breakdown —where "external, situational pressures" are seen as causal.

3. Divorced or separated women score higher on the Immobilization symptom factor than divorced or separated men.

4. Optimism about the future is characteristic of divorced or separated women: 63 per cent of this group think that their future will be "happier" or "much happier," as contrasted to the next most optimistic group, married women, of whom only 45 per cent give a similar report.

To summarize, divorce seems to affect the adjustment of women more than it does the adjustment of men; women experience more disruption, more distress in their lives after a breakup of a marriage. Why should this be so? One reason probably lies in the relative remarriageability of divorced men and women. In looking again for a husband, the divorced woman is often tied down by her children. Her age is a further handicap, more so than for her male counterpart in view of the cultural tendency for men to be older than their wives. Yet what appears to be a bad situation has a note of apparent hopefulness reflected in the divorced woman's optimism about her future happiness.

The Unmarried Statuses—Widows and Widowers

The final solitary status, confronting many more women than men in our society, is loss of a spouse through death. The poignant position of having once experienced a comfortable adjustment in marriage and then facing the problem of living alone—for the most part, in late middle or old age—may change one's perspective on life adjustment. Does widowhood have such an effect?

Widows and widowers are different from other marital statuses and from each other in the following ways (Tables B.38 and B.39):

1. Both widows and widowers say they worry "all the time" more

frequently than any other group but the divorced or separated women, with widows reporting this even more often than widowers.

2. Again with the exception of divorced or separated women, widows and widowers are unusually low in their feelings of present happiness. This is especially true of widowers.

3. Widows and widowers are most pessimistic, with more anticipation of unhappiness and death in the near future than any other group. This, too, is especially true of widowers.

4. Widows and widowers have the lowest scores on the Immobilization symptom factor, with widowers scoring lowest of all.

Because the widowed groups are definitely among the oldest in the population, how many of the above findings can be attributed to age discrepancies? To control for age, we chose a sample of married men and women from the age groups where most of the widows and widowers are concentrated. Since all but a few widowers were fifty-five or more, our comparable group of married men was also fifty-five or more. The widows were a considerably larger group, but almost all of them fell into age categories of forty or more; we therefore set up three age divisions for widows and married women (forty to forty-nine; fifty to fifty-nine; and sixty or over) and made three sets of comparisons in examining the differences between these groups.

These comparisons between married and widowed people of the same ages indicated that age did seem to account for some of the above results. Several previous differences between widows and married women disappeared when age was controlled; but most differences remained, at least for some of the comparisons. Thus, worrying "all the time" is not peculiar to widows between forty and fifty, but does remain a characteristic of the other widow and widower groups; widows and widowers do not differ from married men and women of the same ages in their anticipation of unhappiness, but their anticipation of death remains greater, and the rest of the results reported above remain the same.

In summary, then, widows and widowers are more unhappy, worry more, anticipate death in the near future, and report fewer Immobilization symptoms than married people of the same ages.

The picture of the widowed status is a bleak one; with divorce, it seems to be the solitary status which holds the greatest threat to positive adjustment.

We may end by saying that the unmarried state is generally associated with feelings of unhappiness. But certain of these solitary statuses seem to express more distress than others: the widowed group—the only clearly *non-voluntary* solitary status—reports particularly intense feelings of distress, both in the present and in anticipations of the future; single men seem to experience more difficulty and come to a less satisfactory adjustment than single women; but divorce or separation seems to be more trying for women, although they do maintain hopeful expectations for the future.

RELIGION AND CHURCH ATTENDANCE

Religion can affect adjustment in many ways: it may provide a system of values by which one's life goals and expectations can be set and one's behavior judged; it can provide solace in times of distress, both by making specific resources available to members of church groups and by strengthening personal resources through an internalized set of religious beliefs. The numerous ways that religion can affect life functioning may range in intensity from being focal points in a person's life to playing quite subsidiary roles.

In this section we will consider two sets of questions about the role of religion: (1) Do differences in frequency of church attendance relate to feelings of adjustment? (2) Are there differences between the two major religious groups in America, Protestants and Catholics, in their adjustment patterns? In addition, we will be concerned with the interaction of these two variables—religion and frequency of church attendance—in their relationships to indices of adjustment.

It should be pointed out that the frequency of church attendance is an index that defines how "religious" a person is in terms of formal, institutionalized activities only. Although this is certainly only one of many possible definitions, it has many virtues: it is easily obtainable in a national survey; it is a dimension by which members of any religious group in America can be rated; and it is probably indicative of other aspects of religious involvement, such as intensity of belief in religious teachings or perceptions of the importance of religion for everyday life, both of which should, ideally, be included in an evaluation of how religious a person is.

We would expect that if religion is a positive force in feelings of adjustment, those people who attend church more frequently will experience the least distress. Furthermore, if religious group membership affects adjustment because of the kinds of beliefs and ideologies it nurtures, we not only expect differences between Protestants and Catholics generally, but we also expect that the greatest effects will occur among the most religious Protestants and Catholics, making these groups markedly different from each other, while nonreligious—that is, nonchurchgoing—Protestants and Catholics will be affected least and therefore will be most alike.

We are primarily interested in determining what role religion per se plays in the lives of our respondents, but differences between members of the two large religious groups interest us for other reasons. Even without the support of much systematic theory on the effects of religious group membership on feelings of adjustment, there are some ways in which Protestants and Catholics might be anticipated to differ: the Catholic position on the permanence of the marriage relationship may be particularly relevant to adjustment in the marital and parental roles; the Protestant Ethic may have a unique impact upon adjustment in the occupational role; the institution of the confessional in Catholicism may have special relevance for self-blame, self-doubts, and feelings of inadequacy.

In addition to differences of religious ideology and institutions, Protestants and Catholics have also been found to differ in social characteristics: Catholics, for example, tend to come from the urban areas, and different occupational groups. They are more likely to be recent immigrants, and are a minority group. Indeed, it is these kinds of social, rather than "religious," characteristics that have been linked with such social behavior as voting patterns and preferences.

We may therefore add another dimension to our investigation by recognizing the existence of Protestants and Catholics as two important subcultures in American society.

In presenting our findings, we will discuss the implications of church attendance for Protestants and Catholics separately, contrasting the responses of different church-attending groups within each of the two religious membership categories. We will also point out implications of religious group affiliations for persons at the same level of church attendance, e.g., by comparing Catholics and Protestants who attend church once a week.[1] Variations in church attendance have been categorized into those groups who attend church more than once a week, once a week, a few times a month, a few times a year, and never. Since only nineteen Catholic respondents reported that they never attended church, we excluded them from the analysis as being too small a group for practical use. Respondents whose religious preferences were Jewish (91 people) or other religions (21 people) or who disclaimed any association with the church at all (56 people) were likewise excluded from all analyses.

General Adjustment and Symptom Patterns

Looking first at the influence of church attendance, we see that it does not produce any major variations within our indices of general adjustment. Small differences do occur among measures of extent of worries, extent of happiness, and feelings of having had a nervous breakdown (Table B.41). For Catholics, infrequent church attendance—a few times a month or a few times a year—is accompanied by more worries, less happiness, and higher incidence of feelings of an approaching nervous breakdown; for Protestants, infrequent or complete lack of church attendance is associated with greater unhappiness. It appears that low church attendance, especially among Catholics, is associated with a higher level of felt distress, although we cannot tell whether it is a symptom of such distress or one of its determinants.

Interestingly enough, this distress is not always translated into specific symptoms. Low church-attenders among women tend to show high symptom scores, but for men, although the over-all relationship between church attendance and symptom scores is similar to that for women, it shows highly erratic features (Tables B.44 and B.45).

In addition to indications that infrequent churchgoers give negative evaluations of their general adjustment, we find a tendency for this group to have more negative perceptions of themselves (Table B.43). This tendency is more evident for Protestants.

Turning now to the question of Catholic-Protestant differences, we again find only minimal differences. The general tendency for Protestants to worry less often and to feel happier than Catholics is offset by their greater reports of feelings of imminent nervous breakdowns than Catholics (Table B.41). No consistent differences emerge for women on symptom factor scores (Table B.44); for men, the only consistent pattern is on the Physical Anxiety symptom factor score, on which Catholics score lower than Protestants (Table B.45). As for self-perceptions, Protestants have more differentiated self-images than Catholics (Table B.42), but do not differ from Catholics in degree of self-acceptance (Table B.43).

Adjustment in the Marriage Role

The most striking relationship in this area is between frequency of church attendance and degree of marital happiness (Table B.46). The more frequent church-attenders, both Protestants and Catholics, report happier marriages than less frequent attenders. As with the responses to the question asking for a respondent's evaluation of his *general* happiness, those who report extreme marital unhappiness are the Protestants who never attend church and the Catholics who attend church only a few times a year. It is interesting that church attendance has more striking relationships with marital happiness than with general happiness; this offers support to notions of the special relevance of religion to stability of marriage and the home.

Reports of inadequacy feelings in marriage show, rather than a general relationship like that between church attendance and evaluation of marital happiness, an interaction between religion and church attendance (Table B.46). For Catholics, frequent church attendance is accompanied by fewer feelings of inadequacy as a spouse; for Protestants there is no relationship between church attendance and frequency of felt inadequacy. (We shall return to this finding a little later in the discussion.) The third index of felt marital distress, reports of problems in marriage, is unrelated either to religious group membership or to frequency of church attendance.

A context question strongly related to frequency of church attendance is the inquiry into sources of marital happiness, in the responses to which we find an interesting connection between attendance and locating marital happiness in the relationship with the spouse; frequent Protestant churchgoers are *more* likely to mention relationship sources of happiness than infrequent church-attenders of the same group; for Catholics, frequent church attendance is associated with relatively *low* mention of relationship sources of happiness and high mention of external sources (mainly children) (Table B.46). Other context measures—kinds of problems encountered in marriage, sources of inadequacy feelings—show similar trends.

Turning now from a consideration of church attendance to the question of Catholic-Protestant differences, we again find relationships with marital adjustment measures which are more striking than those obtained with general adjustment. The differences do not derive from religious affiliation alone but are tied to the interaction between such affiliation and church attendance. Regular churchgoing Catholics evaluate their marriages as happier than, or as happy as, regular churchgoing Protestants do, but Protestants who are infrequent churchgoers report greater happiness than Catholics who have the same attendance habits.

Furthermore, the context for judging marital happiness differs for Catholics and Protestants. Except for the group who attend church only a few times a year, Protestants are more likely to mention relationship sources of happiness in marriage and less likely to mention external sources. We find the greatest differences between Protestants and Catholics among the most frequent church-attenders since churchgoing Protestants are the most likely Protestants to dwell on the happiness of their relationships with their spouses, while churchgoing Catholics are the least likely Catholics to do so. As we have noted, churchgoing Catholics focus particularly on external sources of marital happiness.

Let us look more closely at our results, noting first what kinds of responses are coded as external sources of marital happiness. Included in this category are: having a nice house or home, economic security and other situational advantages, and children. The latter response accounts for the bulk of all Catholic replies coded external; for example, a total of 39 per cent of the Catholics who attend church more than once a week mentioned external sources of happiness, and this included 26 per cent of the whole group who specifically mentioned children. It is reasonable to speculate that this tendency is tied to a theological doctrine of Catholicism which does not influence Protestants: Catholic teachings stress the importance of children and the family, the sanctity of the reproductive function, and the sin of using artificial birth control mechanisms. It should therefore not be surprising that the more religious Catholics look upon child-raising and children as very happy, rewarding aspects of marriage.

An interesting complement to other data is presented in comparisons of inadequacy feelings in marriage according to religious affiliation. At all levels of church attendance, Catholics are less likely to report these feelings than Protestants, with the greatest difference between the groups appearing among the regular churchgoers. This finding is surprising when considered in the light of our findings in Chapter IV that highly educated respondents are *more* likely to experience inadequacy feelings as marital partners; for Catholics who attend church most often—more than once a week—are more highly educated than Protestants of the same degree of religiousness. This is a case where religious teachings clearly seem to supersede the ordinary effects of extensive education.

The interpretation of these findings depends upon an assumption about the psychological function of Protestantism as opposed to Catholicism. The formalism of the Catholic religion contrasts with the generally more individualistic Protestantism. It has often been suggested that relatively inflexible formal doctrines offer greater potential for alleviating guilt. If that is so, Catholics may feel inadequate as marital partners less often than Protestants because their religious ideology affords them more opportunity to alleviate any individual guilt they might otherwise have felt. This interpretation is strengthened by adding the fact that Catholics vary in their expression of inadequacy according to their church attendance, with Catholics who attend church most often—presumably having greater opportunities for guilt alleviation—experiencing inadequacy less frequently than less regular churchgoers.

Adjustment in the Parental Role

As in our measures of marital adjustment, reports of problems in raising children are related neither to religiousness nor religious group membership, while feelings of inadequacy are related to both variables. At every church-attendance level, we find that Catholics feel less inadequate than Protestants. Also, as before, more frequent church attendance among Catholics is associated with fewer feelings of inadequacy (Table B.47), whereas for Protestants increased church attendance does not bring fewer inadequacy feelings. As a matter of fact, the relationship in the case of parental inadequacy goes in the opposite direction: the more religious Protestants report *more* feelings of inadequacy.

Adjustment in the Job Role

The picture of frequent churchgoers as happier than other groups, which seems to be emerging from our data, is further substantiated by findings in the job realm. For both Protestant and Catholic employed men, and especially so in the latter, more frequent church attendance is related to greater job satisfaction (Table B.48). There are also differences between Catholics and Protestants. For all groups except the most frequent church attenders, Protestants express greater job satisfaction than Catholics. In addition, except for infrequent church attenders, Protestants indicate having experienced more problems on the job than Catholics, a report we have interpreted, as before, as an indication of greater involvement with the job.

How may we summarize these findings on religion and adjustment? The highlights of the findings on church attendance present a fairly clear picture: low church attendance is associated with a somewhat higher level of distress in the general adjustment measures, a more negative self-percept, less happiness on the job, and strikingly less marital happiness.

No such over-all differences exist between Catholics and Protestants, that is, when church attendance is controlled. (Since Catholics attend church much more frequently, all Catholics and all Protestants should show differences that reflect some of the differences obtained with respect to church attendance.) What seems to obtain, instead, are meaningful differences in the areas on which Catholics and Protestants focus: The Catholic focus on children as a source of marital happiness and the Protestant focus on the marital relationship itself conforms to the great emphasis of Catholicism on the home and family. The Protestants' possibly greater involvement in the job may reflect a Protestant focus on achievement stemming from the Protestant Ethic. And finally, the Catholics' fewer feelings of inadequacy in marriage and as parents may reflect the differential mechanisms provided by the two religions for the handling and alleviation of guilt.

The interactive effects of church attendance and religious group membership serve mainly to accentuate the general Catholic-Protestant differences in the higher church-attending groups, especially with respect to the findings that the Catholics focus more on the children rather than the marital relationship, and that Protestants experience greater feelings of inadequacy in the marital and parental roles.

Some of these findings might be reflections of non-religious aspects of religious affiliation and attendance. Catholics and Protestants differ in urbanization, ethnicity, recency of immigration, majority-minority status as well as ideologically. Church attendance not only is a measure of religious commitment but reflects a person's social integration into the community. These factors should be systematically considered in any intensive exploration of the influence of religion on adjustment patterns.

BROKEN HOME BACKGROUND

It is a common notion—supported partially by clinical observation—that divorce, parental separation, and parental death can have serious consequences for the later adjustment of children from such disrupted homes. We have gathered data on the incidence of broken-home backgrounds which can contribute to the substantiation or refutation of this notion; our study provides the possibilities for a natural experiment. We grouped respondents into three categories: 1915 who did not come from a broken home, 123 who were separated from at least one of their parents through divorce, and 315 who experienced separation through the death of one or both parents. Thus, we may test the general effects of disruption and the special effects of disruption by divorce upon the later adjustment of those who had these experiences as children.

General Adjustment and Symptom Patterns

On the indices of general adjustment, there are surprisingly few differences among the three groups. In particular, growing up in a home disorganized by the death of a parent does not seem to have any special bearing on the experiences of general adjustment. People who were raised in homes in which parents were divorced or separated, however, are distinctive in some respects (Table B.49). For example, proportionately more of the respondents with divorced parents admit to being not too happy; 17 per cent of this group give this response to evaluation of present happiness, compared to only 12 per cent of respondents whose parents died when they were young and 11 per cent of those whose families were intact. Furthermore, 26 per cent of the people with divorced parents mention interpersonal situations as current sources of unhappiness, while only 18 per cent and 15 per cent, respectively, of the other two groups respond similarly. Finally, while only 20 per cent of those separated from their parents by death and 18 per cent of those never separated at all report feelings of having had a nervous breakdown, 31 per cent of the group whose parents were divorced report the same feelings. Another sign of the special effects of coming from a divorce-broken home is the less positive self-percept of these people (Table B.50).

Are these indications of greater psychological distress in people from disrupted home backgrounds reflected in their symptom patterns? Because of the small number of people from disrupted homes in our sample, and because of the necessity to maintain separate analyses of symptom factor scores for men and women, we cannot give a definitive answer to this question. However, for women, among the 83 who come from divorce-broken homes and the 206 who come from death-disrupted homes, there are indications of greater Physical Anxiety, Psychological Anxiety, and Immobilization symptoms (Table B.51). Interestingly enough, only the Physical Health symptom score, which is least directly involved with psychological distress, is unrelated to the nature of the respondents' home background.

We can see, then, that those who come from disrupted homes, particularly homes broken by parental divorce or separation, are likely to experience greater distress and more symptoms. These relationships are, however, minimal, except for the report of having had a nervous breakdown.

Adjustment in the Marriage Role

Does having come from a home broken by divorce or separation have an effect on later marital adjustment? Does early contact with disruption in the marriage of one's parents affect the adjustment a person later makes to his or her own marriage?

There are consistent though not always strikingly large relationships between home background and stability of the respondents' own marriages (Table B.52). While 15 per cent of the people from broken homes are currently divorced or separated from their spouses, only 5 per cent of the people from intact homes and 9 per cent of the people from homes disrupted by death are currently divorced. There are differences as well among marital patterns of those who are presently married: people from divorce-broken homes are distinctive in that 19 per cent of them, as compared to 14 per cent of the group from death-disrupted homes and 8 per cent of the group from unbroken homes, have been married and divorced prior to their current marriages.

Among currently married people, only slight differences show up among the three groups in evaluation of marital happiness, but people from broken homes are least happy. Consistent with this difference, however, are the more frequent admissions of problems and inadequacy feelings in marriage: 68 per cent of the persons from divorce-broken homes admit to some feelings of inadequacy as a spouse, contrasted to 52 per cent and 53 per cent for the other two groups; 60 per cent of those from divorce-broken homes have had some problem in marriage, contrasted to 40 per cent of the other two groups (Table B.53).

It seems clear, from this evidence, that respondents coming from broken homes have a great deal at stake in their marriages. Admission to feelings of inadequacy and the occurrence of problems are reports which we consider indicative of a high level of personal involvement in the marriage role. Nor is it surprising that people who have experienced marital discord in their youth are particularly sensitive to any signs of it within their own marriages.

It is particularly interesting that people from divorce-broken homes not only experience more problems and inadequacy in marriage, but also tend to be less happy. We have seen before that the report of problems in marriage and the evaluation of marital happiness do not necessarily relate in the same ways to social characteristics: young people are not less happy, yet they report more feelings of inadequacy and more problems than older people; highly educated respondents are happier, yet feel more inadequate in marriage than less educated respondents. In these cases, reported feelings of inadequacy and problems seem concomitant with a general commitment to marriage that may produce, under favorable conditions, greater marital happiness. But in cases where great involvement in marriage is accompanied by *serious* reasons for concern about its success—such as previous failures in marriage by one's parents and/or by oneself—we would expect to find problems and inadequacy associated with *less* marital happiness.

A further indication that respondents from broken homes face marital problems of a serious nature may be seen in their proportionately greater tendencies to name their children as the most positive aspect of their marriages, and to mention the marital relationship less frequently than others do (Table B.53). The most central aspect of marriage is generally considered to be the relationship with the spouse; that this is not as satisfying for these people as the fact of having children may reflect either some weakness in the marriage relationship or some special significance attached to the children. It is possible that these people are unusually involved in their children, overreacting to the parental desertion in their own background. However, there are no indications of such unusual involvement from replies to questions dealing directly with their roles as parents; therefore, acknowledging children as the most positive aspect of their marriages is probably indicative of a defect in the relationship with the marriage partner, although some kind of strong involvement in the parent-child relationship is not impossible.

Two points stand out in these configurations of relationships. Persons from intact homes experience less general distress, greater marital stability, and fewer marital difficulties than persons from disrupted homes; and a home disrupted by divorce or separation has more evident effects than a home in which disruption has been caused by the death of one or both parents.

The similarity of the responses of people whose parents died while they were growing up to those of respondents coming from intact homes suggests that the effect of a broken home is more related to the nature of the disruption than to the fact of disruption. Divorce or separation implies that the failure of the parents' marital relationship was emphasized during the respondents' early experiences; death of a parent does not have this direct implication. Although any kind of separation deprives a child of having both parents available as models for the marriage relationship, this does not, in itself, seem crucial, as we examine the relationship between feelings of adjustment and early experiences in the home. It is the disturbed and disorganized marriage relationship, with all its potential effects on a growing child's development, that seems to be the critical factor for this later adjustment.

That coming from a disrupted home has its greatest effects on the marriage relationship itself is therefore not surprising. Personality theorists would probably predict that such a background would have lasting effects on an individual's adaptations to interpersonal interaction; some might posit that witnessing the breakup of their parents' marriage affects the child's expectations about the rewards of intimate interpersonal relationships, while others might suggest that this experience affected the development of the child's personality in a way that has serious implications for the kinds of reactions other people have to him. From either point of view, we can conclude, from our limited sample of people from divorce-broken homes, that there is substantiation of the notion that these early experiences can have important effects upon later adjustments, particularly in the marriage relationship itself.

SUMMARY

This chapter summarizes the findings relevant to the major purpose of Part One—the description of experiences of adjustment and distress among significant subgroups of the national population.

In reviewing the mass of data summarized in this chapter, and comparing the patterns of relationships obtained, the demographic variables seem to differ in two general ways: (1) in the *extent* of their relationships with adjustment experiences, some being critically related to these feelings, others having only negligible relevance; and (2) in their relationships with different *kinds* of adjustment experiences, each subgroup tending to express well-being and distress in particular, characteristic ways.

Two sets of factors seem to be important in differentiating those demographic variables that show extensive relationships with the adjustment measures—sex, age, education, income, marital status—from demographic variables that seem to have little relevance for adjustment. First of all, demographic variables seem to be important in this study when they differentiate population subgroups in terms of the potential rewards and gratifications derived from life, as in the findings on the greater satisfaction of the higher-income and married groups and some of the differences obtained in relation to education, age, and sex. And secondly, they are important when they represent differences in the expectations and demands that the subgroup members make of themselves and life, or differences in introspectiveness and tendencies toward a psychological view of life and the problems it presents. These differences in attitudes and orientations would seem to underlie the sex and education differences we have observed, and to explain to some extent the differences found with respect to age. Those demographic variables that showed little relationship to adjustment—particularly the rural-urban dimension and regional differences—apparently reflect these two sets of factors only minimally.

The question of the demographic variations in the *ways* in which distress and well-being are expressed is important in all but the sex comparisons. Here we could make the generalized statement that women express more distress than men in all the areas of adjustment and on all types of questions explored in this study. But, for the other demographic variables one must specify the area and the particular aspect of adjustment measured.

In attempting to explain these *varying* patterns of adjustment, we have stressed the distinction between the meaning of a demographic variable in terms of gratification-potential and its meaning in terms of involvement and aspirations. This was especially true in the numerous instances where demographic relationships involving happiness and satisfaction did not parallel relationships with worrying, problems, and feelings of inadequacy. The greater satisfaction but greater feeling of inadequacy of the higher educated groups was interpreted in terms of the higher aspirations and greater potential for gratification that come with higher education; the lower feelings of problems and inadequacy, but no greater satisfaction, among the older-aged groups were seen as reflecting the minimization of aspirations and lowering of potential for gratification that comes with increasing age; and so on. We have also given special attention to the meaning of the demographic variables as reflections of differing subcultural emphases on introspectiveness and a psychological as opposed to external or physical approach to problems, looking particularly at some of the age, sex, and education differences in these terms.

That different subgroups of the population differ not so much in "better" or "worse" adjustment as they do in the particular ways in which they experience gratification and adjustment problems raises certain problems if we attempt to make some summary over-all judgment about the adjustment in a group: such a judgment would tend to vary according to the criteria used. This does not mean that if criteria of severe pathology and psychiatric diagnoses were used it would be impossible to differentiate subgroups of the population along some single mental health-mental illness dimension. But in talking of the general population, and dealing with subjective evaluations and experiences of problems within the normal range, it would seem to be more accurate to think in terms of multiple criteria for describing the adjustment patterns as they vary in the population subgroups.

The major purpose of the demographic analysis presented in Part One has been descriptive. But, throughout the discussion of the results we have also been interested in pointing up some of their broader meanings and have drawn implications for etiological hypotheses, cultural and historical trends, mental health definitions, and help-seeking behavior. We will return to some of these implications in Part Two, looking first in Chapter IX at what the data we have examined mean for the help-seeking process.

NOTE

1. The tables in Appendix B of the Tabular Supplement present degree of church attendance within different religious groups rather than the church attendance and Catholic-Protestant differences separately, because religion and church attendance are closely related to each other. In our sample of 542 Catholics, 81 per cent attend church once a week or more, but only 40 per cent of our sample of 1745 Protestants report a similar attendance record. If this had not been done, the high attenders would have a disproportionate number of Catholics, and any relationships obtained between church attendance and adjustment could reflect the effect of either church attendance or Catholic-Protestant membership.

PART TWO

Solving Problems of Adjustment

IX

The Readiness for Self-Referral

Do UNHAPPINESS, worrying, inadequacy, and Psychological Anxiety all lead equally to self-referral? Or do different ways of expressing distress have different implications for help-seeking behavior? Do men and women, old people and young people, highly educated and less educated groups make equal use of professional help resources? One of the major objectives of this study is to answer these questions and assess the distribution of the actual and potential use of professional resources.

In this chapter, we will consider the relationships of the readiness for self-referral to the subjective adjustment indices and the demographic variables examined in Part One. Those adjustment indices that are related to self-referral have implications as self-diagnostic signs that lead a person to therapy. These adjustment indices can also be used as "intervening variables" in an explanatory chain that links demographic variables to subjective adjustment indices, and these in turn to readiness for self-referral. If we find demographic subgroups that are both high in the use of professional resources and high in certain ways of expressing distress, and furthermore, if these particular ways of expressing distress are in turn highly related to the use of professional resources, the use of professional help in these subgroups of the population may be understood in terms of the tendencies of these people to express distress in ways that are maximally relevant for the use of such resources. In this manner we can illuminate both the potential psychological meanings of the relationships between demographic characteristics and the readiness to use professional help and the meaningfulness of the various subjective adjustment indices.

Before turning to a consideration of these analyses, let us examine some of the problems involved in attempting to conceptualize and measure readiness for self-referral. These problems are of special interest, because they bear on broader questions in the general area of public attitudes toward mental health.

MEASURING READINESS FOR SELF-REFERRAL

In attempting to measure the readiness for self-referral, we are, in a sense, concerned with people's general acceptance of psychiatry and the psychiatric view that mental health problems are illnesses rather than defects of character, and should be referred to specialized professional resources for treatment. However, one of the main problems in measuring the readiness for self-referral is manifest in the research previously done in this general area: that intellectual acceptance must be distinguished from personal or emotional acceptance. There is a distinction between the readiness of people to accept a psychiatric point of view as they take an objective, dispassionate view of the question of mental health in general and their readiness to look at *themselves* and some of their *own* problems within such a framework.

Other studies have noted that people seem to be much more ready to accept intellectually the idea that professional help is an appropriate channel for the solution of emotional problems than they are willing to admit the need for seeking such help for their own problems or the problems of people close to them. This conclusion was probably most dramatically suggested by the work of Clausen and his group in their study of the wives of hospitalized patients. They pointed out that women who verbalized all the current notions about mental illness—that mental illness is just like any other illness and calls for the use of specialized professional help—were unwilling to apply this notion to their husbands, even in the face of the most bizarre symptom behavior. Terming this a distinction between "beliefs" and "attitudes," they note that "changes in attitudes toward mental disorders and toward obtaining help with emotional problems do not necessarily follow changed beliefs" (Clausen and Yarrow, 1955, p. 63).

Such findings seem to suggest that people's reactions in this area are still in a process of adjustment between the increasingly popular view that emotional problems represent an illness and older notions that stigmatize these problems as symptoms of personal inadequacy and weakness. These older conceptions, though increasingly rejected intellectually in accordance with the spirit of the times, still operate at a deeper level, so that the idea of going for personal help is still structured as a personal threat and rejected as unacceptable. It might be interesting to speculate how temporary or permanent this process of adjustment is—whether what we are witnessing here is a process typical of the introduction and acceptance of any new ideology, where superficial conformance always tends to precede true interiorization and integration, or whether the peculiarly psychological threats in the mental health area will always induce a personal reluctance in spite of an intellectual acceptance.

What are the implications of these comments as we approach the task of measuring personal acceptance? Measuring what people "really" feel in an area where intellectualized attitudes obscure underlying feelings is always a problem. However, there is an added complication in this particular context, because of the nature of the factors that operate as resistances to the recognition of the underlying feelings. Indications are that resistances in this area operate in such a way as to minimize the extent to which discrepancies between intellectual and personal attitudes will be *experienced* by the individual as a discrepancy. The psychological situation does not seem to be one in which people see themselves as having a serious emotional problem and then resist the idea of going for the help that they intellectually accept as appropriate for that problem. Rather, resistances appear to operate at an earlier stage, by preventing the person from ever recognizing his problem as serious enough to warrant therapy. This again was most dramatically illustrated in the study of the wives of hospitalized patients, where the interviews revealed how the most deviant early manifestations of the husband's psychosis were somehow integrated by the wives into a normal framework.

The nature of the resistance to the use of professional help points up the inadequacy of attempting to measure the readiness for self-referral by the type of straightforward approach used in some studies, in which a person is asked, "If you had any problem like —— do you think you would go to a psychiatrist?" Phrasing the question this way does not necessarily present the respondent with the personal threat necessary to evoke a "personal" rather than "intellectual" response. A respondent may say that he would go to a psychiatrist *if* he had such a problem while feeling that there is no possibility that he ever *would* have such a problem. For such a person, there is no true receptivity to the thought that therapy could ever be a necessary alternative for him. Consequently, the crucial question with respect to the readiness for self-referral relates to a willingness to accept the possibility that one *could* have a problem so bad that it could not be handled by one's own resources, that is, the readiness of an individual to see going for professional help as relevant and appropriate for the problems encountered within his life experience.

It is this perception of professional help as appropriate in terms of one's own experience that we have attempted to measure in the readiness for self-referral index. The respondent was asked to consider problems he encountered in the past and problems he might encounter in the future. We differentiated people who have actually gone for help at some time in their lives, people who see help as relevant for some problem they have faced in life even though they actually did not go for help, people who do not see help as relevant for any problem they have actually faced but see it as something they might possibly need at some time in their lives, and finally, people who reject the possibility of ever having a problem that they could not handle with their own resources.

The index of readiness for self-referral was based on a set of questions following an introduction structuring the questions around personal problems for which help was seen as relevant, help being broadly defined to include ministers, doctors, and social agencies, as well as psychiatric resources. We have already referred to these questions in that part of Chapter II which explored some of the ways people define emotional crises they have faced in the past and which compared those who defined personal problems as relevant for help with those who defined them in terms of "nervous breakdown." We may now look at these questions again within the context of self-referral:

> Sometimes when people have problems like this (i.e., personal problems, described previously as: Sometimes . . . people are very unhappy, or nervous and irritable all the time. Sometimes they are in a marriage—a husband and wife just can't get along with each other. Or, sometimes it's a personal problem with a child or a job) they go someplace for help. Sometimes they go to a doctor or a minister. Sometimes they go to a special place for handling personal problems—like a psychiatrist or a marriage counselor, or social agency, or clinic.
> 1. How about you—have you ever gone anywhere like that for advice and help with any personal problem?
> 2. (If answered "No" to 1.) Can you think of anything that's happened to you, any problems you've had in the past, where going to someone like this might have helped you in any way?
> 3. (If answered "No" to 1 and 2.) Do you think you could ever have a personal problem that got so bad that you might want to go someplace for help—or do you think you could always handle things like that yourself?

From the answers to these three questions, the index of readiness for self-referral was derived as follows:

1. Has used help (answered "Yes" to question 1).
2. Could have used help (answered "Yes" to question 2).
3. Might need help (answered "Yes" to question 3).
4. Self-help (answered "No" to question 3 but with no special emphasis on self-help: e.g., "I could handle it myself," "I think I could handle it myself").
5. Strong self-help (answered emphatic "No" to question 3: e.g., "I'm sure I could manage my own problems," "I'm sure we could always work things out for ourselves," "I'd never go to anyone for help").

In structuring the measurement problem as one of determining whether or not a person would define anything that had or could happen to him as a mental health problem rather than what he would do *if* he did have one, we feel we have structured the questions around the more crucial resistance point in this area. Measurement problems still remain, of course—in the wording of the questions, for example, and particularly in the posing of a hypothetical situation in Question 3, because hypothetical questions must always evoke an intellectual rather than personal response to some extent.

RELATIONSHIP OF READINESS FOR SELF-REFERRAL TO SUBJECTIVE ADJUSTMENT MEASURES

In this section, we will examine the relationships between the readiness for self-referral and the measures of adjustment studied in Part One. We will be interested in relating self-referral both to the different ways of experiencing distress—unhappiness, inadequacy, problems, and the like—and to the content of this distress as measured in the *sources* of unhappiness, inadequacy, and problems.

We will examine these data with three broad questions in mind. First of all, we will investigate the general extent to which feelings of distress become translated into a readiness to rely on professional help resources; secondly, we will explore the extent to which the particular way the distress is phrased and defined is relevant for self-referral—whether phrasing distress as unhappiness has different implications for help-seeking than phrasing it as inadequacy or problems; and thirdly, we will be interested in the extent to which the *content* of the distress is relevant, specifically, whether seeing the sources of distress in psychological terms—personal, interpersonal, relationship aspects of life—will, as one would expect, more often lead to self-referral than seeing the sources of distress as external frustrations.

It would seem fairly obvious that a person who feels he has a problem will more often go for help with it than a person who has no problem, and that one who defines this problem in "personal" terms will more often go for "personal" help with it than one who defines it in material terms. However, for the most part, we will not, in the following data, be relating the experience of a particular problem to self-referral behavior *in relation to that problem*. The readiness for self-referral index is a general measure. In relating it to a specific index of distress in any given adjustment area, we will not be talking specifically of the actual use of help or the readiness to use help for the particular problem represented by that index. Only a handful of people indicating distress on a given index would have actually gone for help for the problem measured by that index. This means that relationships we will be describing between indices of distress and readiness for self-referral are not due solely to the group of people that has sought help for the particular problem under consideration. For example, in the relationship that we will note between feelings of inadequacy as a parent and the readiness for self-referral, we cannot explain the difference between the groups which feel inadequate and adequate by the help that the former have sought for the problems with their child. As will be noted in the following chapter, only a small proportion of the problems that go into the "have had help" category refer to problems with a child. What this relationship means, then, is that a person who feels inadequate as a parent is the kind of person who is more ready for self-referral, even though in most cases the help he has sought or might seek is not for a problem having to do with his child.

Similarly, in talking of the content and sources of distress, we will not be saying that a person who is unhappy in a given area of life for personal or interpersonal reasons will more often seek help *for that problem* than one who structures unhappiness in external ways. Rather, this relationship implies that a person who generally tends to structure distress in personal terms will be more ready to accept the idea that some problem within his life experience might require the help of some professional resource.

In short, although we will be examining the relationship to self-referral of indices in specific adjustment areas, and of contents of particular kinds of problems and inadequacies, these specific measures should be viewed as representative of general tendencies in the person, of the general ways he approaches and structures experiences of distress.

General Adjustment

The relationships between the readiness for self-referral and the measures of general adjustment are presented in Table 9.1. Although we saw in some of the findings in Part One that unhappiness and worrying and the feelings of an impending nervous breakdown had different implications in their relationships with other variables, the results in Table 9.1 indicate that they all are similarly related to self-referral behavior. All of them are clearly related to this index. With respect to self-referral, the crucial thing, as far as these general adjustment measures are concerned, is whether distress is experienced,

Table 9.1—Relationship between Measures of General Adjustment and Readiness for Self-Referral

MEASURES OF GENERAL ADJUSTMENT[a]	READINESS FOR SELF-REFERRAL						Number of People
	Has Used Help	Could Have Used Help	Might Need Help	Strong Self-Help	Not Ascertained	Total	
Extent of worries							
All the time	23%	12	12	32	17	4	100%	(106)
A lot	18%	12	24	31	9	6	100%	(686)
Sometimes	14%	8	33	31	8	6	100%	(166)
Not too much	12%	8	30	34	10	6	100%	(1114)
Never	9%	5	20	43	14	9	100%	(271)
Evaluation of present happiness							
Very happy	11%	7	28	39	9	6	100%	(849)
Pretty happy	14%	10	27	32	11	6	100%	(1325)
Not too happy	21%	14	19	27	12	7	100%	(275)
Feelings of impending nervous breakdown							
Felt impending nervous breakdown	29%	16	23	24	5	3	100%	(464)
Did not feel impending nervous breakdown	10%	8	27	36	12	7	100%	(1991)
Sources of present unhappiness							
Marriage	35%	19	24	15	5	2	100%	(97)
Children	31%	13	17	24	8	7	100%	(107)
Job	16%	9	28	33	7	7	100%	(174)
Respondent's or family's health	11%	6	24	35	18	6	100%	(239)
Economic and material	14%	9	27	34	10	6	100%	(571)
Other	13%	12	28	33	8	6	100%	(699)

[a] The "not ascertained" groups on each adjustment measure were omitted from this table.

not the particular kind of expression it has. People who experience distress—whether as unhappiness or worrying or nervous breakdown—seem to be more psychologically accessible to the use of professional help.

Although different broad ways of phrasing distress in this general adjustment area do not seem to make a difference for self-referral, the sources of distress do seem to be relevant. This was particularly evident in the question on the sources of present unhappiness. It showed, as indicated in Table 9.1, that people whose unhappiness is expressed in terms of relationship problems—in marriage or with the children—are more accessible to the use of help than are those whose problems are seen in more external terms—as problems of health or as economic and material problems.

Perceptions of the Self

In relating the readiness for self-referral to the measures of self-percept, the pattern of findings suggests a relationship between introspection and self-referral (Table 9.2). This does not appear with respect to the question on whether or not a person sees himself as different from others—there was no relationship between this question and self-referral—but it does seem evident in the relationships with the perception of strong points and weaknesses in the self. Here we see that people who say they have no weaknesses (i.e., they do not want a child of theirs to be different from them in any way) and people who say they have no strong points both show the same self-referral pattern. Both of these groups of people tend *not* to go for help. Although one of these responses has negative implications and the other has positive implications, they similarly reflect a non-introspective quality. The crucial variable for self-referral here is the ability to look at and examine the self, rather than the negative or positive quality of the examination.

Congruent with this point is the finding on the degree of self-acceptance (Table 9.2). Although people varying in the degree of self-acceptance do not differ in the extent to which they have actually used help in the past, they do differ in the total measure of readiness for self-referral, a difference that appears particularly in

Table 9.2—Relationship between Measures of Self-Perception and Readiness for Self-Referral

MEASURES OF SELF-PERCEPTION[a]	READINESS FOR SELF-REFERRAL							Number of People
	Has Used Help	Could Have Used Help	Might Need Help	Self-Help	Strong Self-Help	Not Ascertained	Total	
Perception of self as different from others								
Explicitly not different from others	11%	6	30	35	13	5	100%	(390)
Don't know	10%	10	27	36	9	8	100%	(357)
Mention differences from others	15%	10	25	33	10	7	100%	(1690)
Denial of strong points								
Explicitly no strong points[b]	7%	13	29	32	12	7	100%	(84)
Don't know[b]	9%	7	30	36	10	8	100%	(244)
Mention strong points[c]	14%	10	26	34	10	6	100%	(2105)
Admission to shortcomings								
Explicitly do not want child different	5%	5	28	42	10	10	100%	(79)
Don't know; other	9%	4	20	38	22	7	100%	(301)
Explicitly do want child different	14%	10	28	33	9	6	100%	(1965)
Degree of self-acceptance								
Very positive	16%	11	21	30	16	6	100%	(81)
Positive	14%	8	25	36	10	7	100%	(1072)
Neutral	18%	13	28	28	9	4	100%	(224)
Ambivalent	17%	17	30	27	1	8	100%	(86)
Negative	17%	12	25	31	8	7	100%	(227)

[a] The "not ascertained" groups on each measure of self-perception were omitted from this table.
[b] This category represents the initial response to the question on strong points. It includes respondents who mentioned strong points upon interviewer's probing.
[c] Consists of respondents who mentioned strong points in initial response to the question.

the "strong self-help" category. It is interesting that the people who were coded as *ambivalent* in their self-percept appear least frequently in the "strong self-help" category—that is, they are people who are most psychologically accessible for help, more so than those people who see the self in negative terms. Although the difference is not large, it is consistent with the other findings we have noted. What seems to be important, again, is not a purely negative appraisal, but the ability to "weigh" the self, to look at the self in a way that encompasses both positive and negative attributes.

Adjustment in the Marriage Role

Differential relationships between readiness for self-referral and the several measures of adjustment in the marriage role appear to some extent. As indicated in Table 9.3, there is no relationship be-

Table 9.3—Relationship between Measures of Marital Adjustment and Readiness for Self-Referral

MEASURES OF MARITAL ADJUSTMENT[a]	READINESS FOR SELF-REFERRAL							Number of People
	Has Used Help	Could Have Used Help	Might Need Help	Self-Help	Strong Self-Help	Not Ascertained	Total	
Evaluation of marital happiness								
Very happy	10%	7	28	38	11	6	100%	(870)
Above average	15%	10	26	34	10	5	100%	(399)
Average	10%	11	28	34	12	5	100%	(546)
Not too happy	36%	18	6	26	8	6	100%	(50)
Frequency of feelings of inadequacy								
A lot of times; often	18%	13	29	25	11	4	100%	(213)
Once in a while; once or twice	15%	11	30	32	7	5	100%	(782)
Never	6%	5	24	43	15	7	100%	(811)
Report of marriage problems[b]								
Had problems	17%	14	27	30	8	4	100%	(759)
No problems	6%	5	28	41	13	7	100%	(978)
Sources of unhappiness								
Relationship	20%	17	28	29	5	1	100%	(189)
Spouse	17%	11	26	29	11	6	100%	(315)
Self	16%	10	23	35	10	6	100%	(104)
Situation	12%	8	28	36	11	5	100%	(574)
Sources of feelings of inadequacy								
Role functioning	11%	10	33	30	10	6	100%	(456)
Relationship with spouse	20%	15	23	31	5	6	100%	(259)
Other	22%	13	27	27	6	5	100%	(309)
Sources of past problems								
Relationship	15%	14	30	27	9	5	100%	(265)
Spouse	16%	19	29	30	4	2	100%	(180)
Self	17%	15	21	33	5	9	100%	(81)
External	21%	9	24	31	10	5	100%	(233)

[a] The "not ascertained" groups on each marital adjustment measure were omitted from this table.
[b] Does not include 50 married people who evaluated their marriage as "not too happy" and therefore were not asked whether they ever had any marriage problems.

tween readiness for self-referral and the marital happiness measure, except for the "not too happy" group which includes only 2 per cent of the people we interviewed (50 persons). But very clear relationships appear between readiness for self-referral and both feelings of inadequacy and the experience of problems.

The questions on unhappiness, inadequacy, and problems differ not only in the way they express possible psychological distress but in another way as well. The happiness question is phrased in terms of present feelings, whereas the questions on inadequacy and problems are phrased to include the past. Thus, we might expect a difference in the relationships of these questions to the actual use of help in the past. It is not necessarily surprising that there is no relationship (except in the extreme case) between how happy one is in one's marriage now and whether one has ever gone for help in the past. But Table 9.3 also does not show a relationship between feelings of marital happiness and the readiness for self-referral as measured by the feelings about the possibilities of *ever* needing such help. Thus, the table does suggest that a lower level of happiness in itself might not be sufficient to bring a person to the treatment process. What may be required is either extreme unhappiness or a lower level of happiness translated into the perception that there is a "problem" or perceived in terms of one's own inadequacy.

When we turn now to the question of the content of the distress experienced in marriage we see, in Table 9.3, that two of the three relationships examined conform to expectations and to the results already observed in the general adjustment area. There is a relationship between going for help and the structuring of marital unhappiness and inadequacies in interpersonal terms—in stressing defects within the marital relationship rather than situational factors or one's role-functioning inadequacies (inadequacy as a provider or housekeeper). The one exception occurs with respect to the sources of problems; these show little relationship with self-referral and, if anything, suggest that those who structure their problems in external terms sought help more. This finding, which is not consistent with the others in the marital area nor with those observed in the other adjustment areas, may possibly represent a chance relationship.

Adjustment in the Parental Role

As indicated in Table 9.4, the relationships between readiness for self-referral and adjustment in the parental role parallel those we have observed with respect to the marital role. Satisfaction in the

Table 9.4—Relationship between Measures of Adjustment in the Parental Role and Readiness for Self-Referral

MEASURES OF ADJUSTMENT IN THE PARENTAL ROLE [a]	READINESS FOR SELF-REFERRAL							Number of People
	Has Used Help	Could Have Used Help	Might Need Help	Self-Help	Strong Self-Help	Not Ascertained	Total	
Satisfaction as a parent								
Positive	15%	8	27	33	11	6	100%	(894)
Neutral	14%	10	29	31	10	6	100%	(673)
Negative	12%	11	23	38	10	6	100%	(328)
Report of problems in raising children								
Mention problems	15%	12	27	32	9	5	100%	(1430)
No problems	10%	5	24	39	14	8	100%	(477)
Frequency of feelings of inadequacy [b]								
A lot of times; often	21%	19	23	22	8	7	100%	(207)
Once in a while; once or twice	15%	11	31	30	8	5	100%	(398)
Never	10%	7	22	39	14	8	100%	(636)
Content of problems in raising children [c]								
Physical care and material provisions	14%	9	25	34	13	5	100%	(507)
Child's non-family adjustment	16%	9	30	30	8	7	100%	(256)
Obedience, discipline	16%	12	29	30	8	5	100%	(360)
Parent-child affiliative relationship	21%	15	20	29	6	9	100%	(111)
Content of feelings of inadequacy [b, c]								
Physical care and material provisions	11%	12	28	31	10	8	100%	(140)
Obedience, discipline	19%	18	25	26	7	5	100%	(68)
Parent-child affiliative relationship	19%	13	24	31	8	5	100%	(165)
Lack of tolerance for child's behavior	21%	12	32	24	8	3	100%	(137)

[a] The "not ascertained" groups on each parental adjustment measure were omitted from this table.
[b] Includes only parents who answered Forms A or C of the questionnaire.
[c] Does not include people who have not experienced problems or feelings of inadequacy, or those people who gave "other" sources of inadequacy or problems.

parental role does not relate to self-referral, whereas the experience of problems and especially feelings of inadequacy show clear relationships. The lack of relationship with the satisfaction index may be a function of the indirect nature of the question used to derive the index (see pp. 118–119). But because the findings parallel those in the marriage area, this lack of relationship may again imply that distress expressed in terms of unhappiness or dissatisfaction has different implications for self-referral than distress expressed in terms of problems or inadequacy.

The relationships with the content of inadequacies and problems also follow the pattern previously observed. Distress that focuses on aspects of the relationship with the child (affiliative problems and inadequacies, guilt over lack of anger-control and intolerance of the child's behavior) are more related to self-referral than are problems and inadequacies focusing on concern over material considerations and physical care.

Adjustment in the Job Role

With respect to the measures of dissatisfaction, inadequacy, and problems, the findings in the job area parallel those obtained with respect to marriage and children. As indicated in Table 9.5, there is no relationship with dissatisfaction, but relationships do appear with feelings of inadequacy and problems, particularly the latter. As we observed in Chapter VI, feelings of inadequacy on the job tend to be more a reflection of objective status considerations and less a reflection of an introspective self-questioning approach to life than seems to be the case in the comparable questions asked in the marriage and parent areas. But they do seem to reflect such a generalized attitude to some extent, because some relationship does obtain between feelings of inadequacy on the job and readiness for self-referral.

What are the implications of the findings obtained in all three of the role areas—that phrasing distress as an inadequacy or as a problem seems more generally relevant for self-referral than phrasing distress as dissatisfaction or unhappiness? Apparently, unhappiness or dissatisfaction are related to going for help only when they

Table 9.5—Relationship between Measures of Job Adjustment and Readiness for Self-Referral (Employed Men Only)

MEASURES OF JOB ADJUSTMENT[a]	READINESS FOR SELF-REFERRAL							
	Has Used Help	Could Have Used Help	Might Need Help	Self- Help	Strong Self- Help	Not Ascer- tained	Total	Number of People
Job satisfaction								
Very satisfied	12%	5	28	39	10	6	100%	(255)
Satisfied	11%	9	27	36	11	6	100%	(444)
Neutral	12%	8	23	31	16	10	100%	(49)
Ambivalent	9%	5	32	38	8	8	100%	(87)
Dissatisfied	11%	11	23	33	14	8	100%	(76)
Report of work problems								
Had problems	19%	12	26	30	7	6	100%	(267)
Had no problems	8%	6	28	39	13	6	100%	(654)
Perception of adequacy on job[b]								
Very good	12%	7	24	36	12	9	100%	(95)
Little better than average	12%	7	27	37	11	6	100%	(131)
Just average or not very good	15%	11	29	33	7	5	100%	(82)
Sources of job dissatisfaction[c]								
Only ego dissatisfactions	14%	7	26	32	14	7	100%	(182)
Both ego and extrinsic dissatisfactions	18%	8	26	34	10	4	100%	(91)
Only extrinsic dissatisfactions	9%	10	29	37	10	5	100%	(404)
Sources of work problems[d]								
Interpersonal problem	25%	2	20	30	13	10	100%	(40)
Vocational choice	22%	12	26	34	3	3	100%	(83)
Inadequacy on job	24%	10	32	28	3	3	100%	(38)
Extrinsic	16%	14	25	25	12	8	100%	(73)
Other	13%	22	26	35	—	4	100%	(23)

[a] The "not ascertained" groups on each job adjustment measure were omitted from this table.
[b] Includes only employed male respondents who answered Form C of the questionnaire.
[c] Does not include men who said they had no reasons for disliking their job.
[d] Does not include men who said they had no job problems.

represent a general, over-all evaluation of one's life. Unhappiness or dissatisfaction about specific areas of life does not necessarily reflect such a general evaluation and hence seems to be less relevant for self-referral. Inadequacy and problems in specific role areas, on the other hand, do seem to have such general implications, reflecting, perhaps, a general self-questioning attitude toward life that has relevance for self-referral behavior.

The relationship between self-referral and the *content* of the stress is not as clear in the job area as it was for the parental area. Because inadequacy on the job tends to be defined in terms of skill, there was no attempt made to explore different kinds of job inadequacy. The expectation that greater readiness for self-referral would be associated with more ego sources of dissatisfaction was not clearly supported by the findings (Table 9.5), perhaps reflecting the fact that job dissatisfaction, whether attributed to ego or extrinsic sources, tends to imply a blaming of the job or the situation and rarely involves self-blame. Only in terms of sources of job problems do we find the expected relationship (although not a very large one): personal problems—those involving vocational choice, or interpersonal problems, or an experience of inadequacy on the job—show a greater relationship with readiness for self-referral than do the extrinsic problems.

Symptom Patterns

The relationships between readiness for self-referral and the scores on the four symptom factors are presented in Table 9.6 and 9.7. These factors show an interesting distinction between the psychological

Table 9.6—Relationship between Symptom Factor Scores and Readiness for Self-Referral (Men Only)

SYMPTOM FACTOR SCORES[a]	READINESS FOR SELF-REFERRAL							
	Has Used Help	Could Have Used Help	Might Need Help	Self- Help	Strong Self- Help	Not Ascer- tained	Total	Number of People
1. Psychological Anxiety								
High	15%	10	31	27	9	8	100%	(244)
Medium	12%	10	22	41	9	6	100%	(317)
Low	8%	5	27	39	15	6	100%	(510)
2. Physical Health								
High	6%	4	32	29	23	6	100%	(52)
Medium	12%	10	21	26	21	10	100%	(147)
Low	10%	8	27	38	10	7	100%	(871)
3. Immobilization								
High	17%	11	25	31	9	7	100%	(209)
Medium	11%	7	30	35	11	6	100%	(410)
Low	7%	7	25	40	14	7	100%	(439)
4. Physical Anxiety								
High	11%	11	27	29	16	6	100%	(157)
Medium	13%	6	29	35	11	6	100%	(297)
Low	9%	7	25	39	12	8	100%	(606)

[a] The "not ascertained" groups on each symptom factor score were omitted from this table.

Table 9.7—Relationship between Symptom Factor Scores and Readiness for Self-Referral (Women Only)

SYMPTOM FACTOR SCORES[a]	READINESS FOR SELF-REFERRAL							Number of People
	Has Used Help	Could Have Used Help	Might Need Help	Self-Help	Strong Self-Help	Not Ascertained	Total	
1. Psychological Anxiety								
High	22%	14	25	25	8	6	100%	(553)
Medium	14%	11	31	30	8	6	100%	(387)
Low	11%	7	23	41	11	7	100%	(435)
2. Physical Health								
High	11%	14	26	23	14	12	100%	(92)
Medium	16%	10	25	31	12	6	100%	(260)
Low	16%	11	27	33	8	5	100%	(1023)
3. Immobilization								
High	18%	14	28	27	7	6	100%	(359)
Medium	16%	12	28	30	9	5	100%	(591)
Low	13%	7	22	38	12	5	100%	(418)
4. Physical Anxiety								
High	18%	15	21	29	8	9	100%	(295)
Medium	19%	11	29	26	10	5	100%	(440)
Low	13%	9	28	36	9	5	100%	(625)

[a] The "not ascertained" groups on each symptom factor score were omitted from this table.

and physical symptoms in their implications for help-seeking behavior. Psychological Anxiety (Factor 1) has clearest relevance for self-referral; it is highly related to the self-referral index for both men and women. Immobilization (Factor 3) is next in relevance, being clearly related to self-referral in both men and women, although the relationship for women is not as great as the corresponding relationship with Psychological Anxiety. Physical Anxiety (Factor 4) is also related to help-seeking behavior, although the relationship for men is a very slight one. Physical Health (Factor 2) shows a reverse relationship—people with higher scores on the Physical Health symptom factor are *less* likely to go for help (although here the relationship for women is only a slight one.)

Thus, as expected, it would appear that the psychological symptoms are more relevant to self-referral than are the symptoms expressed in physical terms. It was expected that these findings might be affected by age and education factors, since the older and more poorly educated people tend to score higher on the physical symptom factors and somewhat lower on the psychological symptom factors, and, as will be seen in the following section of this chapter, they are also people who are lower in the readiness for self-referral.

Therefore, we examined the relationships between the symptom factor scores and self-referral, with age and education controlled. The tables appear in Appendix C of the Tabular Supplement (see footnote, p. 12).

Looking at the findings with the age control instituted (Tables C.1 to C.4), we see certain changes in the patterns of results relating symptoms to self-referral. Physical Anxiety now shows as high a relationship with self-referral as do the Immobilization and Psychological Anxiety factors, and the Physical Health factor no longer shows a reverse relationship. But there is still no positive relationship between scores on the Physical Health factor and readiness for self-referral. In a sense, this age control clarifies a distinction between the Physical Health and Physical Anxiety factors. Although, as we have seen, Physical Health and Physical Anxiety are highly interrelated factors in terms of factor loadings, self-referral behavior separates the two, with the anxiety aspects of physical symptoms being highly related to self-referral, and the pure physical expression of symptoms having no such relationship. The education control (Tables C.5 to C.8) [1] produces essentially similar results (although here the Psychological Anxiety remains as the most relevant factor for self-referral).

That psychological and anxiety symptoms should lead to self-referral is not surprising, when we recall that the self-referral index was measured in terms of a personal problem for which help was seen as relevant. It is very likely that people with the physical symptoms are also going for help but are defining their problem as a physical one and are seeking nonpsychiatric, medical assistance. If this is so, and if we accept the fact that these symptoms may be taken as possible signs of psychological malfunctioning (as their correlations with independent psychiatric diagnoses would indicate), then this finding underscores the importance of the doctor as the diagnostic agent, as the one who would have to point out the psychological nature of the complaint.

These findings are of interest if we look at the total symptom list as a diagnostic tool. The symptoms, it will be recalled from the discussion in Chapter VII, represent the kinds of items known to correlate with psychiatrists' diagnoses of psychiatric disturbance—particularly 16 of the items (those starred in Table 7.1). Because it is of interest to see whether there is any relationship between criteria that a psychiatrist might use and those seemingly relevant for self-diagnosis and self-referral, we added scores on the 16 items [2] and related them to self-referral. As expected, we found a positive relationship between self-referral and this total symptom score. (Since three of the four factors separately showed positive relationships with self-referral, we would expect that adding them would produce a sizable relationship.) Thus, self-referral would seem to follow experts' judgment of the need for referral, at least as this expert judgment is measured in a symptom list.

An interesting paradox appears, however. In using a symptom list, one tends to diagnose the less educated, lower status groups as the most disturbed. This has been generally true in the cases where symptom lists have been used, for example in the Army studies (Stouffer *et al.*, 1949). It is also true in this study: if we relate the summary score of the 16 symptom items to education, we find a high relationship between low education and a high symptom score. The paradox this presents is as follows: less educated people are high on a symptom list, and a high score on the symptom list tends to lead to self-referral, from which one might surmise that less educated people would be high in self-referral; nonetheless, as we will note in the following section, less educated people tend to be low in self-referral. The findings we have just been exploring on the differential relationship of physical and psychological symptoms to self-referral, coupled with findings reported in Chapter VII on the relationship between education and these two different classes of symptoms, may help to explain this paradox.

We saw in Chapter VII that the factors most clearly related to low education were the physical symptoms—particularly Physical Health. Psychological Anxiety was not clearly related either way, and Immobilization was related in the reverse direction—that is, it was the higher educated who had the higher Immobilization factor scores. Thus, we may surmise that the higher scores of the less educated people on the total symptom list are a function of their high loading on the physical components of the symptom items, particularly the Physical Health component. On the other hand, the self-referral findings discussed above suggest that it is the psychological or the purely nonphysical aspects of the symptoms that are related to help-seeking behavior. In short, those aspects of symptoms—the physical—which make them predominate in lower status groups, are different from those aspects—the psychological—which bring people to help. This may help to explain why higher scores on symptom lists, though related, as a whole, to help-seeking behavior, do not necessarily imply that less educated people will seek help more. (At least, they will not seek help more for problems that they themselves have diagnosed in psychological terms.)

Another interesting point emerges as we examine Tables C.1 to C.4. Although in general these tables demonstrate the pattern of results discussed above, exceptions to these patterns occur within certain of the sex-age subgroups. Not only do exceptions occur but there seems to be a pattern to these exceptions. Specifically, the relationships between symptom factor scores and readiness for self-referral tend to be much stronger in the youngest than in the older groups. This is particularly marked with respect to men: clear relationships were obtained between readiness for self-referral and each of the three symptom factor scores (Psychological Anxiety, Physical Anxiety, and Immobilization) for the youngest and middle-aged groups but not for the oldest age level. In other words, among men over fifty-five years of age, the appearance of psychological and physical anxiety symptoms are apparently not interpreted by them as indicating a need for personal help. It is possible that in older age, with a general decline in physical functioning, the kind of bodily symptom that is represented in the symptom list is either expected or tends more often to be interpreted as a physical rather than psychological complaint.

These differential findings illustrate a significant general point—that something constituting a symptom for self-diagnosis and self-referral in one subgroup of the population may have no such symptomatic implication for the self-diagnosis and self-referral of people in other subgroups of the population.

In this chapter we have been concerned with the implications of various indices and definitions of subjective stress for self-diagnosis and self-referral. It is possible, however, to re-examine all these relationships within different subgroups of the population. In analyzing these relationships in the total population, we have asked the general question of whether a given subjective adjustment index is generally relevant for self-referral. Doing the same analyses in different subgroups, we would see whether different adjustment indices become relevant in different groupings of the population. Do middle class and working class, rich and poor, farmers and city people, Catholics and Protestants all have similar or different criteria for self-diagnosis? Do similar or different distress experiences get them to go for help?

From the results we found in the symptom area in the analysis of sex-age subgroups, and from the analysis of the education control that follows, we would surmise that a differential subgroup analysis does not contradict any of the general relationships presented in this chapter. It is probable that these relationships hold for most elements in the population. But exceptions, when they occur, can have considerable interest. Although systematic exploration of this interest lies beyond the scope of the present report, it is being pursued in further analyses of these data.

Controlling for Education

From the analysis of the relationships presented thus far in this chapter, a consistent pattern of findings has emerged. Readiness for self-referral is associated with introspection, with a structuring of distress in personal and interpersonal terms, with a self-questioning more than with a dissatisfied or unhappy reaction toward life roles, and with psychological rather than physical symptoms. This adjustment pattern that goes with greater readiness for self-referral presents a picture that fits the experiences and orientations of some subgroups of the population more than others. In particular, it conforms to what we have observed to be true of the high education groups (see Chapter VIII). As we will see in the following section, education is also highly related to self-referral. It is possible, then, that the relationships we have observed in this chapter between readiness for self-referral and certain ways of experiencing and defining distress are merely reflections of the fact that both self-referral and these approaches to distress are related to high education. We were interested in observing whether these relationships would remain if education was controlled.

In Tables C.5 to C.14 in Appendix C of the Tabular Supplement we have presented, with education controlled, a number of relationships representative of the findings we have discussed in this chapter. We have chosen, as representative, findings on the symptom patterns (Tables C.5 to C.8), findings from the general adjustment area (C.9 to C.11), and findings from the marriage area (C.12 to C.14). All these tables indicate that the relationships we have observed tend to obtain within each of the three major education groupings. In the marriage area, for example, we find in all three education groups the same pattern of response that we observed for the total population. There is no relationship between self-referral and the evaluation of marital happiness except for the extremely unhappy group, but very clear relationships with feelings of inadequacy and problems in marriage. In general it would appear that the kinds of relationships we have observed in this chapter represent psychological connections between the readiness for self-referral and certain ways of approaching and defining areas of distress, and that these are not just reflections of higher education.

RELATIONSHIP OF READINESS FOR SELF-REFERRAL TO DEMOGRAPHIC CHARACTERISTICS

In Chapter VIII we examined the relationships between various demographic characteristics and different ways of expressing and defining distress, and in the preceding section we looked at the relationships of these latter to the readiness for self-referral. In turning now to the relationships between these demographic characteristics and the readiness for self-referral, we may approach the data with certain expectations in mind. We will look for a high degree of readiness for self-referral within those subgroups of the population that express problems in ways that are also highly related to self-referral.

Table 9.8 presents the relationships between readiness for self-referral and sex, age, and education. As can be seen, all three variables are clearly and consistently related to the self-referral measure. Women, young persons, and the more educated have all gone for help more often in the past, and less often adopt a self-help position when considering future possibilities. In view of the high relationship between age and education, Table 9.8 also presents the relationship of self-referral to these two variables controlled on each other, and we see that the strong relationships remain even when the control is instituted; that is, age and education are independently related to the self-referral index.

The findings with respect to education might be particularly underscored. Data from other studies, for example that of Hollingshead and Redlich (1958), have suggested that higher educated people more often seek out psychiatric services. Since, as will be indicated in the following chapter, only a small proportion of the people who have gone for help have gone to psychiatrists, what Table 9.8 indicates is that the more educated also have gone more often to other help resources as well—these others being mainly, as we shall see, ministers or nonpsychiatric physicians.

When we look at these relationships now in juxtaposition with the relationships between adjustment measures and sex, age, and education, and the relationships between the adjustment measures and self-referral, we see that the three sets of relationships form a highly consistent pattern. This is particularly true for the relationships involving education. The highly educated group fits perfectly the picture presented in the preceding section of the person who is high in readiness for self-referral. The highly educated are more introspective, orient themselves toward life in terms of self-questioning rather than unhappiness or dissatisfaction, express concern over the personal and interpersonal aspects of their lives, predominate in

Table 9.8—Sex, Age, and Education Related to the Readiness for Self-Referral

DEMOGRAPHIC CHARACTERISTICS[a]		READINESS FOR SELF-REFERRAL							Number of People
		Has Used Help	Could Have Used Help	Might Need Help	Self-Help	Strong Self-Help	Not Ascertained	Total	
Sex									
Male		11%	8	26	37	12	6	100%	(1077)
Female		16%	11	27	31	9	6	100%	(1383)
Age									
21–24		18%	14	30	29	4	5	100%	(163)
25–34		16%	11	30	33	6	4	100%	(596)
35–44		18%	11	28	29	8	6	100%	(548)
45–54		13%	8	26	35	12	6	100%	(459)
55–64		7%	6	26	36	17	8	100%	(329)
65 and over		7%	6	19	42	15	11	100%	(352)
Education									
Grade school		7%	8	25	37	14	9	100%	(802)
High school		15%	10	26	33	10	6	100%	(1185)
College		21%	10	31	31	4	3	100%	(457)
Education (within age)									
21–34	Grade school	11%	8	32	31	9	9	100%	(102)
21–34	High school	15%	13	28	34	6	4	100%	(473)
21–34	College	23%	11	33	27	4	2	100%	(184)
35–54	Grade school	9%	11	28	32	13	7	100%	(292)
35–54	High school	17%	9	26	32	10	6	100%	(511)
35–54	College	23%	9	27	32	5	4	100%	(200)
55 and over	Grade school	6%	7	21	39	17	10	100%	(404)
55 and over	High school	9%	6	22	37	19	7	100%	(196)
55 and over	College	10%	9	31	36	7	7	100%	(70)
Age (within education)									
Grade school	21–34	11%	8	32	31	9	9	100%	(102)
Grade school	35–54	9%	11	28	32	13	7	100%	(292)
Grade school	55 and over	6%	7	21	39	17	10	100%	(404)
High school	21–34	15%	13	28	34	6	4	100%	(473)
High school	35–54	17%	9	26	32	10	6	100%	(511)
High school	55 and over	9%	6	22	37	19	7	100%	(196)
College	21–34	23%	11	33	27	4	2	100%	(184)
College	35–54	23%	9	27	32	5	4	100%	(200)
College	55 and over	10%	9	31	36	7	7	100%	(70)

[a] The "not ascertained" groups on each demographic variable were omitted from this table.

psychological rather than physical symptoms. All of these, we have seen, are characteristic of people high on the self-referral index. Thus, the greater use of professional help among the highly educated is very clearly associated with the psychological, introspective orientation towards life and the problems it presents.

It is of particular interest to note that the highly educated people more often go for help despite the fact that they express more happiness and satisfaction on the adjustment indices than do the less educated people. This suggests that it is not the feelings of distress alone that are important for self-referral behavior but rather the ways of defining this distress.

That younger people and women are high in readiness for self-referral is also consistent with the relationships we have observed between age and sex and the adjustment measures. The picture, however, is not so clear as with education. For example, younger people do not appear particularly more introspective in terms of the measures used in the study. However, they do conform to the picture of the high self-referral type in other respects, particularly in more often orienting themselves to life roles in terms of inadequacies and problems, and in their symptom expression (particularly on the Immobilization factor).

Women also present a consistent picture, being more introspective and more oriented toward the personal and interpersonal aspects of life. They also tend to experience distress in ways that are relevant for self-referral, although here the findings are not as unique as they are in the high education group, since women tend to express more distress generally, in unhappiness as well as in feelings of inadequacy, in physical as well as in psychological symptoms.

With education, age, and sex, then, we find that the relationships with self-referral are consistent with what we would expect from the preceding findings in the report. We may now look at the self-referral findings for the other demographic variables of interest in the study.

Table 9.9 presents the relationships between the self-referral index and the six variables we examined in Chapter VIII: income, occupation, place of residence, religion and church attendance, marital status, and broken-home background. Broken-home background, as we have indicated, is not a demographic variable but does represent the kind of early environmental influence that we are interested in exploring in most of these variables. We have also included region in this table, not because of any striking findings, but because a

Table 9.9—Demographic Characteristics Related to the Readiness for Self-Referral

DEMOGRAPHIC CHARACTERISTICS[a]	READINESS FOR SELF-REFERRAL							Number of People
	Has Used Help	Could Have Used Help	Might Need Help	Self-Help	Strong Self-Help	Not Ascertained	Total	
Income								
Under $2,000	10%	10	25	35	11	9	100%	(407)
$2,000–3,999	14%	10	25	34	12	5	100%	(549)
$4,000–4,999	13%	10	28	36	8	5	100%	(390)
$5,000–6,999	13%	10	28	33	10	6	100%	(559)
$7,000–9,999	19%	10	24	31	9	7	100%	(299)
$10,000 and over	15%	5	29	31	13	7	100%	(190)
Occupation—married men								
Professionals, technicians	19%	8	26	33	10	4	100%	(105)
Managers, proprietors	8%	6	31	34	12	9	100%	(116)
Clerical workers	14%	3	32	38	13	—	100%	(37)
Sales workers	20%	8	24	36	2	10	100%	(50)
Skilled workers	11%	8	22	41	13	5	100%	(183)
Semiskilled workers	6%	9	28	38	11	8	100%	(132)
Unskilled workers	12%	4	28	30	20	6	100%	(69)
Farmers	2%	8	23	51	10	6	100%	(66)
Husband's occupation—married women								
Professionals, technicians	19%	15	24	30	8	4	100%	(84)
Managers, proprietors	14%	4	30	38	8	6	100%	(120)
Clerical workers	8%	11	30	37	3	11	100%	(37)
Sales workers	13%	9	34	29	11	2	100%	(66)
Skilled workers	15%	13	24	32	11	5	100%	(178)
Semiskilled workers	13%	10	28	34	11	4	100%	(135)
Unskilled workers	13%	11	31	32	7	6	100%	(83)
Farmers	5%	11	31	31	14	8	100%	(110)
Place of residence								
Metropolitan areas	20%	11	22	27	11	9	100%	(325)
Suburbs	13%	10	24	32	14	7	100%	(326)
Small cities	16%	7	27	38	6	6	100%	(385)
Towns	14%	8	28	33	11	6	100%	(704)
Rural areas	9%	11	28	36	9	7	100%	(720)
Region								
Northeast	15%	6	22	38	14	5	100%	(626)
Midwest	13%	10	28	32	10	7	100%	(716)
West	15%	11	28	31	8	7	100%	(355)
South	13%	11	28	33	9	6	100%	(763)
Religion (church attendance)								
More than once a week								
Protestants	14%	12	31	26	10	7	100%	(193)
Catholics	21%	4	26	36	10	3	100%	(98)
Once a week								
Protestants	14%	9	31	31	8	7	100%	(507)
Catholics	15%	6	25	36	12	6	100%	(310)

THE READINESS FOR SELF-REFERRAL

DEMOGRAPHIC CHARACTERISTICS[a]	READINESS FOR SELF-REFERRAL							Number of People
	Has Used Help	Could Have Used Help	Might Need Help	Self-Help	Strong Self-Help	Not Ascertained	Total	
A few times a month								
Protestants	13%	8	28	37	9	5	100%	(446)
Catholics	11%	17	25	33	8	6	100%	(64)
A few times a year								
Protestants	11%	12	24	36	11	6	100%	(454)
Catholics	16%	10	27	31	14	2	100%	(51)
Never								
Protestants	9%	12	26	35	10	8	100%	(139)
Broken-home background								
Parents divorced or separated	24%	16	23	27	6	4	100%	(123)
Parent(s) died	14%	11	29	28	11	7	100%	(351)
Intact home	13%	8	26	36	11	6	100%	(1915)
Marital status								
Men								
Married	10%	7	26	38	12	7	100%	(908)
Single	15%	11	27	28	11	8	100%	(82)
Widowed	6%	8	26	35	6	19	100%	(47)
Divorced or separated	22%	15	28	20	8	7	100%	(40)
Women								
Married	13%	11	28	33	10	5	100%	(963)
Single	25%	9	33	21	8	4	100%	(76)
Widowed	13%	6	26	37	9	9	100%	(233)
Divorced or separated	40%	22	15	14	5	4	100%	(111)

[a] The "not ascertained" groups on each demographic variable were omitted from this table.

national survey affords an unusual opportunity for obtaining regional distributions of help-seeking patterns.

Turning first to the relationship between income and self-referral, we see no consistent relationship (and even the suggestion of a relationship disappears when education is controlled). Again, this is consistent with the findings on the relationship between income and the subjective adjustment measures. It may be recalled from the discussion in Chapter VIII that very clear relationships were obtained between income and the expression of happiness and satisfaction. However, the income groups did not differ in particular ways of defining and expressing distress, which seem to be more crucial for self-referral. The lack of relationship between income and self-referral, then, is consistent with the findings previously reported.

Digressing for a moment, one further point might be made about this lack of findings with the income variable, particularly in relationship to the high association observed between education and self-referral. In many of the studies made in this area, income and education have been subsumed within a concept of social class, a conceptualization appropriate to the purposes of those studies. The differential income and education findings that we have observed, however, suggest that it may also be meaningful to separate these two variables and note some of their differential effects. In terms of the readiness to go for help, a behavior that other investigations have noted is more common among middle-class than among working-class people, it would appear from our findings that the education rather than the income aspect of class is the crucial variable in getting people to help. We will see in the following chapter, however, that income becomes crucial in the choice of the *particular* therapeutic resource.

We turn now to the relationship between occupation and self-referral. It will be recalled, from Chapter VIII, that occupation was related to the adjustment measures in complex ways, so complex that it is difficult to use those findings as the basis for predicting the relationship between occupation and self-referral. Therefore, we may try to interpret this relationship in terms of other variables than the adjustment measures. The one finding that stands out is that farmers and farmers' wives are very low on the self-referral index, particularly in the actual use of help. This finding may indicate the truth of the stereotype that pictures farm people as self-reliant individualists. On the other hand, this difference may be less a reflection of psychological differences between farmers and other people and more a reflection of differences in the availability of resources, a consideration we will return to later.

Place of residence, it will be recalled, showed little relationship with the adjustment measures. Looking at the relationship between place of residence and the self-referral index in Table 9.9, some difference does appear, particularly in the actual use of help. People in the big cities have used help most, and people in the rural areas have used help least. This parallels the findings with respect to the farmers' low use of help and, as we have suggested, may reflect differential availability of resources.

Region shows no consistent relationship with self-referral, paralleling the lack of differences obtained in relating region to the adjustment measures.

Turning to the religion findings in Table 9.9, we would not have predicted any relationship between religion and self-referral on the basis of the relationships between religion and adjustment measures discussed in Chapter VIII. The most consistent finding in the adjustment area, it may be recalled from Chapter VIII, was that the high church-attenders tended to express more satisfaction and happiness than the low church-attenders. But there were no consistent differences in the ways in which distress was expressed, either between high and low church-attenders or between Catholics and Protestants. Protestants tended to express more inadequacy in the parental and marital roles, but there were no other differences in introspection or psychological orientations toward life.

We do see, in Table 9.9, however, a slight relationship between religion and self-referral. With respect to the church-attendance variable, high church-attenders seem slightly more accessible to the use of professional help. This relationship manifests itself throughout the self-referral scale for Protestants: when compared with the low-attending Protestants, the high-attenders have used more help in the past and also more often say that they might need help in the future. The difference between high- and low-attending Catholics occurs only with respect to the actual use of help: high church-attending Catholics have used help more often than the low-attenders (a difference accounted for mainly by the greater use of religious counsel). And Catholics generally, whether high or low church-attending, show a slightly greater use of help in the past than do the corresponding Protestant groups.

As we have noted, these religious differences do not reflect differences that we have observed in the relationships between religion and the adjustment measures. They probably reflect the influence of variables other than those adjustment variables we have discussed thus far. Since the relationships between religion and self-referral are mainly a function of the use of religious counsel, they probably reflect both the greater availability of these resources for the more religious person, particularly the Catholic, and, particularly in the case of the religious Catholic, the greater traditional support for their use.

In looking at the relationship between marital status and self-referral, we seem to have an instance where the degree of distress, rather than the manner of expressing distress, is related to self-referral. In the discussion in Chapter VIII, it may be recalled, the greatest difference between the married and unmarried groups was in the amount of distress experienced rather than in the manner of expressing this experience. People in the unmarried statuses tended to express much more unhappiness and dissatisfaction than the married people. Although the previous findings have suggested that the ways in which distress is expressed are more relevant for self-referral than is the amount of distress, it is likely that we are dealing here with an experience of distress that is so critical that it makes the use of help imperative, regardless of the particular ways in which the problems are defined.

It is not surprising that divorced people should have gone for help so much more often than people in the other groups, since this difference represents help sought around the period of the breakup of the marriage. What is perhaps more surprising is the fact that a majority of divorced persons, particularly the men, apparently never structured the breakup of their marriage as a personal problem for which they needed some help. The male-female differences in this area are interesting. Whereas 62 per cent of the divorced women either went for help or feel they could have used help at some point in their lives, only 37 per cent of the divorced men responded this way. Since most of these responses refer to trouble in the marriage and the divorce period, this difference is consistent with the indication in Chapter VIII that divorce has a greater impact and more disrupting effect on women than on men.

One interesting aspect of the relationship between self-referral and marital status is the fact that single people who have never been married express greater readiness for self-referral than married people, and that widows, if anything, express less readiness. To some extent, these findings undoubtedly reflect the age differences between these groups, with single people following the greater self-referral behavior of the younger groups, and widows and widowers conforming to the pattern found within their age groups. But these differences may also reflect a difference in the nature of the events creating the difficulties of the single as opposed to the widowed people. Widows and widowers are the victims of external difficulties, whereas the status of the single people, like the divorced, is in many cases a reflection of psychological or internal problems that have kept them from attaining a typically stable marital status. We might expect some recognition of the internal nature of these problems among the single people and a consequent greater readiness to seek help.

This distinction between psychological and external sources of distress may also explain the findings with respect to broken-home background (Table 9.9). People coming from a home disrupted by internal crises which ended in divorce have more often gone for help than people coming from a home disrupted by the death of one of the parents. The latter group is very similar to the people coming from intact home backgrounds.

We may recall, from the discussion in Chapter VIII, that the people from the homes disrupted by divorce have also experienced much more distress than either of the other two groups and more often express it in the introspective, psychological terms more relevant for self-referral. Thus, as in the case of the relationships of self-referral to sex, age, and education, we see that the self-referral behavior of the people from backgrounds disrupted by divorce is consistent with the adjustment patterns evident in that group.

Facilitating or Hindering vs. Psychological Factors

In summarizing the findings on the relationship between demographic characteristics and the readiness for self-referral, it becomes apparent that not all of these relationships are explainable in terms of variations among the subgroups in their psychological orientations and adjustment patterns. In all instances where a given subgroup of the population expressed the adjustment pattern relevant for high self-referral—introspectiveness, the phrasing of distress in terms of self-questioning and problems, a focusing on personal and interpersonal aspects of life, psychological symptoms—this group did in fact turn out to be high in self-referral (e.g., women, young people, and particularly the higher educated).

We found that other conditions and circumstances could also be related to readiness for self-referral. Thus, in the case of the particularly stressful situations of the unmarried groups, self-referral occurred most often in groups high in the amount of distress experienced, even though they were not particularly differentiated in the ways in which they phrased distress. Farmers and rural residents generally tended to be low in self-referral, particularly in relation to people living in big cities, although these rural and urban groups did not differ particularly in adjustment patterns. And high church-attenders, particularly religious Catholics, were higher in self-referral than lower church-attenders, again without any suggestion of why this should be so from the adjustment variables considered in this study.

These findings on the rural and religious groups seem to suggest that in addition to the psychological orientations and motivational factors that make a person receptive to the idea of going for help, there are numerous factors that may be viewed as hindering or facilitating the decision to go. Whereas psychological factors tend to point toward the use of help as desirable, facilitating factors point toward the use of help as available or accessible. Facilitating factors include the actual availability of the resources in the community, an individual's knowledge about the availability of the resources, and the extent to which going for help is "the thing one does" in one's social groups. Thus, the findings on the lower self-referral behavior of the rural and farm groups can probably be partly understood as indicating a lack of facilitating factors—lower availability of resources, less knowledge of resources, and less social support for the use of this channel as a way of dealing with emotional problems. Similarly, the findings of the slightly higher self-referral among higher church-attenders, particularly religious Catholics, may also reflect the presence of facilitating factors. For these people, help (particularly from a minister or priest) is more accessible and is more often a socially accepted, tradition-supported resource.

We may clarify this distinction between psychological and facilitating factors if we think of readiness for self-referral not as a single index but as a composite of a number of decision points. If we ignore the hypothetical question on the potential use of help and think only of the decisions made with respect to emotional problems that a person has faced in the past, we may consider three decision points in the self-referral process. The first decision is whether or not a problem will be defined as a mental health problem—i.e., whether it will be seen as relevant for help. Given such a definition, the next decision is whether or not to go for help with the problem. And finally, given the decision to go for help, the third decision involves the choice of where to go. We may tentatively offer the hypothesis that the kinds of psychological considerations that we examined in this study—the psychological orientation to the self and to one's problems—are most clearly relevant to the first decision point, i.e., to the question of whether or not a problem will be seen as a mental health problem, and that, although these psychological factors are relevant to the second and third decision points as well, facilitating factors are relatively more operative at these latter two points.

Since demographic variables may be viewed as reflecting both psychological and facilitating factors in various degrees, we may explore this hypothesis indirectly by re-examining the relationships between demographic characteristics and self-referral, this time looking not at the total index but rather looking to see whether different demographic characteristics become important at different decision points. If the hypothesis we have offered is correct, we would expect that demographic characteristics strongly reflecting psychological factors would be especially relevant at the first decision point—whether or not a problem is defined as a mental health problem. Demographic characteristics strongly reflecting facilitating factors would be expected to be particularly relevant at the other two points. In the next chapter, we will look at the relationships between demographic characteristics and the third decision point—where does one go, once the decision has been made to go for help? In this section, we will look at demographic relationships at the first two decision points.

To study the relationship between a demographic characteristic and the first decision—whether or not emotional problems are defined in mental health terms—we may re-examine Tables 9.8 and 9.9, looking only at the first two columns in those tables. That is, people who have defined a problem in mental health terms are people who have either gone for help or who can think of a problem for which they could have used some help; thus, the total proportion of a group who have defined some problem in their experience in mental health terms can be obtained by adding the percentages in the first two columns. For example, in Table 9.8 we see that there is a relationship between sex and the tendency to define problems one has experienced as mental health problems—that 27 per cent (16 plus 11) of the women in our sample have done this, as compared to only 19 per cent (11 plus 8) of the men.

For clarity of presentation, we have presented these totals in a separate table, Table 9.10. Here we see the relationship between demographic characteristics and what we have termed the first decision point in the self-referral process—the definition of a problem in mental health terms. (In Table 9.10 we are concerned only with the more traditional demographic characteristics of sex, age, education, income, occupation, rural-urban residence, region, and religion, omitting marital status and broken-home background.) We find that the following demographic variables are related to the tendency to define a problem in one's experience as a mental health problem:

Sex: Women more often define a problem in mental health terms (27 per cent of the women do this, compared to 19 per cent of the men).

Age: Younger people more often define a problem in mental health terms (ranging from 32 per cent of the youngest group to 13 per cent of the oldest). This is also true when education is controlled, with the largest differences occurring among the more educated people.

Education: Higher educated people more often define a problem in mental health terms (31 per cent of the college educated com-

Table 9.10—Demographic Characteristics Related to the Definition of Some Past Problem in Mental Health Terms

Demographic Characteristics [a]	Mental Health Definition of Problem: Has Used or Could Have Used Help	Total Number of People
Sex		
Male	19%	(1077)
Female	27%	(1383)
Age		
21–24	32%	(163)
25–34	27%	(596)
35–44	29%	(548)
45–54	21%	(459)
55–64	13%	(329)
65 and over	13%	(352)
Education		
Grade school	15%	(802)
High school	25%	(1185)
College	31%	(457)
Education (within age)		
21–34 Grade school	19%	(102)
21–34 High school	28%	(473)
21–34 College	34%	(184)
35–54 Grade school	20%	(292)
35–54 High school	26%	(511)
35–54 College	32%	(200)
55 and over Grade school	13%	(404)
55 and over High school	15%	(196)
55 and over College	19%	(70)
Age (within education)		
Grade school 21–34	19%	(102)
Grade school 35–54	20%	(292)
Grade school 55 and over	13%	(404)
High school 21–34	28%	(473)
High school 35–54	26%	(511)
High school 55 and over	15%	(196)
College 21–34	34%	(184)
College 35–54	32%	(200)
College 55 and over	19%	(70)
Income		
Under $2,000	20%	(407)
$2,000–3,999	24%	(549)
$4,000–4,999	23%	(390)
$5,000–6,999	23%	(559)
$7,000–9,999	29%	(299)
$10,000 and over	20%	(190)

Table 9.10—continued

Demographic Characteristics [a]	Mental Health Definition of Problem: Has Used or Could Have Used Help	Total Number of People
Occupation—married men		
Professionals, technicians	27%	(105)
Managers, proprietors	14%	(116)
Clerical workers	17%	(37)
Sales workers	28%	(50)
Skilled workers	19%	(183)
Semiskilled workers	15%	(132)
Unskilled workers	16%	(69)
Farmers	10%	(66)
Husband's occupation —married women		
Professionals, technicians	34%	(84)
Managers, proprietors	28%	(120)
Clerical workers	19%	(37)
Sales workers	24%	(66)
Skilled workers	28%	(178)
Semiskilled workers	23%	(135)
Unskilled workers	24%	(83)
Farmers	16%	(110)
Place of residence		
Metropolitan areas	31%	(325)
Suburbs	23%	(326)
Small cities	23%	(385)
Towns	22%	(704)
Rural areas	20%	(720)
Region		
Northeast	21%	(626)
Midwest	23%	(716)
West	26%	(355)
South	24%	(763)
Religion (church attendance)		
More than once a week		
Protestants	26%	(193)
Catholics	25%	(98)
Once a week		
Protestants	23%	(507)
Catholics	21%	(310)
A few times a month		
Protestants	21%	(446)
Catholics	28%	(64)
A few times a year		
Protestants	23%	(454)
Catholics	26%	(51)
Never		
Protestants	21%	(139)

[a] The "not ascertained" groups on each demographic variable were omitted from this table.

pared to 25 per cent of the high-school educated and 15 per cent of the grade-school educated). When age is controlled, these differences are still maintained, though the differences in the oldest age group (55 and over) are smaller than among the younger people.

Occupation: Several fluctuations obtain within occupation, but the most striking finding is that farmers and farmers' wives are the lowest in defining problems they have experienced in mental health terms.

Place of Residence: People living in big cities more often define a problem in mental health terms (31 per cent of the people living in metropolitan areas, ranging down to 20 per cent of the people in rural areas).

The variables which were *not* related to the tendency to define a problem in mental health terms were *income, region,* and *religion.*

The relationship between demographic characteristics and the second decision point (the decision to go for help, once one has defined the problem as a mental health problem) are also based on the data in the first two columns of Tables 9.8 and 9.9. What we want to consider here is the extent to which a mental health definition of a problem has been translated into a decision to go for help, that is, what proportion of the people who defined a problem in mental health terms have actually gone for help. This question can best be answered by considering only those people who have either gone for help or seen some problem they have experienced as relevant for help, rather than the total sample we interviewed. This is done in Table 9.11.

To see the relationship between the data in this table and Tables 9.8 and 9.9, let us consider the relationship between education and what we have termed the second decision point. In Table 9.8, the figures in the first two columns indicate that of the 31 per cent of college-educated people who defined a problem in mental health terms about two thirds of them (21 per cent) actually went for help as compared to the one third (10 per cent) who did not go for help. This is contrasted with the grade-school group, where of the 15 per cent who defined a problem in mental health terms about an equal number (7 per cent and 8 per cent) did and did not actually use

Table 9.11—Demographic Characteristics Related to Actual Use of Professional Help: Among People who Define Some Past Problem in Mental Health Terms

Demographic Characteristics			Has Used Help	Could Have Used Help	Total	Number of People
Sex						
Male			58%	42%	100%	(194)
Female			60%	40%	100%	(372)
Age						
21–24			57%	43%	100%	(51)
25–34			59%	41%	100%	(162)
35–44			63%	37%	100%	(158)
45–54			62%	38%	100%	(97)
55–64			51%	49%	100%	(43)
65 and over			53%	47%	100%	(49)
Education						
Grade school			47%	53%	100%	(126)
High school			60%	40%	100%	(297)
College			68%	32%	100%	(142)
Education (within age)						
	Grade school		58%	42%	100%	(19)
21–34	High school		53%	47%	100%	(131)
	College		68%	32%	100%	(63)
	Grade school		44%	56%	100%	(57)
35–54	High school		66%	34%	100%	(133)
	College		72%	28%	100%	(64)
	Grade school		46%	54%	100%	(50)
55 and over	High school		62%	38%	100%	(29)
	College		54%	46%	100%	(13)
Age (within education)						
	21–34		58%	42%	100%	(19)
Grade school	35–54		44%	56%	100%	(57)
	55 and over		46%	54%	100%	(50)
	21–34		53%	47%	100%	(131)
High school	35–54		66%	34%	100%	(133)
	55 and over		62%	38%	100%	(29)
	21–34		68%	32%	100%	(63)
College	35–54		72%	28%	100%	(64)
	55 and over		54%	46%	100%	(13)
Income						
Under $2,000			51%	49%	100%	(79)
$2,000–3,999			59%	41%	100%	(132)
$4,000–4,999			56%	44%	100%	(87)
$5,000–6,999			56%	44%	100%	(125)
$7,000–9,999			64%	36%	100%	(87)
$10,000 and over			78%	22%	100%	(49)

USE OF PROFESSIONAL HELP

Demographic Characteristics	Has Used Help	Could Have Used Help	Total	Number of People
Occupation—married men				
Professionals, technicians	71%	29%	100%	(28)
Managers, proprietors	56%	44%	100%	(16)
Clerical workers	83%	17%	100%	(6)
Sales workers	71%	29%	100%	(14)
Skilled workers	59%	41%	100%	(34)
Semiskilled workers	40%	60%	100%	(20)
Unskilled workers	73%	27%	100%	(11)
Farmers	17%	83%	100%	(6)
Husband's occupation—married women				
Professionals, technicians	55%	45%	100%	(29)
Managers, proprietors	77%	23%	100%	(22)
Clerical workers	43%	57%	100%	(7)
Sales workers	62%	38%	100%	(16)
Skilled workers	52%	48%	100%	(50)
Semiskilled workers	56%	44%	100%	(32)
Unskilled workers	55%	45%	100%	(20)
Farmers	33%	67%	100%	(18)
Place of residence				
Metropolitan areas	64%	36%	100%	(101)
Suburbs	57%	43%	100%	(76)
Small cities	68%	32%	100%	(88)
Towns	65%	35%	100%	(153)
Rural areas	46%	54%	100%	(147)
Region				
Northeast	70%	30%	100%	(132)
Midwest	58%	42%	100%	(161)
West	58%	42%	100%	(91)
South	53%	47%	100%	(182)
Religion (church attendance)				
More than once a week				
Protestants	53%	47%	100%	(51)
Catholics	84%	16%	100%	(25)
Once a week				
Protestants	60%	40%	100%	(117)
Catholics	73%	27%	100%	(64)
A few times a month				
Protestants	62%	38%	100%	(95)
Catholics	39%	61%	100%	(18)
A few times a year				
Protestants	48%	52%	100%	(101)
Catholics	62%	38%	100%	(13)
Never				
Protestants	41%	59%	100%	(29)

help. This same relationship between education and the second decision point is more clearly seen in Table 9.11. There we see that 68 per cent of the college-educated group who defined some past problem in mental health terms have used help, while the comparable figure for the grade-school group is only 47 per cent.

Looking at Table 9.11, then, we find that the following demographic variables emerge as most clearly relevant:

Education: Within those defining a problem in mental health terms, the more educated more often go for help (the figures are 68 per cent for the college educated, 60 per cent for the high-school educated, and 47 per cent for the grade-school educated). (When we control for age, we see that this relationship is strongest in the middle-aged groups.)

Occupation: Although again there are several fluctuations within occupation, the most striking finding again obtains for farmers and farmers' wives. Whereas in all but two cases—semiskilled workers and wives of clerical workers—people who define a problem in mental health terms more often go for help than do not go, in the farm group the ratio is strikingly reversed: the large majority of farm people who define a problem in mental health terms do *not* go for help. (The number of cases is very small, but the findings are supported by those for the rural group noted below.)

Place of Residence: Again the rural group stands out. Whereas the large majority of the people in the other categories who define a problem in mental health terms actually go for help, a majority of the rural people who define problems in these terms do *not* go for help.

Region: There is a greater tendency in the northeastern sections of the country for people to go for help once they have defined the problem in terms relevant for help. The other sections of the country do not differ significantly.

Religion: There is little systematic relationship with church attendance, but a striking Catholic-Protestant difference appears among the high attenders. Given a definition of a problem in mental health terms, religious Catholics will more often go for help. This is particularly striking if we compare the highest church-attending groups.

Whereas only a slight majority (53 per cent) of the most religious Protestants who feel they have had a mental health problem went for help, the overwhelming majority (84 per cent) of the most religious Catholics who felt they had such a problem went for help. (Although these findings conform to what one might have predicted, it should be cautioned that they are based on a small number of cases.)

The variable which was most clearly unrelated to this second decision point was sex. Although women more often define a problem in mental health terms, they do not tend to go for help more often. Age also showed no consistent relationships. Income was unrelated except in the two extreme income groups. There is a big difference between the lowest and the highest income groups, with the latter evidencing a greater tendency to activate the mental health definition of a problem into an actual decision to go for help.

We see that, to some extent, a different set of demographic variables becomes relevant at the second decision point—actually going for help—than were relevant in the initial defining of the problem as one that was relevant for help. We may summarize these differences by looking at them within the framework of the distinction between psychological and facilitating factors. The hypothesis was that, while these two sets of factors are interrelated and any demographic variable may reflect both aspects, facilitating factors tend to be more operative at the second decision point than at the first— i.e., at the point of deciding to go for help once one has defined a problem in those terms rather than in the initial definition of the problem.

If we look first at the groups that emerge as clearly distinctive at *both* points, we see that the more highly educated and the non-rural, non-farm groups both more often define a problem in mental health terms and more often go for help once the initial definition has been made. We may look at the education and the rural-urban distinctions as involving both psychological and facilitating factors.

The psychological aspects of education have already been documented in the data examined in this study. We have seen that education is highly related to a psychological orientation to adjustment problems, an orientation which is clearly relevant for defining emotional problems in mental health terms. But it is not surprising that education also seems to reflect facilitating factors. We would expect the higher educated to have more information about the availability of resources and to travel in circles where going for help is a fairly accepted "thing to do."

Farmers and rural people, although not distinguished in terms of the adjustment measures used in the study, may reflect psychological orientations in other areas not measured in the study (for example, individualistic values); these might militate against the definition of emotional problems as relevant for help. Rural people are also the group in which facilitating factors would tend to be minimal, because less resources may be actually available to them, because they may lack information about available resources, or because they live in a social milieu where going for help is not an accepted practice.

If we turn now to the groups that emerge more clearly at the first decision point than at the second, we see that women more often than men define a problem in mental health terms but do not more often translate this definition into an actual decision to go for help. Interpreting this difference in terms of psychological and facilitating factors, it would appear that women differ from men in the kind of psychological orientation toward the self that leads to a definition of problems in mental health terms, but do not differ particularly in facilitating factors—in the resources available to them, in their information, in their social norms relevant to help-seeking once having admitted to a problem.

Age is also a factor operating more at the first decision point than at the second. The younger people more often define their experiences as mental health problems, but, within this definition, they do not go for help more often. This suggests that younger and older people, like sex groups, differ more in their psychological orientations toward problems than in availability of resources, information, or the social climate facilitating or hindering help-seeking decisions.

Finally, we may turn now to the groups that emerge more clearly at the second decision point than at the first. Income, religion, and to some extent region, show no relationship to the tendency to structure personal problems in mental health terms but do show some relationship to the decision to go for help once the basic definition of the problem has been made. That is, they do not seem to operate as psychological factors in this area—which is consistent with the adjustment pictures that they presented—but they do seem to have meaning as facilitating factors.

In what way do income, religion, and region reflect facilitating factors? The influence of income would appear to be obvious. The fact that high income seems to make going for help easier (once a problem has been defined as help-relevant) reflects the importance of money for implementing this kind of decision—particularly for the psychiatric care that, we will see in the following chapter, is especially sought by high-income groups. But the relationship with income may also have less obvious meaning, reflecting group norms and other social factors. Going for help may be a more common, socially accepted, and even encouraged pattern in the high-income groups.

Religious differences appear mainly with respect to the great tendency of the most religious Catholics to go for help, once they have defined a problem as relevant for help. Although based on a small number of cases, this tendency is extremely striking: over 80 per cent of the most religious Catholics who have defined a problem in these terms have actually gone for help, compared to only a little over half of the most religious Protestant group. Assuming that this difference would be maintained in a larger sample, it would appear that for a religious Catholic the basic decision is whether or not a problem becomes defined in help-relevant terms; once this first decision is made, this definition is translated into the decision to go for help in the great majority of the cases. This suggests the importance of the existence of help-seeking as a clearly accepted, tradition-supported pattern, in a group to which one is strongly committed, as a facilitating factor activating the decision to go for help.

Finally in region, although the findings are only suggestive, the indication that people in the Northeast more often implement decisions to go for help suggests the importance of availability and concentration of resources, since there is a greater concentration of help-relevant facilities in that area of the country.

SUMMARY

In this chapter we have examined the readiness for self-referral index, representing a person's psychological preparedness to turn to professional help with an emotional problem (any relevant professional—clergymen and physicians as well as psychiatric specialists). And we have explored its relationships with the two classes of variables examined in Part One of this monograph—the subjective adjustment indices and the demographic variables.

The relationships between the subjective adjustment indices and self-referral supported our assumption that people who seek help for a personal problem tend to be those who have a more psychological orientation toward life and the problems it presents, who are more introspective and self-questioning. The tendency to turn to professional help when faced with personal problems was found to be associated with introspection, with a structuring of distress in personal and interpersonal rather than external terms, with a self-questioning more than a dissatisfied or unhappy reaction toward life roles, with psychological rather than physical symptoms.

The relationships between demographic characteristics and self-referral also partially verified our expectations. We expected that those subgroups of the population that showed more psychological, introspective, self-questioning orientations towards life and its problems (in Chapter VIII) would also show a higher utilization of the formal help resources. And the subgroups of the population that were highest in the expression of these psychological orientations—women, younger people, and particularly the more educated—turned out to be groups that were also high in readiness for self-referral.

But not all of the relationships between demographic characteristics and self-referral behavior were explainable in these terms. Some of the demographic relationships—for example, the greater readiness for self-referral of urban as opposed to rural groups—seemed more understandable in terms of the operation of facilitating factors such as the actual availability of resources in the community, one's knowledge and information about these resources, and the social customs and traditions with respect to help-seeking behavior rather than of psychological or motivational factors. Subgroups of the population differ in these facilitating factors as well as in the extent of their insight and psychological orientations toward life, and the relationships between demographic characteristics and self-referral behavior can reflect both sets of factors.

In a more systematic analysis of the relevance of psychological and facilitating factors in explaining the relationships between demographic characteristics and self-referral, we viewed the latter as a three-stage process, and examined the effects of demographic characteristics at each of the three stages. In this chapter we have presented the demographic analysis of the first two stages: the definition of problems faced as mental health problems and the translation of such a definition into an actual decision to go for help. The third stage of the self-referral process, comparing population subgroups in the particular therapeutic resource that they choose, will be examined in Chapter X.

We would expect that the kinds of psychological factors that we have examined in this study—the psychological orientation to the self and one's problems—would have some relevance at all three stages of the self-referral process, but that such psychological considerations would be most relevant at the first stage—the initial definition of a problem in mental health terms. Facilitating factors were assumed to have increasing significance at the later two stages— the decision to go for help, and the choice of a particular type of help resource.

In the analysis presented, we saw that different demographic characteristics became important at each of the first two stages of the self-referral process, and in ways consistent with the hypothesis that these demographic findings reflect different combinations of psychological and facilitating factors. Following the hypothesis that the tendency to define a problem in mental health terms is relatively more affected by psychological and less affected by facilitating factors than is the decision to go for help once this definition is made, we have attempted to explain the demographic findings in the following terms: the greater readiness for self-referral among women and younger people appears to be mainly due to differences in the psychological orientations of men and women and young and old; the differences in self-referral of different income, religious, and regional groups are more a reflection of facilitating than of psychological factors; and the greater use of help resources by the higher educated and nonrural groups reflects both psychological and facilitating differences between these groups and their lower educated and rural counterparts.

We have stressed this distinction between psychological and facilitating factors not only because of its possible theoretical interest but because the distinction may have certain practical and social implications as well. It would appear to have special implications for any evaluation of the degree to which there is an unfulfilled subjective need for help in the country, and for designating subgroups within which this unfulfilled need is concentrated. For example, other studies have indicated that less educated people seek therapy less often. What our data suggest is that this is not a function of a lack of distress among these people. (In certain respects the less educated express more distress, as this is measured by questions on satisfaction and happiness.) Rather it seems to be a function of two factors: (1) the distress that they experience is less often defined in psychologically relevant terms; and (2) even when distress is defined psychologically—when there is, in a sense, a subjective need for help—this need is less often translated into an actual use of help. In terms of unfulfilled subjective need, then, there would appear to be a special problem in this group, and in other groups where a high proportion of the problems that are experienced as relevant for help do not actually bring people into the treatment process—where the lack is in facilitating rather than psychological and motivational factors.

We have followed people up to the point of going for help. We have explored some of the psychological orientations that help people define their problems as relevant for help, and some of the facilitating factors that serve to activate the decision to seek help. Now we turn to the actual treatment process.

NOTES

1. In these tables, we did not separate men and women because we were interested in comparing the effects that the education control had on the symptom relationships, with its effects on the other relationships in Tables C.9 to C.14.

2. In adding the 16 items together without any differential weighting of items, we did not follow the procedure of the Stirling County study from which these items were taken. In that study, the items were weighted according to a discriminate function analysis, the weights being assigned in such a way as to maximize the relationship of the total score with the diagnoses of the psychiatrists. Because the population in this study was not comparable to the one used in the Stirling County study, we did not adopt their weighting procedure. It should be noted, however, that in the simple additive procedure we used, we are following the usual procedure for arriving at total symptom scores when these have been used as diagnostic tools.

X

People Who Have Gone for Help

SOCIETIES throughout history have set up institutions to provide comfort and aid for their troubled members. In the past, this function was usually performed by religious institutions: the oracle, the priest, the witch doctor were often invested with responsibility for the care and healing of the sick in body or spirit. Their approaches to therapy differed, depending upon the nature of their religious doctrines. The persons who sought their help—practicing widely diverse rites and ceremonies, trusting in totally different powers—had in common with one another the faith that the counsel of these various religious leaders would be effective in helping them establish personal equilibrium. Such leaders, of course, did not always rise from the ranks of churchmen. At various periods, other kinds of individuals were invested with healing powers. "Expert" insight into human nature has been attributed to politicians, scholars, physicians, and others. These men were often credited with having powers of healing as reliable and effective as those attributed to religious leaders.

Modern society is characterized by the multiplicity of resources that share this therapeutic function and by their growing professionalization. Furthermore, there has been a formal expansion of the functions of more traditional professions to include the psychological counselor role. Thus, included among contemporary professional counselors are clergymen, psychiatrists, psychologists, lawyers, marriage counselors, physicians, vocational guidance workers, social workers, and others.

In the preceding chapter, we discussed some of the general background characteristics that are related to the use of these formal facilities for help. A more intensive consideration of those people who have used such help concerns us in the present chapter. The discussion centers around the responses to the following set of questions:

> Sometimes when people have problems like this,[1] they go someplace for help. Sometimes they go to a doctor [2] or a minister. Sometimes they go to a special place for handling personal problems—like a psychiatrist or a marriage counselor, or a social agency or clinic. . . .
> How about you—have you ever gone anywhere like that for advice or help with a personal problem?
> What was that about?
> Where did you go for help?
> How did you happen to go there?
> What did they do—how did they try to help you?
> How did it turn out—do you think it helped you in any way?

We approached the investigation of the group of people who have used help with several practical and theoretical considerations in mind, expressed in a series of interrelated questions which we ask as we review the data. These questions are listed below to give some perspective on the kinds of issues we are interested in and how we intend to deal with them.

1. *Why did these people go for help?* What kinds of personal problems did they perceive as being serious enough to require formal professional services? What was the specific content of the problems, and from what general cause or locus were they seen to arise? The latter specification will permit us to classify respondents according to whether some personal failing, another person, a situational factor, or an interpersonal relationship was seen as the cause of their difficulty. We were interested in this because we anticipated that a choice among professional sources may be related to what was perceived to be the locus of difficulty.

2. *Whom did these people consult for professional help?* What is the differential use of help resources? Of particular interest was the relative use of the clergy, the psychiatric profession, psychiatric agencies, and the medical profession. We also were interested in relationships between kinds of personal problems and the sources to which people turned for help.

3. *How did these people get to their sources of help?* We dealt with the general issue of referral here by asking such questions as: Are people aware of the means by which they selected a particular source of help? What is the extent to which the selection of a help source is dependent upon particular referral agents—i.e., outside referral agents versus self-referral?

4. *Do respondents feel they received help from the sources they consulted? If so, in what ways do they feel they were helped?* We were interested in what proportion of those who sought help perceived some benefit from their course of action, and what the nature of that benefit might have been. Did therapy change something about the person, or did it offer comfort and reassurance? Both issues —whether therapy was felt to be beneficial and what kinds of specific gains were perceived—were further related to the kinds of problems our respondents sought to solve and the sources of help they selected.

The issues dealt with by these general questions were further illuminated by a demographic analysis of the help-seeking group, relating demographic characteristics both to the kinds of problems they perceived as serious and the sources of help they selected as relevant. Will age, education, or income, for example, affect the kinds of problems referred to professional help resources? Will different educational or income groups favor certain help sources over others? We are particularly interested in what groups consult psychiatrists.

WHY PEOPLE GO FOR HELP

In our sample, 345 respondents reported that they have gone somewhere for help with a personal problem. In this group there are undoubtedly some for whom this act represented a last resort, a last attempt to forestall despair. Others, of course, may have acted as they did for far less drastic reasons. In either case, we cannot treat this decision as a casual choice among alternatives. A person who goes for help with a personal problem is, in a sense, revealing at least two assumptions that he has made about his situation: first, that he is faced with a personal problem that distresses him; and second, that he cannot solve this problem by himself or by the help and advice of family or friends.[3] We assume that either of the latter choices would be preferable if they were available and were considered as potentially helpful.

It would therefore be important to determine the nature of the perceived difficulties precipitating a decision to give up, even temporarily, one's own coping devices. A tabulation of the particular problems for which help was sought, presented in Table 10.1, dis-

Table 10.1—Nature of Personal Problems for which People Sought Professional Help

Problem Area	
Spouse; marriage	42%
Child; relationship with child	12
Other family relationships—parents, in-laws, etc.	5
Other relationship problems; type of relationship problem unspecified	4
Job or school problems; vocational choice	6
Nonjob adjustment problems in the self (general adjustment, specific symptoms, etc.)	18
Situational problems involving other people (e.g., death or illness of a loved one) causing extreme psychological reaction	6
Nonpsychological situational problems	8
Nothing specific; a lot of little things; can't remember	2
Not ascertained	1
Total	**
Number of people	(345)

** Here, and in all subsequent tables, this symbol (**) indicates that percentages total to more than 100 per cent because some respondents gave more than one response.

closes that the great majority of them were related to some kind of interpersonal difficulty. Of these, the highest proportion concerned the marriage relationship: 42 per cent went for help because of a problem in the marriage. These problems were either described in terms of the marital relationship—not getting along, sexual difficulties, attempts to forestall divorce or prevent separation—or as an attempt to gain understanding about a maladjusted spouse.

The impression one gains from the interviews is that these were serious problems, not only the marital problems but the others that brought people to the doctors, psychiatrists, and ministers. A large proportion of them (18 per cent), for example, spoke to some professional about their personal adjustments: not getting along, being unhappy, suffering from peculiar psychological symptoms. Only 8 per cent of the entire group mentioned a problem which was coded as nonpsychological and situational, such as a financial difficulty or poor housing; it is evident that we are, for the most part, investigating truly personal problems.

We find, from the manner in which respondents located the difficulties they perceived as being serious, that mentioning a personal problem does not necessarily imply taking responsibility for having caused that problem. In Table 10.2, we note that 25 per cent of the

Table 10.2—Nature and Locus of Personal Problems for which People Sought Professional Help

Locus of Problem

Extreme psychological reaction to situational problems	8%
Personal or interpersonal problem involving defect in the self	23
Problem in other person, or interpersonal problem involving defect in the other	25
Interpersonal problem with defect viewed in the relationship, or locus of defect unspecified	32
Problem structured in impersonal, nonpsychological terms	12
Not ascertained	4
Total	**
Number of people	(345)

group who went for help attribute the blame for their personal problems to *another* person; only 23 per cent specifically trace the difficulty to some defect in themselves. In terms of the motivation for therapy, then, it appears that going for help does not necessarily imply any self-insight or readiness to change. In the next section, we shall determine whether help-seeking channels are different for people who attach blame to themselves as opposed to those who perceive the causal defect in another.

WHERE PEOPLE GO FOR HELP

Once having recognized a personal problem that cannot be solved by one's own resources, a person in trouble can choose among a number of alternatives if he wishes to seek further help. Some of these, however, may be only potentially, rather than actually, available: the person may not be aware of the existence of certain agents or agencies; he may be skeptical about some or unable to afford or not have ready access to others. We do not know why, ultimately, our respondents chose certain sources of help; we only have reports of the fact that they have done so.[4] But we hope to suggest some of the factors that may have influenced them, by inference from the social characteristics of the groups preferring particular sources and from the kinds of problems for which help was sought.

The professional persons approached for help by our respondents have been listed in the categories outlined in Table 10.3. The most

Table 10.3—Source of Help Used by People Who Have Sought Professional Help for a Personal Problem

Source of Help	
Clergyman	42%
Doctor	29
Psychiatrist (or psychologist): private practitioner or not ascertained whether private or institutional [a]	12
Psychiatrist (or psychologist) in clinic, hospital, other agency; mental hospital	6
Marriage counselor; marriage clinic	3
Other private practitioners or social agencies for handling psychological problems	10
Social service agencies for handling nonpsychological problems (e.g., financial problems)	3
Lawyer	6
Other	11
Total	**
Number of people	(345)

[a] Actually only six people specifically mentioned going to a private practitioner. This category should thus be looked upon as representing in the main those people who said "psychiatrist" without specifying that he was part of a mental hygiene agency.

frequently consulted source of help or advice was a clergyman—42 per cent—followed by a doctor—29 per cent (physicians who were not specifically designated as psychiatrists are referred to here as doctors). Thirty-one per cent of the group went to some practitioner or agency subsumed under the heading of "mental health professionals," including psychiatrists, psychologists, marriage counselors, and other private practitioners or institutions that are set up to handle psychological problems. Eighteen per cent specifically mentioned having gone to a psychiatrist or psychologist[5] (6 per cent reported seeing a psychiatrist attached to a clinic, hospital, or other agency; 12 per cent either just referred to a psychiatrist or, in a few instances, specifically mentioned a private psychiatrist). Another 6 per cent mentioned that a lawyer was asked to give help with a personal problem (most of these cases involved counsel associated with divorce proceedings).

Eleven per cent of the responses were coded as using "other sources of help." A content analysis of these "other sources" disclosed that only three responses were directly associated with an agency for mental health rehabilitation, all of these being Alcoholics Anonymous. Five of the remainder referred to consultation with teachers in connection with a child's problems; ten responses referred to nurses or visiting nurses; eight people named policemen or judges as being helpful with personal problems. None of these people, of course, are set up to be psychological counselors. But we feel it is legitimate to include them because, like lawyers, they are associated with situations that may potentially cause intense psychological distress—school problems, health problems, problems with the law—and they have been viewed as having the ability to help with a personal problem and have been asked for such help.[6]

In summary, we find that most of the respondents who went for help in times of personal distress chose a resource that offered, as *one* of its functions, psychological guidance. But it is interesting that those institutions explicitly created for this function alone—such as psychiatry, clinical psychology, social work—were less often consulted than those for which psychological guidance is not a major function—clergymen and physicians in general. It might be contended that clergymen and physicians are more numerous than psychiatric specialists and therefore more available. On the other hand, the greater use of nonpsychiatric specialists may indicate a lack of readiness in the general population to consult mental health professionals in times of crisis, or a lack of knowledge about the availability or effectiveness of such professionals.

To infer what reasons people might have for choosing particular sources of help, we have related the sources of help they chose to the kinds of problems they were interested in solving (Table 10.4). There are slight differences among the kinds of problems that were brought to clergymen, physicians, and psychiatrists. People who consulted clergymen mention marriage problems more often than those who went to physicians or psychiatrists; those who went to psychia-

Table 10.4—Relationship of Source of Help Used to the Problem Area (First-Mentioned Responses Only)

PROBLEM AREA	SOURCE OF HELP						
	Clergy	Doctor	Psychiatrist [a]	Marriage Counselor	Other Psychological Agencies	Nonpsychological Agencies	Lawyer
Spouse; marriage	46%	36%	35%	92%	50%	10%	61%
Child; relationship with child	8	8	20	8	39	10	8
Other family relationships	5	6	4	—	6	—	8
Other relationship problems; type of relationship problem unspecified	8	3	2	—	—	—	8
Job or school	5	2	2	—	—	—	—
Adjustment problems in self (nonjob)	18	22	30	—	5	—	—
Psychological reaction to situational problems	5	6	7	—	—	10	—
Nonpsychological situational problems	2	15	—	—	—	60	15
Nothing specific; can't remember	3	—	—	—	—	—	—
Not ascertained	—	2	—	—	—	10	—
Total	100%	100%	100%	100%	100%	100%	100%
Number of people [b]	(130)	(89)	(46)	(12)	(18)	(10)	(13)

[a] Here and in all subsequent tables this category includes both people who mentioned seeing a "psychiatrist" or a "psychiatrist at a hospital."
[b] Does not include 27 people who mentioned "other" sources of help.

trists were more likely to do so about problems with a child or a personal adjustment problem than those who chose either of the other sources; and physicians are more likely than the other two professions to be confronted with nonpsychological situational problems. In general, however, the three professions seem to be consulted for very similar reasons and are presented with very similar patterns of personal problems; the differences among them are not so striking as we might have expected.

In attempting to understand why the content of the problems that are referred to physicians, ministers, and psychiatrists are so similar, it should be remembered that we are dealing here with answers to a question that focused on personal problems. We are not dealing, therefore, with all problems that people have faced in their lives that may have had psychological implications and for which they received help. The results—that the contents of the problems for which physicians, ministers, and psychiatrists are consulted are very similar

—concern only those problems already defined in personal, psychologically relevant terms. If we were to consider all problems having potential psychological implications, whether or not people defined them in those terms, we might expect to find greater differences in the content of the problems referred to ministers, physicians, and psychiatrists. Specifically, we would expect to find that problems defined in broadly personal or interpersonal terms would be more likely to be handled by psychiatrists than problems not cast in these terms.

This point can be illustrated by comparing the results (on the source of help used) for the question that dealt with personal problems and the question that asked, "Have you ever felt that you were going to have a nervous breakdown?" It will be recalled that in response to this latter question 19 per cent of the sample answered "Yes," indicating, as they talked of the nature of the problem, that they were defining "nervous breakdown" as an individual collapse in the face of some external stress rather than as a personality problem or a problem in interpersonal relationships (Table 2.7). In keeping with this definition, we find, when we asked people what they did about the nervous breakdown problem, that of the 228 people who mentioned going to some professional help resource, only 4 per cent mentioned seeking psychiatric care (Table 10.5). This is in contrast to the 18 per cent of the 345 people reporting having had help for a personal problem who mention a psychiatrist (Table 10.3).[7] As indicated in Table 10.5, the nonpsychiatric physician is the overwhelming choice of people who go for help for a nervous breakdown

Table 10.5—Sources of Professional Help Used by People Who Had Feelings of Impending Nervous Breakdown

Source of Help	
Clergyman	3%
Doctor	88
Lawyer and others	4
Social service agencies (psychological and nonpsychological)	12
Psychiatrist (or psychologist)	4
Total	**
Number of people [a]	(228)

[a] Does not include the 236 people who had feelings of impending nervous breakdown but did not refer the problem to any professional help resource.

—88 per cent of the people who went to any professional resource with the nervous breakdown problem chose a "doctor" (compared to the 29 per cent who chose a physician for help with the personal problem). Not only are psychiatrists seen as inappropriate for handling a nervous breakdown, but clergymen also are largely irrelevant: only 3 per cent of the people went to a clergyman with their nervous breakdown, compared to the 42 per cent who chose this resource when they had a personal problem. Defining tensions and stress as a nervous breakdown apparently emphasizes the physical effects of the experience, making the nonpsychiatric physician the almost inevitable choice when help is sought.

Comparing Tables 10.5 and 10.3—the differences in the professional help resources sought by people defining their problems as a nervous breakdown and those defining them in more psychological terms—we see that the way the person sees the content of his problem is very important in determining the kind of help he will seek. But it is the *initial* definition that is important, whether he structures the problem initially as a personal or interpersonal psychological problem, or sees it in essentially nonpsychological terms. Once a problem is seen in psychological terms, the findings in Table 10.4 indicate that the specific content of the problem is much less important as a determinant of the particular help resource that will be chosen.

These comments are relevant only to the choice of the three major professional help resources—psychiatrists, ministers, and physicians. When we look at the less popular sources of help mentioned in Table 10.4—marriage counselors, psychological agencies, nonpsychological agencies, and lawyers—we see that the particular content of the problem *is* important. These less popular resources were chosen, by and large, for help with specific kinds of problems. To marriage counselors, obviously, were brought problems about marriage; people who chose "other psychological agencies" had marriage problems or problems with their children; those who chose nonpsychological agencies were appropriately troubled by nonpsychological problems; and those who consulted a lawyer, as suggested by the high percentage who mentioned marriage problems, were mostly people who wanted help with divorce proceedings. It is interesting, considering the small number of people in the sample who consulted these less popular sources, how clearly the findings conform to the patterns one would have anticipated.

Table 10.6 presents the relationship between the source of help that was selected and the nature or *locus* of the problem. It will be recalled that respondents were categorized according to whether they localized their difficulties in a personal defect, in the defect of another person, in a particular situation, or in an interpersonal relationship. We find, in Table 10.6, that clergymen were sought to an un-

Table 10.6—Relationship of Source of Help Used to Nature and Locus of the Problem (First-Mentioned Responses Only)

Nature and Locus of the Problem	Clergy	Doctor	Psychiatrist	Marriage Counselor	Other Psychological Agencies	Non-psychological Agencies	Lawyer
Problems involving defect in self	21%	22%	41%	—%	6%	—%	—%
Problems involving defect in other person	22	24	26	33	61	—	31
Interpersonal problems involving defect in relationship or locus unspecified	41	26	24	67	23	—	15
Psychological reaction to situational problems	9	9	9	—	—	10	—
Problems structured in impersonal, nonpsychological terms	5	15	—	—	—	70	39
Not ascertained	2	4	—	—	—	20	15
Total	100%	100%	100%	100%	100%	100%	100%
Number of people ᵃ	(130)	(89)	(46)	(12)	(18)	(10)	(13)

ᵃ Does not include 27 people who mentioned "other" sources of help.

usual extent by people who perceived their problems arising either from a defect in a relationship or an unspecified locus, whereas people who consulted a psychiatrist more often connected their problems with defects in themselves. People who asked a physician for advice, however, were as likely to perceive a defect in the self as a defect in another person or a defect in a relationship.

What is the possible significance of these findings? It is reasonable to assume that people who perceive their problems as arising from some personal defect and who choose to seek assistance in solving them are the ones most willing to effect some internal personal change in order to alleviate their difficulties. They therefore might be most attuned to seeking the kind of treatment appropriate for personality disorders—i.e., psychiatric treatment. In contrast, people who do not localize their problems in a personal defect or in a defect in another person may be seeking help in order to establish the locus of the defect. They may be looking for a person who could judge and evaluate their difficulties and perhaps recommend the "right" course of behavior rather than prescribe some change in personality organization; religious counsel would be most likely to fulfill this requirement. Finally, the fact that people who have gone to a physician for help are likely to specify their problems as arising from any of three sources suggests that there is some ambiguity in the public mind about the ways a doctor of medicine might be helpful in handling personal problems.

In a comparison of Tables 10.6 and 10.4, it is interesting to note that sharper distinctions appear in the relationship between the source of help that was selected and the nature or *locus* of the problem than in the relationships with the specific *content* of the problem. Choice of a psychiatrist, for example, seems more determined by whether or not a person localizes the cause of the problem in himself than by whether or not he sees the problem as expressing itself in the marital relationship or in some other area of life. It is this self-questioning and probably greater motivation for self-change that mainly distinguishes the people who choose psychiatric care (although, as Table 10.6 indicates, even the psychiatrists are approached by many people who localize the problem outside of the self).

As a final note about Table 10.6, we may call attention to the strikingly high proportion—61 per cent—of the group who went to "other psychological agencies" with problems related to a defect in another person. This result may be partially explained by the previous finding that 39 per cent of this group consulted specialists about some problem with a child. But there still remains a high percentage who went to these sources with problems attributed to a defect in another and who were not referring to a problem with a child. Although this finding is based on only 18 cases, it is interesting to speculate on what it might mean, assuming that it was confirmed in a larger sample. Most of the people in this category who did not refer to a child were referring to their spouses as the "other" in whom the defect was located. Perhaps this suggests that agencies specializing in social service work appeal to people who are specifically in need of supportive therapy to tide them over some quite tangible difficulty, such as alcoholism, temporary desertion, or illness of the spouse.

HOW PEOPLE CHOOSE HELP RESOURCES

In order to gain some understanding of the motivating factors underlying the choice of a given source, we have looked at the presenting problems with which people came for help in relation to the particular source of help they chose. We also asked people directly how they happened to get to a particular source of help with the question, "How did you happen to go there?" There were two types of responses to this question. Some people answered the question in terms of the outside referral source that sent them to the particular therapeutic resource. And others spoke in terms of their own motivation for choosing a particular resource. Two kinds of motivation were particularly predominant: Many said they chose a particular resource because of a personal relationship with the therapeutic agent; and many said they went to a particular person or agency because they felt that source of help was appropriate for their problems.

Table 10.7 presents the distribution of these responses. Since the interviewers did not specifically probe to determine whether or not there were any referral agents, the fact that only about one out of four persons mentioned an outside referral source cannot be taken as an indication that no other individuals or agencies were involved in the therapeutic choices of the people in our sample. The lack of specific probing also accounts for the large proportion of responses in the "reason not specified" category. Of special interest in Table 10.7 are the relative figures for the different referral agents. Ministers, for example, apparently see themselves as the final therapeutic agent much more often than physicians do since they do not so often refer

Table 10.7—Reasons for Choice of Particular Source of Help by People Who Have Used Professional Help for a Personal Problem

Spontaneously Mention Referral from Outside Source

Referred by doctor	8%
Referred by clergyman	1
Referred by family or friends	8
Referred by school, court, other civic agencies	3
Referred by mass media (e.g., "I read about it.")	1
Other referral agent	7

Do Not Spontaneously Mention Outside Referral

Personal relationship with help source	19
Help source functionally appropriate for problem	29
Other reasons	7
Reason not specified	41
Total	**
Number of people	(345)

the people that come to them to more specialized therapeutic resources. It is also of interest that family and friends were as important as physicians as referral agents, at least among the people to whom the referral sources were so salient that they mentioned them spontaneously in response to our question.

Clear distinctions also appear in the relationships between channels of referral and sources of help (Table 10.8). As might be expected, most of the people who sought help from doctors and clergymen mention no specific referral agents, and a very large percentage of the group who saw clergymen did so because of a personal relationship with the priest or minister. The source of help that receives the greatest amount of referral by another outside source falls into the general category of "other psychological agencies." This group included such facilities as psychological clinics, mental hygiene clinics attached to hospitals, and social service agencies; few of them are highly publicized or well known to the public, and we would expect that most of the people going to them would be referred. The majority of the people who went to a psychiatrist were also referred, particularly by a physician, although it is interesting to note that a sizable proportion were also referred by family or friends.

In summary, although the data are incomplete, we see marked differences in the paths by which people reach the different help

Table 10.8—*Relationship of Source of Help Used to Reasons for Choice of Particular Source by People Who Have Used Professional Help for a Personal Problem*

SOURCE OF HELP

Kind of Referral	Clergy	Doctor	Psychiatrist	Marriage Counselor	Other Psychological Agencies	Non-psychological Agencies	Lawyer
Spontaneously mention referral from outside source							
Referred by doctor	1%	1%	29%	—%	19%	—%	—%
Referred by clergyman	1	—	6	8	9	—	5
Referred by family or friends	3	4	14	18	18	8	—
Referred by school, court, or other civic agencies	—	—	—	8	12	8	—
Referred by mass media	1	—	—	8	—	8	—
Other referral agent	2	2	8	8	15	33	5
Do not spontaneously mention outside referral							
Personal relationship with help source	27	10	5	8	3	—	10
Help source functionally appropriate for problem	10	22	33	34	15	26	47
Other reason, or reason unspecified	55	59	5	—	9	17	33
Not ascertained	—	2	—	8	—	—	—
Total	100%	100%	100%	100%	100%	100%	100%
Number of people [a]	(145)	(99)	(63)	(12)	(33)	(12)	(21)

[a] Figures are based on all sources of help mentioned by each respondent. People who mentioned more than one source of help are thus included in more than one column. Therefore the number of people totals to more than 345.

resources. The path to a doctor or clergyman is a direct one, almost always unmediated by any formal or even informal referral source. Psychiatrists, clinics and social agencies, however, being less well known to the public, are usually reached through some referral agent. Although the data indicate that the referral source may be a friend or family member, the main ones potentially are the clergyman and the physician. They are the ones most people turn to with their personal problems; they are the major "gatekeepers" in the treatment process, either doing the treating themselves or referring to a more specialized professional resource. The findings indicate that clergymen rarely act as referral sources and see themselves as the final therapeutic agents much more often than physicians do, but even the latter do not usually refer the problems on to some psychiatric or social agency; they are actually no more prominent than family and friends as referral agents. In either event, whether they do the treating themselves or act as diagnostic and referral agents, the findings underscore the crucial importance of physicians and ministers in helping with psychological problems and thus support the oft-made recommendation that these groups receive some psychiatric training, not only for the help that they themselves dispense but in order to know when to refer to an appropriate psychiatric agency.

DO PEOPLE FEEL THEY ARE HELPED?

It is one thing to seek help, and another thing to find it. Although most of the people who received professional counsel felt that it helped them to solve their problems, one out of every five reported that it failed to do so (Table 10.9). To find the theoretical or prac-

Table 10.9—Perception of Helpfulness of Therapy by People Who Have Used Professional Help for Personal Problem

Perception of Helpfulness	
Helped; helped a lot	58%
Helped; qualified	14
Did not help	20
Don't know whether helped	1
Not ascertained	7
Total	100%
Number of people	(345)

tical significance of this result, we shall try to determine whether the content or nature of the problem for which help was sought and the source of help that was selected are related to perceptions of the ultimate benefit of the therapy.

People who went for help with marriage problems were most likely to assert that they did not benefit from it (Table 10.10); similarly, those who localized the source of the problem either in another person or in a relationship were most likely to report the same kind of failure (Table 10.11). Together, these findings suggest that individuals who experienced marital difficulties and attributed them either to their spouses or to some defect in the relationship were least

Table 10.10—Relationship between Area of Problems and Perception of Helpfulness of Therapy (First-Mentioned Responses Only)

AREA OF PROBLEM

How Much Therapy Helped	Marriage	Child	Other Family	Other Relationship	Job	Adjustment (Self)	Situations Involving Others	Non-psychological Situational Problems
Helped, helped a lot	48%	58%	56%	73%	67%	74%	50%	62%
Helped (qualified)	13	16	25	—	16	14	28	14
Did not help	32	13	—	20	11	7	11	14
Don't know	1	5	—	—	—	3	—	—
Not ascertained	6	8	19	7	6	2	11	10
Total	100%	100%	100%	100%	100%	100%	100%	100%
Number of people [a]	(143)	(38)	(16)	(15)	(18)	(58)	(18)	(29)

[a] Does not include ten people for whom the area of the problem was not ascertained.

Table 10.11—Relationship between Nature and Locus of Problems and Perception of Helpfulness of Therapy (First-Mentioned Responses Only)

NATURE AND LOCUS OF PROBLEM

How Much Therapy Helped	Personal Psychological Reaction to Situational Problem	Personal Problem with Defect in Self	Defect in Other	Interpersonal Problem with Defect in Relationship or Unspecified	Impersonal
Helped, helped a lot	65%	73%	47%	55%	56%
Helped (qualified)	19	14	14	13	15
Did not help	4	10	29	24	9
Don't know	—	2	2	1	—
Not ascertained	12	1	8	7	10
Total	100%	100%	100%	100%	100%
Number of people [a]	(26)	(73)	(86)	(105)	(41)

[a] Does not include 13 people for whom the nature and locus of the problem was not ascertained.

amenable to help in working out their problems. In contrast, those who sought help for a personal adjustment problem (Table 10.10), as well as those who perceived their problems arising from some defect in themselves (Table 10.11), claimed more often than any other group in either comparison that therapy had helped them. We may conclude that individuals who recognize that some change in themselves is required to alleviate their difficulties are most likely to believe that professional counsel has helped them.

From these findings one might expect that sources of help that handle marriage problems in which the defects were perceived in the spouse or in the relationship itself would be perceived to have been the least effective. And furthermore, sources of help that handle problems in which the defect was perceived in the person himself would be seen as most effective.

As we saw in Table 10.4, marriage counselors almost exclusively handle marriage problems where the defect is perceived either in the relationship or in the other person. Of all sources of help, the marriage counselors are perceived as least effective (Table 10.12). The number of cases is small, but the differences are striking.

Table 10.12—Relationship of Source of Help Used to Perception of Helpfulness of Therapy (First-Mentioned Responses Only)

SOURCE OF HELP

How Much Therapy Helped	Clergy	Doctor	Psychiatrist	Marriage Counselor	Other Psychological Agencies	Non-psychological Agencies	Lawyer
Helped; helped a lot	65%	65%	46%	25%	39%	60%	62%
Helped (qualified)	13	11	13	8	33	20	15
Did not help	18	13	24	67	17	20	15
Don't know whether it helped	—	1	6	—	—	—	—
Not ascertained	4	10	11	—	11	—	8
Total	100%	100%	100%	100%	100%	100%	100%
Number of people [a]	(130)	(89)	(46)	(12)	(18)	(10)	(13)

[a] Does not include 27 people who mentioned "other" sources of help.

There is no simple way to ascertain whether a professional resource that handles *personal* adjustment problems is seen as most effective, because no professional resource handles this kind of problem exclusively, according to our previous results. One might think, however, that of the three popular resources—clergymen, physicians, and psychiatrists—the psychiatrists should be perceived as most effective inasmuch as psychiatrists receive more problems that are relevant to defects perceived in the self (see Table 10.6). Clergymen should not be as effective as the other two groups because problems handled by clergymen are more often those interpersonal problems where the difficulty is unspecified or ascribed to the relationship (Table 10.6), and we have seen in Table 10.11 that such problems are generally associated with a perception of less help received. However, looking at the results presented in Table 10.12, we see that this expectation is not supported. Of the three most popular resources, psychiatrists are perceived to be the least effective.

We are left with an apparent inconsistency that should, somehow, be accounted for: individuals who recognize personal adjustment problems caused by some personal defect claim to be helped by therapeutic treatment more often than individuals with other kinds of problems; psychiatrists are consulted more often about just these kinds of problems; yet psychiatrists are not perceived to be the most effective source of help. There is apparently some complicated interaction between the content of a problem, the source of help used (among the three alternatives of clergymen, physicians, and psychiatrists) and the perception of therapeutic benefits.

We attempted to discover this interaction by grouping our respondents according to the way they localized their problems—i.e., by controlling the locus of the problem—and relating source of help to perception of success.

For people who went for advice about a problem that they located in another person's defect, we found that psychiatrists are perceived as very much less helpful than clergymen or physicians. Although the number of cases in the groups becomes very small, the discrepancy is a large one and accounts for about half of the difference perceived in the effectiveness of psychiatrists as contrasted to physicians or clergymen.

Assuming again that this difference would be maintained in a larger sample, we can then ask why this discrepancy should exist? Why should psychiatrists who handle problems that are perceived as arising from another person's flaws be thought less effective in their therapy than physicians or clergymen who handle similar problems? It would be logical to suppose that persons who feel they must endure difficulties caused by someone else's faults seek the kind of help from a professional person that would give them comfort and support.

Clergymen and physicians are in a much better professional position to offer this kind of help than are psychiatrists, for psychiatric therapy is oriented toward effecting a change in the attitudes or behavior of an individual. A psychiatrist would be more likely to request treatment for the person in whom the defect is seen than to give supportive therapy to the sufferer. Furthermore, psychiatrists are generally reluctant to administer therapy to people who are facing critical situational difficulties, whether of environmental circumstances or interpersonal relationships, especially if these people do not recognize any need for changes in themselves. Those respondents, therefore, who appeal to psychiatrists for advice about *another* person are likely to feel cheated by the experience; perhaps the psychiatrist refused to handle the case for any length of time, or perhaps he tried to foster self-criticism in the help-seeker, who, unprepared for such an approach, may put up resistance and perceive the psychiatrist as misunderstanding or failing in his role.

It is very likely, then, that the differences in the satisfaction of people who have gone to psychiatrists, clergymen, and physicians reflect differences in the extent to which these help resources have met their expectations. Also, they may reflect differences in the seriousness of the problems referred to different resources; psychiatrists may be receiving the more serious and difficult cases and therefore are less often able to give the help that people seek. Or they may mean, as we have suggested above, that people do not usually go for help with the readiness for self-examination and change demanded in psychiatric therapy and therefore get help from physicians and clergymen that is more at the level that they seek. Some indications of this will be noted in the following section.

HOW PEOPLE FEEL THEY ARE HELPED

We hoped to be able to discover the kinds of criteria people employed to measure therapeutic benefits and whether these criteria differed according to the source that was consulted. Although most of our respondents could not describe explicitly how therapy had helped them, they gave responses generally relevant to this question, and these could be classified into distinct categories (Table 10.13). The more specific of these were the 12 per cent who said they were comforted by the help they received, 14 per cent who said they were changed personally by the experience, 8 per cent who said that the therapy helped another person close to them, and 6 per cent who said that they had received support for breaking up a relationship (mainly by divorce). Twenty-seven per cent indicated having been helped by talking or getting advice, without specifying why this talk or advice had been helpful. Fifteen per cent of those who claimed to have been helped gave no indication at all of how their situations had been improved.

Table 10.13—Perception of Ways in which Therapy Helped

Type of Help

Helped in terms of comfort, ability to endure problem	12%
Helped in terms of cure, change in respondent or relationship	14
Helped by working with other person in relationship	8
Helped by breaking, or by being given support for breaking, relationship (e.g., divorce)	6
Helped in nonpsychological aspect of problem	12
Helped by talking, advice; not ascertained how this helped	27
Helped in other ways	6
Not ascertained	15
Total	100%
Number of people [a]	(260)

[a] Includes only people who said therapy helped.

Are particular sources of help associated with certain ways of perceiving therapeutic benefits? This relationship is presented in Table 10.14. Because only 260 of our help-seeking respondents claim to have been helped, we shall limit this investigation to the three most common sources of help—physicians, clergymen, and psychiatrists—to keep our samples large enough for meaningful analysis.

In most cases, clergymen were appreciated for their ability to offer comfort or, more vaguely, for their capacity to give advice. Both of these benefits were ascribed to clergymen proportionately more often than to either physicians or psychiatrists. These results, taken together, substantiate the assumption that clergymen serve as emotional supporters. Physicians, whose help was frequently perceived as consisting of advice, in addition were thought to have effected

Table 10.14—Relationship between Perception of Ways in which Therapy Helped and Use of Clergyman, Doctor, and Psychiatrist

	SOURCE OF HELP		
Ways in Which Therapy Helped	Clergyman	Doctor	Psychiatrist
Comfort; ability to endure	23%	9%	7%
Cure; change in respondent or relationship	7	26	22
Changed other	10	6	15
Breaking relationship	9	4	—
Nonpsychological aspect	4	12	4
Advice	34	24	15
Other	5	7	11
Not ascertained	8	12	26
Total	100%	100%	100%
Number of people [a]	(100)	(68)	(27)

[a] Includes only people who said therapy helped.

cures in a relatively large number of cases. Psychiatrists were viewed as having helped by bringing about a change in the respondent and, less frequently, in another person; but a large proportion of people who visited psychiatrists could give no indication of a specific way in which therapy had helped them. These findings suggest that, although there may be a fairly clear idea among the public of the kinds of problems psychiatrists handle—i.e., defects in the self— there is not a concomitant clarity about what psychiatrists do to solve these kinds of problems; the aura of mysticism, connected to powers of spiritual healing, may still prevail to some extent, in the public conception of psychiatry.

It appears that people who go for help are, in most cases, not seeking any change in themselves but rather are looking for comfort, reassurance, and advice. This serves to clarify a number of the findings we have presented: that only a minority of the people who went for help defined their problems as a defect in the self; that more people have gone to ministers and physicians than to psychiatrists with their problems; that people are less satisfied with the help received from psychiatrists than they are with the help that clergymen and physicians have given.

In pointing to the lack of motivation for personal change therapy, we do not imply that such motivation is necessarily appropriate in all or even most of the cases where people went for help. But where self-examination and change is called for, the first step in the therapeutic process is only a small step, and any attempts at directing the people toward therapeutic change are likely to meet with resistances. People who seek out ministers and physicians are particularly likely to have such resistances and these practitioners must recognize and be prepared to handle them.

DEMOGRAPHIC CHARACTERISTICS RELATED TO PROBLEMS AND PATTERNS OF HELP-SEEKING

We have already seen that proportionately more women than men, more younger than older persons, more highly educated respondents than less educated respondents, more religious Catholics than religious Protestants, more city people than rural groups have gone for help (Tables 9.8 and 9.9). Our current interest is whether we can observe any relationships between demographic characteristics and the particular *kinds* of problems with which people go for help. We also seek further demographic distinctions among people in terms of the *particular* help resource they choose.

Demographic Characteristics Related to Area of Problem for Which Help Was Sought

Is there a relationship between the demographic characteristics we have considered and the kind of problem for which help was sought? In the following series of tables we examine only those people who have mentioned going for help. Each table reports one or two social characteristics at a time, presenting within a given social dimension the percentage of each social group who went for help regarding a particular problem.

Sex and age. Although men and women do not generally differ in any dramatic way as to the kinds of problems that they present, noteworthy differences between the sexes do appear when they are grouped according to age (Table 10.15).

Two differences are particularly worthy of note. First, 66 per cent of the youngest women have referred interpersonal problems—coded "spouse; marriage," "other family relationships," and "other relation-

PEOPLE WHO HAVE GONE FOR HELP   [325]

Table 10.15—Relationship between Age of Respondent and the Nature of Personal Problems for which People Sought Help: Considered Separately for Men and Women (First-Mentioned Responses Only)

Area of Problem	MEN, AGE 21–34	MEN, AGE 35–54	MEN, AGE 55 and over	WOMEN, AGE 21–34	WOMEN, AGE 35–54	WOMEN, AGE 55 and over
Spouse; marriage	36%[a]	51%	20%	46%	43%	21%
Other family relationships	2	2	—	11	3	3
Other relationship problems; type of relationship problem unspecified	5	5	7	9	1	—
Child; relationship with child	7	12	13	5	14	20
Job or school	19	3	7	—	6	3
Nonjob adjustment problems in self	19	17	20	21	11	18
Psychological reactions to situational problems	—	3	—	1	8	20
Nonpsychological situational problems	10	7	26	6	8	12
Nothing specific; can't remember	2	—	7	—	3	3
Not ascertained	—	—	—	1	3	—
Total	100%	100%	100%	100%	100%	100%
Number of people [b]	(42)	(59)	(15)	(87)	(105)	(34)

[a] Here and in subsequent tables, the figures are presented diagonally so that horizontal comparisons (in this table, between men and women within a given age group) can be made more easily.

[b] Does not include three people whose age was not ascertained.

ship problems"—to an outside source of help, whereas only 43 per cent of the youngest men went for help with interpersonal problems. Furthermore, while 19 per cent of the youngest men sought help for problems related to their jobs or schooling, none of the youngest women have reported ever doing so. These differences between young men and young women appear in areas which reflect an already discussed role differentiation (see Chapter III). We suggested earlier that women in our culture are more personally concerned about social and interpersonal aspects of living and that men attend more to achievement strivings; thus, we would expect women to seek help for interpersonal problems and men to need assistance with problems involving their occupational or scholastic positions.

This difference is strong only among the youngest age groups, however. We might conclude, therefore, that the sex role problems of establishing equilibrium in the interpersonal sphere for women and in the achievement sphere for men are particularly salient for young people, who are trying to make a place for themselves in the world. It appears that these struggles diminish in intensity with increased age, perhaps because the desired equilibrium has been achieved, or perhaps because familiarity with the problems has bred a certain relaxation, or has made them less than all-important.

At any rate, it is notable that older men and women tend to be more alike as to the kinds of problems they perceive as relevant for help than are younger men and women. It can be seen from Table 10.15 that the reason for this growing similarity is that as men's concern about achievement strivings diminishes, their concern about interpersonal problems increases. This increase, taken together with a slackening of concern about interpersonal problems on the part of women who reach thirty-five years of age or more, equalizes the proportions in these two areas.

Precaution should be taken in interpreting relationships between age and help-seeking patterns. The respondents were asked whether they had ever consulted professional help sources during their lives; this gave the older respondents a far longer span of time from which to report such experiences. Furthermore, a sixty-five-year-old person who reports having gone for help may be referring to a visit paid to a clergyman about a marriage problem he had when he was first married at the age of twenty-one. Therefore, the only kinds of relationships with age to which we can ascribe much significance would seem to be decreasing trends—such as older men being less concerned about achievement problems than younger men—or instances of sudden unusual increases at a certain age level.

Such increases do appear in the oldest groups of both men and women. Compared to the women in the other age groups, a higher percentage of the oldest women seek help for problems about psychological reactions to situational problems; many of these are widows, referring to the problems they faced when their husbands died. In the oldest male group, a sudden rise takes place in the frequency with which nonpsychological situational problems are seen as relevant for help, but this finding is based on only a few cases.

Sex and education. Although nothing striking emerges when we compare education groups by sex as to the kinds of problems that led to their seeking help (Table 10.16), there are some slight tendencies that may be noted. For example, college people, particularly men, are likely to be more concerned about achievement problems than are those from other education groups. This conforms to the finding noted in the discussion of job adjustment that the more highly educated men report to having problems on the job more frequently than the less educated men (see Chapter VI).

That college-educated individuals more often go for help about problems in the achievement sphere probably reflects, in part, their greater general willingness to go for help and the wider range of problems for which they see help as relevant. Some of this readiness to go for help may be directly related to the content of their education, which may have made it clear that professional counsel is available—and often effective—for many kinds of problems. Furthermore, counseling about jobs and schools is probably more relevant for more highly educated people: it is to them that many fields of occupation and study are open, in contrast to the limitations imposed upon those with fewer educational advantages. It is more likely to be career problems that beset them—i.e., choosing a job, bucking for promotion, or changing a job. For problems such as these, counsel may be helpful. The kinds of problems that the less educated have to face—boredom, overroutinization, unemployment—are those for which psychological counsel is less likely to offer relief.

A comparatively low percentage of college-educated men report

Table 10.16—Relationship between Education and the Nature of Personal Problems for which People Sought Help: Considered Separately for Men and Women (First-Mentioned Responses Only)

Area of Problem	MEN Grade School	MEN High School	MEN College	WOMEN Grade School	WOMEN High School	WOMEN College
Spouse; marriage	50%	46%	35%	34%	45%	38%
Child; relationship with child	6	16	6	18	11	6
Other family relationships	—	2	2	2	7	6
Other relationship problems; type of relationship problem unspecified	6	6	4	4	4	4
Job or school	—	8	14	—	3	6
Nonjob adjustment problems in self	19	14	21	18	14	21
Psychological reactions to situational problems	—	—	4	9	6	9
Nonpsychological situational problems	13	8	12	9	8	4
Nothing specific; can't remember	6	—	2	4	1	2
Not ascertained	—	—	—	2	1	4
Total	100%	100%	100%	100%	100%	100%
Number of people [a]	(16)	(49)	(51)	(45)	(135)	(48)

[a] Does not include one person whose educational level was not ascertained.

having gone for help about marriage problems, and, similarly, a comparatively small group of college-educated women consulted professionals about problems with children. However, one should not necessarily interpret these figures to mean that either group considers these problems to be unimportant or irrelevant for help. On the contrary, previous results discussed in the chapters on the marriage and parental role indicate that more highly educated people, if they differ significantly at all from the rest of the population, experience more problems in both these areas.

Therefore, the fact that proportionately fewer college-educated persons have gone for help with these problems than have individuals at lower levels of education probably reflects, once again, the greater range of problems considered to be pertinent for professional advice by the most highly educated groups. If these men and women are involved with a great many problems that could conceivably benefit from outside help, then no particular one for which they have contacted such a source will emerge as strikingly important. Thus, in a tabulation of many possible areas of concern leading to some professional source of help, the percentages of people concerned with one particular area will be deceptively small, especially when compared to other respondents who emphasize a few major problems which might be referred for assistance.

Religion and church attendance. In the discussion of indices of adjustment in relation to Protestant-Catholic differences in Chapter VIII, we found that more Protestants than Catholics reported feelings of inadequacy in marriage. Also, within the Catholic group, we found a relationship between these feelings of inadequacy in marriage and church attendance: Catholics who are low church-attenders admit to these feelings more often than regular church-attending Catholics. This relationship was not duplicated in the Protestant group. Thus we might expect marriage problems to be approached in different ways by Catholics and Protestants. Catholic ideology invests a great deal of moral responsibility in the marriage relationship. One might suppose that strong Catholic adherents—those who feel the least inadequacy in marriage—might be less willing than other groups to recognize problems in this relationship as being so serious that they could not be solved without outside help.

Evidence for this idea is the small percentage of regular church-attending Catholics—those most likely to be the strongest adherents—who report having sought help for marriage problems (Table 10.17). This group is not only proportionately smaller than either

Table 10.17—Relationship of Church Attendance and Religion to the Nature of Personal Problems for which People Sought Help (First-Mentioned Responses Only)

Area of Problem	PROTESTANTS Regular Attenders[a]	PROTESTANTS Low Attenders[b]	CATHOLICS Regular Attenders[a]	CATHOLICS Low Attenders[b]
Spouse; marriage	40%	49%	29%	61%
Child; relationship with child	11	10	12	17
Other family relationships	5	3	6	—
Other relationship problems; type of relationship problem unspecified	3	3	10	—
Job or school	3	8	4	6
Nonjob adjustment problems in self	16	13	20	11
Psychological reactions to situational problems	8	3	6	—
Nonpsychological situational problems	9	10	9	—
Nothing specific; can't remember	3	1	3	—
Not ascertained	2	—	1	5
Total	100%	100%	100%	100%
Number of people [c]	(103)	(122)	(69)	(18)

[a] Includes people who attend church once a week or more frequently.
[b] Includes people who attend church less than once a week.
[c] Does not include 33 people whose religion or frequency of church attendance was not ascertained or who had other types of religious affiliation.

of the Protestant groups but is also considerably smaller than the Catholic low-attending group, of whom more than half consulted a professional source about marriage problems. (However, again, the latter group is very small.)

Income. Income shows no systematic association with the kinds of problems that precipitate help-seeking (Table 10.18). Respondents from high-income levels and low-income levels seek help for the same kinds of problems.

Place of residence. Like income, place of residence is not systematically related to the kinds of problems for which people seek help (Table 10.19).

Table 10.18—Relationship between Income and the Nature of Personal Problems for which People Sought Help (First-Mentioned Responses Only)

	INCOME IN DOLLARS					
Area of problem	Under 2,000	2,000– 3,999	4,000– 4,999	5,000– 6,999	7,000– 9,999	10,000 and over
Spouse; marriage	48%	41%	50%	42%	31%	42%
Child; relationship with child	12	6	10	14	12	16
Other family relationships	—	5	2	4	9	8
Other relationship problems; type of relationship problem unspecified	5	6	4	4	3	2
Job or school	5	6	2	7	2	8
Nonjob adjustment problems in self	12	15	24	12	19	21
Psychological reactions to situational problems	3	11	2	4	7	—
Nonpsychological situational problems	12	6	6	8	14	3
Nothing specific; can't remember	3	—	—	4	3	—
Not ascertained	—	4	—	1	—	—
Total	100%	100%	100%	100%	100%	100%
Number of people [a]	(40)	(81)	(50)	(74)	(58)	(38)

[a] Does not include four people whose income level was not ascertained.

Table 10.19—Relationship between Place of Residence and the Nature of Personal Problems for which People Sought Help (First-Mentioned Responses Only)

	PLACE OF RESIDENCE				
Area of Problem	Metropolitan Area	Suburb	Small City	Small Town	Rural
Spouse; marriage	41%	42%	34%	51%	34%
Child; relationship with child	12	7	6	9	20
Other family relationships	6	7	5	2	6
Other relationship problems; type of relationship problem unspecified	3	7	6	6	—
Job or school	6	5	8	6	1
Nonjob adjustment problems in the self	15	20	26	10	18
Psychological reaction to situational problem	4	5	3	6	7
Nonpsychological situational problems	7	7	5	10	11
Nothing specific; can't remember	3	—	5	—	1
Not ascertained	3	—	2	—	2
Total	100%	100%	100%	100%	100%
Number of people	(68)	(43)	(62)	(101)	(71)

The general impression one gathers is that demographic variables have relatively little to do with the kinds of problems that people refer to outside agencies for help. We have seen in the preceding chapter that demographic groupings differ in their original definitions of their problems—in the extent to which they define problems they have experienced as personal, psychologically relevant problems for which professional help is appropriate. But once this definition is made, once a problem is seen in psychological terms and people enter the treatment process, there seem to be fewer subgroup differences in the kinds of problems that are presented.

We have not, however, excluded the possibility that social groups do differ in the kinds of problems for which they seek help in some way which was not measured by our "content of the problem" code. For example, it may be that more highly educated respondents, when seeking help with marriage problems, are referring to difficulties that are much more complicated and reflect a higher level of sophistication regarding interpersonal needs and difficulties than is true of the problems presented by respondents with less education; it may be that problems of various social groups reflect differing aspirations in marriage. The responses to our question about the content of the problems for which help was sought were not detailed enough to enable such fine distinctions. Nevertheless, our findings indicate that social groups do not differ sharply in the *general* problem areas that have brought them to the decision to seek help.

Demographic Characteristics Related to the Source of Help Used

In this section, we will investigate the relationship between demographic characteristics and the choice of a *particular* help resource. In the preceding chapter, we presented the relationships between demographic characteristics and the first two decision points of the self-referral process—the decision to define one's problem in mental health terms and the decision to go for help. We are now interested in seeing which demographic variables become relevant at the third decision point—the decision as to *where* to go for help.

Sex and age. Table 10.20 presents the relationship of sex and age to the source of help that these people used. What is most interesting in this table is that, except for a tendency for more women to go to physicians, there do not seem to be any consistent over-all relationships between choice of a particular help resource and either sex or age. Two possible interactive relationships appear: young men and

Table 10.20—Relationship of Age to Source of Help Used: Considered Separately for Men and Women

Source of Help	MEN, AGE 21–34	MEN, AGE 35–54	MEN, AGE 55 and over	WOMEN, AGE 21–34	WOMEN, AGE 35–54	WOMEN, AGE 55 and over
Clergyman	52%	39%	33%	40%	38%	50%
Doctor	21	24	27	34	30	26
Psychiatrist	12	27	20	13	21	12
Marriage counselor	5	5	—	3	3	3
Psychological agency	5	10	7	14	12	—
Nonpsychological agency	2	—	7	4	4	6
Lawyer	—	10	13	2	8	9
Other	14	7	13	6	15	12
Total	**	**	**	**	**	**
Number of people [a]	(42)	(59)	(15)	(87)	(105)	(34)

[a] Does not include three people whose age was not ascertained.

older women stand out as groups that have gone for help to a clergyman. The greater use of clergymen by older women is not surprising. A good many of these women are widows who at the time of their husband's death turned to their clergymen for support. The finding with respect to the younger men is surprising; it may represent a chance result.

Sex and education. An important, and expected, result appears in Table 10.21, where we have presented the relationship between sex and educational level and the source of help used. This result points to the *greater use of psychiatrists by the more educated men and women* when they seek help with their personal problems. Thus, the highly educated are not only more ready to go for help in times of personal troubles but, when they do go for help, are more likely

Table 10.21—Relationship of Education to Source of Help Used: Considered Separately for Men and Women

	MEN			WOMEN		
Source of Help	Grade School	High School	College	Grade School	High School	College
Clergyman	38%	41%	47%	42%	42%	40%
Doctor	25	31	16	24	34	31
Psychiatrist	13	16	28	4	15	29
Marriage counselor	—	4	6	2	4	2
Psychological agency	13	12	2	7	10	15
Nonpsychological agency	6	2	—	13	3	—
Lawyer	19	6	4	2	7	4
Other	19	6	12	9	11	12
Total	**	**	**	**	**	**
Number of people [a]	(16)	(49)	(51)	(45)	(135)	(48)

[a] Does not include one person whose educational level was not ascertained.

than the less educated to turn to the psychiatric professions. We thus have confirmation of some of the major findings reported in Hollingshead and Redlich's *Social Class and Mental Illness* (1958). This study of the social characteristics of the patients from the New Haven community under psychiatric treatment highlights the greater use of psychiatrists by middle-class patients. It is gratifying that this finding based on a community study seems to be supported in this national survey and that data obtained from psychiatrists' case files and sample survey interviews confirm one another.

Are there any resources used more predominantly by less educated respondents? Men with grade-school education often turn to lawyers with personal problems (although the number of cases is small), and more women with a grade-school education turn to nonpsychological agencies, such as welfare agencies and social service workers and agencies. It is interesting to note that those at the lower education levels tend to use nonpsychological resources. This can be partially interpreted as meaning that the respondents with little education more often face problems that require the attention of those nonpsychological agencies (desertion, nonpayment of alimony, divorce proceedings, criminal offenses, and the like). But it may also mean that psychiatric service is not as available to the less educated groups, not only because of the cost of private psychiatric care but because the less educated may be less aware of channels to psychiatric care.

Another interesting result from Table 10.21 is that, generally speaking, respondents from all educational levels make about equal use of clergymen as a resource for help in handling their personal problems. Religious counsel evidently plays as important a role at one educational level as it does in another, once people have decided that they need help with their personal problems.

Religion and church attendance. Table 10.22 shows the relation-

Table 10.22—Relationship of Church Attendance and Religion to Source of Help Used

Source of Help	PROTESTANTS		CATHOLICS	
	Regular Attenders [a]	Low Attenders [b]	Regular Attenders [a]	Low Attenders [b]
Clergyman	54%	33%	52%	28%
Doctor	28	32	28	22
Psychiatrist	14	20	18	6
Marriage counselor	1	6	1	6
Psychological agency	12	8	4	17
Nonpsychological agency	4	5	1	6
Lawyer	7	8	3	11
Other	12	7	12	28
Total	**	**	**	**
Number of people [c]	(103)	(122)	(69)	(18)

[a] Refers to people who attend church once a week or more frequently.
[b] Refers to people who attend church less than once a week.
[c] Does not include 33 people whose religion or frequency of church attendance was not ascertained, or who had other types of religious affiliation.

ship between church attendance and source of help, presented separately for Protestants and Catholics. We would anticipate that regular attenders—whether Catholic or Protestant—would indicate that they sought help from clergymen to a greater extent than low church-attenders, and so they have. Aside from this difference, there are no major differences in the patterns of help sought between Protestants who were low church-attenders and those who were regular church-attenders. Furthermore, Catholics and Protestants who are regular church-attenders are strikingly similar in the sources of help they turned to. This result was surprising. One might have expected Catholics to have turned to clergymen to a greater extent than Protestants, but this did not appear to be true. Although, as we indicated in the preceding chapter, religious Catholics go for help more often than religious Protestants do, there are no differences among those who do go for help in the particular resources chosen.

The only group which tends to show a pattern of help-seeking which is generally different from the others is the low-attending Catholic group. But here we are again faced with a small number of cases, and the differences that do appear—the lower use of psychiatrists and the higher use of nonpsychological resources in the low-attending Catholic group—probably reflect the lower educational level of that group.

Income. Table 10.23 presents the relationship between income and the source of help used by people who went for help. We again

Table 10.23—Relationship of Income to Source of Help Used

	INCOME IN DOLLARS					
Sources of Help	Under 2000	2000–3999	4000–4999	5000–6999	7000–9999	10,000 and over
Clergyman	48%	43%	56%	39%	36%	29%
Doctor	18	26	28	33	40	24
Psychiatrist	5	15	12	14	24	47
Marriage counselor	—	5	6	3	3	3
Psychological agency	10	14	10	10	9	3
Nonpsychological agency	15	3	2	1	—	3
Lawyer	15	11	2	6	2	—
Other	3	17	8	15	5	8
Total	**	**	**	**	**	**
Number of people [a]	(40)	(81)	(50)	(74)	(58)	(38)

[a] Does not include four people whose income level was not ascertained.

find confirmation of the central theme of Hollingshead and Redlich's report of psychiatric treatment in New Haven. The wealthier respondents are more likely than the poorer ones to turn to psychiatrists with personal problems. The relationship is an extremely striking one. Among the respondents with the lowest incomes ($2,000 a year or less), only 5 per cent consulted a psychiatrist. In the three middle-income ranges—$2,000 to $7,000 a year—the percentage of respondents using psychiatrists is 12 to 15 per cent, with no major variations among these three groups themselves. But of the group that earns the second highest income in the table—$7,000 to $10,000 a year—almost a quarter (24 per cent) report having consulted a psychiatrist. Finally, this figure almost *doubles* for respondents in the highest income group, of which 47 per cent saw a psychiatrist.

These results complement the relationships discovered between selection of sources of help and educational level, leaving one with the conclusion that both higher education and higher income influence a choice of psychiatric treatment for help in handling personal problems. But since high income and high education tend to be associated, it is possible that they are not independently related to the selection of psychiatric treatment. For example, it may be that only education is a factor in this choice and that income does not influence it at all. To determine whether this possibility or its opposite is true, we must compare, for the small group we are interested in, sources of help which were selected by educational groups regardless of income, and by income levels regardless of education.

Income and education. Because we were restricted to a very small sample, we divided the respondents into only two income groups: above and below the median. We maintained our use of three educational levels: grade school, high school, and college. We find that both income and education *are* meaningfully related, independently of one another, to the selection of psychiatric treatment (Table 10.24). Within each income level, the more highly educated groups have made greater use of a psychiatrist's assistance in times of personal crisis. And within each of the educational levels people in the higher income bracket are more likely to go to a psychiatrist than those of lower income.

Table 10.24—Relationship of Education and Income to Use of Psychiatrists [a]

	BELOW MEDIAN INCOME (UNDER $5,000)			ABOVE MEDIAN INCOME ($5,000 AND ABOVE)		
	Grade School	High School	College	Grade School	High School	College
Use of Psychiatrists	4%	11%	23%	16%	20%	32%
Number of people [b]	(47)	(89)	(35)	(12)	(94)	(63)

[a] Based on any mention of psychiatrists.
[b] Does not include five people whose income or education was not ascertained.

The relationship between income and the choice of psychiatric care is an interesting one and, as we have suggested, may have meaning beyond the obvious one that people of higher income can afford the cost of psychiatric care. This finding may reflect the social as well as the material consequences of wealth. It is likely that a wealthy person will have contact with those who are positively oriented to the psychiatric profession or who are at least conversant with what the profession is all about, and for whom going to a psychiatrist is the thing "one does" if one is seeking help for a personal problem.

Place of residence. Several interesting findings appear in the relationship between place of residence and choice of help (Table 10.25). The most striking one is the heavy choice of psychiatrists among people from suburban areas. Forty per cent of the people in this group who have gone for help sought psychiatric care, a figure 24 per cent higher than the proportion mentioning such help in any of the other residential groups. Inasmuch as suburban areas contain concentrations of the highly educated, higher income groups which we have seen are strongly oriented toward the use of psychiatric care, this result is possibly not surprising, although the size of the relationship suggests the possible existence of a "social climate" factor as well.

Other interesting patterns appear in Table 10.25. What seems evident about the people who live in metropolitan areas is that they take advantage of many different resources of help. People residing in metropolitan areas generally have more kinds of facilities available to them. As a result, we find that those in metropolitan areas who

Table 10.25—Relationship of Place of Residence to Source of Help Used

Source of Help	Metropolitan Area	Suburbs	Small City	Small Town	Rural
Clergyman	40%	35%	56%	46%	30%
Doctor	18	28	22	36	35
Psychiatrist	11	40	16	16	15
Marriage Counselor	10	—	3	1	3
Psychological agency	21	12	10	3	7
Nonpsychological agency	3	5	6	2	3
Lawyer	1	—	5	10	10
Other	24	7	8	9	6
Total	**	**	**	**	**
Number of people	(68)	(43)	(62)	(101)	(71)

have sought help have turned to marriage counselors, psychological agencies, and miscellaneous sources (coded "other") to a greater extent than people from other residential localities. These would be the resources more readily accessible to metropolitan residents.

People living in small towns or in rural areas seem to lean more heavily than other groups on doctors for help with personal problems. There appears to be some validity to the stereotype of the "country doctor"—the general practitioner handling all kinds of problems, personally involved in the lives of his patients.

People from small towns and smaller cities, in contrast to those from rural areas, however, are also more likely to mention using the clergy as a resource for help when they have needed it. A clergyman may be more readily perceived as an intimate member of the community by people who live in small towns than by people who live either in the less densely populated and more widely scattered rural communities or in the big cities where the church is not often a "community" institution. And as we have seen, a personal relationship with the clergyman seems to be an important reason for turning to him for help.

We may now integrate the demographic analysis of help-seeking presented here within the framework presented in the last chapter. In that chapter, the psychological orientations that help people define their problems as relevant for help (the first decision point) and the facilitating factors that help activate the decision to seek help (the second decision point) were examined. Now we can follow through to the final decision—the choice of a particular help resource—and examine the facilitating factors important at this point.

Education operates at all three of the decision points: the higher educated more often defined problems they had experienced as mental health problems, more often translated this definition into an actual going for help, and more often chose psychiatric therapy. Thus, education represents both a more psychological orientation toward the self and the facilitating effects of a greater awareness of resources (particularly psychiatric ones) and a social climate more favorable to the use of therapy in general and the use of psychiatric resources in particular.

Place of residence is also relevant at all points of the self-referral process. Rural people less often define problems in mental health terms and, even within such a definition, less often go for help. All points along the place of residence dimension assume significance in terms of the choice of a given resource: the suburbanites are characterized by the use of psychiatric facilities, the small town and city by the greater use of the clergy, the small town and rural areas by the greater use of the physician, and the metropolitan areas by the greater diversity of resources utilized. Except for the rural group, place of residence seems to influence the self-referral process mainly through the differences in the resources that are available to city, town, and country people, a critical distinction in the decision as to *where* to go for help.

Both *income* and *church attendance* conform to the hypothesized pattern of facilitating variables, with no relation to the definition of the problem, some relation to the decision to go for help, and a strong relationship to the particular resource chosen. Persons with high incomes choose psychiatric facilities—a choice that seems to reflect not differences in the psychological insight that would predispose one to the choice of psychiatric care but rather differences in the ability to pay for such care, and perhaps also in the group norms supporting the psychiatric choice. The high church-attenders more often choose a clergyman—a resource more accessible to them, and an accepted help-resource in their social groups.

Finally, *sex* and *age* reflect the reverse pattern. They are more relevant in the initial definition of a problem as a mental health problem than as variables influencing either the decision to go for help or the particular resource chosen. Men and women, and the young and the old, differ more in their psychological orientations toward problems than in availability of resources, information, or the social climate facilitating or hindering help-seeking decisions.

SUMMARY

This chapter has been concerned with one segment of the total sample of people we interviewed—the 14 per cent who report that at some time in their lives they have gone to some professional resource for help with a personal problem.

Our examination of the going-for-help process as the people themselves saw it led us to conclude that in most cases going for help did not seem to represent any real motivation for therapeutic change: Only a minority of the people who went for help (about one in four) explicitly traced the source of the difficulty to some defect in themselves; most of the people going for help chose either a clergyman or nonpsychiatric physician rather than a mental health specialist; people who went to psychiatrists tended to be less satisfied with the help they felt they received than were the people who saw clergymen or physicians; most people described the ways in which they were helped in terms of comfort, reassurance and advice rather than in terms of any change in themselves. Although motivation for change is not always appropriate for the type of problem that was brought for help, these data suggest that where the problem does lie in the person seeking help, any attempts at directing him toward therapy and change are likely to be met with resistances.

These findings underscore the crucial role that nonpsychiatric resources—particularly clergymen and physicians—play in the treatment process. They are the major therapeutic agents: not only do most of the people with personal problems come to them but also, in the great majority of cases, the clergymen and physicians do not refer these people to any psychiatric specialist; they handle the problem themselves. This is particularly true of the clergy.

Physicians and clergymen must also act as diagnostic agents. They must know which of the cases that come to them as personal and psychological problems and which of the cases that are not perceived by the people in difficulty as psychological or personal should be referred to psychiatric specialists. Furthermore, they must be able to handle the resistances of those they wish to refer since many of the people who come with problems do not see the difficulty as psychological or personal and, even when they do, they do not see the cause of the problems in themselves. The physician, for example, faces many of these diagnostic and resistance problems when he treats the disturbed people who come to him with physical symptoms or feelings that they are approaching a nervous breakdown.

In the second set of analyses with which this chapter was concerned, we were mainly interested in carrying to completion the demographic analysis of the help-seeking process that was begun in the preceding chapter by investigating the relationships between demographic characteristics and the particular sources of help chosen —what we have referred to as the third stage in the self-referral process. In general, the findings seemed consistent with the assumption underlying this analysis, that relationships between demographic characteristics and the choice of a particular type of help resource could be interpreted as reflections of the operation of facilitating factors. The influence of place of residence suggests the importance of availability of resources as a facilitating factor—not only the physical presence of resources but the differences in "psychological" availability that are due to the different roles that resources such as clergymen and physicians take in different-sized communities. The greater choice of psychiatrists among high income people suggests the obvious influence of ability to pay for care as a facilitating factor influencing decisions about therapy. The greater choice of clergymen among high church-attenders suggests the importance of the psychological accessibility of the resource—one's social contact and acquaintance with it, and the appropriateness of the resource in terms of one's social and organizational memberships. Finally, the greater choice of psychiatrists among the more highly educated can probably be attributed not only to the greater psychological insight and sophistication associated with education but to such facilitating factors as greater information about psychiatric resources and the patterns of help-seeking behavior utilized in one's social group.

NOTES

1. Refers back to a previous set of questions asking what respondents would do about "being very unhappy all the time," and about problems in marriage, both of which were set in the context of personal problems.

2. The term "doctor" rather than "physician" was used in the question, to conform to the phraseology of daily usage. In the tables in this chapter, "doctor" will refer to non-psychiatric physicians.

3. We will talk about these 345 cases as if they were all individuals who went for help voluntarily. We realize this may involve a slight distortion, for some of these people may have been coerced into seeking help—e.g., schools often insist upon parents taking their children to a professional if they are "problems." However, only a handful of respondents indicated any such coercion.

4. We must remember that we are dealing with *reported* sources of help, and that the public terminology is loose. A general practitioner, for instance, may have been referred to incorrectly as a "psychiatrist," while a psychiatrist may have been simply designated as a "doctor."

5. Since only 6 people mentioned going to a "psychologist," and the public image of psychologists and psychiatrists tends to be confused, we have grouped those who mentioned psychologists with those who mentioned psychiatrists. It should also be noted that, although these figures represent the responses to only one question in the interview, there was only one case where a respondent mentioned seeing a psychiatrist without referring to it in response to this particular question. This 18 per cent figure, then, (2 per cent of the total population we sampled), represents the total number of people that we interviewed who mentioned going for some psychiatric help at some point in their lives.

6. Another twelve respondents mentioned informal sources of help such as friends, relatives, or bosses, although the question was specifically directed toward professional sources. These people—3 per cent of the total number who said they went to professional help with a personal problem—represent

a certain degree of unreliability of response to this, as to any other survey question. In terms of assessing the number of people in the country who have at some time gone for professional help with a personal problem, this figure is very likely counterbalanced by people who did go for help but did not report this to the interviewer.

7. As indicated above (Note 5), the people who mention getting psychiatric care for a "nervous breakdown" are included in the 18 per cent who mentioned psychiatric care in reference to a "personal" problem, with the one exception previously noted.

XI

A Critical Group

IN THIS CHAPTER, we focus our attention on a group of people, most of whom were presumably psychologically accessible to help, who recognized that *professional help could have helped them* with a problem they had faced in the past, and still did not go. We are concerned with why they did not.

All respondents who said they had never gone for help with a personal problem (i.e., all but the 345 respondents considered in the last chapter) were asked the following series of questions:

1. Can you think of anything that has happened to you, any problems you've had in the past, where going to someone like this [1] might have helped you in any way?
(If "Yes"):
a) What do you have in mind—what was it about?
b) What did you do about it?
c) Who do you think might have helped you with that?
d) Why do you suppose that you didn't go for help?

Two hundred twenty respondents—9 per cent of the total sample—said "Yes" to question 1. They could think of some problem in the past for which professional counsel might have helped them in some way.

We will first directly compare these 220 with those we dealt with in the last chapter in order to see if we can infer differences between these two groups that could account for their different behavior. Then we will consider the reasons given for not having actually sought outside help. Finally, we will look at the ways in which these people did in fact handle these problems.

DIFFERENCES BETWEEN PEOPLE GOING FOR HELP AND THOSE WHO "ALMOST" DID

We can best highlight the characteristics of the group who "almost" sought help when faced with personal problems by contrasting them with the group who *did*. We have already explored, in the discussions of the readiness for self-referral in Chapter IX, some of the demographic characteristics and the "facilitating" conditions differentiating these groups. In this section, we will explore two sets of possible differences: do the two groups differ in the kinds of personal problems they said they were facing, and do they differ in the kinds of resources that are psychologically available to them?

Problem Area

Are the problem areas that led one group to seek help similar to or different from those for which the other group said they could have used help? Can we find, in the nature of the problems faced, a reason why one group went for help and the other did not?

When we compare the percentage of each of these groups who mention a particular problem area (Table 11.1), it is clear that the areas tend to be quite similar. But some small differences do appear. There is some suggestion that problems involving children more often led to professional help, but that marriage problems proportionately more often *could have* used help than *did* receive professional attention.

The higher frequency of problems involving children in the group who sought help might occur because many people who become aware of difficulty with children do so only after some outside source (school or court) has brought it to their attention and also referred them to sources of professional help. But why should there be a heavier concentration of marriage problems in the difficulties reported by those who said they could have used help than in the difficulties reported by those who did use help? One might suspect that, when a person is confronted with a marriage problem, he sometimes has difficulty pinpointing the nature of the difficulty. Many people

Table 11.1—Problem Areas Seen as Relevant for Help by People Who Went for Help and Those Who Could Have Used Help

Problem Area	Used Help	Could Have Used Help
Spouse; marriage	42%	52%
Child; relationship with child	12	4
Other family relationships—parents, in-laws, etc.	5	6
Other relationship problems; type of relationship problem unspecified	4	4
Job or school problems; vocational choice	6	4
Nonjob adjustment problems in the self (general adjustment, specific symptoms, etc.)	18	14
Situational problems involving other people (e.g., death or illness of a loved one) causing extreme psychological reaction	6	6
Nonpsychological situational problems	8	6
Nothing specific; a lot of little things; can't remember	2	3
Not ascertained	1	3
Total	**	**
Number of people	(345)	(220)

** Here, and in subsequent tables, this symbol (**) indicates that percentages total to more than 100 per cent because some respondents gave more than one response.

phrased the problem as "we were just incompatible" or "we couldn't get along." When a person structures a marriage problem in this way, he is pointing to a relationship difficulty rather than specifying its nature.

We might hypothesize, then, that the reason there are more marriage problems among the group that never actually went for help is the nature of a marriage problem; it is often difficult to specify, and one less often goes for help when the problem is vague and unstructured. If this line of reasoning is correct, we might expect that people who did not go for help with a marriage problem would be more vague about the problem, would tend to talk about it as a relationship problem, or would not specify the locus of the difficulty.

A comparative look at the data confirms this view. Fifty-eight per cent of the marriage problems mentioned by those who went for help were coded as a "relationship difficulty" or "difficulty unspecified" compared to 68 per cent of the marriage problems of those who did not.

One cannot conclusively interpret data such as these, since we did not interview our respondents at the time they first went for help. It is possible that the greater ability to specify and localize problems of people who sought help was a *result* of the help rather than a precondition that led them to seek it. But the data are at least consistent with our assumption that an important determinant of seeking professional help with a problem is the capacity to specify the locus of the difficulty, whereas vagueness and uncertainty as to where to attribute one's trouble may be a limiting factor.

Sources of Help

We can compare our two groups in another way. What were the resources used by those who went for help in contrast to those suggested as possibly helpful by the people who said they could have used help? (See Table 11.2.)

Table 11.2—Comparison of Source of Help Used by People Who Have Used Help and Source Suggested as a Possible Help by Those Who Could Have Used Help

Source of Help	Used Help	Could Have Used Help
Clergyman	42%	34%
Doctor	29	9
Psychiatrist	18	14
Marriage counselor	3	14
Psychological agency	10	2
Nonpsychological agency	3	—
Lawyer	6	3
Family, friends	3	7
Other	8	10
Don't know	—	12
Not ascertained	—	7
Total	**	**
Number of people	(345)	(220)

Perhaps the most important figure in this comparison is the number of people who said they do not know what source of help could have helped them; 12 per cent of the respondents who said that they could have used help said they did not know to whom they would have turned for this help. Together with the 7 per cent "not ascertained," this means that 19 per cent of those people who said they could have used help did not or could not mention a specific professional resource. In itself, this is an important finding.

The other comparisons in Table 11.2 should be made with this major difference in mind. Since many of those people who said they could have used help do not specify a source, one would expect them to mention any potential source of help considerably less often than those people who actually went for help.

What we find is that one professional resource—marriage counselor—is actually mentioned relatively *more often* by those people who said they could have used help than by those people who actually went for help. One might expect this, since people who feel they could have used help more often point to marriage as a problem area than does the other group. But, beyond this, we would interpret the greater mention of marriage counselor by those who actually did not seek help as another indication of this group's lack of knowledge about the available professional resources. To them, "marriage counselor" probably represents a vague catch-all category rather than a specific professional resource. Marriage counselors are not a very popular resource of those people who actually went for help, and we may assume that, of the second group, many who suggest them as a possible resource would actually have chosen another resource if they had ever arrived at the point of going for help.

What can we conclude about the differences we have mentioned between these two groups? From the impressions one gains as one reads the interviews, both groups seem to have been talking about serious problems, and there is little difference in the content of the problems mentioned. There is a slight difference in that the people who sought help were somewhat more able to specify the nature of the difficulty they were experiencing, especially with regard to problems in marriage. Furthermore, many of the people who did not seek help were also vague about the help resources available—either unable to specify a professional resource that could have helped them, or mentioning a resource that is actually not very popular among those people who did seek help—the marriage counselor.

It is difficult to conclude definitely what this vagueness about help resources means. It may merely mean that these people were never motivated enough to get to the point of really considering help resources. It may imply, however, that this group was unusually handicapped by ignorance about what one does—that many in the group were ready for help, and with an extra impetus from the outside, a referral from a friend or a professional resource, they might have sought help. As we have noted in the preceding chapters, being ready for help is a psychological state that depends a great deal on internal attitudes, beliefs, and motivations. But the mechanics of seeking help, the actual act of self-referral, may depend a great deal upon what we have termed facilitating factors; and the vagueness in the knowledge of the group that never went for help may reflect a lack in some of these factors. If so, it would conform to the demographic analysis discussed in Chapter IX, where differences between those who did and those who did not go for help were also interpreted in terms of differences in these facilitating factors.

WHY PEOPLE DO NOT GO FOR HELP

Of major interest in this chapter are the reasons why people did not go for help when they felt they could have used it. We asked them this question. The reasons they gave are tabulated in Table 11.3,

Table 11.3—Reasons Given for Not Going for Help by People Who Feel They Could Have Used Some Help

Reasons for Not Going for Help	
Self-help—worked it out myself (ourselves)	25%
Lack of knowledge about means—didn't know how to go about it	20
Shame, stigma, hesitancy—ashamed to talk about it	14
Didn't think it would help	7
Temporizing—felt it would work out itself	6
Didn't realize need at the time	5
Problem involved other person who refused to go for help	5
Expense	4
Other	8
Not ascertained; don't know	14
Total	**
Number of people	(220)

indicating the percentage of this group who mentioned each type of reason. Let us examine this table in some detail, pointing out what kinds of responses were coded in each category.

The most popular reason mentioned for not going for help is a reason indicating that the respondent took care of the problem himself, or, if it was an interpersonal problem, that the people involved took care of it themselves. We have called this kind of response "self-help." Twenty-five per cent of the respondents were so coded. Included in this category, then, were all people who indicated that in one way or another they attempted to solve the problem by themselves.

Another large group of respondents (20 per cent) mentioned their lack of knowledge about the means of getting help. Included in this category were such responses as: "didn't know how to go about it," "didn't know about such places," "didn't know what to do," "didn't know a doctor, a minister." These responses all indicate that the channels for help were not accessible to these people, either because they were ignorant of them or because they did not have direct access to the channels of help.

Fourteen per cent indicated that going for help would involve shame. In this category are such responses as "ashamed to talk about it," "didn't feel like talking about it," "felt funny about seeing someone." This is an interesting group to consider. It represents people who were presumably ready for help but refused to go because of what others might think. Mental health programs have often concentrated on this group of people, trying in their educational devices to reassure people that there is nothing socially undesirable about going for help with personal problems. We should probably look at the percentage of people who gave this kind of reason for not going for help as a minimal figure, since fear of social disapproval is a motive not easily admitted to.

The other categories coded were "didn't think it would help," "temporizing—felt it would work out itself," "didn't realize need at the time," "problems involve other person who refused to go," "expense." Each of these categories was mentioned by only 4 to 7 per cent of these respondents.

We would like to draw special attention to two of these categories. Those persons (5 per cent) who said that they did not go for help because they did not realize the need at the time are a special group. In retrospect, they think they had a problem that required help; in a certain sense, they told us that they were not even aware of having the problem when they were experiencing it. All of the other reasons listed in Table 11.3 would indicate that the person was conscious of the problem at the time he experienced the situation mentioned. We point this out because it confirms an assumption we have been making—that the people who said that they could have used help were cognizant of the personal problem at the time that the difficulties were being experienced. This assumption is supported by the reasons given for not going for help; we have evidence that only a handful of people were referring to situations that were *not* recognized as problems requiring help at the time they were experienced.

The other category to which we want to draw particular attention is that labeled "expense"—a finding noteworthy because only a very few mentioned this reason. We highlight this result because findings in the previous chapters might have suggested that this group should have been larger. We have found that high income is one of the factors distinguishing people who have used help from those who feel they could have used it but actually never did, and that income is strongly related to the use of psychiatric care. If many people with low incomes do not make use of professional help or do not go to psychiatrists because they cannot afford these services, then one might expect that there would be a sizable group of people who rejected help-seeking because they felt they could not afford it. However, this does not appear to be true. Only nine respondents in the total sample of 220 said they did not go for professional help because they could not afford it.

This result might mean that the effects of income level discussed in previous chapters, in particular the use of psychiatrists, reflect a much more complicated set of factors than is encompassed by being able or not able to afford professional help. We reiterate a suggestion put forth in the last chapter: income level possibly has a great bearing on the use of professional resources because different income levels often reflect different social climates. The social groups represented by high-income respondents are probably more attuned to the availability of professional help in general, and psychiatry in particular, than those represented by people with lower incomes, and

A CRITICAL GROUP

consequently are more ready to seek potential help from resources that require more money—namely, psychiatrists. In a similar fashion, it would seem that people who may not be able to afford such services do not even consider it for themselves; there are probably few people of lower income who seek out professional help requiring a lot of money and only then find that they cannot afford the services. Not considering such resources, they do not see expense of therapy as a problem.

Social Characteristics Related to Reasons for Not Going for Help

It would be important to discover whether any of the specific reasons given by people for not seeking professional help are more prevalent in certain social groups. If social groups differ in their reasons for not turning to professional help, then any program that is directed toward overcoming resistances to help-seeking must take account of these differences.

Tables 11.4 to 11.7 concern the responses of different social groups to the question on why they did not go for help. Few striking differences appear in these tables, but some of them are suggestive.

Sex. By and large, men and women seem to be very similar in the kinds of reasons they offer for not having gone for help (when they thought they could have used help—Table 11.4). Several possible trends appear in the data, two of which may be noted. First, slightly more women than men give the possible shame going for help might imply as a reason for not going to a professional resource. Secondly, the problem of expense is mentioned more often by women than men.

Although these differences are slight, they appear to be consistent with other information. Several of the results in this monograph have focused on the greater social concerns of women than men; the fact that women tend to worry more about what other people might think if they went for help ties in with these results. The fact that more women than men mention expense as a reason for not seeking help may be linked to women's greater financial dependency. One therefore might expect women more than men to bring up the problem of expense as a deterrent to seeking professional help.

Table 11.4—Relationship of Sex to Reasons Given for Not Going for Help by People Who Feel They Could Have Used Help

Reasons for Not Going for Help	Men	Women
Self-help	26%	25%
Lack of knowledge about means	16	22
Shame	9	17
Didn't think it would help	5	8
Temporizing—felt it would work out itself	9	4
Didn't realize need at the time	8	4
Problem involved other person who refused help	4	6
Expense	1	6
Other	9	7
Not ascertained; don't know	18	12
Total	**	**
Number of people	(77)	(143)

Age. Table 11.5 shows that there is a very similar pattern to the reasons given by the three age levels for not seeking help. The greater reliance on self-help in the oldest group may reflect a generational cultural difference in self-help ideology, although the difference is a very small one.

Table 11.5—Relationship of Age to Reasons Given for Not Going for Help by People Who Feel They Could Have Used Help

	AGE		
Reasons for Not Going for Help	21–34	35–54	55 and Over
Self-help	23%	26%	30%
Lack of knowledge about means	17	22	21
Shame	11	15	14
Didn't think it would help	7	9	5
Temporizing—felt it would work out itself	7	8	—
Didn't realize need at the time	10	2	2
Problem involved other person who refused help	6	4	5
Expense	7	2	2
Other	6	7	14
Not ascertained; don't know	13	14	14
Total	**	**	**
Number of people [a]	(83)	(91)	(43)

[a] Does not include three people whose age was not ascertained.

Education. Likewise, we find nothing particularly different in the patterns of reasons given by people at each educational level. Table 11.6, presenting these education comparisons, shows that the only noteworthy difference appears in the "not ascertained; don't know"

Table 11.6—Relationship of Education to Reasons Given for Not Going for Help by People Who Feel They Could Have Used Help

	EDUCATION		
Reasons for Not Going for Help	Grade School	High School	College
Self-help	22%	29%	26%
Lack of knowledge about means	20	18	23
Shame	12	16	12
Didn't think it would help	5	8	9
Temporizing—felt it would work out itself	6	5	7
Didn't realize need at the time	2	9	2
Problem involved other person who refused help	8	3	9
Expense	3	6	—
Other	8	8	7
Not ascertained; don't know	25	10	9
Total	**	**	**
Number of people	(65)	(112)	(43)

category. Considerably more of the grade-school-educated respondents either gave no reason for not going for help or said they did not know why they did not go for help. Although less educated people generally tend to give more "don't know" and "not ascertained" responses to any attitude question in a survey, the differences in this instance are unusually large. This result would seem to reflect lower introspectiveness of the lower-educated groups.

The absence of any differences among the three education groups is of particular interest in light of the findings, reported in Chapter IX, that more and less educated people differ in the extent to which they translate a definition of a problem in mental health terms into a decision to go for help. Apparently, facilitating factors leading to the use of help are greater among the more highly educated. But the findings in Table 11.6 suggest that these differences between the education groups are not reflected in the factors that are *consciously* involved in the decision not to go for help. It is particularly surprising that these groups do not differ in the proportions who give lack of knowledge as a reason.

One might have anticipated that the respondents from the lower-education groups would be more likely to mention their lack of knowledge as a reason for not seeking help—their ignorance about places to go, their vagueness about professional people to whom they might have turned. The fact that all education groups were just as likely to report this kind of reason is an interesting finding. Evidently, for people who recognize a need for help, level of education has little to do with whether or not they perceive their own ignorance about resources as a deterrent to their obtaining help.

On the other hand, college-educated respondents in this group tended to mention the mental health professions (psychiatrist, marriage counselor, mental hygiene clinic) more often than did the other education groups. Forty per cent of the college group mentioned the mental health professions, while only 24 per cent of the high-school group and 18 per cent of the grade-school group mentioned them. These resources, in contrast to clergymen and physicians, are actually more difficult to know about and gain access to. Therefore, an overall lack of relationship between educational level and "lack of knowledge" as a reason for rejecting help may stem from the possibility that the higher-educated group's greater knowledge about help-seeking is counterbalanced by an interest in those resources that are, in reality, less accessible.

Church attendance. Only a small number of Catholics are included in this group of people who say they could have used help but did not go. In Table 11.7, therefore, we have considered only Protestants in looking at the effect of church attendance on the reasons people give for not going for help. In this comparison, we see that regular and low church-attending Protestants give the same kinds of reasons for having rejected going for help.

Income. If we ignore the figures in the highest income category, based on only 11 cases, only one consistent difference appears in Table 11.8, which compares the reasons for not going for help mentioned by the respondents from different income groups. This difference, one that could be reasonably anticipated, is that all but one of the respondents who do mention an economic barrier to help-seeking came from the lower income groups. (What is perhaps more surprising, as we have previously noted, is that so few people in any category give this reason at all.)

As with respect to education, we see in Table 11.8 that the higher income groups mentioned "lack of knowledge" as a reason for not

Table 11.7—Relationship of Church Attendance (Protestants Only) to Reasons Given for Not Going for Help by People Who Feel They Could Have Used Help

	PROTESTANTS	
Reasons for Not Going for Help	Regular Attenders [a]	Not Regular Attenders [b]
Self-help	20%	26%
Lack of knowledge about means	20	18
Shame	15	15
Didn't think it would help	9	6
Temporizing—felt it would work out itself	5	9
Didn't realize need at the time	5	3
Problem involved other person who refused help	2	5
Expense	5	5
Other	5	8
Not ascertained; don't know	18	15
Total	**	**
Number of people [c]	(65)	(102)

[a] Refers to people who attend church once a week or more.
[b] Refers to people who attend church less than once a week.
[c] Does not include Protestants whose frequency of church attendance was not ascertained.

Table 11.8—Relationship of Income to Reasons Given for Not Going for Help by People Who Feel They Could Have Used Help

	INCOME IN DOLLARS					
Reasons for Not Going for Help	Under 2,000	2,000 3,999	4,000 4,999	5,000 6,999	7,000 9,999	10,000 or More
Self-help	28%	22%	27%	22%	24%	55%
Lack of knowledge about means	18	20	19	22	21	18
Shame	8	24	14	10	17	9
Didn't think it would help	8	8	5	12	—	—
Temporizing—felt it would work out itself	3	2	3	10	14	9
Didn't realize need at the time	5	6	8	10	10	—
Problem involved other person who refused help	—	8	8	6	3	—
Expense	—	10	8	—	3	—
Other	8	12	—	4	14	9
Not ascertained; don't know	28	8	14	14	7	18
Total	**	**	**	**	**	**
Number of people [a]	(39)	(51)	(37)	(50)	(29)	(11)

[a] Does not include three people whose income level was not ascertained.

going for help just as often as this was mentioned by the lower income groups. We might have expected the higher income groups to have more knowledge about resources. Again, the explanation may lie in the differences in the kinds of resources utilized by people at the different status levels. As in the case of the more educated, the higher income groups are much more likely to think of a mental health profession as a resource for help. The differences are even more striking than they were with respect to education, and are noted in Table 11.9: only 7 per cent of the people in the lowest income group, as opposed to over 40 per cent in the highest income groups, mention a mental health profession.

Table 11.9—Relationship between Income and Mention of a Mental Health Profession as Source of Help That Could Have Helped with a Personal Problem

Possible Source of Help	INCOME IN DOLLARS					
	Under 2,000	2,000–3,999	4,000–4,999	5,000–6,999	7,000–9,999	10,000 or More
Some mention of mental health profession	7%	26%	32%	34%	44%	45%
No mention of mental health profession	93	74	68	66	56	55
Total	100%	100%	100%	100%	100%	100%
Number of people ᵃ	(39)	(51)	(37)	(50)	(29)	(11)

ᵃ Does not include three people whose income level was not ascertained.

If we assume that higher income is associated not only with greater general knowledge about resources for help but also with interest in those resources that are in actuality the most difficult to know about and get to, one might expect no over-all difference among income levels in their mentioning lack of knowledge as a reason for rejecting help.

Place of residence. The final table in this series is Table 11.10, in which we consider differences in place of residence. The most striking result here is that the problem of "shame" as a deterrent to going for help is voiced most frequently by respondents who come from a small town. Two factors are probably operative here: The concern about whether the act of going for help might become public knowledge is, in the first place, most realistic in the small-town setting; and secondly, in the atmosphere of a smaller, more integrated community, such as a small town, the concern about the disapproval of one's neighbors is most likely to arise.

In general, few distinctions can be made about who the people are who give one reason for not seeking help as opposed to another. Whatever differences may exist among these groupings in the in-

A CRITICAL GROUP

Table 11.10—Relationship of Place of Residence to Reasons Given for Not Going for Help by People Who Feel They Could Have Used Help

Reasons for Not Going for Help	Metropolitan Areas	Suburbs	Small Cities	Towns	Rural
Self-help	26%	27%	32%	27%	21%
Lack of knowledge about means	20	12	20	23	20
Shame	9	15	4	25	12
Didn't think it would help	3	6	8	6	11
Temporizing—felt it would work out itself	9	6	4	4	7
Didn't realize need at the time	9	6	4	4	5
Problem involved other person who refused help	6	9	8	4	3
Expense	6	9	—	2	4
Other	6	12	16	4	7
Not ascertained; don't know	9	12	16	12	18
Total	**	**	**	**	**
Number of people	(34)	(33)	(25)	(52)	(76)

ternal resistances or external barriers that keep a person who is psychologically accessible to help from the final decision to go for help, these differences are rarely reflected in the reasons that the people in these groupings are consciously aware of.

HOW THESE PEOPLE HANDLE THEIR PROBLEMS

As a final inquiry into patterns of rejecting professional help, we examined what these people actually did do about the problems for which they thought help was relevant. If they did not make use of formal resources of help, did they turn to informal resources (friends or relatives) or did they try to handle these problems by themselves? And if they managed by themselves, how did they go about it? Did they cope actively with the problem? Did they do nothing about it? Did they turn to prayer? There are many different ways that people can choose for handling the problems they face.

An important theoretical dimension to consider in classifying ways of handling problems is an activity-passivity dimension. Does the person cope directly with the problem he encounters, does he attempt an active solution, does he meet it with "problem-solving" activity? Those methods which do directly involve problem-solving activity we called the *coping* ways of handling problems. (We would include going for help in the coping group.) Those that do not directly involve problem-solving activity we called the *passive* ways of handling problems. Some methods of handling problems are difficult to place on this dimension. What does prayer mean in this context? Is it passive—a way of "hoping for the best" but actually doing nothing—or is it an active coping involving turning to spiritual guidance for help in mobilizing one's internal resources and facing the problem? Since it may be one or the other, somewhat depending on the personal meaning of prayer, we have considered the use of prayer as a separate category, placing it in neither the "coping" nor the "passive" group.

In the chapter following we will use this coping-passive dimension to describe methods the respondents in the total sample used for handling the problems and the crises that they face. In the present chapter, we concentrate only on the coping-passive methods used by those people who ended up by themselves handling a problem for which they feel they could have used professional help.

Table 11.11 shows the distribution of the ways that people handled these problems. These methods are grouped according to the coping-passive dimension, with prayer considered separately.

Under passive reactions, we find that only one per cent of the group handled the problem by "denial or displacement," that is, by attempting to "forget about it" or attempting to do or think

Table 11.11—Methods Utilized by People to Handle Personal Problems for Which They Feel They Could Have Used Some Help

Methods of Handling Problems	
Passive reactions:	
Denial or displacement—forgot it; did something else	1%
Did nothing	32
Coping reactions:	
Attempts at coping—tried to work it out myself (or together with another person involved in problem)	26
Withdrawal from situation—left home; separated	13
Sought help from informal sources—family, friends, etc.	9
Sought help from formal sources (but not mental health sources)	8
Prayer	3
Other	3
Not ascertained	8
Total	**
Number of people	(220)

about something else, to "take one's mind off it." This figure is probably spuriously low, since really effective denial should result in no mention of a problem; in a sense, these people are instances of unsuccessful denial. We will see in the following chapter that this denial response appears quite often as a reaction to less serious difficulties. Although the "true" figure is probably greater than one per cent, denial is probably not too readily available as a means of reaction to problems so serious that they were seen as potentially requiring help.

The other reaction coded as a passive reaction was "doing nothing." Although in many cases "doing nothing" probably has elements of denial, it was kept as a separate category because it does not necessarily indicate any attempt at repressing the conflict. "Doing nothing" was mentioned by 32 per cent of the group of people we are considering. This was the most popular category coded, and indicates that a large proportion of this group was essentially helpless in the face of their problem, unable to find either external or internal resources.

Under coping reactions, we find 26 per cent of these respondents mentioning some attempt to handle the problem directly by "trying to work things out." Thirteen per cent withdrew from the situation causing them difficulty, most of these being people who handled a marital problem by divorce or separation. Seventeen per cent went somewhere for help, 9 per cent to informal sources of help (family and friends), the other 8 per cent to formal sources, but not the mental health sources referred to in the question.

Although we have categorized these as coping responses, for the most part they represent essentially a kind of "muddling through." In most of these cases, as in the 32 per cent who said they did nothing, one does not get the feeling that the alternative to the use of help was a reliance on strong internal resources. From the very fact that today, looking back at these problems, people still see them as problems for which they might have used help, there is an implication of a somewhat less than completely satisfactory outcome to these problems. Going for help is, of course, itself no guarantee of cure, but it does represent a hope, and, particularly for those whose only alternative to seeking help was resignation, sometimes it offers the only possibility of solution. How sick these people were, how much they needed help, whether therapy would have helped them, are questions that we cannot answer. It is perhaps the major tragedy of many of these people that these questions are still pertinent—that feeling the distress and seeing and accepting the relevance of help, they never got to a place where these questions might have been answered.

SUMMARY

This chapter has been concerned with an analysis of the 9 per cent of the total sample who recognized the need for personal help at some point in their lives but never went for help. This group is critical for an understanding of the going-for-help process; some of the factors that militate against the use of mental health resources should appear most clearly among these people who do not go for help even though they are psychologically receptive to the idea that such help would be appropriate for their problems.

In the reasons they give for not having sought help, these people most often stressed: the desire to work the problem out themselves, lack of knowledge about where to go or what to do in order to get help, and the shame and stigma attached to going for help with an emotional problem. Experts in the field of mental health have generally considered these factors to be major deterrents to the help-seeking process.

In most cases the methods these people did use to handle their problems indicated a lack of strong internal or external resources to fall back on; the alternative to going for help was either doing nothing, or tentative attempts at resolution that were not completely effective. To a considerable extent, then, this large group of people represents an unmet mental health need.

In comparisons between these people who did not seek help and those people who did go for help with some emotional problem we hoped to highlight the special characteristics distinguishing those who did not go for help. We had already noted certain *demographic* differences between these two groups: those who received help tended to come from the more educated, higher-income and urban groups (Table 9.11, Chapter IX). In this chapter, certain *attitudinal* differences between the two groups were investigated. The group that did not go for help was somewhat more vague and indefinite, both in specifying the locus of the problem and in indicating what resources they might have used if they had gone for help. This vagueness and uncertainty about the nature of the problem and the means of obtaining help may have acted as deterrents to getting help. But there were few other differences between the two groups; they tended to be similar in the ways they viewed the content of their problems and in the professional resources they said they used or might have used.

Within the group that did not go for help, the different demographic subgroups generally tended to be similar in the reasons they gave for not having gone for help, although certain differences were observed; for example, shame and stigma were mentioned more often by women than by men, and by people in small towns more often than by people in big cities and rural areas.

In general, then, few attitudinal differences were observed. The group that went for help and the one that did not, and the different demographic subgroups within the latter group, were more marked for their similarities than their differences. While there may be attitudinal differences among these groups that were not revealed in the study, such attitudinal differences may be truly minimal. Our previous conclusions suggest the latter interpretation; once a problem has been seen in mental health terms, the decision to go for help should be largely a function of facilitating factors, and not necessarily a reflection of attitudinal differences.

NOTE

1. Refers back to the context of the previous question, in which doctors, ministers, psychiatrists, marriage counselors, social agencies, and clinics were established as help sources to whom one might turn with a personal problem.

XII

Personal and Informal Resources

LET US now consider, *for the entire sample,* the question of what people do about their problems if they do not choose to get professional help. Do they seek help from informal resources, turning to family or friends? Do they remain resigned to their problems, doing nothing or attempting to deny the existence of the difficulty? Do they cope actively with the situation that is causing them concern by thinking things out or doing something about the problem? Do they turn to religious resources and pray when things do not go right for them?[1]

We will be specifically concerned with the responses to two sets of questions, one concerning present worries, the other concerning unhappy periods of the past. The relevant questions were:

1. If something is on your mind that's bothering you or worrying you and you don't know what to do about it, what do you usually do? (If doesn't mention "talk it over"): Do you ever talk it over with anyone? (If not mentioned): Who is that?

2. One of the things we'd like to know is how people face the unhappy periods in their lives. Thinking of unhappiness you've had to face, what are some of the things that have helped you in those times?

Anticipating that people might react differently to situations they define as "worries" and those they define as "periods of unhappiness," we were interested in looking for differential reactions to these two questions. We will, therefore, first compare the mechanisms for handling worries with the mechanisms for handling periods of unhappiness, as these were mentioned by all of the respondents, and

PERSONAL AND INFORMAL RESOURCES

then see whether specific patterns of handling these difficulties are more typical of certain social groups than of others.

METHODS OF HANDLING WORRIES AND PERIODS OF UNHAPPINESS

In Chapter II, we discussed the differential meanings of the terms worry and unhappiness, pointing out that, although respondents explicitly mention similar kinds of difficulties in the elaborations of their worries and their sources of unhappiness, there seem to be striking *implicit* differences between worrying and being unhappy. Worrying seems to imply an active coping with life problems and a commitment to the assumption that one can change these disturbing situations. Being unhappy seems, on the other hand, to reflect a passive resignation to troubles, a pessimism about the future, and an absence of positive resources.

Moreover, this difference between worrying and unhappiness, which appeared when we compared responses to the questions on current worries and unhappiness, is even stronger when we consider the question on periods of past unhappiness. Responses to this question, which covers a person's entire past history, include references to catastrophic events which could not very readily be handled by coping behavior, situations in which some form of passive acceptance represented the only real alternative. For example, as we noted in Chapter II, more than one person in four mentioned a death in the family as precipitating the past unhappiness.

Active concern, implied by the term worry, and passive dissatisfaction, implied both by the term unhappy and by the content of the problems referred to in response to the question on past unhappiness, should have direct bearing on what people might do about either kind of personal tension. We might expect, for example, that people would be more inclined to take more direct active measures to handle worries than they would to handle periods of unhappiness.

In Table 12.1, we compare the ways people say they handle worries with the ways mentioned to handle periods of unhappiness. Again we have categorized these responses into three major groups: *passive*

Table 12.1—Comparison of the Ways of Handling Worries and Periods of Unhappiness (First-Mentioned Responses Only)

Methods of Handling Personal Difficulties	Worries		Periods of Unhappiness	
Passive reactions	34%		23%	
Denial or displacement		18%		15%
Do nothing		10		7
Continuing tension		6		1
Coping reactions	44		31	
Do something about it		14		6
Informal help-seeking		26		20
Formal help-seeking		2		2
Help-seeking, not ascertained formal or informal		2		3
Prayer	16		33	
Others	2		5	
Inappropriate: respondent never worried or unhappy	2		4	
Not ascertained	2		4	
Total	100%		100%	
Number of people	(2460)		(2460)	

reactions, *coping* reactions, and the use of *prayer*. Under passive reactions we have three subcategories: denial or displacement (i.e., forgetting about the worries or unhappiness, or doing something else to "take one's mind off" them); doing nothing at all; and "continuing tension," a category which includes such responses as "just keep on worrying" (i.e., responses which indicate that nothing was done about the problem but that the respondent could not forget it). Under *coping* reactions we have distinguished those people who say they do something about their problem—think things through, try to alleviate the situation causing them concern—from those who say they turn to someone else for help; for the latter group, in turn, informal and formal resources have been distinguished.

Again, we have kept the use of "prayer" as a separate category, designating it neither as a passive nor as a coping method, because prayer can have either meaning for a person. For some it can serve to mobilize internal resources, to gather strength to cope with the problems one is facing. To others it is an act of resignation, a recognition that events are beyond one's own control, an appeal not for strength to cope but for strength to endure. From the interviews one gains the impression that, for the majority of the people who mentioned prayer, it seemed a passive rather than a coping reaction. For many it seemed a recourse of despair, a behavior evoked when there are no direct active channels for coping with a problem. For example, this response seemed to be evoked when people faced critical external situations far beyond their direct control—death, illness, and other unchangeable catastrophes—and implied resignation and a quest for spiritual comfort. Consequently, we approach the data in this chapter with the assumption that prayer tends to represent a passive rather than a coping reaction, and see to what extent the findings may be integrated within such an interpretation.

Table 12.1 indicates that the patterns of handling worries and periods of unhappiness are indeed different. Most striking, our respondents more often mention prayer when they describe how they handle periods of unhappiness than when they talk about the ways of handling worries: about one third say they have met periods of unhappiness with prayer, whereas about one-sixth of the sample reports turning to prayer for worries. Because such a large group reports using prayer for periods of unhappiness, proportionately higher percentages reporting *both* passive and active reactions appear in the classification of ways of handling worries. But, interpreting prayer as a passive response, these findings may be viewed as corroborating our assumption that periods of unhappiness would lead more readily to passive reactions, and worrying more readily to coping mechanisms.

Both for handling worries and for handling periods of unhappiness, a frequent reaction was that of turning to some informal resource of help (family or friends). Twenty-six per cent of the respondents mention this as a way of dealing with worries; 20 per cent of the respondents mention this as an aid during periods of unhappiness. But only 2 per cent of the population mention going to professional, formal resources (doctors, clergymen, mental health specialists) for help either with worries or during periods of unhappiness. This is especially interesting when it is recalled that 14 per cent of the population mention having gone for professional help at some time. Evidently, although people admit having received professional help when they are directly questioned about it, they do not, in most cases, generally associate such assistance with the ways in which they cope with unhappiness or worries. We may conclude, for most people, that utilizing resources such as clergymen and family doctors is not usually perceived as being a major method of coping with the problems in their lives.

What are the informal and formal resources that people use? Are they the same for worries and for periods of unhappiness? We find the answers to these questions in Table 12.2, in which we list, for those people who mention talking to someone about worries or unhappiness, the relative frequency with which a certain kind of person was chosen: spouse, children, parents, other family members, friends, clergymen, physicians, mental health specialists. From this table then, we can see to whom these respondents talk and compare the kinds of people who are chosen in times of worry with those chosen in times of unhappiness.

Table 12.2—Comparison of Sources of Outside Help Used in Handling Worries and Periods of Unhappiness (First-Mentioned Responses Only)

Sources of Help	Worries	Periods of Unhappiness
Informal		
Spouse	56%	17%
Parents	4	9
Children	3	4
Other family	8	16
Friends	12	31
Other acquaintances	4	3
Formal		
Clergyman	4	5
Doctor	3	3
Mental health specialist	1	1
Not ascertained	5	11
Total	100%	100%
Number of people [a]	(726)	(613)

[a] Includes only those people who mentioned some outside source of help.

One very striking result appears in Table 12.2. Of those who turned to another person for help with worries, the majority—56 per cent—designate that other person as their spouse. Of those who seek help from others in periods of unhappiness, on the other hand, only 17 per cent mention their spouses. Conversely, people tend to turn to friends to a much greater extent when they are having periods of unhappiness than when they have troublesome worries: 31 per cent contrasted to only 12 per cent.

Why should this big difference occur? Why should worries elicit reliance on the marital partner more than periods of unhappiness? Conversely, why should periods of unhappiness elicit reliance on friends more than times of worry?

Let us consider again our discussion of the differential meaning of worries and unhappiness. The coping, active struggle seemingly implicit in the term worries is one that can conceivably be shared by husband and wife. The helpmate role demand of a husband or a wife can be fulfilled naturally in these periods of distress. During periods of unhappiness, which we consider, generally, to represent resigned passive distress, the helpmate role of the spouse may be less appropriate. Indeed, one might expect that both husband and wife often experience the same resigned states, the same feelings of dissatisfaction in situations defined as periods of unhappiness. It would therefore not be surprising to find many married men and women turning to a third party—a close friend, in particular—for comfort and reassurance. Periods of unhappiness may often be beyond the point of reassurance from a husband or a wife, who has gone through the same misfortune. A third party can lend the comfort and assurance that is temporarily unavailable from the marital partner.

Of course, in a number of cases respondents mentioning periods of unhappiness were referring to times before they were married, or times of marital problems or disruption (death or divorce of a husband or wife), a fact that would tend to lower the number of times the spouse would be mentioned as a source of help during periods of unhappiness. But these instances are not sufficient to account for the large difference found in the data.

DEMOGRAPHIC CHARACTERISTICS RELATED TO WAYS OF HANDLING WORRIES AND PERIODS OF UNHAPPINESS

One might expect that the life situations represented by different demographic groupings would foster different ways of handling personal distress. Therefore, as in the last two chapters, we will be considering sex, age, education, place of residence, income, religion, and church attendance, in an effort to determine whether this hypothesis is borne out by our data.

Table 12.3 presents the relationship of these variables to different ways of handling worries, and Table 12.4 presents relationships between these variables and ways of handling periods of unhappiness. We have combined some of the coding categories: all passive reactions—"denial," "displacement," "doing nothing," and "continuing tension"—have been grouped together; "doing something about the problem" is now titled "direct coping reaction"; those people who said they talked things over with a family member or a friend are included under "informal help-seeking." The category of prayer is maintained, but all other responses are coded under "other." We will consider each demographic grouping separately to note whether, within each one, there is any relationship between that social characteristic and the ways of handling either worries or periods of unhappiness.

Sex

More women than men turn to prayer as a way of handling worries or periods of unhappiness. Social observers have often noted this difference between the sexes—i.e., that prayer and religious matters in general are of greater importance for women as a group than they are for men. If one interprets the mechanism of prayer as a passive mode of problem solving, these observations and results fit into the general picture of sex differences that have been noted in this study. Many of the findings have been discussed in terms of this distinction between the male and female roles, with men, not women, expected to be the actors, the doers, the achievers in the social world. One would expect, then, that women would more often turn to prayer as a means of handling problems, while men would tend to handle problems in a more direct, active way.

Age

The most striking results from examining the relationship between age and ways of handling worries and unhappiness are that older people say they pray more than younger people, with the latter, in turn, talking to family and friends more than older people. We are probably encountering, in these results, the phenomenon of increased resignation to personal difficulties that is likely to occur with age. Such a phenomenon may be explained by assuming that youth is associated with optimism about one's own powers of solving difficulties; as people begin to experience failures in coping with certain areas of distress, they are likely to become more pessimistic about their own powers, more resigned to their fates, and more prone to use passive means of coping with personal distress. The gradual switch from coping mechanisms to passive mechanisms of handling problems as people age is best exemplified in the change from informal help-seeking as a major response of the youngest age groups, to prayer as a major response in the oldest age groups.

The comparatively small proportion of old people who say they turn to family or friends in times of worry or unhappiness is an important factor to consider in an appraisal of the difficulties encountered by the aged in our society. This result reflects a general observation made about old people in the American culture: feeling cut off from human contact in general and lacking a function in the social structure, they feel depersonalized and cannot maintain the personal relationships that were once important to them as young adults.

Education

Education seems to be related to what people do about their worries, but has little to do with the ways they handle periods of unhappiness (Tables 12.3 and 12.4). Generally speaking, more educated respondents report, as ways of handling worries, reactions that reflect more active coping (doing something direct, talking to family and friends) than is reflected in the reactions of less educated respondents; the latter rely more on passive reactions (doing nothing, denying, praying). This differentiation does not occur in ways of handling periods of unhappiness.

How do we account for these differences? If education gives people resources for handling worries, why does it not offer equal

Table 12.3—Relationship between Demographic Characteristics and Ways of Handling Worries (First-Mentioned Responses Only)

	METHODS OF HANDLING WORRIES							
Demographic Characteristics	Passive Reaction (Per Cent)	Prayer (Per Cent)	Direct Coping Reaction (Per Cent)	Informal Help-Seeking (Per Cent)	Other Ways (Per Cent)	Not Ascertained; Not Applicable (Per Cent)	Total Per Cent	Number of People
Sex								
Male	38	8	21	22	6	5	100	1077
Female	30	23	9	28	6	4	100	1383
Age								
21–34	30	7	16	39	5	3	100	759
35–54	34	18	15	24	6	3	100	1007
55 and over	38	23	12	14	6	7	100	681
Education								
Grade school	41	21	8	17	6	7	100	802
High school	31	14	15	32	5	3	100	1185
College	28	11	24	27	7	3	100	457
Income								
Under $2,000	40	26	8	15	4	7	100	407
$2,000–3,999	38	20	9	22	6	5	100	549
$4,000–4,999	30	14	18	30	5	3	100	390
$5,000–6,999	29	11	19	33	6	2	100	559
$7,000–9,999	33	8	17	33	7	2	100	299
$10,000 and over	28	12	24	24	9	3	100	186

Place of residence						
Metropolitan areas	33	12	16	28	7	4	100	325
Suburbs	31	15	19	23	8	4	100	326
Small cities	28	17	13	30	9	3	100	385
Towns	34	17	14	26	4	5	100	704
Rural	39	17	12	23	4	5	100	720
Religion and church attendance						
Protestants						
More than once a week	19	43	10	19	5	4	100	193
Once a week	27	26	11	26	6	4	100	507
A few times a month	33	18	13	28	4	4	100	446
A few times a year	40	6	18	26	5	5	100	454
Never	47	6	20	14	5	8	100	139
Catholics [b]						
More than once a week	21	24	10	34	8	3	100	98
Once a week	36	9	15	28	8	4	100	310
A few times a month	39	3	14	33	6	5	100	64
A few times a year	47	2	20	23	6	2	100	51

[a] The "not ascertained" groups on each demographic variable were omitted from this table.
[b] The Catholic group that "never" attends church was omitted because of its small size (19 people).

Table 12.4—The Relationship between Demographic Characteristics and Ways of Handling Unhappy Periods (First-Mentioned Responses Only)

METHODS OF HANDLING UNHAPPY PERIODS

Demographic Characteristics[a]	Passive Reaction (Per Cent)	Prayer (Per Cent)	Direct Coping Reaction (Per Cent)	Informal Help-Seeking (Per Cent)	Other Ways (Per Cent)	Not Ascertained; Not Applicable (Per Cent)	Total Per Cent	Number of People
Sex								
Male	26	22	9	19	13	11	100	1077
Female	20	40	4	21	9	6	100	1383
Age								
21–34	22	27	5	27	11	8	100	759
35–54	25	32	7	19	10	7	100	1007
55 and over	20	39	7	15	9	10	100	681
Education								
Grade school	22	36	6	17	9	10	100	802
High school	24	31	5	23	10	7	100	1185
College	23	29	9	20	11	8	100	457
Income								
Under $2,000	18	42	6	17	9	8	100	407
$2,000–3,999	25	31	5	22	10	7	100	549
$4,000–4,999	24	32	5	21	11	7	100	390
$5,000–6,999	25	31	6	21	11	6	100	559
$7,000–9,999	22	28	8	22	11	9	100	299
$10,000 and over	25	27	10	16	11	11	100	186

Place of residence						
Metropolitan areas	25	26	7	24	11	7	100	325
Suburbs	25	33	6	18	12	6	100	326
Small cities	21	36	5	19	10	9	100	385
Towns	23	33	7	19	11	7	100	704
Rural	21	32	6	22	10	9	100	720
Religion and church attendance							
Protestants							
More than once a week	11	55	2	19	8	5	100	193
Once a week	18	43	4	20	9	6	100	507
A few times a month	24	33	5	20	11	7	100	446
A few times a year	27	20	9	23	11	10	100	454
Never	29	14	12	19	14	12	100	139
Catholics [b]							
More than once a week	10	65	1	12	4	8	100	98
Once a week	27	35	4	14	13	7	100	310
A few times a month	37	17	17	23	2	4	100	64
A few times a year	10	25	8	31	16	10	100	51

[a] The "not ascertained" groups on each demographic variable were omitted from this table.
[b] The Catholic group that "never" attends church was omitted because of its small size (19 people).

resources for handling periods of unhappiness? For this explanation, we may again turn to the original distinction between worries and unhappiness.

Unhappiness usually implies a passive resignation to a distressed state, whereas worries imply an active coping with distress. Coping behavior in a situation that induces passive resignation does not have the same meaning as such behavior in a situation that has not induced resignation. To do something about unhappiness, to seek help from family or friends about unhappiness, may often mean to seek comfort and reassurance. To do something about worries, to turn to family or friends for advice when worried, would probably mean to engage in fairly direct problem-solving activities.

It may be, then, that for handling worries, people who report coping mechanisms are talking about problem-solving behavior aimed at dealing with the situation *causing the distress,* and that for handling periods of unhappiness people who report coping mechanisms are talking about problem solving directed at *alleviating the felt distress.*

It might be contended that only in the former instance—only when coping means direct problem solving—would a person's educational status be important, for only in direct problem solving would a person who had more education be able to employ coping mechanisms to a greater extent than a person with less education.

Income

Income level seems to relate to ways of handling worries and periods of unhappiness in the same way that educational status does. Higher income statuses are associated with greater mention of coping mechanisms used for handling worries (direct coping or talking with family or friends), while lower income statuses are associated with greater mention of passive mechanisms for handling worries (doing nothing, denying worries, or prayer). Again, this relationship does not obtain when we consider methods of handling unhappy periods of life.

We would give explanations for these findings which are similar to the explanations of the parallel findings with education above. Higher incomes should be associated with increased resources for direct problem-solving behavior, first because income is correlated highly with education, and secondly because higher incomes give people greater actual control over certain problem-solving activities in which they might engage (e.g., solving financial difficulties).

Place of Residence

There is no relationship between place of residence and the informal and personal resources people use in handling the worries and the unhappiness they face. As indicated in Tables 12.3 and 12.4, rural and urban people, small-town and big-city dwellers, do not differ in this respect.

Religion and Church Attendance

The last social comparisons highlighted in Tables 12.3 and 12.4 are ways of handling worries and unhappiness mentioned by Catholic respondents in contrast to Protestants. Again, we compare Catholics and Protestants who report the same frequency of church attendance.

The most interesting comparison is between Catholics and Protestants in the reported use of prayer as a method for handling worries or periods of unhappiness. As one might expect, within each of these religious groups, those respondents who attend church most frequently are more inclined to report the use of prayer as a way of dealing with worries and periods of unhappiness. But a surprising result emerges when Catholic and Protestant respondents are compared within a given frequency of church attendance. *In handling worries, more Protestants than Catholics, at each frequency of church attendance, report that they turn to prayer.* No consistent differences appear in the responses to the question on unhappiness, but prayer seems to be clearly more salient for Protestants than Catholics as a means of handling worries.

What do these results signify? The greater emphasis on prayer by Protestants as a means of handling distress might be taken to mean that Protestantism fosters a more personalized view of prayer, a greater individualistic approach to the determination of one's fate. Prayer for Catholics is often highly ritualized and structured within the church setting itself. In a certain sense, then, prayer may be thought to be less immediately accessible to Catholics. This might explain the fact that the greater emphasis on prayer by Protestants occurs when we examine ways of handling *worries*—active daily struggles—but not when we examine how people deal with periods of unhappiness or more comprehensive, long-term, and often catastrophic problems. If Catholics find prayer less accessible to them, this result is not surprising. The more ritualized structuring of prayer among Catholics might make it less appropriate for everyday concerns. For periods of unhappiness, however, Catholics may make a more special effort to perform the rituals of formal prayer. Indeed, Catholics and Protestants both use prayer more during periods of unhappiness than they do when they are worried, but this difference is sharper for Catholics than for Protestants. As a matter of fact, looking at the figures in Table 12.4, we see that among the very devout, more Catholics than Protestants turn to prayer during periods of unhappiness.

There are apparently other differences in the ways Catholics and Protestants, regular church-attenders and low church-attenders, handle worries and periods of unhappiness, as tabulated in Tables 12.3 and 12.4. Most of these apparent differences, however, seem to stem from the major relationship of these religious variables to the use of prayer. Since low church-attenders do not pray, they mention other passive reactions and coping reactions more often than regular church-attenders in reporting the ways they do handle worries and unhappiness. Similarly, more Catholics than Protestants report reactions other than prayer. There does not, however, seem to be any specific reaction that is particularly striking for low church-attenders or Catholics.

SUMMARY

In this chapter we have looked at some of the alternatives to professional help. What ways besides this relatively extreme course of action do people have for handling the problems that they face, the worries of their daily lives, the periods of unhappiness that they have had to face? The use of informal resources—family or friends—and the internal resources that people draw upon were investigated. Do people meet problems passively, with resignation, doing nothing or attempting to deny the existence of the problem? Or do they attempt to cope actively with the problem? Do they pray?

There are a number of striking differences in the ways different subgroups of the population handle their worries and unhappiness, particularly in their use of prayer. More women than men, more older people than younger people, more regular church-attenders than low church-attenders report turning to prayer as a way of handling their worries and unhappiness. In addition, the less educated, the lower income groups, and Protestants (when compared to Catholics at any given level of church attendance) more often resort to prayer as a way of dealing with their day-to-day worries (although they are not distinctive in their use of prayer in the critical, unhappy periods of their lives).

Direct coping with worries—attempting to do something about the sources of distress—is more common in men, in younger people, in the more educated, and in higher income groups. And reliance on informal ties—on friends and family—is much more common in younger than in older people.

These results point up certain characteristics of the different demographic subgroups: the passivity and loss of personal ties of the older aged groups, the greater passivity and religious involvement of women when compared to men, the increased resources for handling problems that come with increasing education and income.

It is of interest to compare these demographic relationships with those involving the use of formal resources in terms of this question: What alternatives are used by those social groupings of the population that do not make much use of formal help resources?

Those people who do not seek professional help—men, older people, the lower educated, and farm and rural groups—do not make unusual use of either their own or informal group resources. This is most striking in the case of the older and the less educated people where there is much less use of coping mechanisms and, among older people, also much less reliance on the support of friends and family. The major alternative for these people lies in the use of prayer.

The men are the only exception; although they use professional help less than women, they are higher in the use of personal coping mechanisms.

Thus, the groups in our population using professional help less often do not seem to meet their problems unusually well through their own resources; these people are not substituting internal coping resources or informal social ties for the more formal help resources that they are not using. Moreover, it will be recalled that the groups that use professional help less often do not seem to be experiencing less distress, and that their lack of help-seeking reflects lack of facilitating conditions as well as lack of motivation or experienced need. Thus it would appear that the lower use of professional help resources in groups like the lower educated and older ages is a sign neither of their greater mental health nor of a more successful handling of their problems by other means but rather reflects mental health needs that have been less adequately met.

NOTE

1. These personal and informal resources are not the only alternatives to professional help as ways of dealing with personal and emotional problems. For example, there are many "illegitimate" resources that people may use, such as astrologers and fortunetellers. In an attempt to get some idea of the extent to which such resources are used, we asked people whether they had ever gone to an astrologer, fortuneteller, or palmist for help with a personal problem. One per cent of the people we interviewed said that they had gone for such help, and another one per cent said they had gone but added that they had not really been serious and had done so out of curiosity, as a joke. Although these proportions are small, projected onto the total population on which this sample is based, they represent about two million people who have used such resources for help with their problems, half of them admittedly serious in their feeling that they would get such help.

XIII

Availability of Resources

In the preceding chapters of Part Two, we focused on the implications of certain psychological and social characteristics for people's readiness to use and actual use of professional mental health resources. Now we consider another variable potentially relevant to the self-referral process—the availability of psychiatric resources. It seems likely that the relative availability of psychiatric resources would affect the self-referral process at several points: the high or low prevalence of psychiatric facilities in a community might influence that community's social climate by affecting the extent to which people perceive their problems in mental health terms; on the other hand, the prevalence of psychiatric resources may be a reflection of already existing characteristics of the community's social climate. Furthermore, the relative accessibility of psychiatric facilities should influence both the decision actually to go for help with a personal problem defined in mental health terms and the decision as to what type of help to use.

In terms of the distinction we have been making between psychological and facilitating factors that affect the self-referral process, the availability of psychiatric facilities is probably more important as a facilitating factor than as a psychological, motivating factor. Therefore, it would be expected to have its greatest effect at the points of deciding whether or not to seek help and where such help should be sought, rather than at the initial point of defining the problem in mental health terms.

Although this study was not designed to study the "availability" aspect of readiness for self-referral, a unique opportunity was made available to us for combining our data on actual and potential use of psychiatric resources—obtained from a national sample of the population—with data on the availability of such resources obtained from another project sponsored by the Joint Commission on Mental Illness and Health.[1]

The availability data consist of ratings for each county in the United States on three kinds of psychiatric facilities: the presence of a mental health clinic service in the county (rated either "yes" or "no"); the presence of any psychiatric beds in general hospitals, excluding Federal institutions (rated either "yes" or "no"); the presence of psychiatrists in the county—members of the American Psychiatric Association 1955-1956 (rated in terms of the ratio of psychiatrists to the size of the population on a six-point scale, varying from "none" to "one psychiatrist per 1-7499 population").[2] For our purposes we combined the ratings for the three types of psychiatric facilities into one measure that provides a more stable index of the resources available to any particular individual. This combination was done after initial analyses indicated that the three separate ratings all related similarly to our other variables.

Since the county is the primary sampling unit used by the Survey Research Center, we could readily utilize these data. Each county in our sample could be characterized in terms of the availability of psychiatric facilities (just as it was characterized by location in a certain region, or by its degree of urbanization), and each respondent, according to what county he resided in, could be characterized according to whether he lived in an area with relatively few or relatively numerous psychiatric facilities (just as he was categorized as Easterner or Westerner, city-dweller or small-town resident). With these data, we are able to answer the question of whether different help-seeking patterns were reported by people living in areas that have different numbers or patterns of available psychiatric services.[3]

Before discussing our findings, a comment about the use of the county as the unit for describing a community's resources seems relevant. We recognize that the county, for many of our respondents, is only a rough approximation of the boundaries of the "community" which serves as their point of reference; but, with the data available to us, this was the closest approximation that could be made. Furthermore, although the county is not the ideal measure of the psychologically relevant community—that is, the community identified by the respondent as the place in which he lives—it is an important unit to administrators of state and Federal mental health programs.

However, because of these limitations of the county as a measure of the "community," we were led to a separate treatment of metropolitan and nonmetropolitan areas. Metropolitan areas—e.g., New York, Boston, Los Angeles—often include several counties, or parts of counties. This would seem to make the single county a clearly inappropriate estimate of the psychologically relevant community for residents of these areas. For example, the Chicago metropolitan area consists largely of Cook County, but it includes a portion of Kane County; the ratings on psychiatric facilities available in Cook and Kane Counties are appreciably different. But it did not seem reasonable to characterize a resident of Chicago who lives in Kane County as having access to fewer psychiatric facilities than a Chicago resident who lives in Cook County, for both of them probably consider themselves to be residents of the larger Chicago community. For reasons of this nature, we eliminated residents of metropolitan areas and their suburbs from the analysis to be presented in this chapter.

OVER-ALL RELATIONSHIPS WITH SELF-REFERRAL PROCESS

Looking first at the general relationship with readiness for self-referral, we note, in Table 13.1, a slight relationship between the availability of psychiatric facilities and readiness for self-referral which appears largely at the extremes of the index: compared to the people with few facilities available to them, people with more available facilities have had more help (15 per cent versus 9 per cent at the two availability extremes), and are less likely to give strong self-help responses (6 per cent versus 12 per cent).

This general relationship can be considered in more detailed terms by distinguishing between the first two decision points that we have differentiated in the self-referral process. Let us look first at the rela-

Table 13.1—Relationship between the Availability of Psychiatric Resources and Readiness for Self-Referral (Nonmetropolitan Communities Only)

Readiness for Self-Referral	AVAILABLE PSYCHIATRIC RESOURCES			
	None	Some Facility or Some Psychiatrists	Some Facility and Some Psychiatrists	Facilities and Psychiatrists
Had Help	9%	13%	15%	15%
Could have used help	10	8	7	10
Might need help	26	28	30	29
Self-help	36	37	33	34
Strong self-help	12	8	10	6
Not ascertained	7	6	5	6
Total	100%	100%	100%	100%
Number of people	(597)	(362)	(439)	(411)

tionship between the availability of psychiatric resources and the first decision point—the definition of personal problems in mental health terms. (It will be recalled that this relationship can be determined by adding together the percentages for the "had help" and "could have used help" categories of the readiness for self-referral index.) Table 13.1 indicates that there is some relationship between defining personal problems in mental health terms and the availability of psychiatric resources: 19 per cent of the people living in counties where none of the three types of psychiatric resources are available either had help or think they could have used it, whereas 25 per cent of the people living in counties where all three of these resources are available fall into either of these two categories. However, this relationship is not maintained when education is controlled.

Given a definition of a problem as a mental health problem, does the availability of psychiatric resources relate to the next stage in the self-referral process—the decision to go for help? In Table 13.2, where we look only at those people who have either gone for help or seen some problem they have experienced as relevant for help, we see that availability of resources does seem to be related to the decision to go for help. People who have more psychiatric facilities available to them are more likely to have had help, given the definition of a problem in these terms, than people with fewer available resources: less than half (46 per cent) of the group with the least facilities available to them have actually gone for help, as contrasted to 60 per

Table 13.2—Relationship between the Availability of Psychiatric Resources and the Use of Professional Help among People Who Define Some Past Problems in Mental Health Terms (Nonmetropolitan Communities Only)

Use of Professional Help	AVAILABLE PSYCHIATRIC RESOURCES			
	None	Some Facility or Some Psychiatrists	Some Facility and Some Psychiatrists	Facilities and Psychiatrists
Has used help	46%	62%	68%	60%
Could have used help	54	38	32	40
Total	100%	100%	100%	100%
Number of people	(114)	(74)	(100)	(100)

cent or more of the groups with some facilities available. Thus, availability of resources seems to operate as a facilitating factor, serving to translate a psychological readiness to go for help into an actual decision to go.

To consider the meaning of this particular relationship further, we looked at the reasons given for not seeking help by those people who defined a problem in mental health terms but did not actually go for help. The category of reasons for not seeking help that seemed most relevant was that called "lack of knowledge" and included such responses as: "didn't know how to go about it"; "didn't know about such places"; "didn't know how to get one"; "didn't know what to do"; "didn't know a doctor (or minister, or psychiatrist)." We would expect that the fewer the psychiatric facilities in a community, the less information would be generally available about them. Table 13.3,

Table 13.3—Relationship between the Availability of Psychiatric Resources and the Reasons for Not Using Help (Nonmetropolitan Communities Only)

Reasons for Not Using Help	AVAILABLE PSYCHIATRIC RESOURCES			
	None	Some Facility or Some Psychiatrists	Some Facility and Some Psychiatrists	Facilities and Psychiatrists
Lack of knowledge	19%	23%	25%	15%
Shame	14	23	16	5
Other	46	39	47	70
Not ascertained	21	15	12	10
Total	100%	100%	100%	100%
Number of people [a]	(57)	(26)	(32)	(39)

[a] Includes only those people who said they could have used help for a personal problem, but who did not seek such help.

however, indicates that "lack of knowledge" as a reason for not using help is not consistently related to the availability of psychiatric resources. Instead we find that the "shame" response—"I was ashamed to talk about it," "I didn't feel like talking about it"—tends to be the point at which the availability of psychiatric resources is associated with reasons for not going for help. Shame and stigma are mentioned less frequently by people in the counties with the most psychiatric facilities. Perhaps this is due to a correlation between a social climate which condones the use of psychiatric services and the extent to which those services are available in the community. (It should be noted, however, that these findings are based on small numbers of cases.)

Following the self-referral process through to the final decision point—whom to turn to for help—we note (Table 13.4) that greater

Table 13.4—Relationship between the Availability of Psychiatric Resources and the Source of Professional Help Used (Nonmetropolitan Communities Only)

	AVAILABLE PSYCHIATRIC RESOURCES			
Source of Help Used	None	Some Facility or Some Psychiatrists	Some Facility and Some Psychiatrists	Facilities and Psychiatrists
Clergyman	43%	36%	40%	39%
Doctor	39	31	21	30
Psychiatrist	5	10	16	13
Other mental health facilities	2	4	6	10
Informal	—	2	—	1
Others	11	17	17	7
Not ascertained	—	—	—	—
Total	100%	100%	100%	100%
Number of people [a]	(57)	(48)	(68)	(61)

[a] Refers to people who have used help for a personal problem.

availability of psychiatric resources is associated with increased use of both psychiatrists (5, 10, 16, and 13 per cent of the people mention psychiatrists, ranging from low to high availability) and other mental health facilities (the figures here are 2, 4, 6, and 10 per cent).

CONTROLLING FOR EDUCATION AND INCOME

Before we proceed further with a discussion of the effects of the availability of psychiatric resources, several controls will be intro-

AVAILABILITY OF RESOURCES

duced. We reported previously (Chapters IX and X) that education is strongly related to the readiness for self-referral at all points in the self-referral process. Since there is also a relationship between the availability of psychiatric resources in a community and the educational level of the residents (47 per cent of the residents of areas with none of the psychiatric resources we have considered, compared with only 27 per cent of the residents of areas with all three types of psychiatric resources, are in the grade-school group), we will now consider the relationship between the availability of psychiatric resources and the readiness for self-referral separately for the three education groups to see if the relationship between availability and the readiness for self-referral remains when education is controlled.

These relationships are presented in Table 13.5. Table 13.1 indicated that there was a slight relationship between availability of resources and the readiness for self-referral for the population as a whole. Table 13.5 now indicates that slight relationships with self-referral remain at each educational level, but at different points on the readiness scale. Only in the college group is there a clear relationship with the actual use of help.

If we now distinguish, as we did before, the *definition* of a mental health problem from the *use of help* for such a problem, we see that when education is controlled there are no differences in the definition of a problem in mental health terms as a function of availability of resources. (Adding the figures in the first two rows—"had help" and "could have used help"—for each education group, and going from low to high availability, we note the following figures: for the grade-school group—13, 20, 14, 15; for the high school group—24, 19, 23, 27; and for the college group—26, 28, 35, 29.) There are, however, differences within the two more educated groups in the actual use of help, given the definition of a problem in mental health terms (see Table 13.6). For the high-school group the percentage of people reporting a mental health problem who "have used help" varies from 50 in the lowest availability grouping to 60 in the highest availability grouping; for the college-educated respondents, these percentages vary from 54 to 77 in the two extremes of the availability ratings.

Table 13.5—Relationship between the Availability of Psychiatric Resources and the Readiness for Self-Referral: Within Education (Nonmetropolitan Communities Only)

Readiness for Self-Referral (Within Education)	AVAILABLE PSYCHIATRIC RESOURCES			
	None	Some Facility or Some Psychiatrists	Some Facility and Some Psychiatrists	Facilities and Psychiatrists
Grade school				
Had help	5%	12%	9%	5%
Could have used help	8	8	5	10
Might need help	25	22	30	26
Self-help	35	41	35	40
Strong self-help	17	9	14	12
Not ascertained	10	8	7	7
Total	100%	100%	100%	100%
Number of people [a]	(283)	(115)	(122)	(109)
High school				
Had help	12%	11%	15%	16%
Could have used help	12	8	8	11
Might need help	21	30	30	30
Self-help	40	37	30	33
Strong self-help	10	9	11	5
Not ascertained	5	5	6	5
Total	100%	100%	100%	100%
Number of people [a]	(219)	(197)	(218)	(210)
College				
Had help	14%	20%	25%	22%
Could have used help	12	8	10	7
Might need help	38	31	29	34
Self-help	30	29	32	31
Strong self-help	3	6	3	2
Not ascertained	3	6	1	4
Total	100%	100%	100%	100%
Number of people [a]	(90)	(49)	(93)	(91)

[a] Does not include 13 people whose educational level was not ascertained.

Although the latter findings are based on small numbers of cases, they suggest that the effect of increased psychiatric resources is largely as a facilitating factor, affecting the decision to seek help only after the problem is defined in mental health terms. This facilitating effect is somewhat interactive with education, the effect of more psychiatric resources being greatest in the more educated groups, especially among college-educated respondents. This is not surprising; the more educated people are those most likely to be aware of the resources that are available. Given such an awareness, it is not sur-

AVAILABILITY OF RESOURCES

Table 13.6—*Relationship between the Availability of Psychiatric Resources and the Use of Professional Help among People Who Define Some Past Problem in Mental Health Terms: Within Education (Nonmetropolitan Communities Only)*

Use of Professional Help (Within Education)	AVAILABLE PSYCHIATRIC RESOURCES			
	None	Some Facility or Some Psychiatrists	Some Facility and Some Psychiatrists	Facilities and Psychiatrists
Grade school				
Has used help	37%	61%	65%	35%
Could have used help	63	39	35	65
Total	100%	100%	100%	100%
Number of people [a]	(38)	(23)	(17)	(17)
High school				
Has used help	50%	59%	66%	60%
Could have used help	50	41	34	40
Total	100%	100%	100%	100%
Number of people [a]	(52)	(37)	(50)	(57)
College				
Has used help	54%	71%	72%	77%
Could have used help	46	29	28	23
Total	100%	100%	100%	100%
Number of people [a]	(24)	(14)	(32)	(26)

[a] Does not include 13 people whose educational level was not ascertained.

prising that they are most likely to take advantage of the availability of such resources.

When we reconsider the final decision in the self-referral process—what sources of help to use—*two* controls are now important. Not only education but also income must be controlled. Income, as well as education, was found to be related to the *particular* sources of help used (see Chapter X); income is also related to the availability of psychiatric resources (76 per cent of the people in counties with "none" of these psychiatric resources available to them as compared to 47 per cent of the people in counties with all three facilities available, have incomes of under $5000). We saw in Table 13.2 that availability was related to the use of psychiatrists and other mental health facilities when all people were considered together. What we are now concerned with is whether this relationship will be maintained when first education (Table 13.7) and then income (Table 13.8) is controlled.

We observed the relationship between the availability of psychiatric resources and the source of help used (by those 345 people who "had help" for a personal problem), separately for each education group in Table 13.7. An interesting differentiation occurs in the relationships for the three education groupings. For both the high-school- and college-educated groups, the greater availability of psychiatric resources is associated with increased use of psychiatrists (6 per cent versus 13 per cent for the high-school group and 15 per cent versus 21 per cent for the college group), and to a decreased use of nonpsychiatric physicians. The relationship in the grade-school-educated group appears in the decreased turning to ministers and the

Table 13.7—Relationship between Availability of Psychiatric Resources and the Source of Help Used: Within Education (Nonmetropolitan Communities Only)

Sources of Help Used (Within Education)	AVAILABILITY OF PSYCHIATRIC RESOURCES	
	Low [a]	High [a]
Grade school		
Clergyman	50%	41%
Doctor	25	29
Psychiatrist	4	—
Other mental health facilities	—	18
Others	21	12
Total	100%	100%
Number of people [b]	(28)	(17)
High school		
Clergyman	37%	37%
Doctor	41	30
Psychiatrist	6	13
Other mental health facilities	4	7
Others	12	13
Total	100%	100%
Number of people [b]	(51)	(68)
College		
Clergyman	35%	44%
Doctor	35	16
Psychiatrist	15	21
Other mental health facilities	4	5
Others	11	14
Total	100%	100%
Number of people [b]	(26)	(43)

[a] Categories combined due to low frequencies. "Low" includes categories previously labeled "None" and "Some facility or some psychiatrists." "High" includes categories previously labeled "Some facility *and* some psychiatrists" and "Facilities and psychiatrists."
[b] Does not include 13 people whose educational level was not ascertained.

increased use of other mental health facilities, greater availability of psychiatric services being associated with the use of these psychological and social service agencies. Again, although the numbers of cases are small, these findings make sense in terms of previous data we have examined. Apparently, with increased availability the different educational groups choose among the psychiatric facilities in a way that is consistent with the findings reported in Chapter X on the over-all relationship between education and source of help used. The less educated people use mental health clinics, social work agencies, and the like; the more educated respondents use more clearly psychiatric resources.

Similar results are reported in Table 13.8, where we compare the relationships between availability of psychiatric resources and the source of help used, separately for high- and low-income groupings. For the low-income groups—family incomes of less than $5000 a year—the availability of more psychiatric resources is associated with greater use of "other mental health facilities;" for the high-income groups—family incomes of $5000 a year or more—increased availability of psychiatric resources is associated with increased use of both clergymen and psychiatrists. At both income levels, the use of nonpsychiatric physicians decreases when there are more psychiatric services available.

These findings, on the relationships between availability of resources and the use of such resources within different education and income subgroups, further confirms the view of availability as a facilitating factor in the self-referral process. The presence of more psychiatric resources seems to act to accentuate the already present help-seeking tendencies of different population subgroups. Each group chooses its "appropriate" type of psychiatric resource. And the influence is greatest on those groups most ready to be influenced: those groups that are ready to use psychiatric resources will benefit most from their increased accessibility in a community. When more psychiatric services are available, those people who, like the more educated, are more likely to define a problem in mental health terms, will be more likely to translate this definition of their problems into seeking professional help.

Table 13.8—Relationship between the Availability of Psychiatric Resources and the Source of Help Used, by People Who Sought Help for a Personal Problem: Within Income (Nonmetropolitan Communities Only)

Sources of Help Used (Within Income)	AVAILABILITY OF PSYCHIATRIC RESOURCES	
	Low [a]	High [a]
Less than $5,000		
Clergy	45%	42%
Doctor	31	22
Psychiatrist	7	4
Other mental health facilities	1	16
Others	16	16
Not ascertained	—	—
Total	100%	100%
Number of people [b]	(74)	(50)
Over $5,000		
Clergy	29%	38%
Doctor	47	26
Psychiatrist	10	22
Other mental health facilities	3	3
Others	11	11
Not ascertained	—	—
Total	100%	100%
Number of people [b]	(30)	(77)

[a] Categories combined due to low frequencies. "Low" includes categories previously labeled "None" and "Some facility or some psychiatrists." "High" includes categories previously labeled "Some facility *and* some psychiatrists" and "Facilities and psychiatrists."

[b] Does not include three people whose income level was not ascertained.

What are the implications of these and the previous results? From a practical standpoint, if the aim of a mental health program is the improvement of the mental health of people who have, to some extent at least, recognized that they have such problems, an increase in the available psychiatric services seems warranted. Apparently, however, such an increase in the available psychiatric services would not have much impact on those people who might be diagnosed by a psychiatrist as in need of help, but who themselves do not structure their problems in these terms.

One further point should be made about those people who are prone to structure their problems in mental health terms. These people seem to seek out and to obtain professional help for their problems even when there are relatively few psychiatric services readily accessible to them. We can see this by reconsidering the data already presented in Table 13.6, this time looking, within availability groupings, at the relationship between education and the use of professional help when a mental health problem is recognized. We see, in Table 13.9, that *regardless* of the availability of psychiatric resources, the more educated respondents have had more help than the less educated respondents.

We suggested earlier that the more educated are more likely to be aware of existing resources, and therefore to make greater use of these resources in areas where they are available. But we see now that the educated also more often go for help even when living in areas of minimal psychiatric resources. With a greater breadth of information and knowledge, and a greater potential for mobility, the higher-educated are better able to transcend the immediate environment and seek out help, even when it is not readily available in the immediate environment. Although important, the lack of ready availability of psychiatric resources is not an insurmountable problem.

Table 13.9—Relationship between Educational Level and the Use of Professional Help among People Who Define Some Past Problem in Mental Health Terms: Within Availability (Nonmetropolitan Communities Only)

Education (Within Availability)	USE OF PROFESSIONAL HELP			Number of People [a]
	Has Used Help (Per Cent)	Could Have Used Help (Per Cent)	Total (Per Cent)	
None				
Grade school	37	63	100	(38)
High school	50	50	100	(52)
College	54	46	100	(24)
Some facility *or* some psychiatrists				
Grade school	61	39	100	(23)
High school	59	41	100	(37)
College	71	29	100	(14)
Some facility *and* some psychiatrists				
Grade school	65	35	100	(17)
High school	66	34	100	(50)
College	72	28	100	(32)
Facilities and psychiatrists				
Grade school	35	65	100	(17)
High school	60	40	100	(57)
College	77	23	100	(26)

[a] Does not include 13 people whose educational level was not ascertained.

SUMMARY

In this chapter we have looked at the effect that the availability of psychiatric resources in the community has on the help-seeking process. The findings support our expectation that availability of psychiatric facilities would be more important as a facilitator of the self-referral process than as a psychological, motivating factor.

There was little relationship between the availability of psychiatric resources in the community and the extent to which people defined problems they had experienced in mental health terms (and even this disappeared when education was controlled). But among people who have experienced mental health problems, those in communities with some psychiatric facilities have more often gone for help than those in communities with no psychiatric facilities. And availability also influences the particular resources that are chosen: people more often choose psychiatrists and other mental health facilities in communities where more psychiatric resources are available.

This influence of availability as a facilitating factor appears to be somewhat interactive with education and income. The tendency for people in communities with more psychiatric facilities to go for help more often is more marked among the more educated groups; apparently they are more aware of resources that are available and can take greater advantage of them when they are present in the community. And, with respect to the resource chosen, the presence of more psychiatric resources accentuates the already existent help-seeking tendencies in the different education and income subgroups, each group choosing its appropriate type of psychiatric resource: the lower income and education groupings make more use of mental health clinics and social agencies when they are more available, and the higher education and income groups more often utilize psychiatrists.

These findings that availability of resources is a facilitator of existing tendencies rather than an initiator and motivator of the self-referral process imply that increasing the psychiatric facilities in a community probably would not increase the psychological insight of the people in the community nor would it affect their readiness to view the problems they face as mental health problems. But among those who already have such insight, increasing facilities should serve to increase both the numbers who actually do seek help and the proportion who use psychiatric rather than nonpsychiatric resources.

Although availability apparently has some effect, the lack of resources in the immediate environment is not an insurmountable barrier. People motivated strongly enough will get help even in areas of minimal resources. But this ability to transcend the limitations of the immediate environment seems to be greater among the higher educated. Thus, for the lower educated (and lower income) groups, it may be particularly important for clinics and social agencies to be readily available, if the psychiatric needs of these population groupings are to be met.

NOTES

1. We would like to thank Dr. Reginald Robinson, director of the Task Force on Community Resources, for his cooperation in making these data available to us.
2. For a more detailed description of these ratings, and information on how they were obtained see Robinson, De Marche, and Wagle (1960).
3. It should be noted that the relationships we will be presenting between availability of resources and help-seeking patterns will be subject to some error. The relationships are between the resources available in one's *present* county of residence, and help that has been sought in the *past* as well as in the present. Thus, help may have been obtained at a time when the respondent was living in an area that differed in availability of resources from his present area of residence. In most cases, this possible source of error will tend to lower the relationships that we do obtain.

PART THREE

Summary and Conclusions

XIV

Implications

WE HAVE looked at a representative sample of the American population, exploring some of the satisfactions and dissatisfactions they derive from life, their tensions and concerns, their resources and strengths, the problems they face and the ways they cope with them.

The major focus of this report has been epidemiological. We have looked at experiences of adjustment and tensions and ways of handling problems as they are distributed and vary within different subgroups of the population, and have indicated how factors such as a person's sex, age, education, and income may affect his orientations toward life, the gratifications he derives, the ways he experiences tensions and distress, the personal, informal, and formal resources he utilizes in seeking solutions to personal problems.

These demographic relationships have been examined with two interests in mind. First, as descriptive facts, the different ways in which broad subgroups of the population experience and handle adjustment problems provide information relevant to the assessment of the mental health picture on a broad national level. Secondly, these data have etiological implications pointing to some of the possible social and cultural correlates and determinants of different adjustment problems and help-seeking patterns, and we have tried to stress some of these broader meanings.

What are the general "practical"—rather than theoretical—implications of these data?

Looking first at the findings that were stressed in Part One—the delineation of subgroup differences in adjustment patterns—we see these as particularly relevant for people in the mental health field who are working with problems in given population subgroups. For example, these national findings on the problems and tensions associated with aging, indicating that the problems in the older-aged groups seem to be more those of apathy and resignation than of active distress, should be helpful in formulating mental health programs for these groups. Similarly, people interested in programs for lower income, poorly educated, or other population subgroups should find these data relevant. And the findings should also be useful to therapists who are working with patients in a given population subgroup. It may help in the understanding of certain pathological patterns to view them against the backdrop of the problems and life orientations characteristic of the patient's background and cultural environment.

In addition to the subgroup differences, some of the broad cultural implications that have been drawn from these data, particularly the evidence of cultural trends, should be of value to mental health administrators and practitioners. For example, for those concerned with some of the long-range planning in this area, evidence of the generational change toward a greater "psychologizing" of problems, and the implications this has for a constantly increasing demand on psychiatric resources, are crucial for estimates of projected need and resource utilization. For therapists, knowledge of cultural changes may also be helpful. For example, if, as the analyses in Chapter V seemed to suggest, we may expect fathers increasingly to bring relationship problems with their children into the therapeutic session, it may help in evaluating the meaning of these concerns to see them as part of a general cultural pattern.

Broad implications for action may follow even more clearly and directly from the analyses of the help-seeking data that are the focus of Part Two. The distributions of help-seeking patterns and the use of professional resources in the general population and in particular subgroups, such data as those documenting the critical "gate-keeper" position of clergymen and medical doctors, and the findings pointing up some of the effects of availability of psychiatric resources on help-seeking, would all seem to be information valuable to those attempting to formulate broad social decisions for meeting the mental health needs in the country.

In our analysis separating psychological and facilitating aspects of subgroup differences in help-seeking patterns, other findings with possible action implications have emerged with particular relevance to attempts to formulate the mental health programs for different population subgroups. To the extent that a given group's low utilization of professional resources in times of stress seems to reflect psychological rather than facilitating factors, the solution would seem to lie in the realm of education rather than in such things as increased facilities. Where, as in the analysis of the rural-urban differences, there is a suggestion that the lower utilization of resources among farm groups stems from factors other than differences in the psychological orientations of urban and rural people, a more ready availability of facilities would be likely to have some effect.

This analysis might also have implications for the *kind* of education program that might be directed at a given population subgroup. To the extent that the problem of low utilization in any group seems to reflect facilitating rather than psychological factors, the education problem would seem to be one of providing information with respect to the availability of resources and the process to be followed in going for help, rather than of convincing the group members of the need to go for help.

Beyond such possible implications of specific sets of findings, the central practical relevance of the data in this study lies in what they can teach us about the distribution of mental health needs in this country and how these needs are being met. A major interest in interviewing a representative sample of the population was to arrive at some assessment of these needs in the general noninstitutional population. What do our findings tell us about the mental health of the American population? And particularly, what do they tell us about subgroup differences in need, and differences in the extent to which the need that does exist is being met? To the extent these subgroup differentiations exist, a serious social problem is posed, one which has to be considered by people responsible for broad, over-all mental health planning.

In dealing with the question of the health of the total population and different subgroups of the population, we were not concerned with diagnoses of mental health needs in terms of standard psychiatric categories of pathology. We have explored mental health in terms of subjective adjustment indices. And in our analysis of these subjective adjustment indices, we have stressed a multiple criterion approach in interpreting the implications of the findings. Thus, in the subgroup comparisons, we have stressed how judgments of adjustment depend upon the particular criterion of adjustment used, and documented how, in most instances, groups judged "better" in adjustment on some indices would be judged "worse" on others. We have done this, rather than attempt an over-all judgment of the mental health of an individual or a group. In relating our data to formal definitions of mental health, our main interest has been to point up, through the empirical relationships explored, some of the conceptual and value implications of different definitions.

One definition of need, however, has received particular attention in this study. Regardless of the evaluation by the expert observer, the individual's own perception that he needs help has been viewed as crucial. And at this level we have attempted to answer questions about mental health needs and their fulfillment. These subjective definitions of need have particular significance, since it is subjective need that is related to a person's seeking help. Thus, data on the extent and distribution of these felt needs have implications for the utilization and potential use of therapeutic facilities.

Felt need was measured directly by asking the respondents whether they ever had experienced any emotional personal problems that they felt required the assistance of some professional therapeutic resource; and we found that a large number of people—about one quarter of the total adult population—have at some time in their life experienced a serious need for help. The majority of these—14 per cent of the total population sampled—actually went for help.

Of more particular relevance in terms of social significance is that we also found evidence not only that there is a considerable expression of need for help but that in many cases this need is unfulfilled; many distressed people who are to some extent psychologically ready to go for help never actually go. Evidence of this comes from several sources. One is the 9 per cent of the sample who felt they had a problem that could have used help but who did not go for help, even though in many cases the problem apparently was not satisfactorily resolved. A second source is the demographic analysis pointing to the apparent influence of facilitating factors as well as psychological resistances in keeping a person from the actual decision to go for help. Thirdly, the analysis of the effect of availability, discussed in Chapter XIII, suggested that, although strong motivation for therapy can overcome the handicap of low availability of resources, availability is a factor; some people in communities where resources are minimally available would probably have gone for help if they had lived in a community where resources were more accessible.

These unfulfilled needs, these people who have experienced problems and were psychologically accessible to help, yet who never reached a treatment resource, constitute a special social problem and responsibility, especially since the data presented in this study indicate that these unfulfilled needs may be greater in certain subgroups.

That the psychiatric needs of different subgroups are being differentially fulfilled has already been suggested by other research. Studies like that of Hollingshead and Redlich (1958) have dealt with the relationship between social class and the utilization of psychiatric resources, and noted that lower status groups get less psychiatric care. In the relationships we have presented between education and income and the use of psychiatric resources, we have replicated these findings, confirming on a national sample what was revealed in studies in more limited community settings.

But some of the data have amplified these findings in several ways. Because we have been concerned with three sets of relationships—(1) between demographic characteristics and the use of psychiatric facilities; (2) between demographic characteristics and feelings of adjustment; and (3) between demographic characteristics and the utilization of personal, informal, and other formal resources besides psychiatrists—we have been able to see relationships such as those between social status position and the use of psychiatric facilities in a broader context.

That lower status groups get less psychiatric care would seem to represent a social problem. The extent of the problem, however, would depend partially on the emotional distress experienced in these groups and partially on the other means they utilize in dealing with it. It is less of a problem if those groups with lower utilization of psychiatric facilities experience less stress and meet their problems by a greater use of other formal resources or by an unusual use of internal coping resources or informal social ties.

These data have enabled us to explore this question to some extent. They indicate that—if anything—groups using psychiatric facilities less frequently experience *more* distress, *less* often make use of clergymen or physicians (as well as psychiatrists), and more often meet their problems with passivity and resignation rather than with active coping devices.

As we noted at the conclusion of Chapter IX, the problem seems to be twofold. First of all, these groups are less likely to define distress in psychologically relevant terms. But secondly, even when distress is defined psychologically—when there is a realization of the need for some psychological help—this need is less often translated into an actual use of help or an active use of one's own resources. For example, the differences between income groups lie more in the extent to which felt needs get translated into an actual use of help, particularly psychiatric resources, than in the degrees of differential insight, introspection, and subjective need for help. These findings, then, point up the subgroup differences in the fulfillment of needs and tend to accent and underscore the kind of social problem that has been noted by Hollingshead and Redlich and others.

To point out the existence of a large unfulfilled need and the social implications of the subgroup variations in this fulfillment is not to suggest the solution of this problem. With existing psychiatric facilities already overtaxed, and with the prospect of a continuing shortage of psychiatrically trained therapists, perhaps the main import of these findings is to underscore the manpower problem that was outlined in the Albee monograph in this series (1959). The seriousness of this problem is further underscored when we consider the import of the findings that the figures on subjective need for help and utilization of help resources are highest in the higher educated and youngest aged groups. As the education level of the general population increases, and as the growing acceptance of psychiatry now evidenced in the younger generation becomes characteristic of the total culture, we should expect the demand for therapeutic facilities to increase even beyond the figures obtained in the present study.

We must make certain cautionary comments about interpretation of these data on subjective mental health needs. In speaking of the subjective need or psychological readiness for help, we have referred only to a recognition of problems for which some help is needed, and the readiness to take the first step of going to someone for help. This does not imply a readiness or motivation for deep psychiatric therapy; nor does it imply that resistances would not operate once the therapeutic process began. As was noted in Chapter X, only a small minority of those who have gone for help made use of a psychiatric facility. The majority went to a minister or a nonpsychiatric doctor. And there was some evidence that such a choice might have been at least partially determined by a reluctance to enter into the more probing therapy involved in psychiatric treatment. As contrasted to those who went to a psychiatrist, people who sought out a minister or doctor less often localized their problem as a defect in the self, and more often saw the therapeutic help they had received in terms of comfort and advice.

These comments point up a final caution. We have been mainly concerned, in our analysis of the self-referral process, with the factors involved in getting a person to some treatment resource. We have not been concerned with what goes on in the treatment process, or with factors affecting the nature and success of therapy. Going for help is itself no guarantee of cure, even if one reaches the most competent psychiatrist. Some people may be beyond help. Others, lacking the motivation to make the commitment to change that therapy usually involves, leave after the opening sessions. But people who have reached some responsible treatment resource have at least had a possibility for help, a possibility denied those people who, overwhelmed by problems insoluble by their own resources, have never even reached the first step in the treatment process.

We hope that this study will help to clarify the kinds of factors that operate in determining whether or not a person in need of help will use the opportunities available to him. We hope, even more strongly, that it contributes to the formulation of programs designed to make such help available to the maximum number of people in trouble.

Appendixes

Appendix I

The Questionnaire

STUDY OF MODERN LIVING

Legend: Where no letter precedes the question number, this question appears on all forms of the questionnaire.
  a—These questions appear on Forms A and B of the questionnaire.
  b—These questions appear on Forms B and C of the questionnaire.
  c—These questions appear on Forms A and C of the questionnaire.
  d—These questions appear on Form A of the questionnaire.
  e—These questions appear on Form C of the questionnaire.

One of the things we'd like to know is how people spend their time.
  1. For instance—how do you usually spend your time when your work is done—what kind of things do you do, both at home and away from home?
    1a. What other things do you do in your spare time?
    1b. Do you have any other hobbies, or anything like that, that you do regularly in your spare time?
    1c. (If Yes) What sort of things do you do?
  2. Are you a member of any (other) clubs and organizations—like a lodge, PTA, a community group, or any other kind of group?
    2a. (If Yes) What are they?
  3. About how often do you get together with friends or relatives—I mean things like going out together or visiting each other's homes? More than once a week; once a week; few times a month; once a month; less than once a month.
  4. Do you have as many friends as you want, or would you like to have more friends?
    As many friends as wants; would like more friends.
Picture Stories (Show set of male pictures to men, female pictures to women.)

Another thing we want to find out is what people think of situations that may come up in life. I'm going to show you some pictures of these situations and ask you to think of stories to go with them. The situations won't be clearly one thing or another—so feel free to think of any story you want to. (Show Picture 1.) For example, here's the first picture. I'd like you to spend a few moments thinking of a story to go with it. To get at the story you're thinking of, I'll ask you questions like: Who are these people? What do they want? and so on. Just answer with anything that comes to mind. There are no right or wrong answers.

    *a*5. Who are these people? What are they doing?
        5a. What had led up to this—what went on before?
        5b. What do they want—how do they feel?
        5c. What will happen—how will it end?
    *a*6. (Show Picture 2.) Who are these people? What are they doing?
        6a. What had led up to this—what went on before?
        6b. What do they want—how do they feel?
        6c. What will happen—how will it end?
    *a*7. (Show Picture 3.) Who are these people? What are they doing?
        7a. What had led up to this—what went on before?
        7b. What do they want—how do they feel?
        7c. What will happen—how will it end?
    *a*8. (Show Picture 4.) Who is this person? What is (he, she) doing?
        8a. What has led up to this—what went on before?
        8b. What does (he, she) want—how does (he, she) feel?
        8c. What will happen—how will it end?
    *a*9. (Show Picture 5.) Who are these people? What are they doing?
        9a. What has led up to this—what went on before?
        9b. What do they want—how do they feel?
        9c. What will happen—how will it end?
    *a*10. (Show Picture 6.) Who are these people? What are they doing?
        10a. What has led up to this—what went on before?
        10b. What do they want—how do they feel?
        10c. What will happen—how will it end?

One of the things we're interested in is what people think about these days.

    11. Everybody has some things he worries about more or less. What kinds of things do you worry about most?
    12. Do you worry about such things a lot, or not very much?
    13. If something is on your mind that's bothering you or worrying you, and you don't know what to do about it, what do you usually do?
        13a. (If doesn't mention "talk it over") Do you ever talk it over with anyone?
        13b. (If not mentioned) Who is that?

THE QUESTIONNAIRE

14. Now I'd like you to think about your whole life—how things are now, how they were ten years ago, how they were when you were a little (boy) (girl). What do you think of as the happiest time of your life? (I don't mean just a particular day or single happening, but a whole period of your life.)

   14a. (If mentions "present" time as happiest) Why is this a happy time—what are some of the things that you feel pretty happy about these days?

   14b. (If mentions "past" time as happiest) Why was that a happy time—what are some of the things about it that you like to remember?

   14c. (If mentions "past" time as happiest) How about the way things are today—what are some of the things you feel pretty happy about these days?

15. Everyone has things about their life they are not completely happy about. What are some of the things that you're not too happy about these days?

16. Thinking now of the way things were in the *past*, what do you think of as the most unhappy time of your life?

   16a. Why do you think of that as an unhappy time?

17. Taking things all together, how would you say things are these days—would you say you're *very happy, pretty happy,* or *not too happy* these days?

18. Compared to your life today, how do you think things will be five or ten years from now—do you think things will be happier for you than they are now, not quite as happy, or what?

   18a. (If "happier") How is that?

19. One of the things we'd like to know is how people face the unhappy periods in their lives. Thinking of unhappiness you've had to face, what are some of the things that have helped you in those times?

We're interested in how people react to certain typical situations. I'd like to ask you to think about times in your own life when these things happened and tell me what you did.

*b*20. For instance, when you wanted very much to do something well, and tried hard but failed:

   20a. How did you feel?
   20b. What did you do about it?
   20c. What was it?
   20d. (If "never failed") If you had failed, how would you have felt?
   20e. (If "never failed") What would you do?

*b*21. When you like people a lot and try to make friends with them, but they aren't friendly to *you:*

21a. What do you do?
21b. How do you feel?

*b*22. How about when you get angry at someone you're very close to? Think of the last time someone close did something or said something that really made you angry:
22a. What did you do?
22b. How did you feel *then*?
22c. What was it about?

*b*23. Suppose you moved into a new neighborhood and made some new friends. They like you but they criticize certain of your habits and manners. You know that they will like you better if you change.
23a. How would you feel?
23b. What would you do?

Now we'd like to ask you some other questions about yourself.

24. People are the same in many ways, but no two people are exactly alike. What are some of the ways in which you're different from most other people?

Many people, when they think about their children, would like them to be different from themselves in some ways.

25. (Ask men) If you had a son, how would you like him to be different from you?
(Ask women) If you had a daughter, how would you like her to be different from you?

26. How about your good points? What would you say were your strongest points?

Now I'd like to ask you some questions about marriage.

27. (Ask men) First, thinking about a man's life—how is a man's life changed by being married?
(Ask women) First, thinking about a woman's life—how is a woman's life changed by being married?

*e*Now here are a couple of questions I'd like you to use your imagination on.

*e*28. (Ask men) Suppose all you knew about a man was that he didn't want to get married. What would you guess he was like? (If answer in terms of lack of opportunity, never asked, never met a woman to marry, etc.: Well, suppose he had plenty of chances to get married but just didn't want to?)

(Ask women) Suppose all you knew about a woman was that she didn't want to get married. What would you guess she was like? (If answer in terms of lack of opportunity, never asked, never met a man to marry, etc.: Well, suppose she had plenty of chances to get married but just didn't want to?)

28a. (Ask men) Do you think he could live a happy life, or do you think he probably wouldn't be happy?
(Ask women) Do you think she could live a happy life, or do you think she probably wouldn't be happy?

29. Are you married, single, widowed, divorced, or separated?

(If "presently married" ask questions 30 through 37.)

30. We've talked a little about marriage in general. Now, thinking about your own marriage, what would you say were the nicest things about it?
31. Every marriage has its good points and bad points. What things about your marriage are not quite as nice as you would like them to be?

e32. (Ask men) Even in the happiest marriages there are often some things about the husband or wife that we're not completely satisfied with. If you could change one thing about your wife, what would you want to change?
(Ask women) Even in the happiest marriages there are often some things about the husband or wife that we're not completely satisfied with. If you could change one thing about your husband, what would you want to change?

e33. (Ask men) What are some of the ways in which she is a good wife?
(Ask women) What are some of the ways in which he is a good husband?

34. Taking things all together, how would you describe your marriage—would you say your marriage was *very happy, a little happier than average, just about average,* or *not too happy*?

(If "very happy," "a little happier than average," or "just about average," ask questions 34a through 34f.)

   34a. Even in cases where married people are happy there have often been times in the past when they weren't too happy—when they had problems getting along with each other. Has this ever been true for you?
   34b. (If Yes) What was that about?
   34c. What happened—how did you work it out?
   34d. (If "outside help" not mentioned in 34b or 34c) Did you and your wife (husband) work it out yourselves or did you get any advice or help from others?
   34e. (If "got advice or help") Where did you go for help?
   34f. How did it work out?

(If "not too happy" ask questions 34g through 34l.)

   34g. Have you tried to do anything about the things in your marriage that you're not too happy with?

34h. (If Yes) What have you tried to do?
34i. How did it work out?
34j. (If "outside help" not mentioned in 34h or 34j) Did you and your wife (husband) try to work it out yourselves or did you get any advice or help from others?
34k. (If "got advice or help") Where did you go for help?
34l. How did it work out?

35. (Ask men) Many men feel that they're not as good husbands as they would like to be. Have you ever felt this way?
(Ask women) Many women feel that they're not as good wives as they would like to be. Have you ever felt this way?
35a. (If Yes) What kinds of things make you feel this way?
35b. Do you feel this way a lot of times, or only once in a while?

e36. (Ask men) What are some of the ways you've been a *good* husband?
(Ask women) What are some of the ways you've been a *good* wife?

37. We've asked you several questions about your marriage. Is this your first marriage?
37a. (If Yes) How long have you been married?
37b. (If No) How long have you been married to your present wife (husband)?
37c. Did your first marriage end by death or divorce?

(If "divorced" or "separated" ask questions 38 through 40.)

38. We've talked a little about marriages in general. Now, thinking about your own marriage, what would you say were some of the nicer things about it?
39. What were some of the problems in your marriage?
40. What did you and your wife (husband) try to do to work things out?
    40a. (If "outside help" mentioned) How did it work out?
    40b. (If "outside help" not mentioned) Did you and your wife (husband) try to work it out yourselves, or did you try to get any help from others?
    40c. (If "tried to get help") Where did you go for help?
    40d. How did it work out?

And now I'd like to ask you some questions about children.

41. (Ask men) First, thinking about a man's life, how is a man's life changed by having children?
(Ask women) First, thinking about a woman's life, how is a woman's life changed by having children?
42. What would you say is the nicest thing about having children?
    42a. What other kinds of things do you think of?

c43. Some people say that a parent's happiest time is when the children are very little. Others say the happiest time is when the children are older. Which of these times would you say a parent would be happiest? (Show card)
  (1) When the children are very little babies.
  (2) When the children are about three or four years old and haven't started school yet.
  (3) When the children are going to grade school, around the ages of eight or nine.
  (4) When the children are teen-agers, around high school age.
  (5) When the children are grown up and ready to go out on their own.
  43a. Why do you think that's the happiest time?
  43b. Which of these would you say is the *least* happy time for a parent?

(Ask people who are married or were ever married questions 44 through 51, as directed.)

44. Do you have any children?
  44a. (If Yes) How many children have you had?
  44b. Would you tell me whether they're boys or girls, how old they are, and whether they're living with you or away from home?
45. Do you expect to have any (more) children?

(If ever had children ask questions 46 through 48.)

46. Most parents have had some problems in raising their children. What are the main problems you've had in raising your children?
  46a. What did (do) you do when things like that came (come) up?
c47. (Ask men) Many men feel that they're not as good fathers as they would like to be. Have you ever felt this way?
  (Ask women) Many women feel that they're not as good mothers as they would like to be. Have you ever felt this way?
  47a. (If Yes) What kinds of things have made you feel this way?
  47b. Have you felt this way a lot of times, or only once in a while?
c48. (Ask men) What are some of the ways you've been a *good* father?
  (Ask women) What are some of the ways you've been a *good* mother?

(Ask women with children aged sixteen or under questions 49 through 51.)

c49. For every parent, there are times when you enjoy your children more than other times, or things that you enjoy most doing for them. Here is a list of different things and times with children that parents have told us they enjoyed. I'd like you to look this list over and tell me the *two* that you have found nicest about little children. (Show card)
  (1) When they listen to what you tell them to do.

(2) When they are clean and neat.
(3) When they are polite and well behaved with other people.
(4) When they hug and kiss you.
(5) When they play nicely with other children.
(6) When they learn to do something after they have tried for a long time.
(7) Playing with them.

49a. Which two would you say are the next nicest?

Now I have a number of questions which have to do with things you might expect from a child, and when you would expect him to learn them. After I read each one to you, let me know about what age you would think a son of yours should have learned it.

c50. How about
  (a) to try new things for himself without asking for help—at about what age would you think a son of yours should have learned that?
  (b) to be able to lead other children and assert himself in children's groups?
  (c) to make his own friends among children his own age?
  (d) to do well in school on his own?
  (e) to make decisions for himself, such as how he spends his pocket money, what books he reads, what movies he sees?

51. Have you ever tried to get any help in raising your child(ren) by talking to other people, or reading books, or things like that?
  51a. (If Yes) How do you mean—whom have you talked to and what are some of the books you've read?
  51b. Just how much help has that been—would you say it's been a lot of help, some help, or not much help?

Now I'd like to talk to you about your work.

52. What kind of work do you do?
  52a. (If "housewife") Do you do any part-time or full-time work for pay outside the home?
  52b. (If Yes) What kind of work do you do?
  52c. (If "retired") What kind of work did you usually do before you retired?
  52d. (If "unemployed") What kind of work do you usually do?

(Ask all people working "full time" or "part time" questions 53 through 55.)

53. Taking into consideration all the things about your job, how satisfied or dissatisfied are you with it?
54. What things do you particularly like about the job?
55. What things don't you like about the job?

THE QUESTIONNAIRE

(Ask men employed part time or full time questions 56 through 66.)
56. How long have you been doing this kind of work?
57. Have you ever done any other kind of work?
    57a. (If Yes) What was that?
58. Do you work for yourself or for someone else?
    58a. (If works for someone else) About how many people does your company employ—under 100, or over 100?
    58b. (If self-employed) Do you have any people working for you?
    58c. (If Yes) About how many?
59. Regardless of how much you like your job, is there any other kind of work you'd rather be doing?
    59a. (If Yes) What is that?
    59b. Why would you like that better than the work you're doing now?
    59c. Have you ever done anything about getting into this kind of work?
    59d. (If Yes) What happened?
    59e. (If No) Why is that?
60. If you didn't have to work to make a living, do you think you would work anyway?
    60a. (If Yes) What would be your reasons for going on working?
61. Have you ever had any problems with your work—times when you couldn't work, or weren't getting along on the job, or didn't know what kind of work you wanted to do?
    61a. (If Yes) What was that about?
    61b. What did you do about it?
    61c. (If "outside help" not mentioned) Did you go to anyone for advice or help about it?
    61d. (If Yes) Whom did you go to?
    61e. How did it work out?
    61f. (If "Outside help" mentioned) How did it work out?
(If not "self-employed" ask questions 62 through 64.)
d62. Do you work under anyone—a supervisor or anyone in charge of your work?
    62a. (If Yes) Just how much does he (she) have to do with you and your work?
    62b. What kind of a person is he (she) to work for?
d63. Do you have any people working under you?
    63a. (If Yes) How many?
d64. Outside of the people working over you or under you, do you work with any other person or people?

64a. (If Yes) How do you like the people you work with?
*e*65. What does it take to do a really good job at the kind of work you do?
    65a. How much *ability* do you think it takes to do a really good job at the kind of work you do?
    65b. How good would you say you are at doing this kind of work—would you say you were *very good, a little better than average, just average,* or *not very good*?
*b*66. Some people say that you can tell a lot about a man by the kind of job that he has. Other people say that a job isn't that important. How do you feel about this?
    66a. How do you mean?

(Ask women employed part time or full time questions 67 and 68.)

*a*67. Regardless of how much you like your job, is there anything else you'd rather be doing?
    67a. (If Yes) What is that?
    67b. (If mentions "other kind of work") Why would you like that better than the work you're doing now?
    67c. Have you ever done anything about getting into this kind of work?
    67d. (If Yes) What happened?
    67e. (If No) Why is that?
*a*68. If you didn't need the money that you get from working, do you think you would work anyway?
    69a. (If Yes) What would be your reasons for going on working?

(If "full-time housewives," ask questions 69 through 72.)

69. Different people feel differently about taking care of a home—I don't mean taking care of the children, but things like cooking and sewing and keeping house. Some women look on these things as just a job that has to be done—other women really enjoy them. How do you feel about this?
70. Do you get much chance to spend time with other people during the day?
71. Have you ever wanted a career?
    71a. (If Yes) What kind of career?
72. Are you planning to go to work in the future?
    72a. (If Yes) Women have different reasons for working. What would be your main reason for working?
    72b. What kind of work do you think you will do?

(If "retired" ask questions 73 through 77.)

73. Why did you retire?

73a. (If not clear) Did you have to retire, or is this something that you wanted to do?
74. In what way has retirement made a difference in your life?
    74a. Could you tell me more about these changes and what they have meant in your life?
75. When you think of the days when you were working, what do you miss most?
76. Does the fact that you aren't earning a salary make a difference?
    76a. (If Yes) How is that?
77. Did anyone do anything for you in connection with your retirement?
    77a. (If Yes) What did they do?
    77b. (If necessary) Who?

(If "unemployed" ask questions 78 through 82.)
78. Is there any other kind of work you'd like better than the work you usually do?
    78a. (If Yes) What is that?
    78b. Why would you like that better than the work you usually do?
    78c. Have you ever done anything about getting into this kind of work?
    78d. (If Yes) What happened?
79. When did you leave your last job?
80. What happened—why did you leave it?
81. Do you expect to have much trouble getting another job?
    81a. (If Yes) Why do you expect to have trouble?
82. Have you gone to anyone for advice or help during the time you've been out of work?
    82a. (If Yes) Whom have you gone to?
    82b. Did they help in any way? How is that?

Now some questions about your health.
83. Do you have any particular physical or health trouble?
    83a. (If Yes) What is that?
84. Have you had any long illnesses in the past?
    84a. (If Yes) What was that?
85. Have you ever had the following diseases?
    (a) Asthma (If Yes) When was that?
    (b) Hay fever (If Yes) When was that?
    (c) Skin trouble (If Yes) When was that?
    (d) Stomach ulcer (If Yes) When was that?

Now I am going to hand you a sheet which tells about different troubles and complaints people have. After each one, would you check the answer which tells how often you have had this trouble or complaint?

86.

	Nearly all the time	Pretty often	Not very much	Never
a. Do you ever have any trouble getting to sleep or staying asleep?				
b. Have you ever been bothered by nervousness, feeling fidgety and tense?				
c. Are you ever troubled by headaches or pains in the head?				
d. Do you have loss of appetite?				
e. How often are you bothered by having an upset stomach?				
f. Do you find it difficult to get up in the morning?				

	Many times	Sometimes	Hardly ever	Never
g. Has any ill health affected the amount of work you do?				
h. Have you ever been bothered by shortness of breath when you were not exercising or working hard?				
i. Have you ever been bothered by your heart beating hard?				
j. Do you ever drink more than you should?				
k. Have you ever had spells of dizziness?				
l. Are you ever bothered by nightmares?				
m. Do you tend to lose weight when you have something important bothering you?				
n. Do your hands ever tremble enough to bother you?				
o. Are you troubled by your hands sweating so that you feel damp and clammy?				
p. Have there ever been times when you couldn't take care of things because you just couldn't get going?				

87. Here are some more questions like those you've filled out. This time just answer "Yes" or "No."
    87a. Do you feel you are bothered by all sort of pains and ailments in different parts of your body?
    87b. For the most part, do you feel healthy enough to carry out the things that you would like to do?
    87c. Have you ever felt that you were going to have a nervous breakdown?
    87d. (If Yes) Could you tell me about when you felt this way? What was it about?
    87e. What did you do about it?
88. Now here is something different. I have some statements here that describe the way some people are and feel. I'll read them one at a time and you just tell me how true they are for you—whether they're *very true for you, pretty true, not very true,* or *not true at all.*
    (Show card listing alternatives)
    (a) I have always felt pretty sure my life would work out the way I wanted it to.
    (b) I never have any trouble making up my mind about important decisions.
    (c) I often wish that people would listen to me more.
    (d) I often wish that people liked me more than they do.
    (e) I nearly always feel pretty sure of myself even when people disagree with me.

Problems often come up in life. Sometimes they're personal problems—people are very unhappy, or nervous and irritable all the time. Sometimes they're problems in a marriage—a husband and wife just can't get along with each other. Or sometimes it's a personal problem with a child or a job. I'd like to ask you a few questions now about what you think a person might do to handle problems like this.

89. For instance, let's suppose you had a lot of personal problems and you're very unhappy all the time. Let's suppose you've been that way for a long time, and it isn't getting any better. What do you think you'd do about it?
    89a. (If "outside professional source" mentioned) If this didn't work, is there anywhere else you would go to get help? Where is that?
    89b. (If "no outside professional source" mentioned) Do you think you would go anywhere to get some help with these problems? Where would you go?
    89c. (If "outside professional source" still not mentioned) Suppose these problems didn't get better no matter what you tried to do about them yourself, and you felt you had to have some outside

help. Do you know of anyone or any place around here where you could go for help?

89d. (If Yes to question 89c) Where would you go?

89e. Suppose you didn't know of any places yourself. Do you know of anywhere you might go, or anyone you might talk to, where you could find out where to go for help? Where is that?

89f. (If No to question 89c) Do you know of anywhere you might go, or anyone you might talk to, where you could find out where to go for help? Where is that?

(If "married now" ask question 90)

90. Suppose it was a problem in your marriage—you and your (wife) (husband) just couldn't get along with each other. What do you think you would do about it?

90a. (If "no outside professional source" mentioned) Do you think you would go anywhere to get some help with this problem? Where would you go?

90b. (If "outside professional source" mentioned) If this didn't work, is there anywhere else you would go to get help? Where is that?

Sometimes when people have problems like this, they go someplace for help. Sometimes they go to a doctor or a minister. Sometimes they go to a special place for handling personal problems—like a psychiatrist or a marriage counselor, or social agency or clinic.

91. How about you—have you ever gone anywhere like that for advice and help with any personal problems?

91a. (If Yes) What was that about?

91b. Where did you go for help? (Probe for specific names of social agencies.)

91c. How did you happen to go there?

91d. What did they do—how did they try to help you?

91e. How did it turn out—do you think it helped you in any way?

(If No to question 91 ask 92)

92. Can you think of anything that's happened to you, any problems you've had in the past, where going to someone like this might have helped you in any way?

92a. (If Yes) What do you have in mind—what was it about?

92b. What did you do about it?

92c. Who do you think might have helped you with that?

92d. Why do you suppose that you didn't go for help?

92e. (If No to question 92) Do you think you could ever have a personal problem that got so bad that you might want to go someplace for help—or do you think you could always handle things like that yourself?

THE QUESTIONNAIRE [423]

93. There are a lot of other kinds of places that people go to with their problems. I have a list of places here. I'll read them off to you one at a time, and you tell me whether you've ever gone to a person or place like this with any personal problems?
    93a. How about a lawyer, I mean for a personal problem, not a legal problem?
    93b. (If Yes) What was that about?
    93c. What did he do about it—how did he try to help you?
    93d. How did it work out—did he help you in any way?
    93e. How about a policeman, judge, or someone in the courts?
    93f. (If Yes) What was that about?
    93g. What did they do about it—how did they try to help you?
    93h. How did it work out—did they help you in any way?
    93i. How about an astrologer, fortuneteller, or palmist?
    93j. (If Yes) What was that about?
    93k. What did they do about it—how did they try to help you?
    93l. How did it work out—did they help you in any way?
    93m. (If has school-age children) Did you ever talk to a teacher or someone else at school about any problems your child was having?
    93n. (If Yes) What was that about?
    93o. How did it turn out?
94. Have you ever gotten any help from reading a book or a newspaper columnist who advises on personal problems?
    94a. (If Yes) What book or newspaper columnist was that?
    94b. How did they help you?

Now we have finished the regular part of the interview. We need a few facts about you, like age, education, and so on, so that we can compare the ideas of men with those of women, older people with younger people, and one group with another.
(Personal Data)
    PD1 (By observation) Sex: male, female.
    PD2. (By observation) Race: white, Negro, other (specify).
    PD3. (Ask only if R is *not* head of household) What kind of work does (head of household) do?
        PD3a (If head is unemployed) What kind of work does he usually do?
        PD3b. (If head is retired) What kind of work did he usually do before he retired?
    PD4. About how old are you?
        21-24; 25-29; 30-34; 35-39; 40-44; 45-49; 50-54; 55-59; 60-64; 65 or over.
    PD5. What was the highest grade of school you completed?

1; 2; 3; 4; 5; 6; 7; 8; 9; 10; 11; 12; more than 12.
PD5a. (If more than 8) Have you had any other schooling?
PD5b. (If Yes) What other schooling have you had?
PD5c. (If attended college) Do you have a college degree?

PD6. What is your religious preference?
Protestant, Catholic, Jewish, other (specify).
PD6a. (If Protestant) What religious denomination is that?

PD7. About how often do you usually attend religious services?
More than once a week; once a week; two or three times a month; once a month; a few times a year or less; never.

PD8. Where were you born? (If U.S., get state.)
PD8a. (Do not ask of Negroes or foreign born) Were both your parents born in this country?
PD8b. (If Yes) What country did your parents' people originally come from?
PD8c. (If No) In which country was your father born?
PD8d. In which country was your mother born?

PD9. What kind of work did your father do for a living while you were growing up?

PD10. Were you brought up mostly on a farm, in a town, in a small city, or in a large city?

PD11. How long have you lived in (present community)?

PD12. Do you think (present community) is a *friendly* place, or an *unfriendly* place?

PD13. Did you always live together with both of your *real* parents up to the time you were sixteen years old?
PD13a. (If No) What happened?
PD13b. How old were you when it happened?
PD13c. (If step-parent not mentioned) Did your mother (father) remarry?
PD13d. (If had step-parent) How old were you when your mother (father) remarried?
PD13e. How well did you get along with your stepfather (stepmother)?

PD14. About what do you think your total income will be this year for yourself and your immediate family?
Under $1,000; $1,000-1,999; $2,000-2,999; $3,000-3,999; $4,000-4,999; $5,000-5,999; $6,000-6,999; $7,000-7,999; $8,000-9,999; $10,000-14,999; $15,000 or more.

Length of interview.

Appendix II

Sample Design and Sampling Error

SAMPLE DESIGN

The individuals interviewed in this survey are a representative cross section of adults, twenty-one years of age or older, living in private households in the United States. Households on military reservations are excluded; also excluded (because their unusual nature calls for special treatment) are all places where persons have living arrangements of some kind different from the usual family dwelling. Examples of the excluded places are: rooms in hotels and large rooming houses, dormitories for students or workers, barracks, living quarters for inmates of institutions.

The sample was selected by a probability method with procedures known as area sampling.[1] By this method every member of the population sampled has a known chance of being selected. To insure that the sample will have the same characteristics as the total population, a technique known as stratification is used. By this device, the population to be sampled is first sorted into several groups or strata on the basis of geographic location and relevant social and economic variables. Units within each of these strata are selected for the sample, thus insuring that the sample will reflect the diversity of the population with respect to these variables.

The county (or sometimes group of counties or parts of counties) is a convenient unit to use when stratifying the United States population. For this survey, 66 strata were formed from all the counties in the United States. The 12 largest metropolitan areas and their suburbs account for 12 of the strata and contain about 30 per cent of the population. From each of the remaining 54 strata a random selection of one county unit was made to represent the stratum. Thus there are 66 primary sampling units in the survey, one unit from each of the 66 strata. Within the limitations of cost and time, it is, of course, impossible to interview the entire population within a primary sampling unit; hence, some subsampling is necessary. In the 12 largest metropolitan areas, each of the 12 central cities is included in the sample. From a list of the cities, towns, and suburban areas surrounding these central cities, a sample of these places is drawn. The sampling of dwelling units within the central cities and the suburban places follows procedures similar to those described below for cities and towns in the remaining 54 primary units.

Within each of the 54 primary sampling units outside the large metropolitan areas a rather general urban-rural [2] stratification is established. The urban areas are further subdivided by size of place before a probability selection is made to represent each subgroup. Similarly, from the rural part of the primary sampling unit two classifications are formed according to the density of population: (1) rural congested areas, and (2) open country areas. By probability-sampling techniques, selections from each type of rural area are drawn for the sample.

To select the specific dwelling units where interviews were taken, three different procedures were used: (1) In places where an up-to-date city directory was available, addresses were selected from the street addresses section of the directory. These directory addresses were supplemented by an area sample to insure that dwelling units that were not located at directory addresses also had the appropriate probability (greater than zero) of selection for the survey. (2) In all rural areas, and in some urban places where blocks could be easily subdivided, a probability sample of small geographic areas or segments was selected for interviewing. (3) For the remaining urban places, which included almost all of the central cities in the large metropolitan areas, a sample of blocks was selected and sent to the interviewers for prelisting. The listed addresses for each block were returned to the central office where a subselection of addresses was made by probability sampling techniques and sent to the interviewers for inclusion in the survey. The interviewers were also instructed to interview at any unlisted dwelling unit located between a sample address and the next listed address. This procedure, known as the "half-open" technique, provides for the inclusion of a proper sample of new construction addresses and addresses missed at the time of block listing.

Within each sample dwelling unit only one adult was interviewed for this study. The respondent was designated by an objective procedure of selection,[3] and no substitutions were allowed. If the respondent was not at home on the first call, from three to ten call-backs were made in an attempt to reach him. However, even after repeated calls a small proportion (5 per cent) of the designated individuals were not found at home and some (8 per cent) refused to be interviewed.

Although each dwelling unit had an equal chance of selection into the sample, the adults within the sample dwelling units had different probabilities of selection; people living in households with a large number of adults had a smaller chance of being interviewed than people in one- or

SAMPLE DESIGN AND SAMPLING ERROR [427]

two-adult households. Happily, these differences in probabilities of selection were not great; about five sevenths of the households had two adults, about one seventh had one adult, and the remaining one seventh had three to six adults, with three being the majority category in this group. Although the differences can be adjusted through a weighting procedure, this was not done; instead both the weighted and unweighted estimates were computed for a number of critical items. When compared, these estimates showed only small differences relative to the sampling errors. Consequently, the bias resulting from the use of unweighted data is regarded as negligible and all tabulations in the report have been made from unweighted data.

This study used three interview forms, each assigned randomly to one-third of the respondents throughout all primary sampling units. The use of three schedules permitted the employment of a greater variety of questions. The text indicates those items that are based on less than the total sample.

SAMPLING ERROR

Estimates from properly conducted sample interview surveys are subject to errors arising from several sources. Major sources of error are: sampling errors, response and reporting errors, nonresponse errors, and processing errors. Although each is important in evaluating the accuracy of the data, measurement of each type is not available.[4] The discussion which follows will be limited to sampling errors.

Sampling errors can be thought of as the extent to which sample findings may overestimate or underestimate the true figures which would be obtained if the entire population were interviewed. Many factors influence the size of sampling errors; important determinants of sampling errors of proportions are the magnitude of the proportion and the number of interviews on which it is based. In general, the larger the proportion of the population included in the sample, the smaller the sampling error. With a sample of a given size, the smallest sampling error would be achieved if the interviews in the sample were widely scattered throughout the area or the population sampled. However, this kind of sample is prohibitive from the standpoint of time and expense. Consequently, for most surveys—including this study—the interviews are clustered within a limited number of geographic areas. Such clustering increases the sampling error but lowers cost and time expenditures. The procedures used for computing sampling errors in this study take this clustering into consideration.

The sampling error is a measure of the expected variation of a sample statistic from its corresponding population value; it is given in terms of intervals to be used for estimating the population value. However, it does

[428]   APPENDIX II

not measure the actual error of a particular sample estimate; in order to have such a measure, the actual population (true) value would be needed. Rather, it leads to statements in terms of confidence intervals; it estimates the range of sample values that would be obtained if many repeated sample values were obtained using the same sampling and field procedures. The range includes the population (true) value in a specified proportion of cases.

The "sampling error" used in this report is equal to two "standard errors," that is, the sampling error indicates the range on either side of the sample estimate within which the population value can be expected to lie with 95 chances in 100. In about five out of every 100 cases, the population value can be expected by chance to lie outside this range. If one requires a greater degree of confidence than this, a range wider than two standard errors should be used. On the other hand, most of the time the actual error of sampling will be less than the sampling error defined above. In about 68 cases out of every 100 the population value can be expected to lie within a range of one-half the sampling error reported here (i.e., one "standard error") for the estimated sample values.

It is costly to compute sampling errors for every statistic derived from a survey. However, most survey results are presented in the form of percentages of interviews possessing a given attribute, and, fortunately, the sampling errors of these percentages show a fair amount of regularity. This regularity enables the presentation of tables giving approximate estimates of the sampling errors for various percentages based on different numbers of interviews.

Such tables have been developed for this study. Each cell of the table contains two figures—a "high" and a "low" estimate of the sampling error. The low values represent the lower bounds of the sampling errors and are computed from the standard simple random sample formulas. The high values represent the upper bounds of the sampling errors and are derived from estimates of the additional sampling error caused by clustering; these estimates are based on actual calculations of data from this study. Most of the sampling errors computed for particular sample values lie between these limits.

Appendix Table 1 presents the sampling errors for given percentages based on varying size samples. This table provides estimates of the range within which the population value can be expected to lie 95 per cent of the time, given a specified sample percentage and the size of the sample upon which it is based. As an example of the use of this table, let us obtain the sampling errors for the 46 per cent of the 950 married respondents with a high-school education evaluating their marriages as very happy, and for the 60 per cent of the 362 married respondents who have a college educa-

Appendix Table 1—Approximate Sampling Error[a] of Percentages (Expressed in Percentages)

NUMBER OF INTERVIEWS

Reported Percentages	2500	2000	1500	1000	700	500	400	300	200	100
Around 50	2.0–2.8	2.2–3.1	2.6–3.6	3.2–4.5	3.8–5.3	4.5–6.3	5.0–7.0	5.8–8.1	7.1–9.9	10.0–14.0
Around 30 or 70	1.8–2.5	2.0–2.8	2.4–3.4	2.9–4.1	3.5–4.9	4.1–5.7	4.6–6.4	5.3–7.4	6.5–9.1	9.2–12.9
Around 20 or 80	1.6–2.2	1.8–2.5	2.1–2.9	2.5–3.5	3.0–4.2	3.6–5.0	4.0–5.6	4.6–6.4	5.7–8.0	8.0–11.2
Around 10 or 90	1.2–1.7	1.3–1.8	1.5–2.1	1.9–2.7	2.3–3.2	2.7–3.8	3.0–4.2	3.5–4.9	4.2–5.9	6.8–8.4
Around 5 or 95	0.9–1.3	1.0–1.4	1.1–1.5	1.4–2.0	1.6–2.2	1.9–2.7	2.2–3.1	2.5–3.5	3.1–4.3	– – – –

[a] The figures in this table represent two standard errors. Hence, for the most items the chances are 95 in 100 that the value being estimated lies within a range equal to the reported percentages, plus or minus the sampling error.

Two estimates of the sampling error are presented for each cell. The lower values are based on the standard error formula for simple random samples. The higher values are based on the computations of individual sampling errors carried out on the current study data, and allow for the departures from simple random sampling in the survey design such as stratification and clustering.

The sampling error does not measure the total error involved in specific survey estimates since it does not include nonresponse and reporting errors.

[430]   APPENDIX II

tion and say they are very happy in their marriages. (These percentages can be found in Table 4.10.) Appendix Table 1 indicates that the 46 per cent of the 950 respondents is subject to a sampling error of 3.2 to 4.5 per cent. (See the figures in the first row and fourth column of Table 1.) Thus, the chances are at least 95 out of 100 that the population value is

Appendix Table 2—Approximate Sampling Error[a] of Differences (in Percentages)

FOR PERCENTAGES FROM 35 TO 65

	1000	700	500	300	200	100	50
2000	— —	— —	5.0–7.0	6.2–8.7	7.4–10.4	10.3–14.4	14.3–18.4
1500	4.1–5.7	4.6–6.4	5.2–7.3	6.3–8.8	7.5–10.5	10.4–14.6	14.4–18.6
1000	4.5–6.3	4.9–6.9	5.5–7.7	6.6–9.2	7.8–10.9	10.5–14.7	14.5–18.6
700		5.4–7.6	5.9–8.3	6.9–9.7	8.0–11.2	10.7–15.0	14.6–18.9
500			6.3–8.8	7.2–10.1	8.4–11.8	11.0–15.4	14.8–19.2
300				8.2–11.5	9.1–12.7	11.5–16.1	15.4–19.7
200					10.0–14.0	12.2–17.1	15.8–20.7
100						14.1–19.7	17.3–22.4
50							20.0–25.7

FOR PERCENTAGES AROUND 20 AND 80

	1000	700	500	300	200	100	50
2000	— —	— —	4.0–5.6	5.0–7.0	6.0–8.4	8.2–11.5	11.4–14.7
1500	3.3–4.6	3.7–5.2	4.1–5.7	5.1–7.1	6.1–8.5	8.3–11.6	11.5–14.8
1000	3.6–5.0	3.9–5.5	4.4–6.2	5.3–7.4	6.2–8.7	8.4–11.8	11.6–15.0
700		4.3–6.0	4.7–6.6	5.5–7.7	6.4–9.0	8.6–12.0	11.7–15.1
500			5.1–7.1	5.8–8.1	6.7–9.4	8.8–12.3	11.9–15.4
300				6.5–9.1	7.3–10.2	9.2–12.9	12.2–15.9
200					8.0–11.2	9.8–13.7	12.6–16.5
100						11.3–15.8	13.8–18.3
50							16.0–20.6

FOR PERCENTAGES AROUND 10 AND 90

	1000	700	500	300	200	100	50
2000	— —	— —	3.0–4.2	3.8–5.3	4.5–6.3	6.2–8.5	— —
1500	2.4–3.4	2.8–3.9	3.1–4.3	3.9–5.5	4.6–6.4	6.3–8.8	— —
1000	2.7–3.8	3.0–4.2	3.3–4.6	4.0–5.6	4.7–6.6	6.4–9.0	— —
700		3.2–4.5	3.5–4.9	4.1–5.7	4.8–6.7	6.5–9.1	— —
500			3.8–5.3	4.3–6.0	5.0–7.0	6.6–9.2	— —
300				4.9–6.9	5.5–7.7	6.9–9.7	— —
200					6.0–8.4	7.3–10.2	— —
100						8.5–11.9	— —

FOR PERCENTAGES AROUND 5 AND 95

	1000	700	500	300	200	100	50
2000	— —	— —	2.2–3.1	2.8–3.9	3.3–4.6	— —	— —
1500	1.8–2.5	2.1–2.9	2.3–3.2	2.9–4.1	3.4–4.8	— —	— —
1000	1.9–2.7	2.2–3.1	2.4–3.4	3.0–4.2	3.5–4.9	— —	— —
700		2.3–3.2	2.6–3.6	3.1–4.3	3.6–5.0	— —	— —
500			2.8–3.9	3.2–4.5	3.7–5.2	— —	— —
300				3.6–5.0	4.0–5.6	— —	— —
200					4.4–6.2	— —	— —

[a] The values shown are the differences required for significance (two standard errors) in comparisons of percentages derived from two different subgroups of the current survey. Two values —low and high—are given for each cell. See note a to Appendix Table 1.

between 41.5 and 50.5 per cent (using the upper limit). Similarly, the value of 60 per cent based upon the 362 interviews is subject to a sampling error of 5 to 7 per cent. (See the figures in the first row and seventh column.) Therefore, the statement that the population value lies within the range 53 to 67 per cent has at least 95 chances in 100 of being correct (using the upper limit of the sampling error).

Appendix Table 2 presents the sampling errors for the difference between two percentages. This table is most pertinent to the data presented in this report; it provides an estimate of the "significance" of the difference between percentages based on two *different subgroups*. Such an estimate is necessary in evaluating differences between two sample figures since both sample percentages are subject to sampling errors, and the "true" values of each will not necessarily coincide exactly with the obtained values. Let us return to the example used above. We want to know whether married respondents with a high-school education differ from married respondents with a college education on their evaluations of their marital happiness as "very happy." The two percentages in question are 46 and 60, both in the range from 35 to 65 per cent covered by the uppermost section of Appendix Table 2. These percentages are based on samples of sizes 362 and 950. Therefore we look for the intersection of the row dealing with N's of 300 and N's of 1000 in the uppermost section of Table 2, and note that the sampling error is between 6.6 and 9.2 per cent. That is, the two percentages must differ from one another by at least 9.2 per cent (using the upper limit of the sampling error) in order to be significant; in order to be replicated in 95 out of 100 samples. The difference in question is 14 per cent, considerably more than is necessary to be considered significant. Therefore it is reasonable to conclude that in the population as a whole, and not only in our sample, persons with college education are more likely to describe their marriages as very happy than are persons with a high-school education.

NOTES

1. In probability samples the chance of drawing a specific element (dwelling unit, individual) into the sample can be calculated for every element of the population. Probability samples have the distinction of yielding measurable results; that is, the precision of estimates from probability samples can be measured objectively in terms of the sampling errors calculated from the sample.

2. Briefly, places of 2500 or more population at the time of the 1950 Census are classified as urban.

3. Leslie Kish, "A Procedure for Objective Respondent Selection Within the Household," *Journal of the American Statistical Association,* 44 : 380–387, 1949.

4. For a discussion of response and reporting errors see Chapter 1. A discussion of nonresponse errors in this context can be found in William Cochran, *Sampling Techniques,* New York: John Wiley, 1953, pp. 292–317.

Appendix III

Joint Commission on Mental Illness and Health

PARTICIPATING ORGANIZATIONS

American Academy of Neurology
American Academy of Pediatrics
American Association for the Advancement of Science
American Association on Mental Deficiency
American Association of Psychiatric Clinics for Children
American College of Chest Physicians
American Hospital Association
American Legion
American Medical Association
American Nurses Association and The National League for Nursing (Coordinating Council of)
American Occupational Therapy Association
American Orthopsychiatric Association
American Personnel and Guidance Association
American Psychiatric Association
American Psychoanalytic Association
American Psychological Association
American Public Health Association
American Public Welfare Association
Association for Physical and Mental Rehabilitation
Association of American Medical Colleges
Association of State and Territorial Health Officers
Catholic Hospital Association
Central Inspection Board, American Psychiatric Association
Children's Bureau, Dept. of Health, Education and Welfare
Council of State Governments
Department of Defense, U.S.A.
National Association for Mental Health
National Association of Social Workers

National Committee Against Mental Illness
National Education Association
National Institute of Mental Health
National Medical Association
National Rehabilitation Association

Office of Vocational Rehabilitation, Department of Health, Education and Welfare
United States Department of Justice
Veterans Administration

MEMBERS

Kenneth E. Appel, M.D.
Philadelphia, Pa.

Walter H. Baer, M.D.
Peoria, Illinois

Leo H. Bartemeier, M.D.
Baltimore, Maryland

Walter E. Barton, M.D.
Boston, Massachusetts

Otto L. Bettag, M.D.
Springfield, Illinois

Mr. George Bingaman
Purcell, Oklahoma

Kathleen Black, R.N.
New York, New York

Francis J. Braceland, M.D.
Hartford, Connecticut

Hugh T. Carmichael, M.D.
Chicago, Illinois

J. Frank Casey, M.D.
Washington, D.C.

James M. Cunningham, M.D.
Dayton, Ohio

John E. Davis, Sc.D.
Rehoboth Beach, Delaware

Neil A. Dayton, M.D.
Mansfield Depot, Conn.

Miss Loula Dunn
Chicago, Illinois

Howard D. Fabing, M.D.
Cincinnati, Ohio

Rev. Patrick J. Frawley, Ph.D.
New York, New York

Mr. Mike Gorman
Washington, D.C.

Robert T. Hewitt, M.D.
Bethesda, Maryland

Herman E. Hilleboe, M.D.
Albany, New York

Nicholas Hobbs, Ph.D.
Nashville, Tennessee

Bartholomew W. Hogan, Rear Adm. M.C., U.S.N., Washington, D.C.

Louis Jacobs, M.D.
Washington, D.C.

M. Ralph Kaufman, M.D.
New York, New York

William S. Langford, M.D.
New York, New York

Miss Madeleine Lay
New York, New York

Jack Masur, M.D.
Bethesda, Maryland

Berwyn F. Mattison, M.D.
New York, New York

Ernst Mayr, Ph.D.
Cambridge, Mass.

Robert T. Morse, M.D.
Washington, D.C.

Ralph H. Ojemann, Ph.D.
Iowa City, Iowa

Winfred Overholser, M.D.
 Washington, D.C.
Howard W. Potter, M.D.
 New York, New York
Mathew Ross, M.D.
 Washington, D.C.
Mr. Charles Schlaifer
 New York, New York
Lauren H. Smith, M.D.
 Philadelphia, Pa.
M. Brewster Smith, Ph.D.
 Berkeley, California
Mr. Sidney Spector
 Chicago, Illinois

Mesrop A. Tarumianz, M.D.
 Farnhurst, Delaware
David V. Tiedeman, Ed.D.
 Cambridge, Mass.
Harvey J. Tompkins, M.D.
 New York, New York
Beatrice D. Wade, O.T.R.
 Chicago, Illinois
Mr. E. B. Whitten
 Washington, D.C.
Helen Witmer, Ph.D.
 Washington, D.C.
Luther E. Woodward, Ph.D.
 New York, New York

OFFICERS

President: Kenneth E. Appel, M.D.
 Philadelphia, Pa.
Chairman, Board of Trustees: Leo H. Bartemeier, M.D.
 Baltimore, Md.
Vice-President: M. Brewster Smith, Ph.D.
 Berkeley, California
Secretary-Treasurer: Mr. Charles Schlaifer
 New York, N.Y.
Vice-Chairman, Board of Trustees: Nicholas Hobbs, Ph.D.
 Nashville, Tenn.

STAFF

Director: Jack R. Ewalt, M.D.
 Boston, Mass.
Consultant for Scientific Studies: Fillmore H. Sanford, Ph.D.
 Austin, Texas
Consultant in Social Sciences: Gordon W. Blackwell, Ph.D.
 Chapel Hill, North Carolina
Consultant in Epidemiology: John E. Gordon, M.D.
 Boston, Mass.
Associate Director for Administration: Richard J. Plunkett, M.D.
 Chicago, Ill.

Director of Information: Greer Williams
   Boston, Mass.

Associate Director and Consultant on Law: Charles S. Brewton, LL.B.
   Alexandria, Va.

Librarian: Mary R. Strovink
   Boston, Mass.

References

Albee, G. 1959. *Mental Health Manpower Trends.* Basic Books.
Clausen, J. A., and Yarrow, Marian R. (Eds.), 1955. The impact of mental illness on the family. *Journal of Social Issues, 11* (no. 4).
Festinger, L., and Katz, D. (Eds.), 1953. *Research Methods in the Behavioral Sciences.* Dryden Press.
Hollingshead, A. B., and Redlich, F. C., 1958. *Social Class and Mental Illness.* John Wiley.
Jahoda, Marie, 1958. *Current Concepts of Positive Mental Health.* Basic Books.
MacMillan, A. M., 1957. The health opinion survey: technique for estimating prevalence of psychoneurotic and related types of disorder in communities. *Psychological Reports, 3* : 325.
Mead, Margaret, 1949. *Male and Female.* Morrow and Co.
Midtown Survey: See Rennie, T. A. C.
Miller, D. R., and Swanson, G. E. *Inner Conflict and Defense.* Henry Holt. 1960.
Rennie, T. A. C., 1953. The Yorkville community mental health research study. *Interrelations Between the Social Environment and Psychiatric Disorders.* Milbank Memorial Fund. Twenty-ninth Annual Conference, 1952.
Robinson, R., DeMarche, D. F., and Wagle, Mildred K., 1960. *Community Resources in Mental Health.* Basic Books.
Stirling County Survey: See Macmillan, A. M.
Stouffer, S. A., Lumsdaine, A.A., Lumsdaine, Marion H., Williams, R. M., Smith, M. B., Janis, I. L., Star, Shirley A., Cottrell, L. S., 1949. *American Soldier: Combat and Its Aftermath, Vol. 2,* Princeton University Press.

Index

adequacy; *see* job; marriage; parenthood
admission to shortcomings
   and denial of strong points, 61
   as index of self-perception, 54
      related to positiveness of self-percept index, 63–64
   as measure of introspection, 58–59
   and perception of difference from others, 59–60
   and sex, educational level, and age, 66–69
age differences
   summarized, 212–214
   (*see also* happiness; job; marriage; parenthood; professional help; self-perception; self-referral; symptoms; unhappiness; worries)
Albee, G., 404
alienation; *see* job

broken home background
   and marriage, 247–250
   and symptom factors, 246–247
   (*see also* self-referral)

Catholic-Protestant differences; *see* religion and church attendance
child-raising; children; *see* parenthood
church attendance; *see* religion and church attendance
Clausen, J. A., 256–257
clergymen; *see* professional help
conceptual style of expression, 57
coping-passive dimension; *see* professional help
coping reactions; *see* unhappiness; worries (methods of handling)

demographic relationships, implications of, 399–406
demographic variables, 206–208, 250–252
   (*see also* happiness; job; marriage; parenthood; problems; professional help; self-perception; self-referral; symptoms; unhappiness; worries)
denial of strong points
   and admission to shortcomings, 61
   as index of self-perception, 55–56
      related to positiveness of self-percept index, 63–64
   as measure of introspection, 58–59
   and perception of difference from others, 60–61
distress; *see* unhappiness

educational level differences
   and income, 221–223
   summarized, 210–211
   (*see also* happiness; job; marriage; parenthood; professional help; self-perception; self-referral; symptoms; unhappiness; worries)
ego dissatisfactions; *see* job
ego satisfactions; *see* job
extrinsic dissatisfactions; *see* job
extrinsic satisfactions; *see* job

facilitating factors; *see* self-referral
feminine role, 210

gratification; *see* happiness; role adjustment

happiness
   and age, 43–46, 50–51

[439]

INDEX

happiness (*cont'd*)
  anticipation of, 34-36
  and education, 46-48, 50-51
  feelings of, 30-32
  meaning of, 22-24
  and past emotional crises, 36-38, 50
  and sex, 41-43, 50-51
  sources of, 24-30, 48-49
  and worries, 28-36
  (*see also* income level differences; marital status; marriage; nervous breakdown; occupational status; residence; self-referral; unhappiness; worries)
help; *see* professional help
hindering factors; *see* self-referral
Hollingshead, A. B., 277, 334, 403, 404
honesty, problem of, in interview surveys, 9-10

immobilization; *see* income level differences; self-referral; symptoms
inadequacy; *see* job; marriage; parenthood; self-referral
income level differences
  and educational levels, 221-223
  and happiness, 216-218
  and job, 220-221
  and marriage, 218-219
  and parenthood, 219-220
  summarized, 215-223
  and symptom factors, 217-218, 221-222
  and worries, 215-218
  (*see also* professional help; self-referral; unhappiness; worries)
introspection
  admission to shortcomings, as measure of, 58-59
  and age, 68, 80, 82
  associated with readiness for self-referral, 275
  and demographic characteristics, 57-58
  denial of strong points, as measure of, 58-59
  as dimension in self-perception, 57
  and educational level, 69, 81, 82
  perception of difference from others, as measure of, 58-59
  and positive-negative self-percept, 62-67, 81
  as relevant to readiness for self-referral, 58
  and sex, 78
introspectiveness
  and age, 212
  and educational differences, 210-211
  and sex difference, 210

Jahoda, Marie, 6, 7, 13-14, 62, 149
job
  adequacy in, 144-145, 146-150, 156-157, 164-165, 168, 171
    ego vs. extrinsic factors, 156-157
  and age, 168-171
    ego vs. extrinsic dissatisfactions, 168-169
    ego vs. extrinsic satisfactions, 168-169
  alienation from, 143, 148-150, 173
  degree of personal involvement in, 148-150
  dissatisfaction with, 151-154, 160-162, 172-173
    ego vs. extrinsic factors, 151-154, 173
  and education, 165-168
    ego vs. extrinsic dissatisfactions, 165-166
    ego vs. extrinsic satisfactions, 165-166
  inadequacy in, 164-165, 168
    compared to marital and parental relationships, 145, 147-148, 149, 168, 171
  and occupational status, 157-165
    ego vs. extrinsic dissatisfactions, 160-162
    ego vs. extrinsic satisfactions, 158-160
  problems in, 144, 146-150, 154-156, 167-168, 169-171, 172
    ego vs. extrinsic factors, 154-156
  satisfaction with, 144, 146-154, 158-160, 172
    ego vs. extrinsic factors, 149-154, 173
  (*see also* income level differences; religion and church attendance; self-referral)

Macmillan, A. M., 175-176
male role, 209-210

INDEX

marital status
  divorced or separated, 235–236
  single, 233–235
  solitary statuses vs. marriage, 230–233
  widows and widowers, 236–238
  (*see also* self-referral)
marriage
  age difference in, 102–104, 112–113, 116
  as central life adjustment area, 91–92
  and educational level, 104–106, 113–114, 116
  feelings of inadequacy in, 99
  happiness in, and inadequacy, 92–93
  happiness in, and personal problems, 94
  happiness in, and sources of happiness, 97–98
  and parenthood, 117
  personal problems in, and inadequacy, 93
  relational aspects of, 98, 100, 115
  sex difference in, 101–102, 108–112, 115–116
  situational aspects of, 98, 100, 121
  sources of unhappiness in, and personal problems, 99–100
  unhappiness in, and sources of unhappiness, 97–98
  (*see also* income level differences; marital status; occupational status; religion and church attendance; residence; role adjustment; self-referral)
marriage counselors; *see* professional help
Mead, Margaret, 77, 209
Midtown study (Rennie), 175–176
  (*see also* symptoms)
Miller, D. R., 57
moral and virtuous stereotypes; *see* sources of strong points
motoric style of expression, 57
multiple criterion approach, 7–8, 13, 402

nervous breakdown, expectation of
  and age, 43–46, 50–51
  and education, 46–48, 50–51
  related to personal problems, 38–40
  relevance of professional help for, 38–40
  and sex, 41–43, 50–51
  (*see also* broken home background; happiness; marital status; professional help; self-referral; symptoms; unhappiness; worries)

occupational status, 223–228
  (*see also* self-referral)

parenthood
  affiliative inadequacy in, 127
  affiliative satisfactions of, 130
  content of problems of child-raising, and inadequacy feelings in parent, 123
  degree of personal involvement in, 120–123
  measures of, 121–123
  inadequacy feelings and age difference in, 136–140, 140–141
  inadequacy feelings and educational difference in, 134–136, 140–141
  inadequacy feelings and family size, 133–134
  inadequacy feelings and sex difference in, 129–134, 140–141
  modern psychology on, 117–118
  problems of child-raising, and feelings of inadequacy in parent, 119–120
  as psychological stress, 142
  role requirements of, 127–128
  self-evaluations of adjustment to, 124–129
    expressions of inadequacy feelings, 124–126
    expressions of satisfaction, 126–129
  views of society on, 117
  (*see also* income level differences; religion and church attendance; role adjustment; self-referral)
passive reactions; *see* unhappiness; worries (methods of handling)
perception of difference from others
  and admission to shortcomings, 59–60
  and denial of strong points, 60–61
  as index of self-perception, 53–54
  as measure of introspection, 58–59
  and sex, educational level, and age, 66–69
physical anxiety; *see* income level differences; self-referral; symptoms
physical health; *see* income level differences; self-referral; symptoms

physicians; *see* professional help
positive-negative self-percept; *see* introspection
positiveness of self-percept
  associated with "sense of self," 62
  as index of self-perception, 54
  related to admission to shortcomings, 63–64
  related to denial of strong points, 63–64
  related to sources of shortcomings, 64–65
  and sex, age, and educational differences, 69–71
prayer, use of; *see* unhappiness; worries (methods of handling)
problems
  and demographic characteristics, 324–341
  nature of, for seeking professional help, 304–306
  relationship of, to helpfulness of therapy, 317–321
  relationship of, to sources of professional help, 308–314
  (*see also* job; professional help; unhappiness; worries)
professional help
  choice of, 314–317
  demographic characteristics of seekers of, 324–341
    income, 330–331, 336–338, 340, 356–357
    place of residence, 330–331; 338–339, 340, 358–359
    religion and church attendance, 329–330, 335–336, 340, 356
    sex and age, 324–327, 332–333, 341, 353–354
    sex and education, 327–329, 333–335, 340, 354–356
  helpfulness of, 317–321
  and impending nervous breakdown, 310–311
  nature of benefit of, 321–324
    related to source of help, 322–323
  psychiatric resources for, 382–383
    related to self-referral, 383–394
  reasons for seeking, 304–306

refusal of
  coping ways of critical group, 359–362
  demographic analysis of reasons for, 353–359
  passive ways of critical group, 360–362
  problem area of critical group, 346–348
  reasons for, 350–353
  sources of help suggested by critical group, 348–350
sources of, 306–314, 367–369
(*see also* self-referral; unhappiness; worries)
psychiatric resources; psychiatrists; *see* professional help
psychological agencies; *see* professional help
psychological anxiety; *see* income level differences; self-referral; symptoms
psychological factors; *see* self-referral

Redlich, F. C., 277, 334, 403, 404
religion and church attendance
  Catholic-Protestant differences in, 240–245
  and job, 244
  and marriage, 241–244
  and parenthood, 244
  summarized, 245
  and symptom factors, 240–241
  (*see also* professional help; self-referral; unhappiness; worries)
Rennie, T. A. C., 175–176
residence, place of, 228–230
  (*see also* professional help; self-referral; unhappiness; worries)
role adjustment
  degree of personal involvement in, 86–87, 115
  measures of, 91
  dimensions of, 84
  experience of problems, as an aspect of, 85
  feelings of adequacy, as an aspect of, 85
  gratification, as an aspect of, 85

INDEX

measures of, 87–91
and mental health, 174
(*see also* job; marriage; parenthood)
role satisfaction; *see* role adjustment

self-help, 350–351
self-percept; *see* positiveness of self-percept
self-perception; *see* admission to shortcomings; denial of strong points; introspection; perception of difference from others; positiveness of self-percept; self-referral; sources of shortcomings; sources of strong points
self-referral, readiness for
  Clausen and Yarrow on, 256–257
  and demographic factors, 276–298
    age, sex, and education, 277–279, 288–291, 295–296
    (six) demographic variables, 279–285, 289–295
    facilitating and hindering vs. psychological factors, 286–298, 300
  and general adjustment measures, 262–263
  index of, 258–260, 261
  intellectual vs. emotional acceptance of, 256–258
  and introspection, 275
  and job adjustment measures, 268–270
  and marriage adjustment measures, 265–266
  measuring of, 256–260
  and parenthood adjustment measures, 267–268
  related to adjustment indices, 255
  related to demographic variables, 255–256
  related to psychiatric resources, 383–394
  and self-perception measures, 263–264
  and symptom patterns, 270–275
  (*see also* professional help)
sex difference, summarized, 208–210
  (*see also* happiness; job; marriage; parenthood; professional help; self-perception; self-referral; symptoms; unhappiness; worries)
shortcomings; *see* admission to shortcomings; sources of shortcomings
sources of shortcomings
  as index of self-perception, 54–55
  related to positiveness of self-percept index, 64–65
  and sex, age, and educational differences, 71–81
  inadequate personal appearance, 75–76
  interpersonal vs. non-interpersonal personality deficiencies, 74–75
  lack of external achievement vs. personality deficiencies, 73–74
sources of strong points
  as index of self-perception, 56–57
  and sex, age, and educational differences, 71–81
  moral and virtuous stereotypes, 76
  personality strong points, 77
  role characteristics, 76
Stirling County study (Macmillan), 175–176
  (*see also* symptoms)
Stouffer, S. A., *et al.* (army studies), 273
strong points; *see* denial of strong points; sources of strong points
Swanson, G. E., 57
symptoms
  checklist of, 176
  as diagnostic indices, 175
  factor analysis of, 177–205
    according to age, 188–194
    according to education, 194–197
    according to sex, 187–188
    immobilization (Factor 3), 184, 189, 191, 192–193, 195, 196–197, 201, 202, 204
    interrelations among factors, 185–187
    interrelations of factors, and sex, age, and education, 197–203
    physical anxiety (Factor 4), 184, 188, 192, 194, 196, 201–202, 204, 205
    physical health (Factor 2), 184, 188, 190, 194–195, 200–201, 202, 204, 205
    psychological anxiety (Factor 1), 184, 188, 190, 193–194, 197, 199–200, 203, 204
  Midtown study (Rennie), 175–176

symptoms *(cont'd)*
  Stirling County study (Macmillan), 175–176
  (see also broken home background; income level differences; marital status; nervous breakdown; occupational status; religion and church attendance; residence; self-referral)

unhappiness
  and age, 43–46, 50–51
  anticipation of, 34–36
  and education, 46–48, 50–51
  feelings of, 30–32
  meaning of, 22–24
  methods of handling (coping, passive, prayer), 365–369
    formal and informal sources, 367–369
    related to demographic characteristics, 369–378
    summarized, 378–380
  and past emotional crises, 36–38, 50
  and sex, 41–43, 50–51
  sources of, 24–30, 48–49
  and worries, 28–36, 365

(see also happiness; income level differences; marital status; marriage; nervous breakdown; occupational status; self-referral; worries)

worries
  and age, 43–46, 50–51
  and education, 46–48, 50–51
  feelings of, 30–32
  methods of handling (coping, passive, prayer), 365–369
    formal and informal sources, 367–369
    related to demographic characteristics, 369–378
    summarized, 378–380
  related to happiness, 28–36
  related to unhappiness, 28–36, 365
  and sex, 41–43, 50–51
  sources of, 24–30, 49
  (see also happiness; income level differences; nervous breakdown; residence; self-referral; unhappiness)

Yarrow, Marian R., 257

HISTORICAL ISSUES IN MENTAL HEALTH

An Arno Press Collection

American Psychopathological Association. **Trends Of Mental Disease.** 1945

Belknap, Ivan. **Human Problems Of A State Mental Hospital.** 1956

Berkley, Henry J. **A Treatise On Mental Diseases.** 1900

Bond, Earl D. **Thomas W. Salmon: Psychiatrist.** 1950

Briggs, L. Vernon. **Two Years' Service On The Reorganized State Board Of Insanity In Massachusetts,** August, 1914 to August, 1916. 1930

Briggs, L. Vernon. **A Victory For Progress In Mental Medicine.** 1924

Burrow, Trigant. **A Search For Man's Sanity.** 1958

Cahow, Clark R. **People, Patients and Politics.** (Doctoral Dissertation, Duke University, 1967). 1979

The Committee of the American Neurological Association for the Investigation of Eugenical Sterilization. **Eugenical Sterilization.** 1936

Cotton, Henry A. **The Defective Delinquent And Insane.** 1921

Dayton, Neil A. **New Facts On Mental Disorders.** 1940

Fein, Rashi. **Economics of Mental Illness.** 1958

Goldhamer, Herbert and Andrew W. Marshall. **Psychosis And Civilization.** 1953

Gosney, E.S., and Paul Popenoe. **Sterilization For Human Betterment.** 1929

Greenblat, Milton, et al. **From Custodial To Therapeutic Patient Care In Mental Hospitals.** 1955

Grob, Gerald N., editor. **Immigrants And Insanity.** 1979

Grob, Gerald N., editor. **Mental Hygiene In Twentieth Century America.** 1979

Grob, Gerald N., editor. **The Mentally Ill In Urban America.** 1979

Grob, Gerald N., editor. **The National Association For The Protection of the Insane And The Prevention Of Insanity.** 1979

Grob, Gerald N., editor. **Psychiatric Research In America.** 1979

Grob, Gerald N., editor. **Psychiatry and Medical Education.** 1979

Grob, Gerald N., editor. **Public Policy And Mental Illness.** 1979

Grimes, John Maurice. **Institutional Care Of Mental Patients In The United States.** 1934

Gurin, Gerald, et al. **Americans View Their Mental Health.** 1960

Hinsie, Leland. **The Treatment Of Schizophrenia.** 1930

Jahoda, Marie. **Current Concepts Of Positive Mental Health.** 1958

Joint Commission On Mental Illness And Health. **Action For Mental Health.** 1961

Koren, John. **Summaries Of State Laws Relating To The Insane.** 1917

Landis, Carney, and James D. Page. **Modern Society and Mental Disease.** 1938

Lewis, Nolan D.C. **Research In Dementia Praecox.** 1936

Malzberg, Benjamin. **Social And Biological Aspects Of Mental Disease.** 1940

May, James V. **Mental Diseases.** 1922

Myerson, Abraham. **Speaking Of Man.** 1950

The National Committee for Mental Hygiene. **State Hospitals In The Depression.** 1934

National Research Council, The Committee on Psychiatric Investigations. **The Problem Of Mental Disorder.** 1934

Plunkett, Richard J. and John E. Gordon,. **Epidemiology And Mental Illness.** 1960

Rapoport, Robert N., et al. **Community As Doctor.** 1960

Robison, Dale W. **Wisconsin And The Mentally Ill.** (Doctoral Dissertation, Marquette University, 1967). 1979

Sicherman, Barbara. **The Quest For Mental Health In America,** 1880-1917. (Doctoral Dissertation, Columbia University, 1967). 1979

Smith, Stephen. **Who Is Insane?** 1916

Stearns, Henry Putnam. **Insanity.** 1883

United States Surgeon General's Office. **The Medical Department Of The United States Army In The World War.** 1929

Wertheimer, F.I., and Florence E. Hesketh. **The Significance Of The Physical Constitution In Mental Disease.** 1926

White, William A. **The Mental Hygiene Of Childhood.** 1919

White, William A. **William Alanson White.** 1938

RA
790.6
.G87
1980

RA
790.6
.G87

1980